KINANTHROPOMETRY AND EXERCISE PHYSIOLOGY LABORATORY MANUAL

SECOND EDITION

Volume 2: Exercise Physiology
Tests, procedures and data

Edited by Roger Eston and Thomas Reilly

Routledge
Taylor & Francis Group

LONDON AND NEW YORK

First edition published 1996 by E & FN Spon,
an imprint of the Taylor & Francis Group

Second edition published 2001 by Routledge
11 New Fetter Lane, London EC4P 4EE

Simultaneously published in the USA and Canada by Routledge
29 West 35th Street, New York, NY 10001

Reprinted 2004

Routledge is an imprint of the Taylor & Francis Group

Typeset in Palatino by Bookcraft Ltd, Stroud, Gloucestershire

Printed and bound in Great Britain by Bell and Bain, Glasgow

British Library Cataloguing in Publication Data
A catalogue record for this book is available from the British Library

Library of Congress Cataloging in Publication Data
A catalog record for this book has been requested

ISBN 0–415–251877 (hbk)
ISBN 0–415–251885 (pbk)

5
19.6.07

KINANTHROPOMETRY AND EXERCISE PHYSIOLOGY LABORATORY MANUAL

SECOND EDITION

VOLUME 2: EXERCISE PHYSIOLOGY

This is the sec ... *ysiology Labora-*
tory Manual. I ... ometry, sports
science, hum ... y revised and
completely u ... *ise Physiology –*
this manual p ...

- help in the ...
- compreher ... on so that there
  is no need ...
- seven enti ... nd physiology
- eleven self ... other, enabling
  the reader ...
- a wide ran ...

Volume 1: An ... omatotype and
their relatior ... e and range of
motion; asse ... eference to the
assessment (... etry and body
image; statis ... gy.

Volume 2: E ... ling aspects of
neuromuscui ... exercise including haemato ... te, energy and
efficiency inc ... l energy expenditure and co ... rtion.

An entire o ... ext to real-life
practical exa ... niently supple-
mented by a ... cal overviews,
offering an e ...

Dr Roger E ... ercise Sciences,
University o ... search Institute
for Sport an ... s are practising
kinanthropo ... Association for
Sport and Exercise Sciences.

CONTENTS

CONTRIBUTORS

V. BALTZOPOULOS
Department of Exercise and Sport Science
Manchester Metropolitan University, UK

N.T. CABLE
Research Institute for Sport and Exercise
    Sciences
Liverpool John Moores University
Liverpool, UK

C.B. COOKE
School of Leisure and Sports Studies
Leeds Metropolitan University
Leeds, UK

J.H. DOUST
Department of Sports Science
University of Wales
Aberystwyth, UK

R.G. ESTON
School of Sport, Health and Exercise Sciences
University of Wales
Bangor, UK

N.P. GLEESON
School of Sport, Health and Exercise Sciences
University of Wales
Bangor, UK

M. GREAVES
Department of Medicine & Therapeutics
University of Aberdeen, UK

A.M. JONES
Department of Exercise and Sport Science
Manchester Metropolitan University, UK

J. LEIPER
Department of Biomedical Sciences
University of Aberdeen
Aberdeen, UK

D.P. MACLAREN
Research Institute for Sport and Exercise
    Sciences
Liverpool John Moores University
Liverpool, UK

R. MAUGHAN
Department of Biomedical Sciences
University of Aberdeen
Aberdeen, UK

T.P. REILLY
Research Institute for Sport and Exercise
    Sciences
Liverpool John Moores University
Liverpool, UK

J.G. WILLIAMS
Department of Kinesiology
West Chester University
West Chester, PA, USA

E.M. WINTER
Sport Science Research Institute
Sheffield Hallam University
Sheffield, UK

PREFACE

The subject area referred to as kinanthropometry has a rich history although the subject area itself was not formalized until the International Society for Advancement of Kinanthropometry was established in Glasgow in 1986. The Society supports its own international conferences and publication of Proceedings linked with these events. It also facilitates the conduct of collaborative research projects on an international basis. Until the publication of the first edition of *Kinanthropometry and Exercise Physiology Laboratory Manual; Tests, Procedures and Data* by the present editors in 1996, there was no laboratory manual which would serve as a compendium of practical activities for students in this field. The text was published under the aegis of the International Society for Advancement of Kinanthropometry in an attempt to make good the deficit.

Kinanthropometrists are concerned about the relation between structure and function of the human body, particularly within the context of movement. Kinanthropometry has applications in a wide range of areas including, for example, biomechanics, ergonomics, growth and development, human sciences, medicine, nutrition, physical education and sports science. Initially, the book was motivated by the need for a suitable laboratory resource which academic staff could use in the planning and conduct of class practicals in these areas. The content of the first edition was designed to cover specific teaching modules in kinanthropometry and other academic programmes, mainly physiology, within which kinanthropometry is sometimes subsumed. It was intended also to include practical activities of relevance to clinicians, for example in measuring metabolic functions, muscle performance,

physiological responses to exercise, posture and so on. In all cases the emphasis is placed on the anthropometric aspects of the topic. In the second edition all the original chapters have been updated and an additional seven chapters have been added, mainly concerned with physiological topics. Consequently, it was decided to separate the overall contents of the second edition into two volumes, one focusing on anthropometry practicals whilst the other contained physiological topics.

The content of both volumes is oriented towards laboratory practicals but offers much more than a series of laboratory exercises. A comprehensive theoretical background is provided for each topic so that users of the text are not obliged to conduct extensive literature searches in order to place the subject in context. Each chapter contains an explanation of the appropriate methodology and, where possible, an outline of specific laboratory based practicals. This is not always feasible, for example in studying growth processes in child athletes. Virtually all aspects of performance testing in children are reviewed and special considerations with regard to data acquisition on children are outlined in Volume 1. Methodologies for researchers in growth and development are also described in this volume and there are new chapters devoted to performance assessment for field games, assessment of physical activity and energy balance, and anthropometry and body image.

The last two chapters in Volume 1 are concerned with basic statistical analyses and scaling procedures which are designed to inform researchers and students about data handling. The information should promote proper use of common statistical techniques for analysing data obtained on human subjects as well as help to avoid common abuses of basic statistical tools.

The content of Volume 2 emphasizes physiology but includes considerations of kinanthropometric aspects of the topics where appropriate. Practical activities of relevance to clinicians are covered, for example in measuring metabolic and cardiovascular functions, assessing muscle performance, physiological and haematological responses to exercise, and so on. The chapters concerned with electromyography, haematology, cardiovascular function, limitations to submaximal exercise performance are new whilst material in the other chapters in this volume has been brought up to date in this second edition.

Many of the topics included within the two volumes called for unique individual approaches and so a rigid structure was not imposed on contributors. Nevertheless, in each chapter there is a clear set of aims for the practicals outlined and a comprehensive coverage of the theoretical framework. As each chapter is independent of the others, there is an inevitable re-appearance of concepts across chapters, including those of efficiency, metabolism, maximal performance and issues of scaling. Nevertheless, the two volumes represent a collective set of experimental exercises for academic programmes in kinanthropometry and exercise physiology.

It is hoped that the revised edition in two volumes will stimulate improvements in teaching and instruction strategies in kinanthropometry and physiology. In this way we will have made a contribution towards furthering the education of the next generation of specialists concerned with the relationship between human structure and function.

Roger Eston
Thomas Reilly

INTRODUCTION

The first edition of this text was published in 1996. Until its appearance, there was no laboratory manual serving as a compendium of practical activities for students in the field of kinanthropometry. The text was published under the aegis of the International Society for Advancement of Kinanthropometry, in particular its working group on 'Publications and Information Exchange' in an attempt to make good the deficit. The book has been used widely as the subject area became firmly established on undergraduate and postgraduate programmes. The necessity to update the content after a four-year period is a reflection of the field's expansion.

Kinanthropometry is a relatively new term although the subject area to which it refers has a rich history. It describes the relationship between structure and function of the human body, particularly within the context of movement. The subject area itself was formalized with the establishment of the International Society for Advancement of Kinanthropometry at Glasgow in 1986. The Society supports its own international conferences and publication of Proceedings linked with these events.

Kinanthropometry has applications in a wide range of areas including, for example, biomechanics, ergonomics, growth and development, human sciences, medicine, nutrition, physical education and sports science. The book was motivated by the need for a suitable laboratory resource which academic staff could use in the planning and conduct of class practicals in these areas. The content was designed to cover specific teaching modules in kinanthropometry and other academic programmes, such as physiology, within which

kinanthropometry is sometimes incorporated. It was intended also to include practical activities of relevance to clinicians, for example in measuring metabolic functions, muscle performance, physiological responses to exercise, posture and so on. In all cases the emphasis is placed on the anthropometric aspects of the topic.

In the current revised edition the proportion of physiology practicals has been increased, largely reflecting the ways in which physiology and anthropometry complement each other on academic programmes in the sport and exercise sciences.

The six new chapters have a physiological emphasis (focusing on electromyography, haematology, cardiovascular function, submaximal limitations to exercise, assessment of physical activity and energy balance), except for the final chapter on the links between anthropometry and body image. Of the fifteen chapters retained from the first edition, four have incorporated new co-authors with a view to providing the most authoritative contributions available.

As with the first edition, the content is oriented towards laboratory practicals but offers much more than prescription of a series of laboratory exercises. A comprehensive theoretical background is provided for each topic so that users of the text are not obliged to conduct extensive literature reviews in order to place the subject in context. Each chapter contains an explanation of the appropriate methodology and where possible an outline of specific laboratory-based practicals. This is not always feasible, for example in studying growth processes in child athletes. In such cases, virtually all aspects of performance testing in children are covered and special considerations with regard to data acquisition on children are outlined. Methodologies for researchers in growth and development are also described.

Many of the topics included in this text called for unique individual approaches and so it was not always possible to have a common structure for each chapter. In the majority of cases the laboratory practicals are retained until the end of that chapter as the earlier text provides the theoretical framework for their conduct. Despite any individual variation from the standard structure, together the contributions represent a collective set of exercises for an academic programme in kinanthropometry. The relative self-sufficiency of each contribution also explains why relevant concepts crop up in more than one chapter, for example, concepts of efficiency, metabolism, maximal oxygen uptake, scaling and so on. The last section contains two chapters which are concerned with basic statistical analysis and are designed to inform researchers and students about data handling. This advice should help promote proper use of common statistical techniques for analysing data obtained on human subjects as well as help to avoid common abuses of basic statistical tools.

It is hoped that this text will stimulate improvement in teaching and instruction strategies in the application of laboratory techniques in kinanthropometry and physiology. In this way we will have continued to make our contribution towards the education of the next generation of specialists concerned with relating human structure to its function.

Roger Eston
Thomas Reilly

PART ONE
NEUROMUSCULAR ASPECTS OF MOVEMENT

SKELETAL MUSCLE FUNCTION

1

Vasilios Baltzopoulos and Nigel P. Gleeson

1.1 AIMS

The aims in this chapter are to:
- describe specific aspects of the structure and function of the muscular system and the role of muscles in human movement,
- provide an understanding of how neuromuscular performance is influenced by training, ageing and sex-related processes,
- provide an understanding of how neuromuscular performance is influenced by joint angle and angular velocity,
- describe the assessment of muscle performance and function by means of isokinetic dynamometry,
- provide an understanding of the value and limitations of isokinetic dynamometry in the assessment of asymptomatic and symptomatic populations.

1.2 INTRODUCTION

Human movement is the result of complex interactions between environmental factors and the nervous, muscular and skeletal systems. Brain cell activities within the cerebral cortex are converted by supraspinal centre programming into neural outputs (central commands) that stimulate the muscular system to produce the required movement (Cheney, 1985; Brooks, 1986). In this chapter, specific aspects of the structure and function of the muscular system are considered as part of the process for producing movement. Knowledge of basic physiological and anatomical principles is assumed.

1.3 PHYSIOLOGICAL ASPECTS OF MUSCLE AND JOINT FUNCTION

1.3.1 BASIC STRUCTURE AND FUNCTION OF SKELETAL MUSCLE

Each skeletal muscle contains a large number of muscle fibres assembled together by collagenous connective tissue. A motoneuron and the muscle fibres it innervates represent a motor unit. The number of muscle fibres in a motor unit (innervation ratio) depends on the function of the muscle. Small muscles that are responsible for fine movements, such as the extraocular muscles, have approximately 5–15 muscle fibres per motor unit. Large muscles, such as the gastrocnemius, required for strength and power events, have innervation ratios of approximately 1:1800. A muscle fibre comprises a number of myofibrils surrounded by an excitable membrane, the sarcolemma. The basic structural unit of a myofibril is the sarcomere, which is composed of thick and thin filaments of contractile proteins. The thick filaments are mainly composed of myosin. The thin filaments are composed of actin and the regulatory proteins tropomyosin and troponin that prevent interaction of actin and myosin.

Nerve action potentials propagated along the axons of motoneurons are transmitted to the postsynaptic membrane (sarcolemma) by an electrochemical process. A muscle action potential is propagated along the sarcolemma at velocities ranging from 1 to 3 m s^{-1}. It has

Kinanthropometry and Exercise Physiology Laboratory Manual: Tests, Procedures and Data. 2nd Edition, Volume 2: Exercise Physiology
Edited by RG Eston and T Reilly. Published by Routledge, London, June 2001

been reported, however, that the conduction velocity can be increased to approximately 6 m s^{-1} with resistance training (Kereshi *et al.*, 1983). The muscle action potential causes Ca^{2+} release that disinhibits the regulatory proteins of the thin filaments. This freedom from inhibition allows the myosin globular heads to attach to binding sites on the actin filaments and form cross-bridges. The interaction of the actin and myosin filaments causes them to slide past one another and generate force which is transmitted to the Z discs of the sarcomere. This is known as the sliding filament theory. The details of the exact mechanism responsible for the transformation of adenosine triphosphate energy from a chemical to a mechanical form in the cross-bridge cycle is not completely known (Pollack, 1983). For a detailed discussion of the electrochemical events associated with muscular contraction the reader is referred to the text by Gowitzke and Milner (1988).

1.3.2 MOTOR UNIT TYPES AND FUNCTION

Motor units are usually classified according to contractile and mechanical characteristics into three types (Burke, 1981).

- Type S: Slow contraction time, low force level, resistant to fatigue
- Type FR: Fast contraction time, medium force level, resistant to fatigue
- Type FF: Fast contraction time, high force level, fatiguable

Morphological differences are also evident between the different motor unit types. For example, motoneuron size, muscle fibre cross-sectional area and innervation ratio are increased in fast – compared to slow – type motor units.

Another scheme classifies motor units as Type I, IIa or IIb, based on myosin ATPase. An alternative subdivision is slow-twitch oxidative (SO), fast-twitch oxidative glycolytic (FOG) and fast-twitch glycolytic (FG), based on myosin ATPase and anaerobic/aerobic capacity (Brooke and Kaiser, 1974). The relative distribution of different motor unit types is determined by genetic factors. Elite endurance athletes demonstrate a predominance of slow or Type I fibres. Fast-twitch fibres predominate in sprint or power event athletes.

The muscle fibres in a motor unit are all of the same type, but each muscle contains a proportion of the three motor unit types (Nemeth *et al.*, 1986). Motor units are activated in a preset sequence (S–FR–FF) (orderly recruitment) that is determined mainly by the motoneuron size of the motor unit (size principle) (Henneman, 1957; Enoka and Stuart, 1984; Gustafsson and Pinter, 1985). The force exerted by a muscle depends on the number of motor units activated and the frequency of the action potentials (Harrison, 1983). The orderly recruitment theory, based on the size principle, indicates that recruitment is based on the force required, not the velocity of movement. Thus slow motor units are always activated irrespective of velocity. Most human movement is performed within the velocity range of the slow fibres (Green, 1986), although there is evidence of selective activation of muscles with a predominance of fast-twitch motor units during rapid movements (Behm and Sale, 1993).

1.3.3 TRAINING ADAPTATIONS

Resistance training results in neural and structural adaptations which improve muscle function. Neural adaptations include improved central command that generates a greater action potential (Komi *et al.*, 1978; Sale *et al.*, 1983) and a better synchronization of action potential discharge in different motor units (Milner-Brown *et al.*, 1975). Structural adaptations include increases in the cross-sectional area of muscle fibres (hypertrophy) and possibly an increase in the number of muscle fibres through longitudinal fibre splitting. There is no conclusive evidence for development of new fibres (hyperplasia) in humans. The structural changes that are induced by resistance training result in an overall increase in contractile proteins and therefore muscle force capacity (MacDougall *et al.*, 1982). Adaptation of specific motor unit types depends on resistance training that stresses their specific characteristics: this is known as the principle of specificity. For example, during fast high-resistance training movements, slow motor units are activated, but they do not adapt because their specific characteristics are not stressed. Recent evidence suggests that limited transformation between slow- and fast-twitch muscle fibres is possible with long-term specific training (Simoneau *et al.*, 1985; Tesch and Karlsson, 1985).

1.3.4 EFFECTS OF AGE AND SEX ON MUSCLE PERFORMANCE

Sex differences in muscle function parameters have been examined extensively. The absolute muscular force of the upper extremity in males is approximately 50% higher than in females (Hoffman *et al.*, 1979; Morrow and Hosler, 1981; Heyward *et al.*, 1986). The absolute muscular force of the lower extremities is approximately 30% higher in males (Laubach, 1976; Morrow and Hosler, 1981). Because of sex differences in anthropometric parameters such as body mass, lean body mass, muscle mass and muscle cross-sectional area that affect strength, muscular performance should be relative to these parameters. Research on the relationship between body mass and maximum muscular force or moment is inconclusive, with some studies indicating high significant correlations (Beam *et al.*, 1982; Clarkson *et al.*, 1982) and others no significant relationship (Hoffman *et al.*, 1979; Morrow and Hosler, 1981; Kroll *et al.*, 1990). Maximum muscular force expressed relative to body mass, lean body mass or muscle mass is similar in males and females, but some studies indicate that differences are not completely eliminated in upper extremity muscles (Hoffman *et al.*, 1979; Frontera *et al.*, 1991).

Maximum force is closely related to muscle cross-sectional area in both static (Maughan *et al.*, 1983) and dynamic conditions (Schantz *et al.*, 1983). Research on maximum force relative to muscle cross-sectional area in static or dynamic conditions indicates that there is no significant difference between sexes (Schantz *et al.*, 1983; Bishop *et al.*, 1987) although higher force:cross-sectional area ratios for males have also been reported (Maughan *et al.*, 1983; Ryushi *et al.*, 1988). However, instrumentation and procedures for measurement of different anthropometric parameters *in vivo* (for example, cross-sectional area, moment arms, lean body mass, muscle mass) are often inaccurate. Measurement of cross-sectional area in pennate muscles or in the elderly is inappropriate for the normalization of muscular force or moment. Muscle mass, determined from urinary creatinine excretion, is a better indicator of force-generating capacity and is the main determinant of age- and gender-related differences in muscle function (Frontera *et al.*, 1991). The findings of muscle function studies, therefore, must always be considered relative to the inherent problems of procedures, instrumentation and *in vivo* assessment of muscle performance and anthropometric parameters.

Muscular force decreases with advancing age (Dummer *et al.*, 1985; Bemben, 1991; Frontera *et al.*, 1991). This decline has been attributed mainly to changes in muscle composition and physical activity (Bemben, 1991; Frontera *et al.*, 1991). Furthermore, the onset and rate of force decline are different in males and females and in upper–lower extremity muscles (Dummer *et al.*, 1985; Aoyagi and Shephard, 1992). These differences are mainly due to a reduction in steroid hormones in females after menopause and involvement in different habitual-recreational activities. Generally there is a decrease of approximately 5–8% per decade after the age of 20–30 (Shephard, 1991; Aoyagi and Shephard, 1992).

1.4 MECHANICAL ASPECTS OF MUSCLE AND JOINT FUNCTION

1.4.1 MUSCULAR ACTIONS

Muscular activation involves the electro-chemical processes that cause sliding of myofilaments, shortening of the sarcomere and exertion of force. The overall muscle length during activation is determined not only by the muscular force but also by the external load or resistance applied to the muscle. The ratio muscular force:external load determines three distinct conditions of muscle action:

1. *Concentric action*: muscular force is greater than external force and consequently overall muscle length decreases (i.e. muscle shortens) during activation.
2. *Isometric action*: muscular force is equal to external force, and muscle length remains constant.
3. *Eccentric action*: external force is greater than muscular force and consequently muscle length is increased (muscle lengthening) during activation.

During all three conditions, sarcomeres are stimulated and attempt to shorten by means of actin–myosin interaction (sarcomere contraction). The use of the term 'contraction' to mean shortening should be used only to describe the shortening of sarcomeres, not changes in length of the whole muscle. During eccentric activation, for example, the muscle is lengthened and therefore terms such as 'eccentric contraction' or 'isometric contraction' may be misleading (Cavanagh, 1988).

In attempting to examine whole muscle function it is important to consider the different component parts of the muscle, i.e. both the functional contractile (active) and the elastic (passive) components. A simplified mechanical model of muscle includes three components that simulate the mechanical properties of the different structures. The contractile component (CC) simulates the active, force-generating units (i.e. sarcomeres), the series elastic component (SEC) simulates the elastic properties of the sarcolemma, and the parallel elastic component (PEC) simulates the elastic properties of the collagenous connective tissue in parallel with the contractile component (Komi, 1984, 1986; Chapman, 1985).

Muscle architecture describes the organization of muscle fibres within the muscle and affects muscle function. The angle between the muscle fibres and the line of action from origin to insertion is defined as the pennation angle. The pennation angle and the number of sarcomeres that are arranged in series or in parallel with the line of action of the muscle are important factors affecting muscular force.

1.4.2 FORCE–LENGTH AND FORCE–VELOCITY RELATIONSHIPS IN ISOLATED MUSCLE

In muscles isolated from the skeletal system in a laboratory preparation, the force exerted at different muscle lengths depends on the properties of the active (CC) and passive components (SEC and PEC) at different muscle lengths. Force exerted by the interaction of actin and myosin depends on the number of the available cross-bridges, which is maximum near the resting length of the muscle. The force exerted by the passive elastic elements (SEC and PEC) is increased exponentially as muscle length increases beyond resting length (Figure 1.1). The total force exerted, therefore, is the sum of the active and passive forces. At maximum length, there is little force associated with active components because of minimum cross-bridge availability. However, force contributed by the elastic components alone may be even greater than the maximum CC force at resting length (Baratta and Solomonow, 1991).

The effect of the linear velocity during muscle shortening or lengthening on the force output has been examined extensively since the pioneering work of Hill (1938). With an increase in linear concentric velocity of muscle shortening, the force exerted is decreased non-linearly because the number of cross-bridges formed, and the force they exert, are reduced (Figure 1.2). Furthermore, the distribution of different motor unit types affects the force–velocity relationship. A higher output at faster angular velocities indicates a higher percentage of FF–FR motor units (Gregor *et al.*, 1979;

Figure 1.1 Force–length relationship in isolated muscle showing the contribution of the contractile and the elastic elements on total muscular force. Force units are arbitrary.

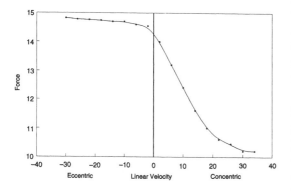

Figure 1.2 Force–velocity relationship of isolated muscle during concentric, isometric and eccentric muscle action. Force and velocity units are arbitrary and do not refer to specific muscles.

Froese and Houston, 1985). However, with an increase in linear eccentric velocity of muscle lengthening, the force exerted is increased (Wilkie, 1950; Chapman, 1976; Thorstensson *et al.*, 1976; Tihanyi *et al.*, 1987).

1.4.3 MUSCLE FUNCTION DURING JOINT MOVEMENT

Examination of the mechanical properties of isolated muscle is of limited use when considering how muscles function during movements in sports or other activities. Movement of body segments results from the application of muscular force around the joint axis of rotation. It is therefore important to consider the relationship between muscle function and joint position and motion (Bouisset, 1984; Kulig *et al.*, 1984). The movement of the joint segments around the axis of rotation is proportional to the rotational effect of the muscular force or moment. This is measured in newton metres (Nm) and is defined as the product of muscular force (in newtons) and moment arm, i.e. the perpendicular distance (in metres) between force line and the axis of rotation of the joint (Figure 1.3). Other physiological, mechanical and structural factors that were described earlier also affect muscle function in a joint system (Figure 1.4).

Joint motion results from the action of muscle groups. Individual muscles in the group may have different origin or insertion points, they may operate over one or two joints and have a different architecture. The moment arm of the muscle group is also variable over the range of motion of the joint. Assessment of dynamic muscle function, therefore, must consider these factors. It must be emphasized that relationships such as force–length or force–velocity refer to individual muscles, whereas moment–joint position and moment–angular joint velocity relationships refer to the function of a muscle group around a joint. For example, the moment of the knee extensor group (rectus femoris, vastus lateralis, vastus medialis, vastus intermedius) at different knee joint angular velocities and positions can be examined during voluntary knee extension using appropriate instrumentation. These terms must not be confused with the force–velocity and force–length relationships of the four individual muscles. These can be examined only if the muscles were separated from a cadaveric joint in the laboratory.

1.4.4 MEASUREMENT OF DYNAMIC MUSCLE FUNCTION – ISOKINETIC DYNAMOMETRY

The most significant development for the study of dynamic muscle and joint function was the introduction of isokinetic dynamometry in the 1960s (Hislop and Perrine, 1967; Thistle *et al.*, 1967). Isokinetic dynamometers have hydraulic or electromechanical mechanisms that maintain the angular velocity of a joint constant, by providing a resistive moment that is equal to the muscular moment throughout the range of movement. This is referred to as optimal loading. Passive systems (Cybex II, Akron, Merac) permit isokinetic concentric movements only, but more recently active systems (Biodex, Cybex 6000, KinCom, Lido) provide both concentric and eccentric isokinetic conditions, with maximum joint angular velocities up to 8.72 rad s^{-1} (500 deg s^{-1}) for concentric actions and 4.36 rad s^{-1} (250 deg s^{-1}) for eccentric actions (see Figure 1.5). It is important to note that it is the joint angular velocity that is controlled and kept constant,

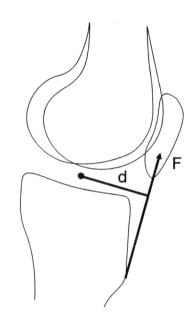

Figure 1.3 The moment arm (*d*) of the knee extensor group is the shortest or perpendicular distance between the patellar tendon and the joint centre. The muscular moment is the product of the force (*F*) along the patellar tendon and the moment arm (*d*).

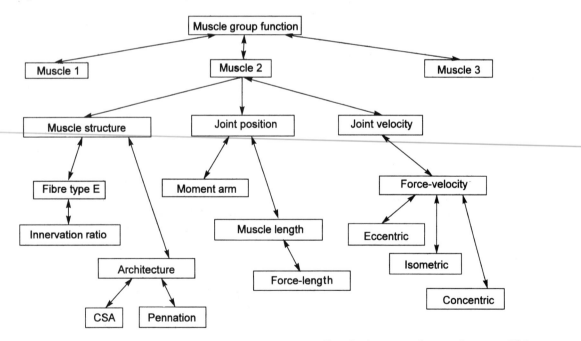

Figure 1.4 The main physiological and mechanical factors that affect the function of a muscle group. This simple model is not exhaustive and any interactions between the different factors are not indicated for simplicity.

Figure 1.5 Measurement of knee extensor strength on an isokinetic dynamometer (KinCom 500H, Chattex, Chattanooga, TN, USA).

not the linear velocity of the active muscle group (Hinson *et al.*, 1979). Dynamometers that control the rate of change of joint angular velocity have also been developed (Westing *et al.*, 1991). Most commercial isokinetic systems have accessories that allow testing of all the major joints of the upper and lower limbs and the back. Apart from isolated joint tests, workplace manual activities, such as lifting and handling materials and equipment, can be simulated on adapted dynamometers using dedicated attachments. Methodological problems such as subject positioning and motivation during the test require standardized protocols. Mechanical factors such as the effect of gravitational moment or the control of the acceleration of the segment affect measurement of muscular moment but appropriate correction methods have been developed and used routinely (Baltzopoulos and Brodie, 1989). Excellent test reliability and computerized assessment of muscle function permit widespread application of isokinetics for testing, training and rehabilitation.

1.4.5 MOMENT–ANGULAR VELOCITY RELATIONSHIP

The moment exerted during concentric actions is maximum at slow angular velocities and decreases with increasing angular velocity. Some authors have reported a constant moment output (plateau) for a range of slow angular velocities (Lesmes *et al.*, 1978; Perrine and Edgerton, 1978; Wickiewicz *et al.*, 1984; Thomas *et al.*, 1987), whereas others have found a continuous decrease from slow to fast concentric angular velocities (Thorstensson *et al.*, 1976; Coyle *et al.*, 1981; Westing *et al.*, 1988). Although the plateau has been attributed to neural inhibition during slow dynamic muscular activation, it is also affected by training level and testing protocol (Hortobagyi and Katch, 1990). The rate of decrease at higher angular velocities is affected by activity, sex and the physiological/mechanical factors discussed above. The maximum concentric moment of the knee extensors decreases by approximately 40% from 1.05 to 4.19 rad s^{-1} (60 to 240 deg s^{-1}), whereas the knee flexor moment decrease varies between 25 and 50% (Prietto and Caiozzo, 1989; Westing and Seger, 1989). The eccentric moment remains relatively constant with increasing angular velocity and approximately 20% higher than the isometric moment. There are considerable differences in muscular moment measurements at different concentric–eccentric angular velocities between the large number of studies on dynamic muscle function. These result mainly from differences in methodology, anthropometric, physiological and mechanical parameters (Cabri, 1991; Perrin, 1993).

The moment–velocity relationship is influenced by the physiological principles of isolated muscular action and the mechanical factors affecting muscle function in a joint system. Figure 1.4 is a simple representation of the different mechanical and physiological factors that affect the function of a muscle group during joint movement. Direct comparisons of the moment–angular velocity relationship during isokinetic eccentric or concentric joint motion, with the force–linear velocity relationship of isolated muscle, is of limited use, given the number of variables affecting muscle and joint function (Bouisset, 1984; Bobbert and Harlaar, 1992).

1.5 ISOKINETIC DYNAMOMETRY APPLICATIONS

1.5.1 MEASUREMENT ISSUES: INDICES OF NEUROMUSCULAR PERFORMANCE AND RELATIONSHIPS TO FUNCTIONAL CAPABILITY

Applications of isokinetic dynamometry are manifold. Its deployment as a 'safe' tool for conditioning to enhance neuromuscular performance has been established in the literature. The most significant aspects of isokinetic training are velocity-specific adaptations and the transfer of improvements to angular velocities, other than the training velocity. Training at intermediate velocities 2.09–3.14 rad s^{-1} (120–180 deg s^{-1}) produces the most significant transfer to both slower and faster angular velocities (Bell and Wenger, 1992; Behm and Sale, 1993). Eccentric training at 2.09 rad s^{-1} improves muscle function in both slower (1.05 rad s^{-1}) and faster (3.14 rad s^{-1}) angular velocities (Duncan *et al.*, 1989). There is no conclusive evidence of improvements in eccentric muscle function after concentric training and vice versa.

Earlier studies reported no hypertrophy following isokinetic training (Lesmes *et al.*, 1978; Cote *et al.*, 1988) although more recent findings suggest isokinetic training can induce increases in muscle size (Alway *et al.*, 1990). Further research is required to examine the effects of both concentric and eccentric isokinetic training programmes on muscular hypertrophy.

Isokinetic dynamometry has also become a favoured method for the assessment of dynamic muscle function in both clinical, research and sports environments. Several indices, such as peak torque, are used in the literature to characterize individual, group or larger population performance.

The relevance of isokinetic dynamometry may be better understood by consideration of the specificity of this mode of testing in relation to the criterial physical activity. This comparability may be achieved at different levels which include identification and assessment of the involved muscle group; simulation of the activity's movement pattern and muscle action type during testing; and simulation of the movement velocity during testing (Sale, 1991). The muscle group of interest may be tested using anatomical movements that employ this muscle group as an agonist. Further test specificity in terms of simulation of the movement pattern may be limited because, while commercially available isokinetic dynamometers are capable of testing unilateral single-joint movements, most are not suitable for testing the multi-joint movements common to many sports. Similarly, replication of the stretch–shortening cycle (eccentric–concentric) pattern of muscular action, which occurs in some sports and physical activities, is limited to those commercially available isokinetic dynamometers which offer assessment of both concentric and eccentric types of muscular action. This limitation may further extend to compromised replication of the temporal sequencing of these types of muscular action during testing.

Attempted replication of the eccentric component of sport-specific movements may offer increased potential for injury during the testing of symptomatic and asymptomatic individuals completing rehabilitation or conditioning programmes. Attempts to mimic aspects of sport-specific movement also demand greater attention be given by the test administrator to accommodation and habituation responses of the participant to the testing protocols. Isokinetic dynamometers are often compromised in their ability to replicate sport-specific movement velocities, for example, offering concentric muscle action test velocities up to only 58% (~7 rad s^{-1}) of the maximum unresisted knee extension velocity (~12 rad s^{-1})

(Thorstensson *et al.*, 1976) and up to 20% (~3.4 rad s^{-1}) of the maximal eccentric action velocity of the knee flexors during sprint running (~17 rad s^{-1}) (Sale, 1991).

The validity of isokinetic dynamometry is complicated by a myriad of factors that interact to influence the externally registered estimate of the net torque or work associated with a joint system. Strength performance constitutes only one aspect of the cascade of the neuromuscular and musculoskeletal machinery necessary to achieve temporal neuromuscular control and coordinated rapid force production. The relative importance of absolute strength to the sports-performance of interest will be influenced by torque–velocity and power–velocity relationships (Fenn and Marsh, 1935; Hill, 1938) interacting with sport-specific neuromuscular recruitment and activation patterns (Edman, 1992). The magnitude of the correlation between indices of isokinetic neuromuscular performance and functional performance has been shown to be variable and accounts for only low to moderate portions of the shared variance. During the rehabilitation of high-performance soccer players from musculoskeletal injury and dysfunction through to full functionality and return to match-play condition, absolute strength performance of the involved musculature varied relatively little across the period of rehabilitation (15–20% change relative to post-injury asymptomatic functional performance and time of return to match-play condition) (Rees and Gleeson, 1999). In contrast, indices of temporal neuromuscular control (electromechanical delay (see Chapter 2 by Gleeson), rate of force development, and static and dynamic proprioception (discussed later), demonstrated relatively dramatic performance changes over the same period (70–85%), suggesting a more potent role for the latter factors in functional performance. Assessment of strength using isokinetic dynamometry constitutes one component of a wider multivariate model of neuromuscular performance (Cabri, 1991; Perrin, 1993). In this respect, it may contribute partially to an informed decision about the timing of a 'safe' return to play for the athlete rehabilitating from injury (Rees and Gleeson, 1999). However, the preceding discussion suggests that there are limitations associated with this mode of assessment and that it cannot be used unreservedly.

Sensitivity of a criterion test protocol may be defined as the ability to detect small changes in an individual's performance, or relative positional changes of an individual's performance within a sub-sample (Gleeson and Mercer, 1996). This ability to discriminate relates directly to the reliability and reproducibility characteristics of the isokinetic test protocol. Within the context of a given application, the selection of minimum or threshold reliability and reproducibility criteria to meet the demand for appropriate measurement rigour will in turn regulate the selection of suitable protocol characteristics (for example, required number of replicates, inter-replicate time duration and mode of action). In a 'case-study', less stringent sensitivity criteria may be appropriate for the discrimination of gross muscle dysfunction in the clinical setting, whereas relatively greater sensitivity may be needed to interpret correctly the effects of intervention conditioning in an elite strength-trained athlete, whose performance levels may vary by only ±5% over the competitive season (Gleeson and Mercer, 1992).

Once a mandate for the valid use of isokinetic dynamometry has been established within an intended measurement application, there are several competing demands within measurement protocol design which may affect the measurement of isokinetic strength and its subsequent suitability for meaningful evaluation and interpretation. The desire to increase measurement rigour, reliability and sensitivity to suit the intended application by using more elaborate multiple trials may be hampered by logistical and financial constraints or reduced subject compliance. The net effect of the interaction of such demands may be considered to be the utility of the isokinetic dynamometry protocol. Of the factors that impinge on utility, those relating to reliability afford the most control of measurement quality by the test administrator.

Research data suggest that, in many measurement applications, the reliability and sensitivity associated with many frequently-used indices of isokinetic leg strength which are estimated by means of single-trial protocols are not sufficient to differentiate either performance change within the same individual or between individuals within a homogeneous group. While such limitations may be addressed by the use of protocols based on 3–4 inter-day trials for the index of peak torque, other indices which demonstrate reduced reliability, for example, the ratio of knee flexion to extension peak torque, may require many more replicates to achieve the same level of sensitivity. Here, the measurement utility of the index may not be sufficient to justify its proper deployment. Such issues are important for the utility of all aspects of dynamometry, and the reader is directed to more complete reviews (for example, Gleeson and Mercer, 1996).

1.5.2 DATA COLLECTION AND ANALYSIS CONSIDERATIONS

One of the most important considerations in testing muscle function is the positioning of the subject. The length of the muscle group, contribution of the elastic components, effective moment arm, development of angular velocity and inhibitory effects by the antagonistic muscle groups are all influenced by positioning and segment–joint stabilization during the test. For these reasons, the above factors must be standardized between tests, to allow valid comparisons.

Isokinetic testing of an isolated joint does not employ a natural movement. Accurate instructions are required concerning the operation of the isokinetic dynamometers and the testing requirements, together with adequate familiarization. Eccentric conditions, particularly fast angular velocities, require special attention in order to avoid injury in novices or subjects with musculoskeletal weaknesses.

Simple isometric measurements can be performed using force transducers or cable tensiometers, hand dynamometers and simple free weights or resistive exercise equipment (Watkins, 1993). The force output using these devices depends on the point of attachment on the limb, moment arm of muscle group and the joint position. It is therefore essential to express joint function in terms of moment (N m), i.e. as the product of the force output of the measuring device (N) and the perpendicular distance (m) between the force line and the joint axis of rotation. Accurate determination of the joint centre is not possible without complicated radiographic measurements and therefore an approximation is necessary. An example is the use of the femoral epicondyle in the knee as a landmark.

Computerized, isokinetic dynamometers allow more accurate positioning of the subject and of the joint tested, and a more precise assessment of muscle function. However, the cost of these devices may prohibit their use as tools in teaching. The moment recorded by isokinetic dynamometers is the total (or resultant) moment exerted around the joint axis of rotation. The main component of this total joint moment is the moment exerted by the active muscle group. The contribution of other structures such as the joint capsule and ligaments to the total joint moment is minimal and therefore the moment recorded by isokinetic dynamometers is considered equal to the muscular moment. During testing of a knee extension, the moment exerted by the quadriceps is the product of the force exerted by the patellar tendon on the tibia and the moment arm, i.e. the perpendicular or shortest distance between the patellar tendon and the centre of the knee joint (Figure 1.3). The moment arm is variable over the range of movement (Figure 1.6), being least at full knee extension and flexion and greatest at approximately 0.78 rad of knee flexion (Baltzopoulos, 1995a). Moment arms at different joint positions are usually measured

Figure 1.6 The patellar tendon moment arm during knee extension from different studies.

directly on the subject using radiography or derived indirectly from cadaveric studies. If the knee extensor isometric moment of a subject with body weight of 800 N (body mass 81.5 kg) is 280 N m at 0.87 rad (50 deg) of knee flexion, and assuming that the moment arm at this joint position is 0.035 m, then the muscular force exerted by the patellar tendon is 8000 N or 10 times the body weight (BW) of that subject. This method can be applied to the moment measurements from isokinetic or isometric tests in order to obtain the actual muscular force exerted. This is usually expressed relative to body weight to allow comparisons. Using a similar method, it was estimated that the maximum muscular force exerted during isokinetic knee extension ranged from 9 BW at 0.52 rad s^{-1} (30 deg s^{-1}) to 6 BW at 3.66 rad s^{-1} (210 deg s^{-1}) (Baltzopoulos, 1995b).

Another important aspect of muscle function assessment is the expression of maximum performance parameters, such as moment, force and power, as a ratio relative to different anthropometric parameters (e.g. body mass, lean body mass, cross-sectional area) without considering the underlying relationship between the two parameters. This ratio is usually obtained by dividing the mean force, for example, by the mean body mass, without considering the regression line between force and

body mass. A ratio relationship assumes that the regression line crosses the origin of the axes (or that the intercept is approximately zero). If, despite a high correlation, a ratio relationship does not exist between moment and body mass, then expressing the moment relative to body mass (N m kg^{-1}) is representative of subjects with body mass close to the mean body mass. This, however, will overestimate or underestimate the moment for subjects with body mass further away from the mean body mass. Indeed the magnitude of the error in estimating the maximum moment from the ratio, instead of the regression line, depends on the intercept (i.e. difference between regression and ratio lines) and the deviation of the subject's body mass from the mean body mass (see Volume 1, Chapter 11 by Winter and Nevill).

Another consideration when comparing muscle function between different groups over time is the use of an appropriate statistical technique. Analysis of covariance (ANCOVA) is necessary if the initial level of the dependent (measured) variable (e.g. maximum isokinetic moment) is different between the groups and the effects of training programmes over time are assessed. Multivariate ANOVA (MANOVA) or multivariate ANCOVA (MANCOVA) is necessary if a number of different muscle function parameters that are likely to affect each other are measured and compared simultaneously.

1.5.3 ASSESSMENT OF SHORT-TERM MUSCLE POWER AND FATIGUE USING ISOKINETIC DYNAMOMETRY

The work capacity of a muscle or muscle group may be determined by calculating the total area under one or a series of torque–angular position curves. Power is determined by assessing the time required to complete the relevant period of work. Many isokinetic dynamometry systems have software that is capable of determining these indices of performance. Protocols have been used to assess the capability of the neuromuscular system to produce all-out short-term work by means of varying simultaneous contributions from the ATP-PC and glycolytic energy pathways (Abernethy *et al.*, 1995; Kannus *et al.*, 1991). Depending on the methodology used for the assessment of power during single or repeated muscle actions, isokinetic indices of peak or mean power may be compromised by the intrusion of the effects of acceleration and deceleration periods associated with limitations of the angular velocity control mechanisms. Furthermore, limitations in the maximum sampling rates for data acquisition offered by commercially available dynamometers would tend to limit the accuracy of analogue-to-digital conversions and attenuate the highest frequencies of work patterns and associated power outputs.

Various isokinetic dynamometry protocols involving serial muscle actions have been used to assess the effects of fatigue on neuromuscular performance. Protocols have ranged from 50 unidirectional maximal voluntary actions of the knee extensor muscle group (Thorstensson *et al.*, 1976) to bidirectional (reciprocal) all-out exercise tasks consisting of 25–30 reciprocal maximal voluntary actions of the knee extensors and flexors of the leg at moderate movement velocities (3.14 rad s^{-1}) with no rest between movements (Burdett and van Swearingen, 1987; Baltzopoulos *et al.*, 1988; Montgomery *et al.*, 1989; Mathiassen, 1989; Gleeson and Mercer, 1992). In the case of bidirectional protocols, total work and indices of fatigue may be determined during both extension and flexion movements. The latter indices may be calculated automatically using the dynamometer's control software. A least-squares regression may be applied to the actual work done in all repetitions, and the index of fatigue can be determined as the ratio of the predicted work done in the last repetition compared to the first repetition and expressed as a percentage. Alternatively, Thorstensson *et al.* (1976) defined endurance as the torque from the last three contractions as a percentage of the initial three contractions of 50 contractions, and Kannus *et al.* (1992) reported that the work performed during the last 5 of 25 repetitions and the total work performed were valuable markers in the documentation of progress during endurance training. The isokinetic protocols may be designed to reflect the 'worst-case' scenario for fatiguing exercise within the context of the sport of interest (Gleeson *et al.*, 1997) or be associated with a particular duration in which a bioenergetic pathway is considered to have prominence (Sale, 1991).

Indices of leg muscular fatigue demonstrate significantly greater variability in inter-day assessments of reproducibility compared with indices of strength (9.1% vs. 4.3%, respectively) (Burdett and van Swearingen, 1987; Gleeson and Mercer, 1992). The ability to reproduce exactly the pattern of work output and fatigue responses over repeated day-to-day trials appears to be compromised. The latter trend may be due in part to an intrusion of conscious or unconscious work output pacing strategies as suspected for this and other exercise modalities during tests of similar duration (Perrin, 1986; Burke *et al.*, 1985). The inflated variability associated with the assessment of isokinetic endurance parameters may be explained by the problems of subjects having to sustain a higher degree of self-motivation to maximum effort throughout 30 repetitions lasting approximately 40 seconds, compared to the relatively short duration of 3 maximal voluntary muscle actions associated with strength assessment protocols. As the series of bidirectional agonist–antagonist muscle group actions associated with the fatigue test protocols progresses, it may be that inherently higher variability of the interaction of motoneuron recruitment, rate coding, temporal patterning and co-activation phenomena, and ultimately changes to the recorded net torque about the joint of interest (Enoka, 1994; Milner-Brown *et al.*, 1975) may underscore these findings. While the dynamometer provides a 'safe' environment in which to stress the musculoskeletal system with high-intensity fatiguing exercise tasks, the 'work–rest' duty cycles and motor unit recruitment patterns associated with the isokinetic testing cannot mimic faithfully the loading during the sports activity. The results from such isokinetic tests of muscle endurance must be interpreted cautiously.

1.5.4 CLINICAL APPLICATIONS OF ISOKINETIC DYNAMOMETRY

Isokinetic dynamometry provides a relatively 'safe' and controlled environment in which to stress the neuromuscular performance of a joint system. Clinical applications of isokinetic dynamometry include assessment of bilateral and agonist–antagonist muscle group performance ratios in symptomatic populations and prophylactic assessments of asymptomatic populations.

It is often assumed that net torque performance scores for the uninjured extremity can be used as the standard for return of the injured extremity to a normal state. This marker for a safe return to play may be compromised by the influence of limb dominance or the effect of neuromuscular specificity of various sport activities on bilateral strength relationships. Bilateral differences are minimal in healthy non-athletes or in participants in sports that involve symmetrical action. However, differences of up to 15% have been reported in asymmetrical sport activities (Perrin *et al.*, 1987). Importantly, in most circumstances involving

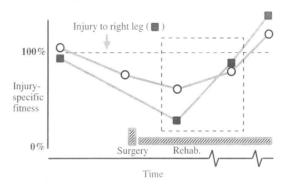

Figure 1.7 A schematic diagram illustrating the dilemma faced by the clinician in assessing safe return-to-play for the injured athlete. The figure shows the progression of performance associated with both the involved right leg (square markers) and contralateral (circular markers) leg prior to and following injury to the right leg. Pre-injury levels of performance are associated with injury. Post-injury conditioning should exceed pre-injury levels of performance for protection from the threat of injury. The clinician has data and contralateral leg comparisons within the dashed box available to help in the decision of when it is safe to return to play (see text).

sports injury, prospective pre-injury performance scores for both involved and contralateral limbs are unavailable to the clinician. Furthermore, the condition of the contralateral 'control' limb is often compromised substantively by deconditioning associated with changed motor unit recruitment patterns during reduced volume and intensity of habitual exercise and injury-related bilateral inhibitory effects. This often serves to lessen the utility of concurrent contralateral limb comparisons and effectively masks the pre-injury baseline performance of the contralateral limb. The latter may be compromised as an optimal marker for a safe 'return to play' because it was associated with the occurrence of the injury. Figure 1.7 illustrates the dilemma faced by the clinician in assessing a safe 'return to play' for the injured athlete.

The bilateral assessment of the injured athlete presents further issues that may hinder the

Figure 1.8 95% confidence limits constructed around a single torque–angular position curve derived from maximal voluntary muscle actions of the knee extensors and flexors at 1.05 rad s^{-1}. The *x* axis denotes the time over which the muscle actions take place (approximately 3 seconds).

proper interpretation of performance scores. The injury may cause unilateral restriction to the range of motion available for isokinetic assessment. While this may be an interesting clinical finding in itself, contralateral comparisons through unequal ranges of motion could be compromised by greater pre-stretch and metabolic potentiation to a muscle, enabling that muscle to produce a higher level of peak torque within the subsequent range of motion tested. Similarly, the differential movement patterns would confound contralateral comparisons of average torque and work values. Variations or modifications in placement of the fixation point between the dynamometer and the patient may affect the recorded peak or average torque. It is essential that appropriate anatomical measurements or mapping techniques be used in these circumstances to minimize the intrusion of these aspects of technical error (Gleeson and Mercer, 1996).

Reciprocal muscle group ratios (e.g. knee flexor/extensor) may indicate aspects of joint balance and possible predisposition to joint or muscle injury. Concentric knee flexion/extension moment ratios range from 0.4 to 0.6 and are mainly affected by activity, methodological measurement problems and gravitational forces (Appen and Duncan, 1986; Fillyaw *et al.*, 1986; Figoni *et al.*, 1988). Studies that use moment data uncorrected for the effect of gravitational forces demonstrate higher ratios and a significant increase in the ratio with increasing angular velocity. This increase is a result of gravity. Gravity-corrected ratios are approximately constant at different angular velocities (Appen and Duncan, 1986; Fillyaw *et al.*, 1986; Baltzopoulos *et al.*, 1991). During joint motion in sport or other activities, concentric action of agonist muscles requires eccentric action of the antagonist muscles to control the movement and ensure joint stability. For this reason, ratios of agonist concentric to antagonist eccentric action (e.g. eccentric knee flexion moment/concentric knee extension moment) are more representative of joint function during sport activities.

It is intuitively appealing for isokinetic dynamometry to offer the capability to discriminate, and potentially diagnose, pathologies in muscle–tendon units and bony articulations of a joint system. Various artefacts in the torque–angular position curves have been attributed to conditions such as anterior cruciate ligament deficiency, and chondromalacia patella (Perrin, 1993). There are many factors, including subject–dynamometer positioning, limb fixation characteristics, the compliance of soft tissue, the compliance of padding and structures of the dynamometer, injury-related neuromuscular inhibitory and pain responses, differential accommodation, habituation and warm-up effects, that influence neuromuscular performance (Gleeson and Mercer, 1996). These factors contribute to the technical and biological variability in the recorded net torque associated with the interaction between a given assessment protocol, patient and the dynamometry system. Figure 1.8 illustrates 95% confidence limits constructed around a single torque–angular position curve derived from maximal voluntary muscle actions of the knee extensors and flexors at 1.05 rad s^{-1}. The limits are estimated from empirical data from reproducibility and single-measurement reliability studies involving asymptomatic participants (Gleeson and Mercer, 1992, 1994). Potential anomalies to the torque–angular position curve would typically need to exceed such limits consistently before further investigation was warranted.

1.5.5 ASSESSMENT OF PROPRIOCEPTION PERFORMANCE USING ISOKINETIC DYNAMOMETRY

A model for dynamic joint stability comprises primary ligamentous restraints interacting with other static stabilizers (osseous geometry, capsular structures and menisci) and with dynamic stabilizers such as the musculature associated with the joint (Fu, 1993). An important function of skeletal muscle is to contribute both sensory and torque-generating machinery to this model. In the functionally stable knee, such factors interact to maintain joint stability. Optimal functioning relies on enhanced awareness of joint position and motion sensation. Proprioception can be thought of as a complex neuromuscular process that involves both afferent and efferent signals and allows the body to maintain stability and orientation during both static and dynamic activities (Lephart *et al.*, 1992).

Proprioceptive input is derived from mechanoreceptors located in the skin, joint capsules, ligaments, and musculotendinous units which relay afferent feedback to the central nervous system (CNS) for continuous processing. Different types of afferent joint receptors have been identified: Ruffini

Figure 1.9 Example data from a single trial of an assessment involving the ability to regulate volitional force (net torque). Performance is expressed as the discrepancy between the blinded attainment of a prescribed force (e.g. 50% maximal voluntary muscle force of the knee flexors, static (first response above baseline)) and subsequent reproduction of this target force (second response above baseline). The exact force data for comparison on the force–time record are indicated by the points at which there are rapid and sustained declines of force as the subject relaxes the musculature (see vertical cursors).

receptors, Paciniform, Golgi Tendon Organs (GTO), and nociceptive type fibres. The latter have high response thresholds, and slowly adapting in the detection of pain. All types of receptors may play a role in the regulation of muscle stiffness around the joint by means of the gamma-muscle spindle system and ultimately contribute to the control of joint stiffness and functional stability (Johannsen *et al.*, 1986; Johannsen, 1991). Information from proprioceptive receptors offers sensory awareness in the form of both feedback and feed-forward mechanisms. Feedback processes are thought to regulate motor control continually through reflex pathways and be associated with reactive muscle activity. Feed-forward neuromuscular control involves planning movements based on sensory information from past experiences and are responsible for preparatory muscle activity (Swanik *et al.*, 1997). It is possible that a protective feedback reflex would be too slow to provide protection in a rapid ligamentous injury scenario (Pope *et al.*, 1979; Rees and Gleeson, 1999). Thus sensory awareness in the form of both feedback and feed-forward mechanisms may underpin the integrity and stabilization of the joint as well as the coordination of complex movement systems (Hasan and Stuart, 1988; Krauspe *et al.*, 1992). For example, the main function of ligamentous afferents may be to provide a continuous preparatory adjustment (or pre-programming) of intrinsic muscle stiffness through the reflex-mediated stiffness.

Proprioceptive performance has been assessed in the contemporary clinical literature using tests such as the ability to reproduce passive positioning of the injured and contralateral limbs (Lattanzio and Petrella, 1998). These tests are undertaken at relatively slow angular velocities of movement. More recently, dynamic proprioception assessments have been developed which may be more applicable to the dynamic model of knee joint stability (Rees and Gleeson, 1999; Gleeson *et al.*, in press). These tests involve the ability to regulate volitional force and results are expressed as the discrepancy between the blinded attainment of a prescribed force (for example, 50% maximal voluntary muscle force of the knee flexors) and subsequent reproduction of this target force. Figure 1.9 shows data from a single trial of a blinded attainment of a prescribed force. In controlled clinical trials involving populations with anterior cruciate ligament deficiency, the patterns of change in the dynamic proprioception performance of the musculature of the knee joint prior to and following bone–patella tendon–bone anterior cruciate ligament reconstruction surgery and subsequent rehabilitation appear to predict improvements in the functional stability of the knee joint.

An isokinetic dynamometry system and its associated control software offer a useful facility for employing both the traditional clinical tests of joint proprioception (reproduction of passive positioning of the involved and contralateral limbs) and more recent dynamic proprioception tests.

The practical exercises in this chapter describe assessment of knee joint function at different joint angular velocities and positions. Similar parameters of muscle function during maximal voluntary activation (isokinetic or isometric) can be assessed in different groups of subjects using other muscle groups to examine the effects of age, sex and sport, and the relationship of muscle function with various anthropometric measures.

1.6 PRACTICAL 1: ASSESSMENT OF MUSCLE FUNCTION DURING ISOKINETIC KNEE EXTENSION AND FLEXION

1.6.1 PURPOSE

The purpose of this practical is to assess the maximum muscular moment (dynamic strength) of the knee extensor and flexor muscles at different concentric and eccentric knee joint angular velocities. This practical requires an isokinetic dynamometer for data collection. As these devices are very expensive, and so may not be available in all laboratories, data collected from a group of young female age swimmers using a Biodex dynamometer are presented in Tables 1.1–1.3. These can be used for data analysis and discussion of the topics examined in this practical.

Table 1.1   Body mass, lean body mass and height of subjects ($n = 10$)

Subject no.	Body mass (kg)	Lean body mass (kg)	Height (m)
1	51.6	39.5	1.57
2	49.4	38.1	1.57
3	58.1	41.2	1.69
4	48.1	37.0	1.62
5	62.5	46.0	1.62
6	58.7	42.9	1.55
7	54.5	38.9	1.52
8	46.5	37.2	1.62
9	68.4	54.1	1.76
10	56.2	39.4	1.53
Mean	55.4	41.4	1.60
SD	6.8	5.2	0.07

1.6.2 PROCEDURE

1. Record all data on the data sheet shown in Figure 1.10.
2. Calibrate the equipment according to the manufacturer's instructions. Record the date, the subject's name, gender, age, body mass, height and training status.
3. Measure or estimate other anthropometric parameters if required (e.g. lean body mass, cross-sectional area of muscle groups, segment circumference and volume, muscle mass etc.).
4. Allow the subject to perform general warm-up/stretching exercises.

Table 1.2 Knee flexion moment (Nm) during isokinetic eccentric and concentric angular velocities

| | Angular velocity (rad s⁻¹)[a] | | | | | | | |
| | Eccentric | | | | Concentric | | | |
Subject no.	4.19	3.14	2.09	1.05	1.05	2.09	3.14	4.19
1	65	61	63	59	52	52	42	39
2	69	71	74	71	57	49	38	38
3	76	83	80	82	67	67	50	45
4	63	61	59	56	43	47	39	34
5	77	81	84	78	68	64	52	47
6	93	90	89	92	69	57	43	42
7	56	65	63	59	50	61	47	39
8	65	72	70	68	54	50	37	29
9	104	110	116	118	96	108	98	105
10	88	90	86	81	62	60	50	44

[a] 1 rad s⁻¹ is equal to an angular velocity of 57.296 deg s⁻¹

Table 1.3 Knee extension moment (Nm) during isokinetic eccentric and concentric angular velocities

| | Angular velocity (rad s⁻¹)[a] | | | | | | | |
| | Eccentric | | | | Concentric | | | |
Subject no.	4.19	3.14	2.09	1.05	1.05	2.09	3.14	4.19
1	137	140	139	132	123	105	105	101
2	128	131	134	130	122	104	78	83
3	179	183	195	186	169	141	116	105
4	152	153	151	144	132	108	82	72
5	179	184	173	169	157	115	96	87
6	180	185	187	191	168	128	98	87
7	171	169	173	166	154	119	97	84
8	159	157	161	112	131	103	82	71
9	253	249	245	238	202	162	139	121
10	159	179	175	169	152	118	98	85

[a] 1 rad s⁻¹ is equal to an angular velocity of 57.296 deg s⁻¹

Side	Action	Parameter	Eccentric					Concentric			
			4.19	3.14	2.09	1.05	0	1.05	2.09	3.14	4.19
R	EXT	Maximum Moment (Nm)									
		Angular Position (rad))									
	FLX	Maximum Moment (Nm)									
		Angular Position (rad)									
		FLX/EXT Moment Ratio									
L	EXT	Maximum Moment (Nm)									
		Angular Position (rad)									
	FLX	Maximum Moment (Nm)									
		Angular Position (rad)									
		FLX/EXT Moment Ratio									
L/R EXT Moment Ratio											
L/R FLX Moment Ratio											

Figure 1.10 Data collection sheet (R = right, L = left, EXT = extension, FLX = flexion).

5. Position the subject on the dynamometer without attaching the input arm. A sitting position with the hips flexed at approximately 1.74 rad (100 deg) is recommended. A supine position may be preferable in order to increase muscular output and simulate movements where the hip angle is approximately neutral.
6. Carefully align the approximate joint axis of rotation with the axis of the dynamometer by modifying the subject's position and/or the dynamometer seat adjustments. For the knee test, align the lateral femoral epicondyle with the dynamometer axis and ensure that it remains in alignment throughout the test range of movement.
7. Attach the input arm of the dynamometer on the tibia above the malleoli and ensure that there is no movement of the leg relative to the input arm. Generally a rigid connection is required between the segment and the various parts of the input arm.
8. Secure all the other body parts not involved in the test with the appropriate straps. Ensure that the thigh, opposite leg, hips, chest and arms are appropriately stabilized. Make a note of the seat configuration and the joint positions in case you need to replicate the test on another occasion.
9. Provide written, clear instructions to the subject concerning the purpose of the test and the experimental procedure. Explain in detail the requirement for maximum voluntary effort throughout the test and the use of visual feedback to enhance muscular output. Allow the subject to ask any questions and be prepared to explain in detail the test requirements.
10. Familiarize the subject with the movement. Allow at least five submaximal repetitions (extension–flexion throughout the range of movement) at all the test angular velocities.

11. Allow the subject to rest. During this period, enter the appropriate data on the computer system, set the range of movement and perform the gravity correction procedure according to the instructions provided by the manufacturer of the dynamometer.
12. Start the test and allow 5–6 reciprocal repetitions (extension followed by flexion). The order of the test angular velocity should be randomized. Visual feedback and appropriate test instructions are adequate for maximum effort. If other forms of motivation are required (e.g. verbal encouragement) then make sure they are standardized and consistent between subjects.
13. After the test is completed, record on the data sheet the maximum moment for knee extension and flexion and the angular position where the maximum was measured. Allow the subject to rest for 1–2 minutes and perform the test at the other angular velocities. Repeat the procedure for the other side.

1.6.3 DATA ANALYSIS

1. Plot the maximum moment of the knee extensors and flexors against the angular velocity of movement (moment–angular velocity relationship).
2. Compare the increase/decrease of the moment during the eccentric and concentric movements with previously published studies examining this relationship.
3. Discuss the physiological/mechanical explanation for these findings.
4. Calculate the flexion/extension ratio by dividing the corresponding maximum moment recorded at each speed and plot this ratio against angular velocity. What do you observe? Explain any increase or decrease at the different eccentric and concentric velocities.
5. Plot the angular position (knee flexion angle) of the maximum moment at different angular velocities. Is the maximum moment recorded at the same angular position at different angular velocities? What is the physiological/mechanical explanation for your findings?
6. If data for both sides have been collected, then calculate the bilateral moment ratio (left joint moment/right joint moment) at the different angular velocities. See if you can explain any bilateral differences.
7. Establish the relationship between maximum moment, body mass and lean body mass. Can you express the maximum moment relative to body mass or lean body mass as a ratio? Explain the rationale for your answer.

1.7 PRACTICAL 2: ASSESSMENT OF ISOMETRIC FORCE–JOINT POSITION RELATIONSHIP

1.7.1 PURPOSE

The purpose of this practical is to assess the maximum isometric moment (static strength) of the knee extensor muscles at different knee joint positions. Isometric force can be measured using relatively inexpensive instruments that are commercially available.

1.7.2 PROCEDURE

Record all data on the data sheet for this practical (Figure 1.10).
1. Calibrate equipment according to the manufacturer's instructions. Record the date, the subject's name, gender, age, body mass, height and training status.
2. Measure or estimate other anthropometric parameters if required (for example lean body mass, cross-sectional area of muscle groups, segment circumference and volume, muscle mass etc.).
3. After some general warm-up/stretching exercises, position the subject on a bench lying on his/her side. A position with the hips flexed at approximately 1.74 rad (100 deg) is recommended. An extended position may be preferable to increase muscular output and simulate movements where the hip angle is approximately neutral.
4. Secure all the other body parts not involved in the test with appropriate straps. Ensure that the thigh, opposite leg, hips, chest and arms are appropriately stabilized. Make a note of the joint positions in case you need to replicate the test on another occasion. Attach the tensiometer or portable dynamometer to the limb near the malleoli. Ensure that the instrument is perpendicular to the tibia and on the sagittal plane (i.e. the plane formed by the tibia and femur). The movement must be performed on a plane parallel to the ground in order to avoid the effect of the gravitational force on the measurements. If the test is performed with the subject seated in a chair then the measurements of muscular moment are affected and must be corrected for the effect of the gravitational moment. For details of this procedure see Baltzopoulos and Brodie (1989).
5. Provide written, clear instructions to the subject concerning the purpose of the test and the experimental procedure. Explain in detail the requirement for maximum voluntary effort throughout the test and the use of feedback to enhance muscular output.
6. Familiarize the subject with the movement and allow at least two submaximal repetitions. An important aspect of isometric testing is the gradual increase of muscular force, avoiding sudden, ballistic movements. Allow the subject to ask any questions and be prepared to explain and demonstrate the test requirements.
7. Position the knee at approximately 90 degrees of knee flexion, start the test and maintain maximum effort for 5–7 seconds. Ensure that the presentation of test instructions and the use of verbal and visual feedback is standardized and consistent between subjects.
8. After the test is completed, record the maximum force measured. Measure the distance between the point of application and the joint centre of rotation and calculate the moment for knee extension as the product of force and moment arm. Record the isometric moment and the angular position where the maximum was measured, on the data sheet for this practical (Figure 1.10). Allow the subject to rest for 1–2 minutes and perform the test at angular position intervals of 10 degrees until full extension.

1.7.3 DATA ANALYSIS

1. Plot the maximum moment of the knee extensors against the angular joint position (moment–joint position relationship).

2. Explain the increase/decrease of the moment during the range of movement and compare these findings with previously published studies examining this relationship in other muscle groups.
3. Establish the physiological/mechanical explanation for these findings.
4. Calculate the muscular force from the equation: Force = Moment / Moment Arm. The moment arm of the knee extensors at different joint positions is presented in Figure 1.6. Is the force-position similar to the moment position relationship? What are the main determinants of these relationships during knee extension and other joint movements such as knee and elbow flexion?

1.8 PRACTICAL 3: ASSESSMENT OF KNEE JOINT PROPRIOCEPTION PERFORMANCE: REPRODUCTION OF PASSIVE JOINT POSITIONING

1.8.1 PURPOSE

The purpose of this practical is to assess the error associated with the passive reproduction of a series of blinded target knee flexion angles in a sagittal plane. Knee flexion angles can be measured using a isokinetic dynamometer goniometer system and movement of the lever input arm can be achieved manually or in an automated fashion under software control as appropriate.

1.8.2 PROCEDURE

1. Calibrate the equipment according to the manufacturer's instructions. Record the date, the subject's name, gender, age, body mass, height and training status.
2. Allow the subject to perform general warm-up/stretching exercises. Position the subject on the dynamometer without attaching the input arm. A sitting position with the hips flexed at approximately 1.74 rad (100 deg) is recommended. A supine position may be preferable in order to increase muscular output and simulate movements where the hip angle is approximately neutral.
3. Select a random assessment order for involved and contralateral limbs. Carefully align the approximate joint axis of rotation with the axis of the dynamometer by modifying the subject's position and/or the dynamometer seat adjustments. For the knee test, align the lateral femoral epicondyle with the dynamometer axis and ensure that it remains in alignment throughout the test range of movement.
4. Attach the input arm of the dynamometer on the tibia above the malleoli and ensure that there is no movement of the leg relative to the input arm. Generally a rigid connection is required between the segment and the various parts of the input arm.
5. Secure all the other body parts not involved in the test with the appropriate straps. Ensure that the thigh, opposite leg, hips, chest and arms are appropriately stabilized. Make a note of the seat configuration and the joint positions in case you need to replicate the test on another occasion.
6. Provide written, clear instructions to the subject concerning the purpose of the test and the experimental procedure. Explain in detail the requirement for a blinded

presentation of the target knee flexion angle (the participant should be blindfold or a screen should be placed so as to visually obscure the knee position). In the case of automated control of the input arm movement and associated knee flexion, the participant may need to wear ear-plugs in order to minimize the intrusion of the dynamometer's motor noise and potential cueing of knee position. Allow the subject to ask any questions and be prepared to explain in detail the test requirements.

7. Familiarize the subject with the procedures and allow at least three practice repetitions. Potential distractions to the participant should be minimized and a minimal number of investigators should be present in the laboratory during data capture.

8. The participant's musculature should remain passive throughout the test procedures.

9. Enter any preliminary information required by the data acquisition software and set the blinded target knee flexion angle. This can be achieved by using the on-screen visual display of knee flexion angle (which should be kept hidden from the participant) and either moving the input arm manually or using the control software to 'drive' the input arm into position. The specific target knee flexion angle may be selected from several angles spanning the knee range of motion, e.g. 15, 30, 45, 60, 75 and 90 degrees. Ensure that each movement is initiated from a different knee flexion angle which is selected at random to minimize potential cueing effects. Attempt to standardize the movement velocity of the input arm to 5 deg s^{-1} or to a value which is permitted by the dynamometer's control software. Once the blinded target knee flexion angle is achieved, maintain this target position for 5 seconds. Move the input arm to another position selected at random. After a 15 second period, initiate movement of the input arm at the standardized velocity throughout the knee joint range of movement. The initial direction of movement (either towards or further away from the target angle before returning from the extreme of the range of motion) should be selected at random. During this movement, the participant should indicate the position at which equivalence of knee joint angle with the blinded target angle is achieved.

10. Repeat the ipsilateral assessment process at the other knee flexion angles of interest in random order. Repeat the whole series of assessments.

11. Repeat the whole assessment protocol on the contralateral limb.

1.8.3 DATA ANALYSIS

1. Calculate the average error for joint position estimation across selected target knee flexion angles and duplicate trials.

2. Determine performance differences associated with contralateral limb comparisons.

3. Are there systematic differences in performance at the extremes and mid-range of the knee joint range of motion?

4. What improvements to the test procedures could be made to further limit the intrusion of potential cueing effects?

5. Discuss the physiological/mechanical basis for the findings.

6. On dynamometer systems which permit 'closed-chain' joint loading, repeat the above procedures. Discuss potential differences in responses between knee joint proprioception performance under 'closed-chain' (weight-bearing) and 'open-chain' (non-weight-bearing) joint loading conditions.

1.9 PRACTICAL 4: ASSESSMENT OF KNEE JOINT PROPRIOCEPTION PERFORMANCE: REPRODUCTION OF NET JOINT TORQUE

1.9.1 PURPOSE

The purpose of this practical is to assess the error associated with reproduction of a series of blinded target net torques in the knee flexors in a sagittal plane. This protocol was designed to assess the ability of the subject to actively regulate or control the force production in the knee flexors. Knee flexion torques can be measured using the isokinetic dynamometry system at 0 deg s^{-1} (static).

1.9.2 PROCEDURE

1. Calibrate equipment according to the manufacturer's instructions and record the date, the subject's name, gender, age, body mass, height and training status.
2. Allow the subject to perform general warm-up/stretching exercises.
3. Position the subject on the dynamometer without attaching the input arm. A sitting position with the hips flexed at approximately 1.74 rad (100 deg) may be used. A supine position may be preferable in order to increase muscular output and simulate movements where the hip angle is approximately neutral.
4. Select a random assessment order for involved and contralateral limbs. Carefully align the approximate joint axis of rotation with the axis of the dynamometer by modifying the subject's position and/or the dynamometer seat adjustments. For the knee test, align the lateral femoral epicondyle with the dynamometer axis and ensure that it remains in alignment throughout the test range of movement.
5. Attach the input arm of the dynamometer on the tibia above the malleoli and ensure that there is no movement of the leg relative to the input arm. Generally a rigid connection is required between the segment and the various parts of the input arm.
6. Secure all the other body parts not involved in the test with the appropriate straps. Ensure that the thigh, opposite leg, hips, chest and arms are appropriately stabilized. Make a note of the seat configuration and the joint positions in case you need to replicate the test on another occasion.
7. Assessments may be undertaken in random order at several knee flexion angles of interest (for example, 0.44 rad (25 deg), 0.87 rad (50 deg) and 1.31 rad (75 deg)).
8. Assess peak torque (PT) associated with maximal voluntary muscle actions of the knee flexors at each of the above knee flexion angles.
9. Provide written, clear instructions to the subject concerning the purpose of the test and the experimental procedure. Explain in detail the requirement for a blinded presentation of the target knee flexion torque. The participant should be blindfolded or a screen should be placed so as to visually obscure the knee musculature and any feedback from the computer control software. This minimizes the intrusion of the potential cueing of effort. Allow the subject to ask any questions and be prepared to explain in detail the test requirements.
10. Familiarize the participant with the procedures and allow at least three practice repetitions. Enter the appropriate data on the computer system.
11. Using the previously measured PT, ask the participant to produce muscle actions eliciting a blinded target knee flexion torque of 50% PT under verbal direction from the test

administrator. On attainment of the prescribed force level, ask the participant to maintain this prescribed torque for 3 seconds. The subject should then be requested to relax the involved musculature for a period of 15 seconds before reproducing the prescribed force within a period of 5 seconds. The participant should be requested to indicate perceived equivalence between the prescribed target torque and reproduced torque by relaxing the involved musculature immediately. The initiation of a rapid and sustained reduction in torque associated with muscle relaxation will effectively place a marker on the torque–time record. After allowing a 120-second recovery period, repeat this procedure.

12. Repeat the whole assessment protocol on the contralateral limb.

1.9.3 DATA ANALYSIS

1. The observed discrepancy between the prescribed and reproduced force levels may be expressed as a percentage of PT (torque error (TE%)). The TE% may be defined as the mean of the two intra-session replicates and calculated as the quotient of the difference between prescribed and perceived torque divided by the maximal voluntary knee flexion torque multiplied by 100.
2. Calculate the average torque error across selected knee flexion positions and duplicate trials.
3. Determine performance differences associated with contralateral limb comparisons.
4. Are there systematic differences in performance at the extremes and mid-range of the knee joint range of motion?
5. What improvements to the test procedures could be made to further limit the intrusion of potential cueing effects?
6. Discuss the physiological/mechanical basis for the findings.
7. Repeat the assessments at blinded target knee flexion torques of 75% peak torque and 25% peak torque in random order and suggest what effect this would have on torque error.

REFERENCES

Abernethy, P., Wilson, G. and Logan, P. (1995). Strength and power assessment. *Sports Medicine,* **19**, 401–17.

Alway, S., Stray-Gundersen, J., Grumbt, W. and Gonyea, W. (1990). Muscle cross-sectional area and torque in resistance trained subjects. *Journal of Applied Physiology,* **60**, 86–90.

Aoyagi, Y. and Shephard, R. (1992). Ageing and muscle function. *Sports Medicine,* **14**, 376–96.

Appen, L. and Duncan, P. (1986). Strength relationship of knee musculature: effects of gravity and sport. *Journal of Orthopaedic and Sports Physical Therapy,* **7**, 232–5.

Baltzopoulos, V. (1995a). A videofluoroscopy method for optical distortion correction and measurement of knee joint kinematics. *Clinical Biomechanics,* **10**, 85–92.

Baltzopoulos, V. (1995b). Muscular and tibio-femoral joint forces during isokinetic knee extension. *Clinical Biomechanics,* **10**, 208–14.

Baltzopoulos, V. and Brodie, D. (1989). Isokinetic dynamometry: applications and limitations. *Sports Medicine,* **8**, 101–16.

Baltzopoulos, V., Eston, R.G. and Maclaren, D. (1988). A comparison of power outputs on the Wingate test and on a test using an isokinetic device. *Ergonomics,* **31**, 1693–9.

Baltzopoulos, V., Williams, J. and Brodie, D. (1991). Sources of error in isokinetic dynamometry: effects of visual feedback on maximum torque output. *Journal of Orthopaedic and Sports Physical Therapy,* **13**, 138–42.

Baratta, R. and Solomonow, M. (1991). The effects of tendon viscoelastic stiffness on the dynamic performance of isometric muscle. *Journal of Biomechanics*, **24**, 109–16.

Beam, W., Bartels, R. and Ward, R. (1982). The relationship of isokinetic torque to body weight in athletes. *Medicine and Science in Sports and Exercise*, **14**, 178.

Behm, D. and Sale, D. (1993). Velocity specificity of resistance training. *Sports Medicine*, **15**, 374–88.

Bell, G. and Wenger, H. (1992). Physiological adaptations to velocity-controlled resistance training. *Sports Medicine*, **13**, 234–44.

Bemben, M. (1991). Isometric muscle force production as a function of age in healthy 20 to 74 yr old men. *Medicine and Science in Sports and Exercise*, **23**, 1302–9.

Bishop, P., Cureton, K. and Collins, M. (1987). Sex differences in muscular strength in equally trained men and women. *Ergonomics*, **30**, 675–87.

Bobbert, M. and Harlaar, J. (1992). Evaluation of moment angle curves in isokinetic knee extension. *Medicine and Science in Sports and Exercise*, **25**, 251–9.

Bouisset, S. (1984). Are the classical tension-length and force-velocity relationships always valid in natural motor activities? In *Neural and Mechanical Control of Movement*. ed. M. Kumamoto (Yamaguchi Shoten, Kyoto, Japan), pp. 4–11.

Brooke, M. and Kaiser, K. (1974). The use and abuse of muscle histochemistry. *Annals of the New York Academy of Sciences*, **228**, 121–44.

Brooks, V. (1986). *The Neural Basis of Motor Control*. (Oxford University Press, New York).

Burdett, R.G. and Van Swearingen J. (1987). Reliability of isokinetic muscle endurance tests. *Journal of Orthopaedic and Sports Physical Therapy*, **8**, 485–9.

Burke, E.J., Wojcieszak, I., Puchow, M. and Michael, E.D. (1985). Analysis of high intensity bicycle tests of varying duration. *Exercise Physiology: Current Selected Research*, **1**, 159–70.

Burke, R. (1981). Motor units: anatomy, physiology, and functional organization. In *Handbook of Physiology*. ed. V. Brooks (American Physiological Society, Bethesola, MD), pp. 345–422.

Cabri, J. (1991). Isokinetic strength aspects of human joints and muscles. *Critical Reviews in Biomedical Engineering*, **19**, 231–59.

Cavanagh, P. (1988). On muscle action versus muscle contraction. *Journal of Biomechanics*, **21**, 69.

Chapman, A. (1976). The relationship between length and the force-velocity curve of a single equivalent linear muscle during flexion of the elbow. In *Biomechanics IV*. ed. P. Komi (University Park Press, Baltimore, MD), pp. 434–8.

Chapman, A. (1985). The mechanical properties of human muscle. In *Exercise and Sport Sciences Reviews*. ed. L. Terjung (Macmillan, New York), pp. 443–501.

Cheney, P. (1985). Role of cerebral cortex in voluntary movements. A review. *Physical Therapy*, **65**, 624–35.

Clarkson, P., Johnson, J., Dexradeur, D., *et al.* (1982). The relationship among isokinetic endurance, initial strength level and fibre type. *Research Quarterly for Exercise and Sport*, **53**, 15–19.

Cote, C., Simoneau, J., Lagasse, P., *et al.* (1988). Isokinetic strength training protocols: do they include skeletal muscle fibre hypertrophy? *Archives of Physical Medicine and Rehabilitation*, **69**, 281–5.

Coyle, E., Feiring, D., Rotkis, T., *et al.* (1981). Specificity of power improvements through slow and fast isokinetic training. *Journal of Applied Physiology*, **51**, 1437–42.

Dummer, G., Clark, D., Vaccano, P., *et al.* (1985). Age related differences in muscular strength and muscular endurance among female master´s swimmers. *Research Quarterly for Exercise and Sport*, **56**, 97–102.

Duncan, P., Chandler, J., Cavanaugh, D., *et al.* (1989). Mode and speed specificity of eccentric and concentric exercise. *Journal of Orthopaedic and Sports Physical Therapy*, **11**, 70–5.

Edman, P.K.A. (1992). Contractile performance of skeletal muscle fibres. In *Strength and Power in Sport*. ed. P.V. Komi (Blackwell Scientific Publications, Oxford), pp. 96–114.

Enoka, R. and Stuart, D. (1984). Henneman's 'size principle': current issues. *Trends in Neurosciences*, **7**, 226–8.

Enoka, R.M. (1994). *Neuromechanical Basis of Kinesiology*. (Human Kinetics, Champaign, IL).

Fenn, W.O. and Marsh, B.S. (1935). Muscular force at different speeds of shortening. *Journal of Physiology*, **85**, 277–97.

Figoni, S., Christ, C. and Massey, B. (1988). Effects of speed, hip and knee angle, and gravity on hamstring to quadriceps torque ratios. *Journal of Orthopaedic and Sports Physical Therapy*, **9**, 287–91.

Fillyaw, M., Bevins, T. and Fernandez, L. (1986). Importance of correcting isokinetic peak torque for the effect of gravity when calculating knee flexor to extensor muscle ratios. *Physical Therapy*, **66**, 23–9.

Froese, E. and Houston, M. (1985). Torque-velocity characteristics and muscle fibre type in human vastus lateralis. *Journal of Applied Physiology*, **59**, 309–14.

Frontera, W., Hughes, V., Lutz, K. and Evans, W. (1991). A cross-sectional study of muscle strength and mass in 45- to 78-yr-old men and women. *Journal of Applied Physiology*, **71**, 644–50.

Fu, F.H. (1993). Biomechanics of knee ligaments. *Journal of Bone and Joint Surgery*, **75A**, 1716–27.

Gleeson, N.P. and Mercer, T.H. (1992). Reproducibility of isokinetic leg strength and endurance characteristics of adult men and women. *European Journal of Applied Physiology and Occupational Physiology*, **65**, 221–8.

Gleeson, N.P. and Mercer, T.H. (1994). An examination of the reproducibility and utility of isokinetic leg strength assessment in women. In *Access to Active Living: 10th Commonwealth and International Scientific Congress*. eds. F.I. Bell and G.H. Van Gyn (University of Victoria, Victoria, BC), pp. 323–7.

Gleeson, N.P. and Mercer, T.H. (1996). Influence of prolonged intermittent high intensity running on leg neuromuscular and musculoskeletal performance. *The Physiologist*, **39**, A–62.

Gleeson, N.P., Mercer, T.H., Morris, K. and Rees, D. (1997). Influence of a fatigue task on electromechanical delay in the knee flexors of soccer players. *Medicine and Science in Sports and Exercise*, **29**, S281.

Gleeson, N.P., Rees, D., Doyle, J., *et al.* The effects of anterior cruciate ligament-reconstructive surgery and acute physical rehabilitation on neuromuscular modelling associated with the knee joint. *Journal of Sports Sciences*. (In press).

Gowitzke, B. and Milner, M. (1988). *Scientific Basis of Human Movement*. (Williams and Wilkins, Baltimore, MD).

Green, H. (1986). Muscle power: fibre type recruitment metabolism and fatigue. In *Human Muscle Power*. eds. N. Jones, N. McCartney, and A. McComas (Human Kinetics, Champaign, IL), pp. 65–79.

Gregor, R., Edgerton, V., Perrine, J., *et al.* (1979). Torque velocity relationships and muscle fibre composition in elite female athletes. *Journal of Applied Physiology*, **47**, 388–92.

Gustafsson, B. and Pinter, M. (1985). On factors determining orderly recruitment of motor units: a role for intrinsic membrane properties. *Trends in Neurosciences*, **8**, 431–3.

Harrison, P. (1983). The relationship between the distribution of motor unit mechanical properties and the forces due to recruitment and to rate coding for the generation of muscle force. *Brain Research*, **264**, 311–15.

Hasan, Z. and Stuart, D.G. (1988). Animal solutions to problems of movement control: the role of proprioceptors. *Annual Reviews in Neuroscience*, **11**, 199–223.

Henneman, E. (1957). Relation between size of neurons and their susceptibility to discharge. *Science*, **126**, 1345–7.

Heyward, V., Johannes-Ellis, S. and Romer, J. (1986). Gender differences in strength. *Research Quarterly for Exercise and Sport*, **57**, 154–9.

Hill, A. (1938). The heat of shortening and the dynamic constants of muscle. *Proceedings of the Royal Society of London*, **126B**, 136–95.

Hinson, M., Smith, W. and Funk, S. (1979). Isokinetics: a clarification. *Research Quarterly*, **50**, 30–5.

Hislop, H. and Perrine, J. (1967). The isokinetic concept of exercise. *Physical Therapy*, **47**, 114–17.

Hoffman, T., Stauffer, R. and Jackson, A. (1979). Sex difference in strength. *American Journal of Sports Medicine*, **74**, 264–7.

Hortobagyi, T. and Katch, F. (1990). Eccentric and concentric torque-velocity relationships during arm flexion and extension. *European Journal of Applied Physiology*, **60**, 395–401.

Johannsen, H. (1991). Role of knee ligaments in proprioception and regulation of muscle stiffness. *Journal of Electromyography and Kinesiology*, **1**, 158–79.

Johannsen, H., Sjolander, P. and Sojka, P. (1986). Actions of y-motoneurons elicited by electrical stimulation of joint afferent fibers in the hind limb of the cat. *Journal of Physiology (London)*, **375**, 137–52.

Kannus, P., Jarvinen, M. and Lehto, M. (1991). Maximal peak torque as a predictor of angle-specific torques of hamstring and quadriceps muscles in man. *European Journal of Applied Physiology and Occupational Physiology*, **63**, 112–8.

Kannus, P., Cook, L. and Alosa, D. (1992). Absolute and relative endurance parameters in isokinetic tests of muscular performance. *Journal of Sport Rehabilitation*, **1**, 2–12.

Kereshi, S., Manzano, G. and McComas, A. (1983). Impulse conduction velocities in human biceps brachii muscles. *Experimental Neurology*, **80**, 652–62.

Komi, P. (1984). Biomechanics and neuromuscular performance. *Medicine and Science in Sports and Exercise*, **16**, 26–8.

Komi, P. (1986). The stretch-shortening cycle and human power out-put. In *Human Muscle Power*. eds. N. Jones, N. McCartney, and A. McComas (Human Kinetics, Champaign, IL), pp. 27–39.

Komi, P., Viitasalo, J., Rauramaa, R. and Vihko, V. (1978). Effects of isometric strength training on mechanical, electrical and metabolic aspects of muscle function. *European Journal of Applied Physiology*, **40**, 45–55.

Krauspe, R., Schmidt, M. and Schaible, H.G. (1992). Sensory innervation of the anterior cruciate ligament. *Journal of Bone Joint Surgery (Am)*, **74**, 390–7.

Kroll, W., Bultman, L., Kilmer, W. and Boucher, J. (1990). Anthropometric predictors of isometric arm strength in males and females. *Clinical Kinesiology*, **44**, 5–11.

Kulig, K., Andrews, J. and Hay, J. (1984). Human strength curves. In *Exercise and Sport Sciences Reviews*. ed. R. Terjung (Macmillan, New York), pp. 417–66.

Lattanzio, P.J. and Petrella, R.J. (1998). Knee proprioception: A review of mechanisms, measurements, and implications of muscular fatigue. *Othopaedics*, **21**, 463–70.

Laubach, L. (1976). Comparative muscular strength of men and women: a review of the literature. *Aviation, Space and Environmental Medicine*, **47**, 534–42.

Lephart, S.M., Kocher, M.S., Fu, F.H., *et al.* (1992). Proprioception following anterior cruciate ligament reconstruction. *Journal of Sports Rehabilitation*, **1**, 188–96.

Lesmes, G., Costill, D., Coyle, E. and Fink, W. (1978). Muscle strength and power changes during maximum isokinetic training. *Medicine and Science in Sports and Exercise*, **10**, 266–9.

MacDougall, J., Sale, D., Elder, G. and Sutton, J. (1982). Muscle ultrastructural characteristics of elite powerlifters and bodybuilders. *European Journal of Applied Physiology*, **48**, 117–26.

Mathiassen, S.E. (1989). Influence of angular velocity and movement frequency on development of fatigue in repeated isokinetic knee extensions. *European Journal of Applied Physiology and Occupational Physiology*, **59**, 1/2, 80–8.

Maughan, R., Watson, J. and Weir, J. (1983). Strength and cross-sectional area of human skeletal muscle. *Journal of Physiology*, **388**, 37–49.

Milner-Brown, H., Stein, R. and Lee, R. (1975). Synchronization of human motor units: possible roles of exercise and supraspinal reflexes. *Electroencephalography and Clinical Neurophysiology*, **38**, 245–54.

Montgomery, L.C., Douglass, L.W. and Deuster, P.A. (1989). Reliability of an isokinetic test of muscle strength and endurance. *Journal of Orthopaedic and Sports Physical Therapy*, **8**, 315–22.

Morrow, J. and Hosler, W. (1981). Strength comparisons in untrained men and trained women athletes. *Medicine and Science in Sports and Exercise*, **13**, 194–7.

Nemeth, P., Solanki, L., Gordon, D., *et al.* (1986). Uniformity of metabolic enzymes within individual motor units. *Journal of Neuroscience*, **6**, 892–8.

Perrin, D.H. (1986). Reliability of isokinetic measures. *Athletic Training*, **10**, 319–21.

Perrin, D. (1993). *Isokinetic Exercise and Assessment*. (Human Kinetics, Champaign, IL).

Perrin, D., Robertson, R. and Ray, R. (1987). Bilateral isokinetic peak torque, torque acceleration energy, power, and work relationships in athletes and nonathletes. *Journal of Orthopaedic and Sports Physical Therapy*, **9**, 184–9.

Perrine, J. and Edgerton, V. (1978). Muscle force-velocity and power-velocity relationships under isokinetic loading. *Medicine and Science in Sports and Exercise*, **10**, 159–66.

Pollack, G. (1983). The cross-bridge theory. *Physiological Reviews*, **63**, 1049–113.

Pope, M.H., Johnson, R.J., Brown, D.W. and Tighe, C. (1979). The role of the musculature in injuries to medial collateral ligament. *Journal of Bone and Joint Surgery (Am)*, **61**, 398–402.

Prietto, C. and Caiozzo, V. (1989). The in vivo force-velocity relationship of the knee flexors and extensors. *American Journal of Sports Medicine*, **17**, 607–11.

Rees, D. and Gleeson, N.P. (1999). The scientific assessment of the injured athlete. *Proceedings of the Football Association – Royal College of Surgeons Medical Conference*, Lilleshall Hall National Sports Centre, October.

Ryushi, T., Hakkinen, K., Kauhanen, H. and Komi, P. (1988). Muscle fibre characteristics, muscle cross-sectional area and force production in strength athletes, physically active males and females. *Scandinavian Journal of Sports Sciences*, **10**, 7–15.

Sale, D., McDougall, D., Upton, A. and McComas, A. (1983). Effect of strength training upon motoneuron excitability in man. *Medicine and Science in Sports and Exercise*, **15**, 57–62.

Sale, D.G. (1991). Testing strength and power. In *Physiological Testing of the High Performance Athlete*, 2nd edn. eds. J.D. MacDougall, H.A. Wenger and H.J. Green (Human Kinetics, Champaign, IL), pp. 21–106.

Schantz, P., Randal-Fox, A., Hutchison, W., *et al.* (1983). Muscle fibre type distribution of muscle cross-sectional area and maximum voluntary strength in humans. *Acta Physiologica Scandinavica*, **117**, 219–26.

Shephard, R. (1991). Handgrip dynamometry, Cybex measurements and lean mass as markers of the aging of muscle function. *British Journal of Sports Medicine*, **25**, 204–8.

Simoneau, J., Lortie, G., Boulay, M., *et al.* (1985). Human skeletal muscle fibre type alteration with high-intensity intermittent training. *European Journal of Applied Physiology*, **54**, 250–3.

Swanik, C. B., Lephart, S.M., Giannantonio, F.P. and Fu, F.H. (1997). Re-establishing proprioception and neuromuscular control in the ACL-injured athlete. *Journal of Sport Rehabilitation*, **6**, 182–206.

Tesch, P. and Karlsson, P. (1985). Muscle fibre type and size in trained and untrained muscles of elite athletes. *Journal of Applied Physiology*, **59**, 1716–20.

Thistle, H., Hislop, H., Moffroid, M. and Lohman, E. (1967). Isokinetic contraction: a new concept of resistive exercise. *Archives of Physical Medicine and Rehabilitation*, **48**, 279–82.

Thomas, D., White, M., Sagar, G. and Davies, C. (1987). Electrically evoked isokinetic plantar flexor torque in males. *Journal of Applied Physiology*, **63**, 1499–502.

Thorstensson, A., Grimby, G. and Karlsson, J. (1976). Force-velocity relations and fibre composition in human knee extensor muscle. *Journal of Applied Physiology*, **40**, 12–16.

Tihanyi, J., Apor, P. and Petrekanits, M. (1987). Force-velocity-power characteristics for extensors of lower extremities. In *Biomechanics X-B*. ed. B. Johnson (Human Kinetics, Champaign, IL), pp. 707–12.

Watkins, M. (1993). Evaluation of skeletal muscle performance. In *Muscle Strength*. ed. K. Harms-Ringdahl (Churchill Livingstone, London), pp. 19–36.

Westing, S. and Seger, J. (1989). Eccentric and concentric torque-velocity characteristics, torque output comparisons, and gravity effect torque corrections for the quadriceps and hamstring muscles in females. *International Journal of Sports Medicine*, **10**, 175–80.

Westing, S., Seger, J., Karlson, E. and Ekblom, B. (1988). Eccentric and concentric torque-velocity characteristics of the quadriceps femoris in man. *European Journal of Applied Physiology*, **58**, 100–4.

Westing, S., Seger, J. and Thorstensson, A. (1991). Isoacceleration: a new concept of resistive exercise. *Medicine and Science in Sports and Exercise*, **23**, 631–5.

Wickiewicz, T., Roy, R., Powell, P., *et al.* (1984). Muscle architecture and force velocity in humans. *Journal of Applied Physiology*, **57**, 435–43.

Wilkie, D. (1950). The relation between force and velocity in human muscle. *Journal of Physiology (London)*, **110**, 249–54.

ASSESSMENT OF NEUROMUSCULAR PERFORMANCE USING ELECTROMYOGRAPHY

2

Nigel P. Gleeson

2.1 AIMS

The aims of this chapter are to:
- describe the application of electromyography to the study of neuromuscular performance,
- describe the relationship between physiological and recorded electromyographic signals,
- provide an understanding of how the fidelity of the recorded electromyographic signal may be influenced by factors intrinsic to the muscle and by factors which may be controlled by the test administrator,
- describe some of the characteristics of the recording instrumentation associated with electromyography,
- evaluate the value and limitations of using electromyography in the assessment of temporal neuromuscular control,
- describe factors which affect the validity and reliability of measurements that are derived from electromyographic techniques.

2.2 INTRODUCTION

Muscle is an excitable tissue that responds to neural stimulation by contracting and attempting to shorten within its articular system. The many functions that are served by associated changes to the stiffness or movement of a joint system permit effective and safe interaction with our environment. Any mechanical response is preceded by an asynchronous pattern of neural activation and an electrical response from the muscle fibres. Electromyography (EMG) is a technique for recording the changes in the electrical potential of a muscle when it is caused to contract by a motor nerve impulse.

The fundamental structural and functional unit of neuromuscular control (Enoka, 1994; Aidley, 1998) is the motor unit which consists of a single motor nerve fibre (efferent α-motoneuron) and all the muscle fibres it innervates. Such fibres can be spread over a wide area of the muscle (Nigg and Herzog, 1994). Each muscle is composed of multiple motor units. The contractile force produced by the whole muscle is partly determined by the number of motor units that are activated by neural stimulation and by the rate at which stimulation occurs.

Stimulation of the muscle fibre at the neuromuscular junction (motor end-plate) elicits a reduction of the electrical potential of the cell and propagation of the action potential throughout the muscle fibre. The waveform resulting from this depolarization is known as the motor (fibre) action potential (MAP). Each nerve impulse produces an almost simultaneous contraction in all the muscle fibres of the motor unit before being followed by a repolarization wave. The spatial and temporal summation of MAPs from the fibres associated with a given motor unit is termed a motor unit action potential (MUAP). Repeated neural stimulation elicits a train of MUAPs (MUAPT)

Kinanthropometry and Exercise Physiology Laboratory Manual: Tests, Procedures and Data. 2nd Edition, Volume 2: Exercise Physiology
Edited by RG Eston and T Reilly. Published by Routledge, London, June 2001

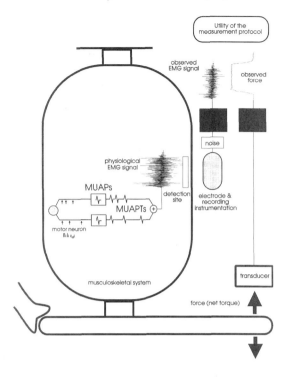

Figure 2.1 A schematic representation of the electromechanical sequelae of neural activation of the muscle.

(Basmajian and De Luca, 1985) and the summation over time of these trains from the various motor units is referred to as the physiological electromyographic signal (Figure 2.1). Of the electrical and mechanical events that follow neural activation, it may be somewhat easier to detect the electrical events. Electromyography is a fundamental tool in functional anatomy and clinical kinesiology. It offers the only method of objectively assessing when a muscle is active (Grieve, 1975) and is commonly used to evaluate the roles of specific muscles in movement situations (Basmajian and De Luca, 1985) and to present biological feedback for the improvement of motor performance. It has also been used to investigate the effects of neuromuscular conditioning.

While electromyography offers important and useful applications of kinanthropometric interest, it is also fraught with potential limitations which threaten to detract from its utility.

The recorded signal is an intrinsically complex history of the muscular electrical activity that can be influenced at any given time by many variables. It is thus a proxy of the physiological electromyographic signal. Its interpretation is considered to be even more complex.

2.3 FACTORS INFLUENCING THE ELECTROMYOGRAPHIC SIGNAL

The primary factors which have an influence on the recorded signal and ultimately its interpretation can be segregated into intrinsic and extrinsic factors. 'Intrinsic' factors reflect physiological, anatomical and biochemical characteristics within the muscle. 'Extrinsic' factors include the external system for detecting the electromyographic signals. In this respect, the quality of the recorded signal and its proper interpretation are very much dependent on the electrode structure and placement. However, depending on the application, the recorded electromyographic signal and its interpretation can also be influenced by other components of this system during modification of the signal (amplifier) and the storage of the resulting waveform (digital recording system).

2.3.1 THE MUSCULATURE AND INTRINSIC FACTORS INFLUENCING THE RECORDED ELECTROMYOGRAPHIC SIGNAL

This intrinsic group includes the number of active motor units at any specified time of the muscle action; fibre-type composition of the muscle; blood flow in the muscle; fibre diameter; depth and location of the active fibres within the muscle relative to the electrode detection surfaces; amount of tissue between the surface of the muscle and the electrode; firing characteristics of the motor units (firing rates of the motor units and potential for synchronization); and the motor unit twitch.

These factors contribute in various ways to changes in the amplitude and frequency content (spectrum) of the electromyographic signal by means of spatial filtering and changes to the conduction velocity. For example, the fibre diameter may influence the amplitude, shape and conduction velocity of the action potentials that constitute the signal; increased distance of the fibres of active motor units from the detection electrode hinders the detection of separate MUAPs. Also, the type and amount of subcutaneous tissue modifies the characteristics of the signal by rejecting some of the high-frequency components of the signal.

Limitations in current technology and knowledge mean that for the most part such intrinsic factors cannot be controlled. The contributions of some of the factors (for example, the depth and location of the active fibres within the muscle relative to the electrode detection surfaces) would be expected to add to the background experimental error (noise) associated with the measurement of the recorded signal. Others, for example, fibre diameter and firing characteristics of the motor units, may be influenced systematically by changes to the neuromuscular system associated with specific conditioning interventions. The relative importance of these factors to the utility of the electromyographic signal remains elusive.

2.3.2 THE SYSTEM FOR DETECTING THE ELECTROMYOGRAPHIC SIGNALS: EXTRINSIC FACTORS

Electrode configuration describes the shape and area of the electrode detection surfaces and determines the number of active motor units that are registered by the detecting electrodes. The distance between the electrode detection surfaces determines the bandwidth (the range of frequencies) that the differential electrode configuration will be capable of detecting. The location of the electrode with respect to the musculotendinous junction and the motor end-plates in the muscle moderates the amplitude and frequency characteristics of the detected signal. The location of the electrode on the surface of the muscle, with respect to the anatomical border of the muscle, regulates the potential for crosstalk (the term

crosstalk is used to describe the interference of electromyographic signals from muscles other than the ones under the electrode (Basmajian and De Luca, 1985). The orientation of the detection surfaces relative to the pennation characteristics of the muscle fibres influences the value of the measured conduction velocity of the action potentials and ultimately the frequency content and amplitude of the signal. Extrinsic factors such as those listed above can be controlled by the test administrator. Optimized practice should increase the utility, validity and reliability (reproducibility) of measurements involving electromyography.

Other aspects of the instrumentation associated with electromyography can contribute to the utility of the measurement. The following sections provide an overview of the key aspects of instrumentation used to optimize detection and recording of the signal.

2.4 ELECTRODES

The electromyographic signal can be recorded by means of invasive and surface electrodes. Invasive electromyography is necessary for recording activity in deep muscles but involves the use of indwelling (fine wire) electrodes which are inserted with a hypodermic needle. While the fine wire electrodes have a very small diameter (approximately 0.025 mm) which means that they are relatively painless in use, several problems limit the potential utility of such invasive procedures in sports medicine and science. These include ethical issues relating to possible breakage during dynamic manoeuvres and associated risks of infection. The method also requires clinical imaging techniques such as ultrasound to overcome the difficulties of locating deep muscles precisely. High electrode impedance, potential distortion of the recorded signal due to deformation and changes in the effective length of the electrode, and damage to adjacent muscle fibres during insertion are technical issues which have also contributed to the fact that these procedures are rarely deployed outside specialist research applications or where indicated clinically. Fine wire electrodes have been advocated clinically when the patient is obese, oedematous or in cold conditions but are rarely used even under such circumstances (Engbaek and Mortensen, 1994).

Surface electromyographic techniques generally permit access to electrical signals from superficial muscles only. Both active and passive surface electrodes require placement on the surface of the skin above the musculature of interest. Active surface electrodes require a power supply to operate and thus demand electrical isolation. This type of surface electrode has the advantage of not requiring any skin preparation or electrode gels but they are likely to increase the overall noise level during the amplification of the signal (De Luca and Knaflitz, 1990).

Passive surface electrodes are routinely used for monitoring neuromuscular transmission in a bipolar configuration in which the difference in potential between two adjacent electrodes is utilized to reduce mains-related interference during subsequent amplification (see later section). Paediatric electrodes are often recommended due to their increased current density. These are generally up to 10 mm in diameter although 10 mm × 1 mm rectangular-shaped electrodes are likely to interact with greater numbers of muscle fibres. Disposable, self-adhesive, surface electrodes are of the Ag/AgCl type consisting of a silver metal base coated electrolytically with a layer of ionic compound, silver chloride and pre-gelled with electrolyte gel. This type of electrode is electrochemically stable and reduces polarization potentials which cause signal distortion. A full discussion of electrode characteristics can be found in Geddes and Baker (1989).

Surface electrodes are subject to movement artefacts which in turn disturb the electrochemical equilibrium between the electrode and skin and so cause a change in the recorded electrode potential. Electrode gel minimizes this change by moving the metal and electrolyte away from the skin so that movement of the electrode does not disturb the metal–electrolyte junction and the potential is unaltered. Electrode gel contains Cl⁻ as the principal anion in order to maintain good contact. Lewes (1965) showed that electrolyte gel with high chloride and abrasive content is unnecessary with an amplifier input impedance in excess of 2 MΩ. Reduction of impedance at the electrode–skin barrier is important to minimize induced currents from external electrical and electromagnetic sources. Without skin preparation, skin impedance can be in of the order of 100 kΩ depending on the measuring technique. Impedance has components of resistance, capacitance and inductance, making it frequency-dependent. In tissue such as muscle, fat and skin the capacitance and resistance are significant components (Basmajian and De Luca, 1985).

In most circumstances it is desirable to reduce skin impedance and contact resistance by means of appropriate skin preparation. Many techniques have been used to reduce electrode–skin impedance and motion artefacts. Medina *et al.* (1989) and Tam and Webster (1977) measured offset potential and showed a decrease with 'light' abrasive skin preparation. More invasive methods include a skin-puncture technique with a micro-lancet (Burbank and Webster, 1978) and scratching with a needle and the reverse side of a sterile lancet to break the superficial layer of dead skin (Okamoto *et al.*, 1987). De Talhouet and Webster (1996) suggested that motion artefact incurred by stretching of the skin could be reduced by stripping skin layers with adhesive tape. Degreasing the skin with acetone or alcohol is the least skin preparation technique employed prior to application of electrodes. Patterson (1978) found no significant difference between either solvent when considering impedance measurements. However, Almasi and Schmitt (1974) suggested differences between genders and, in addition, wide and systematic variation depending on where the electrodes were placed on the body. All strategies should aim to minimize (less than 10 kΩ and preferably less than 5 kΩ), standardize and maintain the measured impedance (measured across the expected signal frequency range) between sets of recording electrodes after the electrode sticker and sterilized electrode have been attached. These precautions will maximize the detected electromyographic signal compared to the noise inherent in the remainder of the recording instrumentation. The latter is particularly important where high performance (high-input impedance) amplifiers are not available.

2.4.1 POSITIONING OF THE ELECTRODES

Whatever the type of surface electromyographic electrode, the location of the electrodes is of fundamental importance. This should be away from the location of the motor end-plate (De Luca and Knaflitz, 1990). The amplitude and frequency spectrum of the signal are affected by the location of the electrode with respect to the innervation zone, the musculotendinous junction and the lateral edge of the muscle. The preferred location is in the mid-line of the belly of the muscle between the nearest innervation zone and the musculotendinous junction. In this location the electromyographic signal with the greatest amplitude is detected. The latter process requires the use of an external device to elicit activation of the muscle. Where a stimulator is not available, electrodes may be placed over the mid-point of the muscle belly (Clarys and Cabri, 1993), which may offer a reasonable approach to the standardization of the recorded signal. Further consistency is afforded to the recorded electromyographic signal by siting the two detector electrodes with the line between them parallel to the direction of the muscle fibres or pointing to the origin and insertion of the muscle where the muscle fibres are not linear or without a parallel arrangement (Clarys and Cabri, 1993).

Since surface electromyographic electrodes are susceptible to crosstalk, the separation of the electrodes determines the degree of localization of the detected signal. A standard electrode separation distance of 10 mm has been recommended (Basmajian and De Luca, 1985). Furthermore, as discussed previously, several factors have the potential to influence the spatial filtering, amplitude and frequency characteristics of the detected signal. These include the depth and location of the active fibres within the muscle with respect to the electrode detection surfaces, the amount of tissue between the surface of the muscle and the electrode, and the fibre diameter. Thus, even subtle deviations in the positioning of the detecting electrodes relative to the motor units and muscle fibres originally contributing to the physiological signal may alter the spatial filtering characteristics of the detection volume and may be sufficient to place a new set of active motor units within the detection volume of the electrode and to remove some of the motor units from the detection volume. Incorrect positioning would be expected to produce additional error or noise in the recorded electromyographic signal as well as in associated indices of neuromuscular performance. Under the most unfavourable circumstances of relative migration of the electrode and active fibres, this could actually invalidate the recorded electromyographic signal. This potential for error raises concern for inter-trial assessments of the same muscle where electrodes are re-affixed on each test occasion or during dynamic muscle actions. There is an inevitability about relative movement between detecting electrode and active muscle fibre population. Tattooing of the skin at the site of the electrode position or preserving the geography of the site by mapping on an acetate sheet the electrode position relative to moles, small angiomas and permanent skin blemishes would be expected to facilitate signal stability and comparability across inter-trial assessments of the neuromuscular performance of the same musculoskeletal system.

2.5 OVERVIEW OF HARDWARE

A typical physiological recording system will consist of an isolated connection to the participant, signal conditioning in terms of amplifiers and filters and an analogue-to-digital converter, before collection and storage on a PC.

As outlined earlier, where the electrode assembly connects directly to the participant circuit an isolation barrier is necessary for participant's electrical connection safety. These terms are defined under the relevant safety requirements for medical electrical equipment (see British Standards Institute documentation, BS/EN 60601–1: 1993, and international equivalents, International Electrotechnical Commission 60601–1). The safety implication for the amplifier circuitry is that the participant circuit is electrically isolated from the amplifying equipment and the connection provides no path to ground. This isolation barrier is often provided by an isolation transformer and a frequency modulator. After passing through a transformer with a low primary-to-secondary ratio, the modulated carrier is demodulated and the original signal is recovered. This isolated input demands that the electrical potential of the participant is floating, the participant is isolated from earth and the mains equipment is under a single fault condition and protected by an allowable participant leakage current.

2.5.1 SIGNAL AMPLIFICATION

The detected electromyographic signal will have an amplitude in the order of 5–9 mV with surface electrodes. This relatively low level signal typically requires amplification to match the electrical characteristics of a variety of suitable signal recording instrumentation systems. The gain describes this process and is calculated as the ratio of output to input voltages. The gains used in electromyography are typically high and vary in the range 10^2 to 10^4 depending on the instrumentation system and application.

There are several important aspects concerning design of amplifiers which are critical to the meaningful collection of the surface electromyographic signal and related physiological data (Basmajian and De Luca, 1985). The amplifier should be situated close to the participant during the recordings in order to minimize the potential intrusion of noise from many sources. This interference can be from the participant, from the environment, or from the instrumentation being used close to the participant. In particular, these sources can be due principally to electrostatic or electromagnetic induction from mains or radio-frequency sources.

In conjunction with other close equipment, the participant may contribute to the electrical capacitance associated with the assessment system. Capacitatively linked electrostatic potentials will vary as the potential path to ground varies with the object and they may appear at the input of the amplifier at the frequency associated with the alternating current of the mains. In addition, interference occurs close to cables carrying alternating current due to the constantly changing flux linkage across a conductor within its field. An electromagnetically induced current flowing at the same frequency as the source would be produced. Furthermore, mains-related interference can be introduced due to earth-loop interference where two earth points have slightly different potentials and a leakage current can flow due to the potential difference between the two. Finally, radio frequency, i.e. greater than 100 kHz, can enter the recording system by a number of routes. This may be through the mains mixed with the frequency of the alternating current, or directly propagated through the air. These interference effects can all be accentuated by high electrode impedance. If the electrode impedance is low then the induced current due to the interference will not cause a significant potential drop at the amplifier input. This will be exhibited as interference at the frequency of the alternating mains current on the input signal.

Good amplifier design aims to reduce interference; all amplifiers used in biological applications are of a differential type with a good Common Mode Rejection Ratio (CMRR). The CMRR is a measure of how well the amplifier rejects any interference or common-mode signal that will appear at both input terminals of a differential amplifier. The amplifier magnifies the difference between the voltages appearing at the two input terminals (a triphasic wave derived from the bi-phasic wave associated with each electrode from the bipolar electrode configuration) so that the common-mode signal is rejected (Basmajian and De Luca, 1985). The CMRR is defined as:

$$CMRR = \frac{differential\ voltage\ gain}{common\ mode\ voltage\ gain}$$

When expressed in decibels then:

$$CMRR\ (dB) = 20\log_{10}(CMRR)$$

Another feature of a biological amplifier that ensures faithful reproduction of the signal of interest is the high input impedance of the amplifier. The high input impedance ensures that most of the signal voltage is presented at the input of the amplifier. If the input impedance was similar to that of the skin and tissue impedance then a high proportion of the signal voltage would be lost due to the potential drop across the electrodes. The signal voltage at the input to the amplifier would be much less.

2.6 RECORDING OF DATA

Many systems have been used to record the amplified electromyographic signal. In contemporary practice, analogue-to-digital conversion and computer processing are the most commonly used recording methods. Where excessive connection cabling threatens to intrude on the ecological validity of the recording of electromyographic data during sports manoeuvres, radio telemetry and portable digital data loggers have also been used to transmit and provide intermediate storage for signals, respectively.

The highest frequency expected in the spectrum of the evoked muscle compound action potential is of the order of 500 Hz – 1 kHz when using surface electrodes. This will be higher when using wire electrodes (~1 kHz) and much higher with needle electrodes (10 kHz). In order to prevent erroneous measurement of the sampled signal (aliasing), the rate of digitization must be at least twice that of the highest frequency expected in the sample. This is termed the *Nyquist* frequency. Any frequency above the Nyquist frequency will be recorded as an artefact. This would suggest that an analogue-to-digital sampling rate of at least 2 kHz should be employed so as not to introduce additional error into the recorded signal during surface electromyography, for example. Ideally, the sampling rate should be several times higher than the Nyquist frequency (Basmajian and De Luca, 1985). However, depending on the application and the number of recording channels, the need to use such high sampling rates may exceed the capacity of some systems. An alternative strategy would be to digitally filter the signal with an anti-aliasing hardware filter in order to make sure only frequencies below this optimum frequency pass into the recording system. Wherever possible from a technical and logistical perspective, it may be prudent to attempt to record the electromyographic signal in an unadulterated fashion in the first instance. Recording in this way would involve maintaining the analogue-to-digital sampling rates at a level that ensures a significant margin of 'safety' between the highest frequency expected in the detected signal and the Nyquist frequency, and no additional filtering except for that intrinsically linked with the detection site. This procedure would preserve the integrity of the original recorded signal and make it available for a variety of appropriate subsequent manipulations involving software-derived digital filtering and data smoothing procedures.

The recorded electromyographic data offer potential utility when used in conjunction with other markers of neuromuscular and musculoskeletal performance to investigate the temporal and sequential activation of the musculature associated with exercise. A critical evaluation and comparison of all applications which have used electromyography in this way would be an impracticable task. In the next section selected applications will be described and potential limitations to their successful deployment highlighted.

2.7 SELECTED APPLICATIONS UTILIZING ELECTROMYOGRAPHIC TECHNIQUES

2.7.1 ASSESSMENT OF TEMPORAL MUSCULOSKELETAL AND NEUROMUSCULAR CONTROL

In many sports and daily activities, precise motor acquisition and rapid reaction time are as important as the capacity to produce force. This is perhaps best illustrated when considering the protection from injury offered to a joint system by the musculature associated with its movement. A conceptual model which defines the limits of normal joint movement comprises primary ligamentous restraints interacting with the other static stabilizers (osseous geometry, capsular structures, and menisci) and with the dynamic muscle stabilizers (Fu, 1993). An unfavourable interaction of the dynamic and static stabilizing factors may predispose sports participants to an increased threat of ligamentous disruption (Gleeson *et al.*, 1997a). The time-course of ligamentous rupture can be very rapid (300 ms; Rees, 1994). Optimal functioning of the dynamic muscle stabilizers of the joint system may be fundamental to the prevention or limiting of the severity of ligamentous injury. The neuromuscular system has a limited reaction time response to dynamic forces applied to the joint. Electromechanical delay (EMD) is defined as the time delay between the onset of muscle activity and the onset of force generation (Norman and Komi, 1979). The EMD may be associated with the unrestrained development of forces of sufficient magnitude to damage ligamentous tissue during exercise

(Mercer and Gleeson, 1996). The EMD is determined by the time taken for the contractile component to stretch the series elastic component of the muscle (Winter and Brookes, 1991). Exercise-related increases in connective tissue compliance have been observed and attributed to the visco-elastic behaviour of collagen under repetitive stress loading (Weisman *et al.*, 1980). The visco-elastic behaviour may be indicative of transient impairment to joint musculoskeletal robustness. According to this model, it is possible that fatigue-related slowing of excitation–contraction coupling or altered visco-elastic behaviour of collagen within the series elastic component of muscle and ligamentous structures of the knee may be reflected in an increased EMD. This alteration to temporal neuromuscular control has been observed in maximal voluntary actions of the musculature associated with the knee joint using EMG and static force assessment techniques. Studies involving acute bilateral cycling fatigue tasks (Zhou *et al.*, 1996), single-leg control trials involving prolonged cycling fatigue tasks (Mercer *et al.*, 1998), isokinetic fatigue trials (Gleeson *et al.*, 1997b) and under more ecologically-valid fatigue trials involving the simulation of metabolic and mechanical stresses of team games and high-intensity running (Gleeson *et al.*, 1998), have shown EMD latencies to have been increased by up to 60%. Alternative techniques for the assessment of voluntary EMD under dynamic muscle actions have been suggested (Vos *et al.*, 1991).

2.7.2 ASSESSMENT OF EMD INVOLVING STATIC AND DYNAMIC MUSCLE ACTIVATIONS

While EMD may offer potentially important insights into the neuromuscular and musculoskeletal performance of a joint system, attempts to estimate the precise time at which a muscle begins and ends being activated and at which net torque is provided by the joint system to do useful work are fraught with difficulties. The latter have not yet been completely resolved in the literature and offer a threat to the validity of the measurement. In addition, the protocols deployed to assess EMD are associated with technical and biological variability (noise) which may decrease measurement reproducibility and reliability and compromise ultimately the specificity, sensitivity and utility of the measurement. Nevertheless, the measurement of EMD serves as a useful model from which to appreciate some of the limitations associated with the assessment of neuromuscular performance by way of EMG.

2.7.3 MEASUREMENT TECHNIQUES

The validity of the measurement protocol used to assess EMD and other neuromuscular indices of performance may be inexorably linked to how well it mimics the stresses imposed on the neuromuscular system by the 'real-world' activity. In the case of ligamentous injury to the joint system, this has been observed in a spectrum involving high- and low-velocity episodes of joint movement (Rees, 1994). It may be appropriate therefore to attempt to assess EMD across this joint movement velocity-spectrum of joint movements. Of fundamental importance to the assessment of EMD involving both static and dynamic muscle actions is the determination of whether any segment of

the muscle in the vicinity of the electrode becomes active. This requires that the recorded surface EMG signal should not be substantively contaminated by crosstalk from adjacent muscles and that the amplitude of the EMG signal exceeds the amplitude of the noise in the detection and recording equipment. The issue of crosstalk is particularly important because the amplitude of the signal being analysed is relatively low at the initiation of muscular activity (Figures 2.2 and 2.3) and progressively emerges from the background noise level. Similar problems afflict the detection of significant force (net torque) generation relative to the electrical noise inherent in the transducer. While the placement of the electrode in the mid-line of the belly of the muscle may offer considerable protection against the intrusion of crosstalk in the detection of minimal signal, it may not always be a sufficient precaution (De Luca and Knaflitz, 1990). The assessment of EMD associated with dynamic muscle actions (for example, assessments involving isokinetic dynamometry; Vos *et al.*, 1991) may be more susceptible to issues such as crosstalk since there is a greater potential for repetitive deviations in the positioning of the detecting electrodes relative to the motor units and

Figure 2.2 A time plot of force (upper trace) and electromyographic signal (lower trace) associated with a single static maximal voluntary muscle action of the m. biceps femoris at 0.44 rad of knee flexion.

Figure 2.3 A time plot of force (upper trace) and electromyographic signal (lower trace) associated with the initial phase of a single static maximal voluntary muscle action of the m. biceps femoris at 0.44 rad of knee flexion. The time difference between left vertical line (muscle activation) and right vertical line (initiation of force response) may be defined as the electromechanical delay (EMD) (see text).

muscle fibres contributing to the physiological signal at any moment in time.

2.7.4 FACTORS INFLUENCING THE MEASUREMENT OF EMD

The delay between the detected EMG signal and the force would be expected to depend on several physiological and mechanical factors, including the fibre type composition and firing rate dynamics of the muscle and the visco-elastic properties of the muscle and tendon tissues. It may also be influenced by protective neuromuscular inhibitory mechanisms associated with joint injury, deconditioning and limited motor unit recruitment patterns (Doyle *et al.*, 1999; Rees and Gleeson, 1999). In general, a muscle consisting of a greater percentage of fast-twitch muscle fibres may be expected to have a shorter time delay between the EMG signal and the registration of force. The estimate of EMD may be influenced also by the signal propagation velocity and its effect on differential positioning of the detection surfaces of the electrodes relative to the sites of innervation of the muscle. This may influence

inter-individual comparisons in particular. It may also contribute a limitation to the precision with which estimates of EMD can be made in intra-individual comparisons where the detection surfaces have been relocated and reference cannot be made to anatomical mapping of electrode positioning. A simple approach to the discrimination of the recorded EMG signal and joint net torque from background noise that has been adopted in the author's laboratory is to consider each recorded signal as a stochastic variable in which 95% confidence limits can be constructed around the mean noise amplitude. The time at which the EMG signal exceeds the 95% confidence limits associated with the background noise for a minimal period defined beforehand can be considered to indicate the initiation of activation of the muscle. The minimal amount of time can be based on the likely limits to the precision of EMD measurements considered earlier. In the absence of laboratory instrumentation to identify innervation points within the muscle of interest and thus physiological limits to the precision of the estimate of EMD, this period may need to be set to exceed 7 ms, given likely mean velocities of propagation through the muscle tissue (up to 6 m s^{-1}: Enoka, 1994) and possible distances between electrode positions (40 mm) and innervation points in large lower limb muscles. A similar approach can be deployed to detect significant force generation relative to the background noise of the transducer and associated instrumentation. The point of force generation may be defined as a sustained separation of confidence limits associated with the mean of the recorded force signal over and above those for the background noise. Alternatively, a criterion threshold for force generation may be set relatively to the peak force signal and which exceeds the likely confidence limits for the noise of the transducer system, for example, 1.0% of peak force.

2.7.5 ELECTROMECHANICAL DELAY AND FATIGUING EXERCISE

There are conflicting reports in the literature about the influence of fatiguing exercise on EMD. There is accumulating evidence from the recent literature (Horita and Ishiko, 1987; Mercer and Gleeson, 1996; Zhou *et al.*, 1996; Mercer *et al.*, 1998; Gleeson *et al.*, 1997b; Gleeson *et al.*, 1998) that EMD during maximal voluntary muscle actions in the knee extensors and flexors is influenced by fatiguing exercise. Other reports involving submaximal muscle actions suggest the opposite (Vos *et al.*, 1991).

The potential fatigue-related impairment of EMD may be attributed to a complex interaction of neuromuscular and biomechanical factors. The rate of shortening of the series elastic component of muscle may be the primary cause of EMD in a given muscle (Norman and Komi, 1979) and this compliance predominates over tendon compliance during movement requiring submaximal tension development (Alexander and Bennet-Clark, 1977). However, the limb segment orientation and moment of inertia and unfavourable joint position for net muscle torque development near to full knee extension may present substantive challenges to the whole musculotendinous unit. Thus,

any increases in compliance of the musculotendinous unit associated with the exercise would tend to increase the EMD. Increased muscle temperature may be an important moderator in the latter process. Such changes are associated with an increase in neural propagation velocity and an increase in compliance in the connective tissue (Shellock and Prentice, 1985). Since the time to shorten the series elastic component of muscle exceeds substantially the time leading to the activation of cross-bridges during concentric muscle actions (Norman and Komi, 1979), the influence of increased compliance may prevail and contribute to increase in EMD.

It is assumed that the asymptomatic, well-conditioned and motivated individual undertaking exercise involving maximal voluntary muscle actions is able to recruit heavily from populations of larger high-threshold fast-acting motor units to contribute to the measured neuromuscular performance. Larger high-threshold fast-contracting motor units have been observed to be recruited preferentially over slow-contracting in tasks demanding rapid ballistic muscle actions (Grimby and Hannerz, 1977; Sale, 1992) and it is known that normal recruitment order according to the 'size-principle' may be violated under some conditions (Enoka, 1994). This premise cannot be assured under all circumstances involving volitional efforts. For example, it is unclear how well orderly recruitment is preserved under conditions of fatigue (Enoka, 1994). It is possible that under conditions of fatigue or involving sub-maximal muscle actions, the determination of 'voluntary' EMD reflects variable contributions from slow-acting, fatigue-resistant motor units since these motor units are recruited first according to the 'size-principle' under most circumstances.

Although not yet widely used in contemporary clinical practice, evoked M-wave and fused tetanic responses from the knee extensor and flexor muscle groups by means of magnetic stimulation of the femoral nerve and anterior horn cells associated with the sciatic nerve (L4–L5), respectively, offer interesting insights into the ultimate physiological performance capability of these muscle groups (Figure 2.4). It is interesting to note that under conditions of muscle activation in which the musculature is not protected by central and peripheral nervous system inhibitory responses, EMD latency responses are significantly reduced compared to their volitional counterparts in all asymptomatic and symptomatic populations with musculoskeletal injury. The latter population has shown some of the greatest reductions in latency between volitional and evoked EMD performance (up to 70% relative to volitional performance) (Rees and Gleeson, 1999).

Other techniques for the estimation of temporal neuromuscular control have been proposed which offer utility under both static and dynamic assessment conditions. The estimation of EMD by means of cross-correlation techniques entails constructing a linear envelope without phase shift with respect to the raw, rectified EMG signal data. Subsequently the phase difference between the linear envelope and the force recorded during static or dynamic muscle actions is established by cross-correlation procedures (Vos *et al.*, 1990, 1991). The technique offers an estimate of EMD performance based on a large proportion of the rising phase of the force production and EMG response (for example, between 0% and 75% of peak force, Figure 2.5) and therefore provides a 'holistic' view of the muscle activation characteristics which may be averaged over several cycles of muscle activation and relaxation. The EMD may be defined

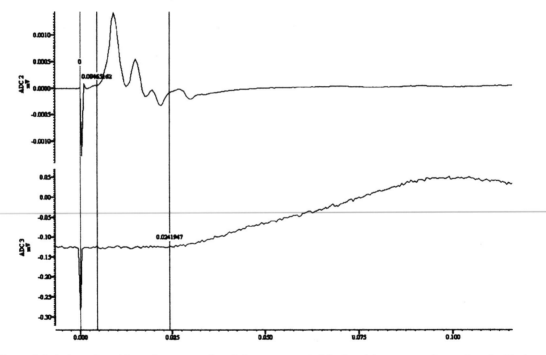

Figure 2.4 A time plot of force (lower trace) and electromyographic signal (upper trace) associated with the initial phase of a single evoked M-wave response from the knee flexor muscle group (m. biceps femoris) at 0.44 rad of knee flexion by means of magnetic stimulation of anterior horn cells associated with the sciatic nerve (L4–L5). The time difference between stimulation (0.0 ms) and middle vertical line (muscle activation) represents latency of neural propagation (4.6 ms). The time difference between muscle activation and the right vertical line (initiation of force response) may be defined as the electromechanical delay (EMD; 19.5 ms) (see text).

Figure 2.5 A time plot of force (lower trace) and electromyographic signal (rectified, raw, upper trace) associated with the initial phase (0% to 75% of peak force) of a single static maximal voluntary muscle action of the m. biceps femoris at 0.44 rad of knee flexion. The phase difference between muscle activation initiation of force response may be measured using cross-correlation techniques (see text).

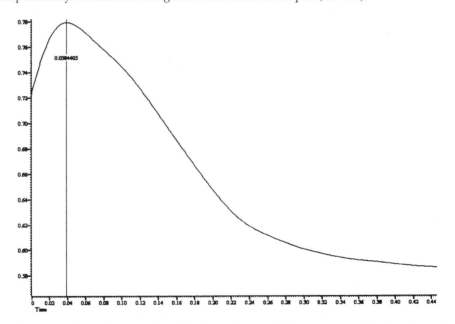

Figure 2.6 Cross-correlation (r, vertical axis) between force and electromyographic signal associated with the initial phase (0% to 75% of peak force) of a single static maximal voluntary muscle action of the m. biceps femoris at 0.44 rad of knee flexion. An index of EMD may be defined as the time (phase difference) at which the highest correlation is observed (vertical line, 38 ms).

as the delay at which the highest correlation is observed (Figure 2.6). It may be considered particularly effective in assessment conditions involving voluntary muscle activations and in which there are difficulties associated with precisely controlling the dynamic movements, for example in assessments involving bidirectional isokinetic dynamometry (Gleeson *et al.*, 1997b).

2.8 MEASUREMENT UTILITY: PRINCIPLES OF MEASUREMENT AND EVALUATION IN INDICES OF NEUROMUSCULAR PERFORMANCE INVOLVING EMG

While the appreciation of the factors which threaten to compromise the fidelity of the recorded EMG signal is fundamental to the integrity of the index of neuromuscular performance, other measurement issues contribute equally to the utility of the index within a specific measurement context. The assessment of indices of neuromuscular performance such as EMD has been deployed in a variety of measurement environments. The application continuum spans single-subject investigations in which the focus may be the rehabilitation or the monitoring of individual athletes, through use within relatively small-sample descriptive and intervention studies, and finally to a potential relevance within epidemiological studies involving relatively large sample populations. Each type of application presents unique demands in respect of an appropriate test protocol to achieve both acceptable utility and rigour during the data acquisition process.

(a) Reproducibility and reliability

Once repeated exposures to the criterion test elicit negligible increases in performance, subjects may be considered to have become habituated to the criterion test and its associated environment. This process may be verified using repeated-measures analysis of variance (ANOVA) techniques for sub-samples of appropriate size (Verducci, 1980; Kirkendall *et al.*, 1987; Thomas and Nelson,

1996). The process of learning will include an accommodation phase in which the specific movements, neuromuscular patterns and demands of the test will become familiar to the subject. Subsequent multiple measurements on the criterion test will be prone to random measurement variability or error, with smaller variations being indicative of greater reliability, consistency or reproducibility of the criterion test (Verducci, 1980; Sale, 1991; Thomas and Nelson, 1996).

(b) Variability in performance

The two principal sources of variability in the index of neuromuscular performance are biological variation, which is the relative consistency with which a subject can perform, and experimental error, which describes variations in the way the test is conducted (Sale, 1991). Examples of these categories of variation include time-of-day effects on indices of neuromuscular performance (Reilly *et al.*, 1993) and technological / instrumentation variation, respectively. Selected contributions to the latter sources of variation have been considered in the previous sections. The goal of the test administrator may be considered to be to dilute the error variance to best reveal the true performance score, consequently permitting the proper interpretation of the effects of physiological intervention or adaptation.

In situations where the assessment of reliability of the criterion test is intended to be reflected mainly in terms of the consistency or reproducibility of observed scores, reliability may be estimated effectively using the coefficient of variation ($V\%$), corrected for small-sample bias (Sokal and Rohlf, 1981). Such a process would allow the quantification of a test-response 'window of stability' for an individual and subsequently the minimum number of intra-subject replicates which are required to attain a criterial measurement error. Group mean estimates of the reproducibility of the index of EMD and related latencies of muscle activation have ranged between 3.2% and 6.9%

for repeated inter-day assessments (Viitasalo *et al.*, 1980; Gleeson *et al.*, 1998).

Reliability models relating to the fluctuations of a participant's repeated test scores within the context of sub-sample performance variability may be estimated using the intra-class correlation coefficient (r_i). This estimate of reliability is based on partitioning models in ANOVA but is susceptible to misinterpretation where significant inter-subject heterogeneity exists. For example, scores of greater than 0.80 have been considered acceptable in clinical contexts (Currier, 1984), whereas this criterion may be entirely inappropriate when attempting to discriminate amongst a group of high-performance athletes demonstrating homogeneous performance characteristics. Bland–Altman plots and the construction of 95% confidence limits associated with repeated measurements of EMD may also be useful in estimating the reproducibility responses in this context (Bland and Altman, 1986; Nevill and Atkinson, Volume 1, Chapter 10).

Sensitivity of a criterion test may be defined as the ability to detect small changes in an individual's performance, or relative positional changes of an individual's performance within a sub-sample. This discrimination ability relates directly to the reliability of the test and may be estimated and further quantified using standard error of measurement (SEM) in conjunction with r_I and the sub-population standard deviation (a measure of homogeneity/heterogeneity) (Gleeson and Mercer, 1992). For given levels of measurement reproducibility, greater heterogeneity amongst measurements would be expected to enhance measurement sensitivity. For example in 'case-study' interventions, assuming an appropriate current trainability phenotype, sensitivity should be enhanced in situations where there is greatest potential for improvement in performance. This would include situations in which the individual has undertaken limited prior strength conditioning or is rehabilitating following injury. The reader is directed to more complete reviews of measurement issues relating to the assessment of neuromuscular performance (Gleeson and Mercer, 1996).

(c) Measurement objectivity and standardization

Objectivity is the degree to which a test measurement is free from the subjective influences and concomitant additional variability due to the differential styles of test administrators (Thomas and Nelson, 1996). Standardization of all aspects of the test administration, including, for example, the test administrator, test instrumentation, calibration of the instrumentation, subject positioning and restraint, lever-arm length, delivery and content of test instructions, will minimize the intrusion of measurement error from extraneous variables and so enhance reliability (Sale, 1991).

(d) Measurement validity

A criterion test which does not yield consistent results is compromised in its validity because the results cannot be depended upon (Thomas and Nelson, 1996). As such, the identification of protocols that will confer appropriate test reproducibility and reliability is a prerequisite for establishing test validity. Validity of a test or measurement instrument refers to the degree of soundness or appropriateness of the test in measuring what it is designed to measure (Vincent, 1995). The validity of the index of EMD may be ascertained by a logical analysis of the measurement procedures, or an estimate of its concurrent validity may be obtained by correlating measurements with those from other established factors contributing to muscle contractile performance, such as predominance of a particular type of myofibrillar protein (Thomas and Nelson, 1996). The relevance and relative importance of the use of EMD within sports medical applications may be estimated by considering its likely predictive validity (Thomas and Nelson, 1996). The predictive validity of EMD as a discriminator of predisposition to musculoskeletal injury may be supported if individuals who reported knee injury had demonstrated prior insufficiency in EMD capability compared to uninjured counterparts, or compared to their own uninjured limb.

(e) Utility of the protocol

A fundamental attribute of any assessment of EMD must be that it offers at least a minimal level of measurement rigour and integrity commensurate with its intended use, i.e. the utility of the test protocol may be considered to be the net outcome from several competing demands (Gleeson and Mercer, 1996).

Within the context of a given application, the selection of threshold reproducibility and reliability criteria to meet the demand for appropriate measurement rigour will in turn regulate the selection of suitable protocol characteristics (for example, required number of replicates, inter-replicate time duration and mode of action). The logistical constraints, time-related pressures and costs associated with replicate testing of the same individual may be considerable in the context of 'case-study' investigations. Furthermore, the concerns regarding the subject waning in motivation as a result of multiple replicate testing over protracted periods may compromise the validity of a test involving maximal voluntary muscle actions. The proper manipulation of the inter-replicate periods to minimize confounding physiological adaptation effects would tend to lengthen further the test period and exacerbate the problem.

Those factors which contribute to the measurement utility of EMD, and which may be directly manipulated by the test administrator, need to be fully appraised and optimized. This category includes factors such as electrode positioning, number of replicates, inter-replicate interval, presentation of test instructions, and isolation of the involved muscle groups. Other factors, such as the available EMG instrumentation, associated technological error, and biological variation in performance, are relatively immutable. The net overall effect of factors that tend to enhance measurement rigour but detract from ease of administration of testing and participant compliance may be to override any practical utility for the measurement in relation to its intended purpose. These issues remain a substantive challenge for the administrator of the test.

2.9 PRACTICAL 1: ASSESSMENT OF ELECTROMECHANICAL DELAY OF THE KNEE FLEXORS ASSOCIATED WITH STATIC MAXIMAL VOLUNTARY MUSCLE ACTIONS

Prior to conducting this practical, ensure that any conditions imposed by the local ethics committee for experimentation on humans have been met and that any participants are asymptomatic.

2.9.1 PURPOSE

The purpose of this practical is to assess the electromechanical delay (EMD) of the knee flexors associated with static maximal voluntary muscle actions and knee flexion angles at which key ligamentous structures are placed under mechanical strain and non-contact knee joint injuries have occurred (Rees, 1994). This practical requires appropriate surface electrodes, an electromyographic recording system as described previously and a dynamometry system permitting prone gravity-loaded knee flexion movements in the sagittal plane.

2.9.2 PROCEDURES

1. Test apparatus calibration. Prior to and repeatedly during testing, the technical error performance of the measurement instrument should be subject to validity assessments using inert gravitational loading. Experimentally recorded force transducer responses should be compared to those expected during the application of standard known masses through a biologically valid range (e.g. 0–600 N). Recorded forces should demonstrate an overall mean technical error (± standard error of the estimate) which is acceptable in the context of the assessment to be undertaken. For example, low technical error associated with the force transducer (0.2 ± 0.03 N across a total of more than 10 calibrations) facilitates the test administrator's ability to identify the point at which force generation is initiated. Similarly, where the appropriate instrumentation is available to generate known patterns of voltage potential, the calibration of the electromyographic signal voltage recording system can be verified.

2. Record the date, the participant's name, sex, age, relevant anthropometric details and training status.

3. The detected electromyographic signals may be recorded with bipolar surface electrodes (self-adhesive, silver–silver chloride, 10 mm diameter, inter-electrode distance 20 mm centre to centre) applied to the preferred leg following standard skin preparation (inter-electrode impedance $< 5 \,\text{k}\Omega$). In the absence of muscle stimulation apparatus to identify sites of muscle innervation, electrodes should be placed longitudinally distal to the belly of the m. biceps femoris on the line between the ischial tuberosity and the lateral epicondyle of the femur. It may also be helpful if the participant were to perform a submaximal voluntary muscle action in the musculature of interest. This would facilitate the identification of the palpable part of the musculature and, by means of the appropriate surface anatomical landmarks, help to identify the longitudinal axis of the muscle. The reference electrode may be placed over the lateral femoral epicondyle, which is one of several possible anatomical sites that may be used for this purpose. The m. biceps femoris is of interest in this investigation as a contributor to the restraint of anterior tibio–femoral displacement in the knee joint and the restraint of the lateral rotation of the femur relative to the tibia, both of which are implicated in the disruption of the anterior cruciate ligament (Rees, 1994). As was discussed earlier, if further assessment trials are to be conducted on the same participant, it would be prudent to make a map of the thigh of each subject to ensure the same electrode placement in subsequent trials. This could achieved by marking on acetate paper the position of the electrodes, moles and small angiomas.

4. Following habituation to procedures, allow each participant to perform a standardized warm-up (5 minutes cycling at an exercise intensity of 120 W for males and 90 W for females, followed by 5 minutes of stretching of the involved muscles).

5. Position the participant in a prone position on the dynamometer with the knee flexed passively to 0.44 rad (25 deg) (0 deg = full knee extension). While seated positions can be used, a prone position may be preferable since it allows simulation of movements where the hip angle is approximately neutral. The lower leg should be supported at a position 0.1 m proximal to the lateral malleolus by a rigid adjustable system. The latter system should incorporate a load cell (range 2000 N) interfaced to a voltage signal recording system which provides appropriate signal amplification and analogue-to-

Figure 2.7 An example experimental set-up for the assessment of neuromuscular performance (EMD). The participant may be positioned prone on the dynamometer with the knee flexed passively to 0.44 rad (25°) (0° = full knee extension). The system incorporates a load cell (range 2000 N) interfaced to a voltage signal recording system which provides appropriate signal amplification and analogue-to-digital conversion of muscle force at more than 2 kHz and provides temporal synchronization of the load cell and EMG signal data.

    digital conversion of muscle force at 2 kHz (see Figure 2.7). The signal recording system should provide temporal synchronization of the load cell and EMG signal data.

6. Carefully align the approximate joint axis of rotation with the axis of the dynamometer by modifying the participant's position and/or by adjusting the relative position of the dynamometer's seat and plinth. For this assessment involving the knee, align the lateral femoral epicondyle with the dynamometer's axis and ensure that it remains aligned throughout the participant's maximal intensity efforts.

7. Secure all the other body parts not involved in the test with the appropriate straps. Ensure that the thigh, contralateral leg, hips, chest and arms are appropriately stabilized. Record the seat configuration and the joint positions in case subsequent intra-participant comparisons are to be made.

8. Provide written, clear instructions to the participant concerning the purpose of the test and the experimental procedure. Explain in detail the requirement for muscular relaxation prior to the test and for maximum voluntary effort throughout the test, including the need to initiate the maximal force effort absolutely as rapidly as possible after receipt of the stimulus to start the muscle activation. Visual feedback may also be used to enhance muscular output. Allow the subject to ask any questions and be prepared to explain in detail the test requirements. Potential distractions to the participant should be minimized during data capture including the number of investigators present in the laboratory in addition to the participant.

9. Allow the participant to undertake a specific muscle warm-up against the resistance offered by the static immovable structure incorporating the load cell and allow at least five intermittent submaximal repetitions (nominally $3 \times 50\%$, $2 \times 75\%$ and $1 \times 95\%$ of maximal effort). It is worthwhile recording the latter trial as an estimate of the likely signal-to-noise ratios to be expected during the subsequent maximal voluntary assessments. Modifications to skin preparation, electrode to data acquisition system connections and potential intrusions from electromagnetic interference can be made at this juncture as appropriate.

10. Gravity moment correction. Compensation procedures for gravitational errors in recorded forces during maximal voluntary muscle actions in the vertical plane should be undertaken either immediately before or just after testing. Angle-specific torque data generated by the effect of gravity acting on the mass of the involved lower extremity of each participant and the weight of the relevant input accessories at the prescribed knee flexion angles of 0.44 rad (25 deg) should be recorded with the participant resting passively. These scores should then be used to correct all subsequent force measurements as appropriate.

11. Allow the participant to rest (more than 60 s).

12. After a verbal indication, an auditory signal should be given to the participant randomly within a 1–4 s period. On hearing the signal the participant should attempt to flex the knee joint as forcefully and rapidly as possible against the immovable restraint offered by the apparatus. After a suitable period of maximal voluntary muscle activation (~3 s) to elicit peak force (PF), another auditory signal should be given to cue the conscious withdrawal of muscle activation and associated neuromuscular relaxation by the participant as rapidly as possible. This procedure can be completed twice more with an appropriate inter-trial rest period (approximately 60 s or more). The electromyographic and force transducer signals should be saved to hard disk for subsequent software processing.

2.9.3 DATA ANALYSIS AND ADDITIONAL PRACTICAL ACTIVITIES

1. The EMD, in this practical, may be defined as the time interval from the onset of electrical activity of the biceps femoris muscle to the observed development of muscle force (Winter and Brookes, 1991). An example of the assessment output is displayed in Figure 2.2 (a time plot of a single maximal voluntary muscle action of the m. biceps femoris associated with the assessment protocol). Figure 2.3 shows a time plot of a single maximal voluntary muscle action from the onset of the electromyographic signal to the force generation (electromechanical delay, EMD).

2. Record the time at which the onset of electrical activity occurs in the m. biceps femoris and the development of force by means of visual inspection.

3. Using the relevant data capture and analysis software, identify and record the peak force from the data record as the highest force observed during the three muscle activations.

4. Compare the observed EMD for the m. biceps femoris with values from previously published studies examining this index of neuromuscular performance.

5. In order to assess the inter-tester reliability of the visual inspection method for the determination of EMD, perform 'blinded' assessments of a random sample of force–EMG records associated with single maximal voluntary muscle actions on three other test individuals. Undertake appropriate statistical analyses of the data (for example, intra-class correlation). Discuss factors that may contribute to measurement variability and error in the visual inspection method. For example, while the data presented in Figure 2.2 show relatively good signal-to-noise characteristics, how might responses in which greater noise levels have intruded be accurately assessed for the onset of the response of interest?

6. How might an objective determination of the onset of muscle electrical activity and force generation be achieved? Discuss the factors which may contribute to measurement error in the visual inspection method.

7. Repeat the experimental protocols with exercise intensities of nominally 50% and 75% of peak force. What differences, if any, would you expect to observe in EMD derived from maximal and submaximal voluntary muscle actions? Discuss the physiological basis for the recruitment of motor units during the onset of voluntary muscle activations.

8. Repeat the experimental protocols to assess EMD in the knee extensor muscle group (m. vastus lateralis or m. rectus femoris) associated with maximal voluntary muscle actions. Compare the observed EMD scores for the agonist–antagonist muscle groups. Discuss the physiological and mechanical basis on which EMD might contribute to joint stability and protection from injury. Similarly, assess this index of neuromuscular performance in the non-preferred leg and comment on ipsi- and contralateral performance differences. Sample data for contralateral leg comparisons are presented in Table 2.1.

9. Using the acetate sheet anatomical mapping of the electrode positions which was prepared earlier, select alternative electrode positions which should be 20 mm lateral and medial, and 40 mm proximal and distal, to the original detection site, respectively. Repeat the assessment of EMD derived from maximal and submaximal voluntary

muscle and discuss the physiological basis for any systematic changes that might be observed in EMD performance.

10. Repeat all or selected aspects of the above protocols at different times of the day matching those used in contemporary practice (e.g. 07 00 – 09 00 hr, 12 00 – 14 00 hr and 17 00 – 19 00 hr) to assess for variations in performance. Similarly, these protocols may be repeated on different days to assess the contributions of inter-day technical and biological variation to measurement error.

11. Repeat the experimental protocols to assess EMD in the knee flexor muscle group associated with maximal voluntary muscle actions before and after an acute fatiguing task. An example of a fatigue task may involve a 'work–recovery' cycle of 5 s static maximal voluntary exercise at the knee flexion angle used for the assessment followed by 5 s recovery which is repeated throughout a 60 s period. Investigate the effects of the acute fatigue task on the observed EMD scores for the muscle group of interest and the recovery. Data illustrating the effects of an acute fatigue task on the EMD values for the m. biceps femoris at 0.44 rad knee flexion are presented in Table 2.1.

Table 2.1   Example EMD data associated with static maximal voluntary muscle actions of the m. biceps femoris at 0.44 rad knee flexion in male high-performance soccer players ($n = 12$) presenting with unilateral recurrent m. biceps femoris injury (caput longus, greater than three episodes of serious injury (4 weeks absence from training or match-play))

Contralateral leg; pre-fatigue (ms)	Involved leg; post-fatigue (ms)	Contralateral leg; pre-fatigue (ms)	Involved leg; post-fatigue (ms)
45.4	56.1	78.5	88.2
39.2	49.8	67.8	73.2
30.5	37.5	56.8	64.2
37.6	45.2	89.7	102.3
52.5	60.4	63.2	73.3
47.5	52.1	58.2	64.8
34.7	39.9	41.7	48.8
36.7	47.8	51.3	60.0
47.8	55.0	64.5	69.8
45.7	48.9	72.1	73.7
37.9	54.2	56.2	59.3
40.9	46.1	49.6	55.5

Data were collected according to the procedures described in 'Practical activities' for the contralateral and involved legs, prior to and after an acute fatigue task (60 s duration, 5 s static maximal voluntary muscle action, 5 s passive recovery) (Gleeson and Rees, unpublished data).

2.10 PRACTICAL 2: ASSESSMENT OF ELECTROMYOGRAPHIC SIGNAL AMPLITUDE AND FORCE OF THE KNEE FLEXORS ASSOCIATED WITH STATIC VOLUNTARY MUSCLE ACTIONS

2.10.1 PURPOSE

The purpose of this practical is to assess the relationship between electromyographic signal amplitude and force of the knee flexors associated with static voluntary muscle. This practical requires appropriate surface electrodes, an electromyographic recording system as described previously and a dynamometry system permitting prone gravity-loaded knee flexion movements in the sagittal plane.

The previous practical activities show that the electromyographic signal can be detected with mimimal insult to the participant. Electromyography is therefore a favourable alternative for more direct methods of assessing muscular effort in many applications. However, considerable controversy exists in the contemporary literature regarding the description of the electromyographic signal–force relationship. This practical introduces the reader to the description of the electromyographic signal–force relationship in a relatively large muscle group (m. biceps femoris) associated with static muscle actions.

2.10.2 PROCEDURES

1. Test apparatus calibration should be undertaken in accordance with schedules described in the previous experimental procedures.
2. Record the date, the participant's name, sex, age, relevant anthropometric details and training status.
3. The detected electromyographic signals may be recorded with bipolar surface electrodes (self-adhesive, silver–silver chloride, 10 mm diameter, inter-electrode distance 20 mm centre to centre) applied to the preferred leg following standard skin preparation (inter-electrode impedance < 5 kΩ). Electrodes should be placed longitudinally distal to the belly of the m. biceps femoris on the line between the ischial tuberosity and the lateral epicondyle of the femur. The reference electrode may be fixed on the pre-amplifier and placed over the lateral femoral epicondyle. The m. biceps femoris is of interest in this investigation as a contributor to knee flexion performance.
4. Following habituation to procedures, allow each participant to perform a standardized warm-up (5 minutes cycling at an exercise intensity of 120 W for males and 90 W for females, followed by 5 minutes of stretching of the involved musculature).
5. Position the participant in a prone position on the dynamometer with the knee flexed passively to 0.44 rad (25 deg) (0 deg = full knee extension). While seated positions can be used, a prone position may be preferable since it allows simulation of movements where the hip angle is approximately neutral. The lower leg should be supported at a position 0.1 m proximal to the lateral malleolus by a rigid adjustable system. The latter system should incorporate a load cell (range 2000 N) interfaced to a voltage signal recording system which provides appropriate signal amplification and analogue-to-digital conversion of muscle force at 2 kHz (see Figure 2.7). The signal recording system should provide temporal synchronization of the load cell and electromyographic signal data.

6. Align carefully the approximate joint axis of rotation with the axis of the dynamometer by modifying the participant's position and/or the adjustments of the dynamometer's seat. For this assessment involving the knee, align the lateral femoral epicondyle with the dynamometer's axis and ensure that it remains aligned throughout the participant's efforts.

7. Secure all the other body parts not involved in the test with the appropriate straps. Ensure that the thigh, contralateral leg, hips, chest and arms are appropriately stabilized. Record the seat configuration and the joint positions in case subsequent intra-participant comparisons are to be made.

8. Provide written, clear instructions to the participant concerning the purpose of the test and the experimental procedure. Allow the subject to ask any questions and be prepared to explain in detail the test requirements. Potential distractions to the participant should be minimized during data capture including the number of investigators present in the laboratory in addition to the participant.

9. Allow the participant to undertake a specific muscle warm-up against the resistance offered by the static immovable structure incorporating the load cell and allow at least five intermittent submaximal repetitions (nominally $3 \times 50\%$, $2 \times 75\%$ and $1 \times 95\%$ of maximal effort). It is worthwhile recording the latter trial as an estimate of the likely signal-to-noise ratio to be expected during the subsequent maximal voluntary assessments. Modifications to skin preparation, electrode to data acquisition system connections and potential intrusions from electromagnetic interference can be made at this juncture as appropriate.

10. Gravity moment correction. Compensation procedures for gravitational errors in recorded forces during maximal voluntary muscle actions in the vertical plane should be undertaken just prior to testing. Angle-specific torque data generated by the effect of gravity acting on the mass of the involved lower extremity of each participant and the weight of the relevant input accessories at the prescribed knee flexion angles of 0.44 rad (25 deg) should be recorded with the participant resting passively. These scores should then be used to correct all subsequent force measurements as appropriate.

11. Allow the participant to rest (more than 60 s).

12. After a verbal warning, an auditory signal should be given to the participant. On hearing the signal the participant should attempt to flex the knee joint as forcefully as possible against the immovable restraint offered by the apparatus. After a suitable period of maximal voluntary muscle activation (~3 s) to elicit peak force, another auditory signal should be given to cue the conscious withdrawal of muscle activation and associated neuromuscular relaxation by the participant as rapidly as possible. This procedure can be repeated once more with an appropriate inter-trial rest period (approximately 60 s or more). The electromyographic and force transducer signals should be stored to hard disk for subsequent software processing. The recording of peak force as the average for the two trials serves as a reference from which various submaximal forces for each participant may be calculated (for example 10%, 20%, 30% of peak force).

13. Participants should be requested to produce in random order, muscle actions eliciting 'blinded' target knee flexion forces of 10%, 20%, 30%, 40%, 50%, 60%, 70%, 80% and 90% of peak force under verbal direction from the test administrator. The random ordering of the prescribed forces minimizes the potential for intrusion of fatigue and

other carry-over effects on the recorded scores. On attainment of the prescribed force level, the participant should be asked to maintain this prescribed net force for 3 seconds, before being requested to relax the involved musculature. Following a 120 s recovery period, this procedure should be repeated for the next target force prescribed at random. These procedures may be extended to include several efforts for each of the prescribed forces and several participants. The recorded force and corresponding electromyographic signal may be averaged over the number of repeated samples.

2.10.3 DATA ANALYSIS AND ADDITIONAL PRACTICAL ACTIVITIES

1. For each participant, plot the recorded force (as a percentage of peak force) against the normalized amplitude of the electromyographic signal in the m. biceps femoris (amplitude associated with peak force is recorded as 100%) for all of the prescribed force levels. Parameters that may be used to describe the amplitude of the electromyographic signal include mean rectified amplitude, mean-squared amplitude and versions of integrated amplitude (Basmajian and De Luca, 1985).

2. Describe the relationship between normalized force and electromyographic signal amplitude for these experimental conditions. Where appropriate, use statistical techniques to assist in the quantification of the relationship as linear or non-linear. An example relationship between signal amplitude and force normalized for their respective peak values is shown in Figure 2.8 for the m. biceps femoris.

3. Compare the observed relationship for the m. biceps femoris with those from previously published studies examining this aspect of neuromuscular performance. Further, examine interparticipant variability in the relationship between amplitude of the signal

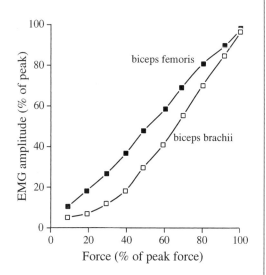

Figure 2.8 Amplitude of electromyographic signal–force relationship for m. biceps femoris and m. biceps brachii associated with static muscle actions. The electromyographic and force responses have been normalized to their respective peak values. Data points represent the mean response of six trials at each prescribed force (various percentages of peak force; see text) for a single participant. Standard error bars associated with electromyographic amplitude are omitted for visual clarity.

and force associated with static voluntary muscle actions. Example data illustrating the relationship between amplitude of the electromyographic signal and force associated with static voluntary muscle actions of the m. biceps femoris at 0.44 rad knee flexion in three male soccer players is presented in Table 2.2.

4. Where the appropriate experimental apparatus is available, repeat the whole assessment protocol on different muscle groups including, for example, smaller muscle

groups of the arm or hand. An example relationship between signal amplitude and force normalized for their respective peak values is shown in Figure 2.8 for the m. biceps brachii.

5. Discuss the factors which may moderate the relationship between the amplitude of the electromyographic signal and the force output associated with static muscle actions.

Table 2.2 Example data illustrating the relationship between amplitude of the EMG signal and force associated with static voluntary muscle actions of the m. biceps femoris at 0.44 rad knee flexion in three male soccer players

	Normalized EMG amplitude (%)		
Normalized force (%)	Participant 1	Participant 2	Participant 3
10	10.7 ± 2.2	9.2 ± 2.4	12.1 ± 3.8
20	17.9 ± 3.6	14.3 ± 3.7	16.1 ± 4.1
30	27.4 ± 5.1	24.4 ± 6.1	28.8 ± 5.5
40	38.1 ± 7.2	34.3 ± 8.6	40.1 ± 9.2
50	48.2 ± 7.3	44.2 ± 9.4	49.2 ± 7.9
60	57.9 ± 11.2	55.9 ± 12.7	58.9 ± 15.1
70	69.6 ± 12.8	66.1 ± 14.2	70.1 ± 12.3
80	81.7 ± 17.4	78.7 ± 18.3	82.4 ± 13.7
90	90.4 ± 19.1	91.3 ± 23.2	91.6 ± 19.3
100	98.9 ± 18.3	100.7 ± 24.1	99.4 ± 17.6

Data collected are from the preferred leg according to the procedures described in 'Practical activities'. The EMG and force scores have been normalised to their respective peak values.

REFERENCES

Aidley, D.J. (1998). *The Physiology of Excitable Cells,* 4th edn. (Cambridge University Press, Cambridge).

Alexander, R. McN. and Bennet-Clark, H.C. (1977). Storage of elastic strain energy in muscle and other tissues. *Nature,* **265**, 114–7.

Almasi, J.J. and Schmitt, C.H. (1974). Automated measurement of bioelectric impedance at very low frequencies. *Computing in Biomedical Research,* **7**, 449–56.

Basmajian, J.V. and De Luca, C.J. (1985). *Muscles Alive: Their Functions Revealed by Electromyography,* (Williams & Wilkins, Baltimore, MD).

Bland, J.M. and Altman, D.G. (1986). Statistical methods for assessing agreement between two methods of clinical measurement. *The Lancet,* **i**, 307–10.

Burbank, D.P. and Webster, J.G. (1978). Reducing skin potential motion artefact by skin abrasion. *Medical and Biological Engineering and Computing,* **16**, 31–8.

Clarys, J.P. and Cabri, J. (1993). Electromyography and the study of sports movements: a review. *Journal of Sports Sciences,* **11**, 379–448.

Currier, D.P. (1984). *Elements of Research in Physical Therapy,* 2nd edn. (Williams and Wilkins, Baltimore, MD).

De Luca, C.J. and Knaflitz, M. (1990). *Surface Electromyography: What's New?* Neuromuscular Research Centre, Boston, MA.

De Talhouet, H. and Webster, J.G. (1996). The origin of skin-stretch caused motion artefacts under electrodes. *Physiological Measurement*, **17**, 81–93.

Doyle, J., Gleeson, N.P. and Rees, D. (1999). Psychobiology and the anterior cruciate ligament (ACL) injured athlete. *Sports Medicine*, **26**, 379–93.

Engbaek, J. and Mortensen, C.R. (1994). Monitoring of Neuromuscular Transmission. *Annals Academy of Medicine*, **23**, 558–65.

Enoka, R.M. (1994). *Neuromechanical Basis of Kinesiology.* (Human Kinetics, Champaign, IL).

Fu, F.H. (1993). Biomechanics of knee ligaments. *Journal of Bone and Joint Surgery*, **75A**, 1716–27.

Geddes, L.A. and Baker, L.E. (1989). *Principles of Applied Biomedical Instrumentation.* (John Wiley & Sons, New York).

Gleeson, N.P. and Mercer, T.H. (1992). Reproducibility of isokinetic leg strength and endurance characteristics of adult men and women. *European Journal of Applied Physiology and Occupational Physiology*, **65**, 221–8.

Gleeson, N.P. and Mercer, T.H. (1996). The utility of isokinetic dynamometry in the assessment of human muscle function. *Sports Medicine*, **21**, 18–34.

Gleeson, N.P., Mercer, T. and Campbell, I. (1997a). Effect of a fatigue task on absolute and relativised indices of isokinetic leg strength in female collegiate soccer players. In *Science and Football III.* eds. T. Reilly, *et al.* (E & F.N. Spon, London), pp. 162–7.

Gleeson, N.P., Mercer, T.H., Morris, K. and Rees, D. (1997b). Influence of a fatigue task on electromechanical delay in the knee flexors of soccer players. *Medicine and Science in Sports Exercise*, **29(5)**, S281.

Gleeson, N.P., Mercer, T.H., Reilly, T., *et al.* (1998). The influence of acute endurance activity on leg neuromuscular and musculoskeletal performance. *Medicine and Science in Sports and Exercise*, **30**, 596–608.

Grieve, D.W. (1975). Electromyography. In *Techniques for the Analysis of Human Movement.* eds. D.W. Grieve, D.L Miller, D. Mitchelson, *et al.* (Lepus Books, London).

Grimby, L. and Hannerz, J. (1977). Firing rate and recruitment order of toe extensor motor units in different modes of voluntary contraction. *Journal of Physiology*, **264**, 865–79.

Horita, T. and Ishiko, T. (1987). Relationships between muscle lactate accumulation and surface EMG activities during isokinetic contractions in man. *European Journal of Applied Physiology*, **56**, 18–23.

Kirkendall, D.R., Gruber, J.J., and Johnson, R.E. (1987). *Measurement and evaluation for physical educators*, 2nd edn. (Human Kinetics, Champaign, IL).

Lewes, D. (1965). Electrode jelly in electrocardiography. *British Heart Journal*, **27**, 105–15.

Medina, V., Clochesy, J. M. and Omery, A. (1989). Comparison of electrode site preparation techniques. *Electromyography and Clinical Neurophysiology*, **18**, 456–60.

Mercer, T.H and Gleeson, N.P. (1996). Prolonged intermittent high intensity exercise impairs neuromuscular performance of the knee flexors. *Physiologist*, **39**, A–62.

Mercer, T.H., Gleeson, N.P., Claridge, S. and Clement, S. (1998). Prolonged intermittent high intensity exercise impairs neuromuscular performance of the knee flexors. *European Journal of Applied Physiology and Occupational Physiology*, **77**, 560–2.

Nigg, B.M. and Herzog, W. (1994). *Biomechanics of the Musculoskeletal System.* (John Wiley, Chichester).

Norman, R.W. and Komi, P.V. (1979). Electromechanical delay in skeletal muscle under normal movement conditions. *Acta Physiologica Scandinavica*, **106**, 241–8.

Okamoto, T., Tsutsumi, H., Goto, Y. and Andrew, P. (1987). A simple procedure to attenuate artifacts in surface electrode recordings by painlessly lowering skin impedance. *Electromyography and Clinical Neurophysiology*, **27**, 173–6.

Patterson, R.P. (1978). The electrical characteristics of some commercial electrodes. *Journal Cardiology*, **11**, 23–6.

Rees, D. (1994). Failed ACL reconstructions. *Proceedings of the Football Association – Royal College of Surgeons, Edinburgh 6th Joint Conference on Sport Injury*, Lilleshall Hall National Sports Centre, 2nd–3rd July.

Rees, D. and Gleeson, N.P. (1999). The scientific assessment of the injured athlete. *Proceedings of the Football Association – Royal College of Surgeons Medical Conference*, Lilleshall Hall National Sports Centre, October.

Reilly, T., Atkinson, G. and Collwells, A. (1993). The relevance to exercise performance of the circadian rhythms in body temperature and arousal. *Biology of Sport*, **10**, 203–16.

Sale, D.G. (1991). Testing strength and power. In *Physiological Testing of the High Performance Athlete,* 2nd edn. eds. J.D. MacDougall, H.A. Wenger and H.J. Green (Human Kinetics, Champaign, IL), pp. 21–106.

Sale, D.G. (1992). Neural adaptations to strength training. In *Strength and power in sport.* eds. P.V. Komi (Blackwell Scientific Publications, Oxford), pp. 249–65.

Shellock, F.G. and Prentice, W.E. (1985). Warming-up and stretching for improved physical performance and prevention of sports-related injuries. *Sports Medicine*, **2**, 267–78.

Sokal, R.and Rohlf, F. (1981). *Biometry*, 2nd edn. (W.H. Freeman, Oxford).

Tam, H.W. and Webster, J.G. (1977). Minimising electrode motion artifact by skin abrasion. *IEEE Transactions of Biomedical Engineering*, **BME–24**, 134–9.

Thomas, J.R. and Nelson, J.K. (1996). *Research Methods in Physical Activity*, 3rd edn. (Human Kinetics, Champaign, IL).

Verducci, F.M. (1980). *Measurement Concepts in Physical Education.* (C.V. Mosby, St. Louis, MO).

Viitasalo, J.T., Saukkonen, S. and Komi, P. (1980).

Reproducibility of selected neuromuscular performance variables in man. *Electromyography and Clinical Neurophysiology*, **20**, 487–501.

Vincent, W.J. (1995). *Statistics in Kinesiology.* (Human Kinetics, Champaign, IL).

Vos, E.J., Mullender, M.G. and Van Ingen Schenau, G.J. (1990). Electromechanical delay in vastus lateralis muscle during dynamic isometric contractions. *European Journal of Applied Physiology*, **60**, 467–71.

Vos, E.J., Harlaar, J. and Van Ingen Schenau, G.J. (1991). Electromechanical delay during knee extensor contractions. *Medicine and Science in Sports and Exercise*, **23**, 1187–93.

Weisman, G., Pope, M.H. and R.J. Johnson. (1980). Cyclic loading in knee ligament injuries. *American Journal of Sports Medicine*, **8**, 24–30.

Winter, E.M. and Brookes, F.B.C. (1991). Electromechanical response times and muscle elasticity in men and women. *European Journal of Applied Physiology*, **63**, 124–8.

Zhou, S., McKenna, M.J., Lawson, D.L., *et al.* (1996). Effects of fatigue and sprint training on electromechanical delay of knee extensor muscles. *European Journal of Applied Physiology*, **72**, 410–6.

PART TWO

OXYGEN TRANSPORT SYSTEM AND EXERCISE

LUNG FUNCTION

Roger G. Eston

3.1 AIMS

The aims of this chapter are to:
- provide students with an understanding of the assessment of lung function at rest and during different modes of exercise,
- describe the relevance of anthropometric, postural and environmental factors on lung function,
- outline practical exercises and data to exemplify techniques of assessing lung function using open and closed circuit spirometry procedures.

3.2 INTRODUCTION

3.2.1 PULMONARY VENTILATION AT REST AND DURING EXERCISE

Pulmonary ventilation refers to the mass movement of gas in and out of the lungs. It is regulated to provide the gaseous exchange necessary for aerobic energy metabolism. Inhaled volumes and exhaled volumes are usually not equal, since the volume of inspired oxygen is usually greater than the volume of expired carbon dioxide. Inspiratory volumes are therefore usually larger than expiratory volumes. **Pulmonary ventilation** is commonly assessed by measuring the volume of air that is exhaled per minute and is abbreviated $\dot{V}E$. It is dependent on the rate (frequency) and depth (tidal volume) of ventilation per breath. Under normal resting conditions, pulmonary ventilation varies between 4 and 12 litres per minute. Naturally, this figure varies with body size and is smaller in women than in men. At rest, typical values for tidal volume and frequency are 400–600 ml and 10–20 breaths per minute, respectively.

3.2.2 FACTORS AFFECTING PULMONARY VENTILATION

Pulmonary ventilation varies with exercise intensity not only within the same individual, but also between individuals. Factors causing this variation mainly relate to body size, age and sex. Peak values for pulmonary ventilation are reached at about 15 years of age for females and 25 years of age for males. It then decreases with age when it declines to less than half the peak value (Figure 3.1). Increases in ventilation from young age to adulthood are caused primarily by physical maturation. As children grow in weight and particularly in stature, total lung capacity and pulmonary ventilation increase accordingly. However, adults over 25 years of age who have reached full physical growth experience reduced ventilation, even though body size remains the same or increases. The decline after young adulthood is due to a decrease in the inspiratory volumes and expiratory volumes as a consequence of physical inactivity and to a reduction of the elastic components in the wall of the thoracic cage. The greater pulmonary ventilation in males compared to females after the age of about 14 years is primarily the result

Kinanthropometry and Exercise Physiology Laboratory Manual: Tests, Procedures and Data. 2nd Edition, Volume 2: Exercise Physiology Edited by RG Eston and T Reilly. Published by Routledge, London, June 2001

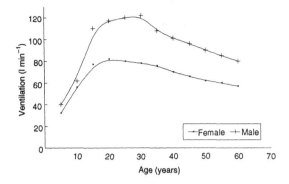

Figure 3.1 Relationship between pulmonary ventilation and age among males and females. (Data from Åstrand, 1952.)

of body size. When the male hormone testosterone is secreted in larger quantities, the skeletal and muscle mass of males increase rapidly. As the rib cage enlarges, the thoracic cavity can accommodate larger quantities of air, which increases pulmonary ventilation.

3.2.3 ALVEOLAR VENTILATION AND DEAD SPACE

Only part of the inspired tidal volume (V_T) of air reaches the alveoli where gaseous exchange takes place. This process is known as **alveolar ventilation** (V_A). The air that remains in the respiratory passages that do not participate in gaseous exchange is referred to as the **dead space volume** (V_D). The average resting value of the dead space volume is about 150 and 100 ml in men and women, respectively, although this depends on body size. The total expired gas is therefore a mixture of dead space and alveolar gas, or

$$V_T = V_A + V_D$$

If, at a ventilation of 6.0 l min^{-1}, the respiratory frequency is 10, and the dead space is 0.15 l, the alveolar ventilation is

$$60 - (10 \times 0.15) = 4.5 \text{ l min}^{-1}$$

If the respiratory rate is 20, and the gross ventilation dead space is unchanged, the alveolar ventilation becomes

$$6.0 - (20 \times 0.15) = 3.0 \text{ l min}^{-1}$$

During exercise, dilation of the respiratory passages may cause anatomical dead space to double, but since the tidal volume also increases, an adequate alveolar ventilation, and therefore gas exchange, is maintained. When submerged in water, breathing through a snorkel presents a considerable challenge to gaseous exchange. The snorkel represents an extension of the respiratory dead space, and the tidal volume has to be increased by an amount equal to the volume of the tube if alveolar ventilation is to be maintained unchanged. Although it is not possible to measure the dead space exactly, it is possible to estimate the dead space volume with the aid of Bohr's formula, which is explained in Practical 1 of this chapter.

3.3 EVALUATION OF PULMONARY VENTILATION DURING EXERCISE

In light to moderate exercise, ventilation increases linearly with oxygen consumption $\dot{V}O_2$, with a relatively greater increase at the heavier exercise intensities (Figure 3.2). It is notable from this relationship that pulmonary ventilation does not limit the maximal oxygen uptake. Maximal ventilation can reach values as high as 180 l min^{-1} and 130 l min^{-1} for male and female athletes, respectively. When pulmonary ventilation is expressed in relation to the magnitude of oxygen uptake, it is termed the **ventilatory equivalent** ($\frac{\dot{V}E}{\dot{V}O_2}$). It is maintained at about 20–25 litres of air breathed per litre of oxygen consumed. In non-steady-rate exercise, ventilation increases disproportionately with increases in oxygen consumption, and $\frac{\dot{V}E}{\dot{V}O_2}$ may reach 35–40. In children under 10 years of age, the values are about 30 during light exercise and up to 40 during maximal exercise (Åstrand and Rodahl, 1986). When the partial pressure of ambient oxygen is reduced,

Figure 3.2 Relationship between pulmonary ventilation and oxygen consumption in trained and untrained individuals. (Data from Saltin and Åstrand, 1967.)

Figure 3.3 Pulmonary ventilation (BTPS) in relation to oxygen uptake at different altitudes. (Modified from Åstrand, 1954.)

such as during exposure to high altitude, the ventilation equivalent increases to compensate for the hypoxic conditions (Figure 3.3).

During exercise of low intensity, it is primarily the tidal volume rather than the breathing frequency that is increased. In many types of exercise, tidal volume may amount to approximately 50% of the vital capacity when the rate of exercise is moderately heavy or heavy. Children about 5 years of age may have a respiratory frequency of about 70 breaths min^{-1} at maximal exercise, 12-year-old children about 55 breaths min^{-1}, and 25-year-old individuals 40–45 breaths min^{-1}. In well-trained athletes with high aerobic power, respiratory frequencies of about 60 breaths min^{-1} are usual (Åstrand and Rodahl, 1986).

3.3.1 THE VENTILATORY THRESHOLD

As exercise intensity increases, the $\dot{V}O_2$ increases linearly, but the blood lactate level changes only slightly until about 60–80% of $\dot{V}O_2$ max is reached, depending on training status. After this, the blood lactate increases more rapidly (see Figure 10.2 in Chapter 10 by Jones and Doust). Because blood acidity is one of the factors that increases $\dot{V}E$, the abrupt increase in $\dot{V}E$ during exercise is often used to indicate the inflection point in the blood lactate

curve. This has been termed the **anaerobic threshold** and procedures for its derivation are explained in detail by Wasserman *et al.* (1987) and Jones and Doust (see Chapter 10). The concept is considered to be a misnomer by some experts as the physiological reasons for the rapid increase in $\dot{V}E$ beyond the inflection point are not necessarily due to metabolic acidosis. Consequently, the disproportionate rise in $\dot{V}O_2$ is preferably referred to as the **ventilatory threshold** (T_{vent}). The T_{vent} for the trained and untrained person is indicated in Figure 3.2 by the solid arrows.

One of the most pertinent refutations of the **anaerobic threshold** was the study by Hagberg *et al.* (1982) on patients with McArdle's syndrome. Victims of this disease lack the enzyme phosphorylase, which renders them incapable of catabolizing glycogen and forming lactate. Hagberg *et al.* (1982) showed that these patients possess ventilatory thresholds despite the fact that there is no change in blood lactate concentrations (Figures 3.4 and 3.5).

3.3.2 PULMONARY VENTILATION AND TRAINING

Endurance training reduces total ventilation volumes at given exercise intensities in

Figure 3.4 Blood lactate response in normal controls and in victims of McArdle's disease during continuous, progressive exercise on a cycle ergometer.

Figure 3.5 Both groups display a ventilatory threshold (arrow), despite the fact that there is no corresponding lactate threshold in the McArdle's patients. (Modified from Hagberg *et al.*, 1982.)

adolescents and adults (Jirka and Adamus, 1965; Tzankoff *et al.*, 1972; Fringer and Stull, 1974; Rasmussen *et al.*, 1975). In general, the tidal volume becomes larger and the breathing frequency is reduced with endurance training. Consequently, air remains in the lungs for a longer period of time between breaths. This results in an increase in the amount of oxygen extracted from the inspired air. The exhaled air of trained individuals often contains only 14–15% oxygen during submaximal exercise, whereas the expired air of untrained persons may contain 18% oxygen at the same workload

(McArdle *et al.*, 1996). The untrained person must therefore ventilate proportionately more air to achieve the same oxygen uptake (Figure 3.2). This is important for performing prolonged vigorous exercise because the lower breathing rate reduces the fatiguing effects of exercise on the ventilatory musculature and allows the extra oxygen available to be used by the exercising muscles.

Aerobic training also brings about changes in pulmonary ventilation during maximal exercise. Maximal ventilatory capacity increases with improvements in maximal oxygen uptake. This is an expected response, since an increase in maximal oxygen uptake results in a larger oxygen requirement and a correspondingly larger production of carbon dioxide that must be eliminated through increased alveolar ventilation (McArdle *et al.*, 1996).

3.3.3 ACUTE AND CHRONIC VENTILATORY ADAPTATIONS TO ARM AND LEG EXERCISE

Ventilatory adaptations appear to be specific to the type of exercise performed. The ventilatory equivalent is greater during arm exercise than during leg work (Rasmussen *et al.*, 1975; Eston and Brodie, 1986). As arm exercise elicits higher lactate levels for any given work-rate (Stenberg *et al.*, 1967), it is likely that this factor, in conjunction with the higher sympathetic outflow for arm work (Davies *et al.*, 1974) is the most likely reason for the higher ventilation during arm exercise. Bevegard *et al.* (1966) have suggested that the higher ventilation rate during arm exercise could be an important factor in maintaining ventricular filling pressures and stroke volume in the absence of the mechanical effect of the leg muscle pump. Additional factors which influence pulmonary ventilation during arm exercise may include (a) a mechanical limitation of tidal volume by static contractions of the pectoralis and abdominal musculature and (b) a metering or synchronization of respiratory rate caused by the rhythmic movement of the arms (Mangum, 1984).

The reduction in ventilatory equivalent that occurs through training is also dependent on the specificity of training. Rasmussen *et al.* (1975) observed that reductions in ventilatory equivalent occurred only when the mode of exercise training matched the activity. In a comparison of groups trained either by arm ergometry or leg ergometry, the ventilatory equivalent was reduced only in arm exercise for the arm-trained group (from 30 to 25) and only in leg exercise for the leg-trained group (from 26 to 23). Arm training did not reduce the ventilatory equivalent during leg exercise and vice versa.

3.4 POST-EXERCISE CHANGES IN LUNG FUNCTION

Changes in lung volumes and function occur *after* acute exercise. After all-out exercise, some people, particularly rowers (Rasmussen *et al.*, 1988) experience coughing with expectoration and dyspnoea. The cough may persist for several days. A decrease in the forced vital capacity (FVC) immediately following exercise (Miles *et al.*, 1991), reductions in peak expiratory flow rate (Rasmussen *et al.*, 1988) and increases in residual volume have been reported (Buono *et al.*, 1981). Shifts in central blood volume, changes in lung mechanics, respiratory muscle fatigue and the development of subclinical extravascular pulmonary fluid retention have all been suggested as contributing factors for the observed transitory changes in lung volume following exercise.

3.5 ASSESSMENT OF RESTING LUNG FUNCTION

Lung function tests are widely employed to assess respiratory status. In addition to their use in clinical case management, they are routinely used in health examinations in respiratory, occupational and sports medicine, and for public health screening. Assessment of lung function, particularly in the clinical and occupational health settings, is mostly concerned with the testing of lung volumes and capacities observed in the resting state. It is common practice for the results of lung function tests to be interpreted in relation to reference values, and in terms of whether or not they are considered to be within the 'normal' range of values. Many published reference values and prediction equations are available for this purpose. The American Thoracic Society (1991) has summarized the most common equations for use with black and white adults. Some of these equations are shown in Tables 3.1–3.3. Equations for children and adolescents have also been provided by Cotes (1979) and Polgar and Promadhat (1971) (Table 3.4).

It is appropriate here to describe and distinguish the various volumes, capacities and peak flow rate classifications which are frequently measured. The lung volumes can be classified as either *static* – referring to the quantity of air with no relation to time – or *dynamic*, which are measured in relation to time.

3.5.1 STATIC LUNG VOLUMES

Lung volumes are measured by a spirometer (Figure 3.6). The bell of the spirometer falls and rises as air is inhaled and exhaled from it. As the bell moves up and down the movement is recorded on a rotating drum (kymograph) by a stylus or pen. This provides a record of the ventilatory volume and breathing frequency (spirogram), as depicted in Figure 3.7. The capacity of the spirometer is usually 9 litres or 13 litres. If it is to form part of a closed-circuit system to measure oxygen uptake, as in Practical 4, it should include a soda-lime canister on the inlet to absorb carbon dioxide.

The volume of air moved during a normal breath is the **tidal volume** (V_T). At rest V_T usually ranges between 0.4 and 0.6 litre per breath. During exercise it increases linearly with the ventilatory requirement of the subject up to a limiting value, which is about 50% of the vital capacity (Cotes, 1979). The reserve ability for inhalation beyond the tidal volume is termed the **inspiratory reserve volume** (IRV). This is the amount of air that can be inspired

Table 3.1 Predicted values for FEV_1 and FVC from selected regression equations for non-smoking Caucasian men and women (modified from American Thoracic Society (1991))

Source	Age	Number studied	$FEV_{1.0}$				FVC			
			$FEV_{1.0}$ for ht and age[a]	Regression coefficient Ht	Age	SEE	FVC for ht and age[a]	Regression coefficient Ht	Age	SEE
Men										
Morris et al. (1971)	20–84	517	3.63	3.62	–0.032	0.55	4.84	5.83	–0.025	0.74
Knudson et al. (1983)	25–84	86	3.81	6.65	–0.029	0.52	4.64	8.44	–0.030	0.64
Crapo et al. (1981)	15–91	125	3.96	4.14	–0.024	0.49	4.89	6.00	–0.021	0.64
Women										
Morris et al. (1971)	20–84	471	2.72	3.50	–0.025	0.47	3.54	4.53	–0.024	0.52
Knudson et al. (1983)	20–87	204	2.79	3.09	–0.020	0.39	3.36	4.27	–0.017	0.49
Crapo et al. (1981)	15–84	126	2.92	3.42	–0.026	0.33	3.54	4.91	–0.022	0.39

Format of equation
Men
Predicted $FEV_{1.0}$ or FVC = Predicted value[a] for: ht 1.75 m, Age 45 + {ht Coefficient × (ht – 1.75)} + {Age Coefficient × (Age – 45)}
Women
Predicted $FEV_{1.0}$ or FVC = Predicted value[a] for: ht 1.65 m, Age 45 + ht Coefficient × (ht – 1.65)} + {Age Coefficient × (Age – 45)}

Figure 3.6 Subject breathing from a *Harvard* 9 Litre Spirometer (Harvard Apparatus Ltd, Kent, UK).

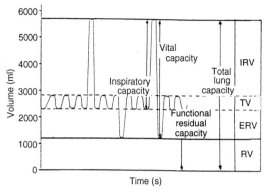

Figure 3.7 Spirogram showing the various lung volumes and capacities. IRV, inspiratory reserve volume; ERV, expiratory reserve volume; RV, residual volume; TV, tidal volume.

maximally at the end of a normal inspiration. At rest it is normally about 2.5–3.5 litres. The volume of air that can be expired maximally after normal expiration is the **expiratory reserve volume** (ERV), which ranges from 1.0 to 1.5 litres for the average-sized man. The IRV and ERV show large variations with posture on account of changes in the **functional residual capacity** (FRC). This function is defined as the volume of air in the chest at the end of a normal expiration when the elastic recoil of the lung and the thoracic cage are equal and opposite. In normal subjects the FRC is affected by posture, which affects the position of the chest wall and reduces FRC by about 25% in the supine position compared to the upright position. In the upright position, in healthy adults, FRC is in the range 0.8–5.5 and 0.7–4.9 litres for men and women, respectively. The FRC is increased in the presence of emphysema (a condition which causes an increase in the size of air spaces distal to the terminal bronchioles) when this is accompanied by a reduction in the elastic recoil of the chest wall. It is reduced when V_T is increased, such as during exercise, or by breathing a gas mixture of carbon dioxide in air. The **total lung capacity** (TLC) is defined as the volume of gas in the thorax at the end of a full inspiration. In healthy adults, depending on size, the TLC is in the range 3.6–9.4 and 3.0–7.3 litres for males and females, respectively. The TLC is reduced if there is a

decrease in the strength of the respiratory muscles, as in diseases such as interstitial fibrosis or muscular dystrophy. It is enlarged when the compliance of the lung is increased by emphysema or as a result of physical training. Hanson (1973) observed TLC values ranging from 7.0 to 9.8 litres in seven international cross-country skiers. During exercise, the IRV, particularly, and the ERV are reduced, which is a natural consequence of an increase in V_T.

The total volume of air that can be moved voluntarily from the lung from full inspiration to full expiration is the **vital capacity** (VC). It is the sum of V_T, IRV and ERV. In healthy adults, depending on age and size, VC is in the range 2.0–6.6 litres and 1.4–5.6 litres for males and females, respectively. It is reduced in emphysema and in other conditions which cause an increase in residual volume. Vital capacities of 6–7 litres are not uncommon for tall individuals and athletes. Ekblom and Hermansen (1968) observed a value of 7.7 litres in a champion male athlete. Although the size of the lung is influenced by the same anthropometric factors that may also predispose an individual to athletic success, VC can be increased by training, but this is only in certain circumstances and with special types of training. Cotes (1979) reported that training of the muscles of the shoulder girdle probably leads to an

Table 3.2 Predicted values for $FEV_{1.0}$ and FVC from selected regression equations for black men and women (modified from American Thoracic Society, 1991)

Source	Age	Number studied	$FEV_{1.0}$				FVC			
			$FEV_{1.0}$ for ht and age[a]	Regression coefficient		SEE	FVC for ht and age[a]	Regression coefficient		SEE
				Ht	Age			Ht	Age	
Men										
Lapp et al. (1974)	34.9 ± 11.9	79	3.53	3.54	−0.025	0.23	4.11	3.94	0.021	0.32
Cookson et al. (1976)	43.6 ± 15.1	141	3.12	2.20	−0.024	0.50	3.74	3.90	0.017	0.65
Women										
Johannsen and Erasmus (1968)	20–50	100	2.25	2.18	−0.013	0.34	2.74	2.51	0.015	0.35
Cookson et al. (1976)	36.7 ± 11.6	102	2.35	2.35	−0.028	0.41	2.86	3.00	0.019	0.42

Format of equation
Men
Predicted $FEV_{1.0}$ or FVC = Predicted value[a] for: ht 1.75 m, Age 45 + {ht Coefficient × (ht − 1.75)} + {Age Coefficient × (Age − 45)}
Women
Predicted $FEV_{1.0}$ or FVC = Predicted value[a] for: ht 1.65m, Age 45 + {ht Coefficient × (ht − 1.65)} + {Age Coefficient × (Age − 45)}

Table 3.3 Predicted values for total lung capacity (TLC) and residual volume (RV) from selected regression equations for men and women (modified from American Thoracic Society, 1991)

Source	Age	Number studied	TLC				RV			
			TLC for ht and age[a]	Regression coefficient Ht	Age	SEE	RV for ht and age[a]	Regression coefficient Ht	Age	SEE
Men										
Boren et al. (1966)	20–62	422	6.35	7.80	—	0.87	1.62	1.90	0.012	0.53
Crapo et al. (1982)	15–91	123	6.72	7.95	0.003	0.79	1.87	2.16	0.021	0.37
Women										
Hall et al. (1979)	27–74	113	5.30	7.46	0.013	0.51	1.80	2.80	0.016	0.31
Crapo et al. (1981)	17–84	122	5.20	5.90	—	0.54	1.73	1.97	0.020	0.38

Format of equation
Men
Predicted TLC or RV = Predicted value[a] for: ht 1.75m, Age 45 + {ht Coefficient × (ht − 1.75)} + {Age Coefficient × (Age − 45)}
Women
Predicted TLC or RV = Predicted value[a] for: ht 1.65m, Age 45 + {ht Coefficient × (ht − 1.65)} + {Age Coefficient × (Age − 45)}

Table 3.4   Regression relationships for the prediction of indices of lung function from height and sitting height in healthy boys and girls of European descent (modified from Cotes, 1979)

Index	Sex	Height (H)		Sitting height (SH)	
		Relationship	SD%	Relationship	SD%
Cotes (1979)					
TLC (l)	M	$1.227\ H^{2.80}$	9	$7.242\ SH^{2.90}$	11
	F	$1.189\ H^{2.64}$	10	$6.554\ SH^{2.90}$	
VC (l)	M	$1.004\ H^{2.72}$	11	$5.641\ SH^{2.80}$	11
	F	$0.946\ H^{2.61}$	10	$5.053\ SH^{2.80}$	
FEV_1 (l)	M	$0.812\ H^{2.67}$	11	$4.807\ SH^{2.93}$	12
	F	$0.788\ H^{2.73}$	10	$4.527\ SH^{2.93}$	
RV (l)	M + F	$0.237\ H^{2.77}$	27	$1.448\ SH^{3.12}$	31
PEFR ($l\ s^{-1}$)	M + F	$7.59\ H^{-5.53}$	13	$15.94\ SH^{-6.87}$	13
Polgar and Promadhat (1971)					
TLC (l)	M	$1.226\ H^{2.67}$	11.6		
	F	$1.153\ H^{2.73}$			
VC (l)	M	$0.963\ H^{2.67}$	13.0		
	F	$0.909\ H^{2.72}$			
FEV_1 (l)	M + F	$0.796\ H^{2.80}$	9.0		
RV (l)	M + F	$0.291\ H^{2.41}$	22.8		

increase in VC by virtue of the increased strength of the accessory muscles of inspiration. This is a feature of rowers, weightlifters and participants in archery and other sports in which these muscles are employed. When differences for body size and age are taken into account, middle-distance runners, cyclists and swimmers tend to have a higher than normal vital capacity. A larger lung leads to the V_T contributing more to the ventilation minute volume than in subjects with smaller lungs. The increased VC is not usually accompanied by a corresponding increase in the forced expiratory volume and thus the proportion of the VC which these subjects can expire in 1 s tends to be relatively low. In this respect, Hanson (1973) observed $FEV_{1.0\%}$ values ranging from 61 to 85% in male cross-country skiers whose VCs ranged from 4.8 to 7.3 litres. In swimmers, the increase in VC due to muscle training is superimposed on that associated with a long trunk length which probably also confers a competitive advantage (Cotes, 1979). Vital capacity is reduced by about 7% when the subject lies down. This change is due to the displacement of gas by blood which enters the thorax from the lower parts of the body.

The volume of air that cannot be exhaled after a maximal expiration is the **residual volume** (RV). Functionally, this makes sound physiological sense or there would be complete collapse (closure) of all airways as well as cessation of all gaseous exchange at the lung. In healthy adults, depending on size and age, the RV is in the range of 0.5–3.5 and 0.4–3.0 for males and females, respectively. The RV tends to increase with age, whereas the IRV and ERV become proportionately smaller. The loss in breathing reserve and the concomitant increase in RV with age are generally attributed to the loss of elasticity in the lung tissue (Turner *et al.*, 1968), although there is evidence to suggest that the effects of ageing on lung function can be altered with training (Hagberg *et al.*, 1988). As indicated previously, various studies have shown that RV is temporarily increased during and after recovery from acute bouts of exercise of both short- and long-term duration. The precise reason for an increase in RV with exercise is unknown, although it has been postulated that it is partially attributed to closure of the small peripheral airways and an accumulation of pulmonary extravascular fluid with exercise, which prevents a person from achieving a maximal exhalation (McArdle *et al.*, 1996).

3.5.2 DYNAMIC LUNG VOLUMES (INDICES OF MAXIMAL FLOW)

An important consideration is the individual's ability to *sustain* high levels of flow. This capability depends on the speed at which the volumes can be moved and the amount that can be moved in one breathing cycle. Dynamic function can be considered in terms of either a short period of hyperventilation or a single maximal respiratory effort. The term usually given to the former is maximal voluntary ventilation (MVV), which involves rapid and deep breathing for 15 s. The exact procedure for this measurement is explained in Practical 1. The MVV in adults, depending on age and size, is in the range of 47–253 and 55–139 l min^{-1} in males and females, respectively. The MVV is usually about 25% higher than the ventilation volume observed during maximal exercise $\dot{V}E$ max This is because the ventilatory system is **not** stressed maximally in exercise. Figure 3.2 clearly shows that the rate of ventilation ($\dot{V}E$) is not the limiting factor for maximal oxygen uptake, as $\dot{V}E$ continues to increase

Figure 3.8 Procedure for measuring maximal voluntary ventilation (MVV). The student photographed here (ht 1.97 m, mass 97 kg, age 24) had an abnormally high MVV of 294 l min^{-1} (BTPS).

when maximal oxygen uptake is reached. McArdle *et al.* (1996) have reported values of 140–180 and 80–120 l min^{-1} in college-aged males and females, respectively. Hanson (1973) reported average values of 192 l min^{-1} for the men's US Ski Team, with the highest value being 239 l min^{-1}. Figure 3.8 shows a young athletic male performing the MVV test. This subject, a former amateur boxer, had an abnormally high MVV, which was measured at 294 l min^{-1} (BTPS). Patients with obstructive lung disease can achieve only about 40% of the MVV predicted for their age and size (Levison and Cherniack, 1968).

The MVV can be increased by exercises that increase the strength of the respiratory muscles. This applies both to normal subjects and to pulmonary patients (Sonne and Davis, 1982; Akabas *et al.*, 1989).

Figure 3.9 Subject performing a forced expiratory volume test on a Vitalograph spirometer.

When the ventilatory capacity is considered in terms of a single forced expiration or inspiration, it is expressed as either the maximal flow rate at a defined point in the respiratory cycle (e.g. the forced expiratory volume after the first or third second, $FEV_{1.0}$ and $FEV_{3.0}$ respectively, see below), the average over part of the breath, or portion of the vital capacity. This portion is usually the middle half (for example, $FEF_{25-75\%}$, see below).

The peak expiratory flow rate (PEFR) is the maximum flow rate that can be sustained for a period of 10 ms. The PEFR in healthy adults, depending on age and size, is in the range of 6–15 l s^{-1} and 2.8–10.1 l s^{-1} in males and females, respectively.

Figure 3.10 *Vitalograph* spirogram on a normal healthy male, an asthmatic male and a male smoker, which illustrates how the various static and dynamic lung function parameters can be calculated. (Vitalograph chart reproduced with permission of Vitalograph Ltd, Buckingham, UK.)

Table 3.5   Comparison of lung function values for the three spirograph tracings illustrated in Figure 3.10

Value		Subject A (Normal)	Subject B (Asthmatic)	Subject C Pre smoking	30 min after smoking
FVC	(l)	6.4	6.3	5.1	4.6
$FEV_{1.0}$	(l)	5.2	2.9	3.7	3.3
$FEV_{1.0\%}$	(l)	81	46	73	72
$FVC_{25\%}$	(l)	1.6	1.6	1.3	1.2
$FVC_{75\%}$	(l)	4.8	4.7	3.8	3.5
$FVC_{85\%}$	(l)	5.4	5.4	4.3	3.9
$FEF_{25-75\%}$	$(l\ s^{-1})$	5.1	1.6	2.5	2.0
$FEF_{75-85\%}$	$(l\ s^{-1})$	1.5	0.8	0.7	0.5
FMFT	(s)	0.65	2.0	0.95	1.05

Figure 3.9 shows a subject performing a forced expiratory volume test on a Vitalograph spirometer (Vitalograph Ltd., Buckingham, UK).

Figure 3.10 shows four spirometer tracings taken from a Vitalograph™ spirometer, to illustrate some of the static and dynamic characteristics of a single 6 s forced expiratory effort in a fit, healthy male, an asthmatic male and a regular smoker. The various lung function values are shown in Table 3.5.

The amount of air expired over a specific time period of a forced expiration is termed the forced expiratory volume qualified by the time over which the measurement is made, for example, $FEV_{1.0}$, $FEV_{3.0}$. In healthy adults, depending on age and size, the $FEV_{1.0}$ is in the range of 1.2–5.7 l and 0.8–4.2 l in males and females, respectively. In Figure 3.10, the $FEV_{1.0}$ for the healthy, non-smoking subject (A) and the asthmatic subject (B) is 5.2 and 2.9 l, respectively.

The forced mid-expiratory flow (FMF) is the average flow rate over the middle half of the FVC. It is also called the Forced Expiratory Flow (FEF) for the appropriate segment of the FVC, for example, $FEF_{25-75\%}$. Graphic analysis involves location of 25% and 75% volume points on the spirogram. The two points are then connected by a straight line and

protracted to intersect the two time lines that are one second apart. The number of litres per second is then measured between the points of the intersection. This method is demonstrated for subject A in Figure 3.10. The 25%, 75% and 85% FVC values are shown on the time–volume curve. In this case, the $FEF_{25-75\%}$ was calculated by taking the difference between two intersection points at time lines 0 and 1 s, i.e. 1.1 and 6.2 l. The average flow rate between these two points is therefore 5.1 l s^{-1}. Alternatively, but less accurately, the FMF can be calculated by dividing the change in volume by the time period between FEV at 25% FVC ($FVC_{25\%}$) and at 75% FVC ($FVC_{75\%}$) on the Vitalograph. Another conventional flow rate is $FEF_{75-85\%}$, which is calculated in a similar manner. For subject A, it was calculated as the difference between 6.7 l (at 2 s) and 5.2 (at 1 s). The 25%, 75% and 85% FVC values are also indicated for the asthmatic subject (B), as a further example of this procedure. The average flow for one litre of gas starting at 200 ml after the beginning of a forced expiration is also used as an index ($FEF_{200-1200}$).

A frequently used ratio is the forced expiratory volume in a second ($FEV_{1.0}$) expressed as a proportion of the vital capacity ($FEV_{1.0\%}$ = ($FEV_{1.0}$ / FVC) × 100). This value provides an indication of the respiratory power and the resistance to air flow. The ratio in healthy adults, depending on age and size, is 51–97% and 59–93% in males and females, respectively. Normally, the demarcation point for airway obstruction is the point at which less than 70% of the FVC can be expired in 1 s. It can be seen from Figure 3.10 and Table 3.5 that, although there is no difference between the FVC values for the healthy lung (A) and the asthmatic lung (B), the dynamic values for the latter are much lower. It is also interesting to note the acute increase in airway resistance after smoking a cigarette. In this example, the student, who was a regular smoker, was tested before (C1) and 30 minutes after smoking a cigarette (C2). Smoking resulted in a 10% reduction in FVC and a 20% reduction in the mid-expiratory flow rate.

3.6 PULMONARY DIFFUSING CAPACITY

The pulmonary diffusing capacity (D_L) is an indication of the rate of diffusion from the alveoli membrane to the pulmonary vascular bed. As greater volumes of air are brought into the alveoli during exercise, the increased volume is matched by a greater volume of pulmonary blood flow (ventilation:perfusion ratio). The rate of gaseous exchange is therefore increased considerably. The D_L therefore provides an indication of the available surface area interface of the alveolar and capillary membrane at any given point in time. It is theoretically dependent upon (a) the surface area of the pulmonary capillaries in contact with alveolar gas, (b) the thickness of the pulmonary membrane and (c) the specific resistance to gas diffusion of the tissue making up the membrane (Ogilvie *et al.*, 1957). It is commonly measured by a single breath-hold of a gaseous mixture of 0.03% CO, 10.0% He, 21% O_2 balanced with N_2. The technique is abbreviated as DL_{COsb}. A practical example of the method is described in Practical 3.

The measurement of D_L at rest provides an additional clinical measure which may be used in the diagnosis of disease, and which may not be apparent from the normal FVC, $FEV_{1.0}$ and $FEV_{1.0\%}$ measurements. In normal subjects, values at rest range from about 20 to 30 ml CO min^{-1} $mmHg^{-1}$ but this is dependent on body size and sex, since oxygen consumption increases with body size. Ogilvie *et al.* (1957) observed that D_L was directly related to surface area and could be calculated by the equation:

$$D_L = \text{surface area (m}^2) \times 18.55 - 6.8 \ (r = 0.81),$$
$$\text{SEE} = 3.92 \text{ ml min}^{-1} \text{ mmHg}^{-1}$$

This equation was derived on subjects in the sitting position, since D_L, like residual volume, increases progressively as the person assumes a change in position from standing erect to supine. The increase in D_L is ascribed to a large pulmonary capillary blood volume and a more uniform balance between ventilation and perfusion in the supine position (Turino *et al.*, 1963).

Below-normal values are observed in patients who have suffered from such ailments as chronic obstructive emphysema, asthma, pulmonary arterial disease, pulmonary carcinoma and kyphoscoliosis, and in patients who have suffered chemical burns or who have been exposed to asbestos dust (refer to Ogilvie *et al.*, 1957, for specific examples).

3.6.1 EFFECTS OF EXERCISE ON PULMONARY DIFFUSING CAPACITY

An increase in D_L with exercise was first reported by Krogh (1915). Using the DL_{COsb} technique, the pulmonary diffusing capacity increases to about 55–70 ml min^{-1} $mmHg^{-1}$ (Turino *et al.*, 1963; Turcotte *et al.*, 1992), depending on the intensity of the exercise. Turino *et al.* compared the diffusing capacity of the lung during exercise in the upright and supine positions. Although they observed differences at rest, they showed that during exercise the body position has less of an effect on the determinants of D_L. They observed that D_L continued to increase as the intensity of the exercise increased and concluded that it was unlikely that D_L limited maximum oxygen uptake. This conclusion is consistent with the proposition that circulatory performance, rather than pulmonary diffusing capacity, sets the ceiling for physical exertion. There is also evidence to suggest that pulmonary diffusing capacity increases with training (Newman *et al.*, 1962).

3.7 SOURCES OF VARIATION IN LUNG FUNCTION TESTING

Measurements of pulmonary function are subject to a number of sources of variation. Variation can be attributed to technical factors, such as instrumentation, procedure, observer error, and so on. The variation could also be due to dysfunction, or disease, or a result of biological variation. The major focus here is on biological sources of variation within individuals and between individuals. For a more detailed discussion of all sources of variation in lung function testing, the reader is guided to the position statement of the American Thoracic Society (1991).

3.7.1 WITHIN-SUBJECT VARIATION

The main sources of within-subject variation in ventilatory parameters both at rest and during exercise that are not related to disease, environment, drugs or subject compliance are body position, head position and the degree of effort exerted during the test. There is also a circadian rhythm.

The FVC is 7–8% lower in the supine compared to the standing position and 1–2% lower in the sitting compared to the standing position (Townsend, 1984; Allen *et al.*, 1985). The standing position is also preferable for obese subjects. Systematic increases in maximal expiratory flows have been documented during neck hyperextension. This change may be due to elongation and stiffening of the trachea. Conversely, neck flexion may decrease peak expiratory flow rate and increase airway resistance (Melissinos and Mead, 1977). The $FEV_{1.0}$ may be 100–200 ml lower when the effort is maximal compared to submaximal, because the airway is narrower in relation to the exhaled volume (Krowka *et al.*, 1987). In some subjects,

repeated maximal efforts may trigger bronchospasm, resulting in a progressive decrease in FVC and $FEV_{1.0}$ (Gimeno *et al.*, 1972). Residual volume also increases by about 20% on changing from a standing to a sitting position and by about 30% on changing from a sitting to a supine position (Blair and Hickam, 1955).

Another source of intra-subject variation is the time of day due to circadian rhythms. For maximal expiratory flows, the lowest values are usually found in the morning (04:00 to 06:00 hours) and the largest values usually occur around midday (Hetzel, 1981). Guberan *et al.* (1969) observed significant increases in $FEV_{1.0}$ of 150 ml in the morning which decreased by 50 ml in the afternoon in nocturnal workers, demonstrating a disturbance of the normal circadian rhythm. Data on FVC from my laboratory on asthmatic and normal subjects were 7% higher at 16.00 hours compared to 08.00 hours ($p < 0.01$). The $FEV_{1.0}$ was also increased by about 200 ml ($p < 0.01$). In both studies the changes were more marked in the asthmatic subjects. Hetzel and Clark (1980) have reported that PEFR peak-to-trough amplitude of the circadian rhythm is about 8%. A rhythm in $\dot{V}E$ is also evident during submaximal exercise, and is closely related to the circadian curve in body temperature (Reilly, 1990).

3.7.2 BETWEEN-SUBJECT VARIATION

The main anthropometric factors responsible for inter-subject variation in lung function are sex, body size and ageing. These alone account for 30%, 22% and 8%, respectively, of the variation in adults (Becklake, 1986). Other factors are race and past and present health.

Although sitting height explains less of the variability in lung function than standing height (Ferris and Stoudt, 1971; Cotes, 1979), it may be a useful predictor when dealing with mixed ethnic origins due to the fact that blacks have a lower trunk–to–leg ratio than whites (Van de Wal *et al.*, 1971). It is also used to predict lung function in children, particularly during periods of rapid growth. Arm span measurements provide a practical substitute for stature in subjects unable to stand or those with a skeletal deformity such as kypho-scoliosis (Hibbert *et al.*, 1988). Measurements of chest circumference may also slightly improve the prediction of lung function (Damon, 1966). After correcting for body size, girls appear to have higher expiratory flows than boys, but men have larger volumes and flows than women (Schwartz *et al.*, 1988). With regard to *age*, after adult height is attained, there is either an increase (usually in young men) or little or no decrease in function (usually in young women) after which lung function decreases at an accelerating rate with increasing age (American Thoracic Society, 1991). *Race* is an important determinant of lung function (American Thoracic Society, 1991). Caucasians of European descent have greater static and dynamic lung volumes and greater forced expiratory flow rates than black people, but they have similar or lower $FEV_{1.0}$ / FVC ratios. In this respect, regression equations derived from white populations using standing height as the measure of size usually over-predict values measured in blacks by about 12% for TLC, $FEV_{1.0}$ and FVC and by about 7% for FRC and RV (Cotes, 1979). Differences have been attributed to body build differences and frame size (Jacobs *et al.*, 1992). It has already been noted that blacks have a lower trunk:leg ratio than whites.

A factor related to the size of the lung is *growth in standing height*, as this affects lung function measurements in childhood and adolescence. Growth in stature is not in phase with lung growth during the adolescent growth spurt (DeGroodt *et al.*, 1986) and growth in chest dimensions lags behind that of the legs (DeGroodt *et al.*, 1988). In males, standing height and VC are often not maximal by the age of 17 years. The VC continues to increase after increases in height cease and may not be maximal until about 25 years of age. Girls, however, attain their maximal values around the age of 16 years (DeGroodt *et al.*, 1986).

The ratio $FEV_{1.0}$ / FVC and the ratio of maximal expiratory flow (derived from flow–volume curves) to the FVC are almost constant from childhood to adulthood. Girls have larger expiratory flows than boys of the same age and stature (DeGroodt *et al.*, 1986). This is partly due to the fact that girls have a smaller VC for the same TLC than boys. It may also reflect the smaller muscle mass and the smaller number of alveoli found in girls (Thurlbeck, 1982). The American Thoracic Society (1991) recommended that such sex differences warrant the use of different prediction equations for boys and girls at all ages. Ideally, developmental rather than chronological age should be included in prediction equations for children and adolescents, although such equations are neither available nor practical.

The size of the lung determines the total lung capacity, its subdivisions and the indices that are dependent on lung size, for example, forced expiratory flow rates. In children up to the age of puberty, these indices are related to stature, usually in a curvilinear manner; the relationship is linear when height is raised to the power of about 2.6 (Cotes, 1979; Table 3.4).

After stature has been taken into account, the indices are independent of age and usually independent of body weight and sitting height. During the adolescent growth spurt, the rate of growth of the trunk and its contents, including the lungs, is relatively greater than that of the legs. It is therefore useful to use sitting height as an alternative reference variable during this stage of growth (Cotes, 1979; Cotes *et al.*, 1979). Equations which use stature and sitting height to predict lung function in children are shown in Table 3.4. Relative to stature, boys and girls have similar values for residual volume, peak expiratory flow rate and flow rate at 50% of vital capacity. The ERV is slightly larger and the inspiratory capacity is about 12% larger for boys than for girls. Thus, boys have larger values for the functional residual capacity, the vital capacity and the total lung capacity. As a consequence of these differences in lung size, boys also have larger values for $FEV_{1.0}$.

3.8 LUNG FUNCTION IN SPECIAL POPULATIONS

3.8.1 HIGH-ALTITUDE NATIVES

Like the acclimatized visitor, the high-altitude native hyperventilates relative to a normal sea-level person. This increases alveolar ventilation and limits the fall in the partial pressure of oxygen in the alveoli which lessens the reduction in the oxygen pressure gradient across the alveolar membrane. At any given altitude, the ventilation of the acclimatized visitor is greater by about 20% than that of the native highlander (Minors, 1985). Thus, the high-altitude native seems to have lost some respiratory sensitivity to hypoxia.

Native highlanders developed certain anthropometric differences enabling them to tolerate the hypobaric conditions experienced at high altitude. They have a smaller stature than lowlanders of the same age. Although the difference in height varies by about 10%, the chest circumference of native highlanders is about 5% greater (Frisancho, 1975). This is accompanied by a larger vital capacity, larger lung volume and residual lung volume than sea-level subjects. In addition, morphometric measurements of the lungs of high-altitude natives resident at 4000 m have shown alveoli that are larger and greater in number than those in lowland natives of the same body size. The increased alveolar surface area in contact with functioning pulmonary capillaries, in combination with an increased pulmonary capillary blood volume, leads to an increased pulmonary diffusing capacity in the high-altitude native's lung. The combination of increased alveolar ventilation and pulmonary diffusing capacity increases the total alveolar gas exchange in the highlander.

3.8.2 LUNG FUNCTION IN DIVERS

Certain physical adaptations to long-term diving have been noted in US Navy Escape Training Tank Instructors (Carey *et al.*, 1956) and to a lesser extent in male recreational divers (Hong *et al.*, 1970). These changes include an increase in VC, a decrease in RV and a lowered RV / TLC ratio.

Differences have also been observed in the Korean diving women known as the *ama*. Before each dive an *ama* hyperventilates then dives between 5–18 metres for 20–40 s in repeated dives for approximately 3 h per day. Song *et al.* (1963) observed VC and MVV maximal volumes to be 125% and 128%, respectively, of predicted values. They also observed a higher inspiratory capacity, but no difference in ERV between the *ama* and a group of controls. The RV, expressed as a proportion of total lung capacity, was also lower in the *ama*.

The reason for the increased VC was attributed to the increased inspiratory capacity of the *ama*. This difference was attributed to better developed inspiratory muscles thought to be an adaptation to the constant hydrostatic pressure which the *ama* must overcome on inspiration before a dive. The lower RV / TLC ratio was considered to be important since it determines the maximal depth of diving.

3.9 PREDICTION OF LUNG FUNCTION

Reference equations provide a context for evaluating pulmonary function in comparison to the distribution of measurements in a reference population. Linear regression is the most common, but not the only model used to describe pulmonary function data in adults. These types of equations perform less well at the edges of the data distribution. Further, estimates are likely to be misleading if they go beyond the range of the independent variables used to create the equation. The most commonly reported measures of how well regression equations fit the data they describe are the square of the correlation coefficient (r^2) and the standard error of the estimate (SEE). The proportion of variation in the observed data explained by the independent variables is measured by r^2. The SEE is the average standard deviation of the data around the regression line. This will decrease and r^2 will increase as regression methods reduce the differences between predicted and observed values in the reference population. When the same equations are used to describe a different population, SEE will invariably be larger, and r^2 will be smaller.

Tables 3.1–3.4 contain a listing of various regression equations that predict the various lung function indices in black and white adults and children. The American Thoracic Society (1991) has recommended that, ideally, publications describing reference populations should also include a means of defining the lower limits of the regression equations. Nevertheless, it is possible to estimate lower limits of normal from a regression model.

3.9.1 ESTIMATION OF *LOWER* LIMITS OF NORMAL

Values below the 5th percentile are conventionally taken as below the expected range and those above the 5th percentile are taken as within the expected range (American Thoracic Society, 1991). It is possible to calculate percentiles if there are sufficient measurements within each category. The value of the 5th percentile can be roughly estimated as:

$$\text{Lower limit of normal} = \text{predicted value} - 1.645 \times \text{SEE}$$

For example, the predicted value of FVC for a 45-year-old male, stature 1.75 m (Table 3.1) is 5.83 l according to the prediction equation of Morris *et al.* (1971). The standard error of estimate is 0.74 l for this equation. Thus, the lower limit of normal (i.e. the lower 5% of the population) for a man of this age and stature would be 4.61 litres (5.83 l – (1.645 × 0.74)).

Defining a fixed $FEV_{1.0}$ / FVC ratio as a lower limit of normal (e.g. 80%) is not recommended in adults because $FEV_{1.0}$ / FVC is inversely related to age and stature (American Thoracic Society, 1991). The use of a fixed ratio will therefore result in an apparent increase in dysfunction associated with ageing. In addition, some athletes have values of FVC that are relatively larger than those for $FEV_{1.0}$, which results in a lower $FEV_{1.0}$ / FVC ratio. Thus, the definition of the lowest 5% of the reference population is also the preferred method to predict abnormality in this parameter.

3.10 DEFINITION OF OBSTRUCTIVE AND RESTRICTIVE VENTILATORY DEFECTS

3.10.1 OBSTRUCTIVE DEFECT

An obstructive ventilatory defect is defined as a disproportionate reduction in maximal airflow from the lung with respect to the maximal volume (vital capacity) that can be displaced from the lung (American Thoracic Society, 1991). It implies narrowing of the airway during expiration.

Indications of an obstructive defect can be seen in the latter stages of a flow–volume curve. The slowing is reflected in a reduction in the instantaneous flow after 75% of the FVC has been exhaled ($FEF_{75-85\%}$) or in the $FEF_{25-75\%}$. In the event of airway disease becoming more advanced, the $FEV_{1.0}$ becomes reduced out of proportion to the reduction in VC.

3.10.2 RESTRICTIVE DEFECT

One may infer the presence of a restrictive ventilatory defect when VC is reduced and $FEV_{1.0}$ / FVC is normal or increased. A reduction in VC may occur because airflow is so slow that the subject cannot continue to exhale long enough to complete emptying or because airways collapse.

3.10.3 INTERPRETATION OF LUNG FUNCTION TESTS

The basic parameters used to interpret spirometry are the VC, $FEV_{1.0}$ and $FEV_{1.0}$ / FVC ratio (American Thoracic Society, 1991). Although FVC is often used instead of VC, it is preferable to use the largest VC, whether obtained on inspiration (IVC), slow expiration (EVC) or forced expiration (FVC) for clinical testing. The FVC is usually reduced more than IVC or EVC in airflow obstruction.

The $FEV_{1.0}$ / FVC ratio is the most important measurement for distinguishing an obstructive impairment. According to the American Thoracic Society (1991), expiratory flow measurements other than the $FEV_{1.0}$ and $FEV_{1.0}$ / FVC should be considered only after determining the presence and clinical severity of obstructive impairment using the basic parameters measured above. When $FEV_{1.0}$ and the $FEV_{1.0}$ / VC ratio are within the normal range, abnormalities in flow occurring late in the maximal expiratory flow–volume curve should not be graded as to severity and, if mentioned, should be interpreted cautiously. When there is a borderline value of $FEV_{1.0}$ / FVC, these values may help to confirm the presence of airway obstruction. The same is true for average flows such as $FEF_{25-75\%}$. It is important to note that there is wide variability of these measurements in healthy subjects and this variation must therefore be taken into account in the final interpretation.

3.11 PRACTICAL EXERCISES

In the following section four laboratory practicals are suggested. Lung function in the resting state is determined in Practical 1 and lung function during exercise is determined in Practical 2. Practical 3 describes a procedure for measuring D_L with examples of values and calculations. Practical 4 also describes how oxygen uptake may be demonstrated by the closed circuit system, during which lung function measures may also be demonstrated. Each practical contains actual data to exemplify the relationships between variables and provides examples and applications of the various formulae for assessing lung function.

3.12 PRACTICAL 1: ASSESSMENT OF RESTING LUNG VOLUMES

3.12.1 PURPOSE

- To measure static and dynamic lung volumes in the resting state
- To determine relationships between lung function and anthropometric variables
- To assess the effects of changes in posture on lung function.

Some data are presented in Table 3.6 to exemplify some of these measurements.

3.12.2 PROCEDURES

(a) Closed circuit spirometry

1. Record the subject's age, stature, mass, physical activity/training status.
2. Record ambient conditions (temperature, barometric pressure).
3. Record sitting height, arm span and chest circumference.
4. Measurement of inspired and expired volumes using a wet spirometer with kymograph.
    (a) Sanitize all equipment and mouthpiece.
    (b) The subject puts on a nose clip.
    (c) Procedure:
    (i) The recording pen is best placed just below half-way on the kymograph.
    (ii) Set the drum rotation speed to 10 mm s^{-1}.

Table 3.6 Assessment of resting lung volumes: example of lung volumes at rest in a 38-year-old active male

Descriptive data

Name	RGE	Age	38
Stature (m)	1.78	Mass (kg)	86.0
Sitting height (m)	0.91	Arm span (m)	1.84

Ambient conditions

Laboratory temperature (°C)	20	P_{Bar} (mmHg)	750

(a) Resting measurements (dry spirometer)[a]

	FVC (l)	$FEV_{1.0}$ (l)	$FEV_{1.0\%}$ (l)	$FEF_{25-75\%}$ (l s^{-1})	$FEF_{75-85\%}$ (l s^{-1})	$FEF_{0.2-1.2}$ (l s^{-1})	FMFT (s)	MVV (l min^{-1})
Standing	6.65	5.41	81.2	5.37	1.2	13.0	0.62	230
Supine	6.32	5.1	80.6	5.21	1.1	11.0	0.81	190
Predicted values	5.02	4.04	80.0	4.60	1.27	9.00	0.73	200

(b) Resting measurements (wet spirometer)[a]

	V_T (l)	IRV (l)	ERV (l)	FVC (l)	RV (l)	FRC (l)	TLC (l)
Measured	0.60	3.20	1.65	6.65	1.80	3.45	8.45
Predicted values	0.60	2.91	1.39	5.02	1.90	2.70	6.8

(c) Resting measurements (Douglas bag)[a]

	$\dot{V}E$ (l s^{-1})	f (breaths min^{-1})	V_T (l)	V_T as %FVC	MVV (l min^{-1})
	7.0	10.0	0.70	10.0	210.0

a All values should be recorded at BTPS.

(iii) Ask the subject to breathe normally into and out of the spirometer to allow measurement of *tidal volume* (V_T) and breathing frequency (*f*).

(iv) At the end of a normal inspiration, ask the subject to inhale as deeply as possible to measure *inspiratory reserve volume* (IRV) and return to normal breathing.

(v) At the end of a normal expiration, ask the subject to expire as much as possible to determine the *expiratory reserve volume* (ERV) and return to normal breathing.

(vi) The subject is then requested to inhale as deeply as possible and exhale as forcefully as possible to measure the *forced vital capacity* (FVC).

(vii) *Residual volume* can be predicted from the relevant equation in Table 3.3 or it can be measured by the method explained in the laboratory practical described in Volume 1, Chapter 1 by Hawes and Martin. This will allow *total lung capacity* (TLC) and *functional residual capacity* (FRC) to be calculated.

(b) Open circuit spirometry (Vitalograph)

5. Measurement of FVC, $FEV_{1.0}$, $FEV_{1\%}$, FMF ($FEF_{25-75\%}$), $FEF_{75-85\%}$, PEFR, $FEF_{0.2-1.2}$, FMFT.
   (a) Set the Vitalograph spirometer to zero.
   (b) From the standing position, ask the subject to inhale as deeply as possible, place the spirometer mouthpiece into the mouth, and exhale as forcefully as possible over a period of 5–6 s. Record the best of three readings.
   (c) Calculate the various lung function parameters as indicated in Figure 3.10.
   (d) Compare individual scores with predicted scores using one of the appropriate regression equations listed in Tables 3.1–3.4 and record all data.
   (e) Repeat the above procedures with the subject in the supine position.

6. Measurement of maximal voluntary ventilation (MVV) (Figure 3.8).
   (a) Predict MVV using the formula:

$$MVV = FEV_{0.75} \times 40 \text{ (Cotes, 1979)}$$

where:

$$FEV_{0.75} = 0.92 \times FEV_{1.0} - 0.07 \text{ (95\% limits} \times 8\%)$$

   (b) Insert respiratory valve and attach the nose clip.
   (c) Ask the subject to breathe as deeply and rapidly as possible for 15 s into either a Douglas bag or directly into a dry gas spirometer. Convert the values into litres per minute (BTPS).
   (d) Record values on data sheet.

7. Measurement of V_T, *f* and pulmonary ventilation ($\dot{V}E$) at rest. The subject sits quietly for 5 minutes. Expired air is collected into a Douglas bag in the final minute. The respiratory frequency can be counted by rise and fall of the chest wall or by movement of the respiratory valves. Tidal volume can be calculated from the following:

$$V_T = \frac{V_{BTPS} \ (l) \ \text{min}^{-1}}{f}$$

8. Computation of dead space. The volume of dead space can be calculated using Bohr's formula, which is based on the fact that the expired volume of oxygen at each

respiration ($V_T \times FEO_2$) is equal to the sum of the volume of oxygen contained in the dead space compartment ($V_D \times FIO_2$) and the volume of oxygen coming from the alveolar air $V_A \times FAO_2$. We therefore arrive at the following formula:

$$V_T \times FEO_2 = (V_D \times FIO_2) + (V_A \times FAO_2)$$

Since $V_A = V_T - V_D$, the formula may be simplified as follows:

$$V_D = V_T \times \frac{FEO_2 - FAO_2}{FIO_2 - FAO_2}$$

If the oxygen content of the inspired air is 21%, the oxygen content of the expired air is 16%, the oxygen content of the alveolar air is 14%, and the depth of the respiration (V_T) is 500 ml, the dead space volume (V_D) is:

$$V_D = 500 \times \frac{16-14}{20-14} = 143\,ml$$

3.12.3 ASSIGNMENTS

1. Examine the spirogram from the wet spirometry practical. Comment on the relative magnitude of the various volumes, e.g. compare IRV with ERV.
2. Comment on the relationship between height, sitting height, weight, chest circumference, arm span and the lung function measurements ($FEV_{1.0}$, FVC).
3. Compare the accuracy of the prediction of MVV by the $FEV_{1.0}$ method with the 15 s Douglas bag method.
4. Compare the measured values with the predicted values in Tables 3.1–3.4.
5. Compare the spirometry values in the standing and supine position.
6. Compare the resting $\dot{V}E$, V_T and f measurements with expected values. Consider the effects of body size on these measurements.
7. Calculate the relative size of each breath as a proportion of the vital capacity in the standing and supine positions (%FVC = (V_T / FVC) × 100).
8. Compare values between males and females.
9. Is there any relationship between the level of physical training and lung function values?

3.13 PRACTICAL 2: ASSESSMENT OF LUNG VOLUMES DURING EXERCISE

3.13.1 PURPOSE

To assess the influence of arm and leg exercise on pulmonary ventilation, alveolar ventilation, breathing frequency, tidal volume and the ventilatory equivalent. Some data are presented in Table 3.7 to exemplify these measurements.

3.13.2 PROCEDURES

All data for this practical should be recorded on a data sheet similar to that shown in Table 3.7.

Table 3.7 Assessment of lung volumes during exercise: Example of lung volumes at rest and during different modes of exercise in a 38-year-old active male

Descriptive data

Name	RGE	Age	38
Height (m)	1.78	Mass (kg)	86.0
Sitting Height (m)	0.91	Arm span (m)	1.84

Ambient conditions

Laboratory temperature (°C)	20	P_{Bar} (mm Hg)	760

(a) Resting values

VE l min⁻¹	V_T (l)	V_T as%FVC	f	%O₂	%CO₂	$\dot{V}O_2$ (l min⁻¹)	$\dot{V}E_{eq}$	$V_D(ml)^a$
9.1	0.70	10.0	13	15.7	4.00	0.36	25.0	172.0

(b) Arm exercise

Watts	V_e (l) min⁻¹ (BTPS)	V_T (l)	V_T (as%FV)	f	%O₂	%CO₂	$\dot{V}O_2$	VE_{eq}
25	21.6	1.20	18.0	18	16.4	4.1	0.82	26.3
50	32.2	1.40	21.0	23	16.2	4.3	1.29	25.0
75	50.4	1.80	27.0	28	16.4	4.3	1.91	26.3
100	70.5	2.13	32.0	33	16.4	4.5	2.63	26.6
125	95.5	2.45	37.0	39	17.0	4.5	2.97	32.1
150	118.4	2.80	42.0	42	17.2	4.5	3.43	34.4

(c) Leg exercise

Watts	V_e (l) min⁻¹ (BTPS)	V_T (l)	V_T (as%FV)	f	%O₂	%CO₂	$\dot{V}O_2$	VE_{eq}
25	16.0	1.0	15.0	16	16.3	4.0	0.63	25.4
50	24.3	1.43	21.4	17	16.0	4.0	1.03	23.6
75	29.4	1.47	22.1	20	16.0	4.1	1.24	23.7
100	38.6	1.68	25.2	23	16.3	4.2	1.51	25.7
125	47.1	1.96	29.5	24	16.5	3.9	1.80	26.2
150	53.3	2.05	30.8	26	16.4	4.0	2.05	26.0
200	69.1	2.03	30.5	30	16.6	4.4	2.44	28.3
250	96.3	2.91	43.8	33	16.8	4.6	3.18	30.2
300	130.0	3.51	52.8	37	17.0	4.6	4.02	32.3

Formulae:

$V_T = VE_{BTPS}/f$

V_T as %FVC $= (V_T/FVC) \times 100$

$\dot{V}O_2 = \dot{V}E_{STPD} \times (((1 - (FEO_2 + FECO_2)) \times 0.265) - FEO_2)$

$\dot{V}O_2 = \dot{V}E \times 0.04$

$\dot{V}E = \dot{V}O_2 \times 20 - 25$

$V_{Tmax} = 0.74 \, FVC \times 1.11$

$VE_{eq} = \dot{V}E_{BTPS}/\dot{V}O_{2STPD}$

$V_D = V_T \times \dfrac{FEO_2 - FAO_2}{FIO_2 \; FAO_2}$

$FEO_2 = \%O_2/100$

Correction of gas volumes:

From ATPS to STPD $V_{STPD} = V_{ATPS} \times (273 / (273 + T°C)) \times ((P_{BAR} - P_{H2O}) / 760)$

From ATPS to BTPS $V_{BTPS} = V_{ATPS} \times (310 / (273 + T°C)) \times ((P_{BAR} - P_{H2O}) / (P_{BAR} - 47)$

From STPD to BTPS $V_{BTPS} = V_{STPD} \times (310 / 273) \times (760 / (P_{BAR} - 47)$

$P_{H2O} = 13.955 - 0.6584T + 0.0419T^2$

1. Record the subject's age, stature, weight, physical activity/training status.
2. Record ambient conditions (temperature, barometric pressure).
3. *Assessment of resting pulmonary values*: The subject rests and breathes normally for 5 minutes. Expired air is collected in the final minute in a Douglas bag. Record the respiratory frequency and compute tidal volume as described in Practical 1. Lung volumes should be recorded at BTPS (i.e. convert ATPS to BTPS using the formula in Table 3.7).
4. Determine the oxygen and carbon dioxide fraction in the Douglas bag.
5. *Incremental exercise test*: The subject exercises at 25 W on the arm ergometer with increments of 25 W every 3 minutes until maximal volitional exhaustion (or 150 W). Expired air is directed into a Douglas bag to obtain the oxygen and carbon dioxide fractions. Respiratory frequency is measured. The volume of expired air is then determined through a dry gas meter.
6. The subject rests for 10–15 minutes.
7. Repeat the procedure described in steps 5 and 6 on a cycle ergometer at identical work-rates (for comparison of arm and leg values). Work-rates are then increased by 50 W every 3 minutes until maximal volitional exhaustion. Collect expired air over the final minute of each increment.
8. The subject rests for 5 minutes.
9. Perform the FVC test to obtain a spirogram for analysis of post-exercise static and dynamic volumes.

3.13.3 ASSIGNMENTS

1. Determine V_T and the relative size of each breath in relation to the FVC for arm and leg work ($\%FVC = (V_T / FVC) \times 100$).
2. Determine the ventilatory equivalent (VE_{eq}) at rest, and during submaximal and maximal work intensities for arm and leg ergometry.

$$VE_{eq} = \frac{VE_{BTPS}}{\dot{V}O_2}$$

3. What do you notice about the pulmonary ventilation for arm ergometry at submaximal and maximal work-rates?
4. Are there any differences in the $\dot{V}_E$ and VE_{eq} responses for trained and untrained individuals?
5. Compare the post-exercise spirogram results with those taken at rest. What do you notice about the static and dynamic lung volumes and flow rates?
6. How accurate are the following equations for predicting $\dot{V}_E$, $\dot{V}O_2$ and V_{Tmax}?

$$\dot{V}_E = (\dot{V}O_2 \, (l \, min^{-1}) \times 20) - 25$$

$$\dot{V}O_2 = \dot{V}_E \, (l \, min^{-1}) \times 0.04$$

(Datta and Ramanathan, 1969)

$$V_{Tmax} = 0.74 \, FVC - 1.11 \qquad \text{(Jones, 1984)}$$

7. How does the relationship between V_E and VO_2 compare to previously observed values from the literature? Does V_E limit $\dot{V}O_2$ max?
8. Compare the MVV obtained from the 15 s test to the maximum V_E obtained in the exercise test. Why is MVV greater than $V_E$max?

3.14 PRACTICAL 3: MEASUREMENT OF PULMONARY DIFFUSING CAPACITY

3.14.1 PURPOSE

Pulmonary diffusing capacity (D_L) is commonly measured by the single-breath method. This technique requires the subject to inspire a mixture of 0.3% carbon monoxide (CO), 10% helium (He), 21% oxygen (O_2) and a balance of nitrogen (N_2). Specifically, the technique measures the rate of diffusion of CO from the alveoli to the pulmonary vascular bed in a single full 10 s breath-hold of the gas mixture and is hence abbreviated DL_{COsb}. The rationale for its measurement was described in Section 3.6.

3.14.2 PROCEDURES

The method is described in detail by Ferris (1978) and is summarized here for ease of reference.

3.14.3 APPARATUS (FIGURE 3.11)

1. A 30 litre Douglas bag is flushed several times with the He–CO mixture.
2. Just before the test, the inspiratory tubing and valve section is also flushed with the He–CO mixture.
3. The subject is seated, fitted with a nose clip, and breathes ambient air (valve directed to A).
4. With the valve directed to A (ambient air), the subject is instructed to (1) exhale maximally to residual volume, signal by hand, and on instruction (2) inhale rapidly and maximally from the Douglas bag and hold the breath for 10 s. On a signal, the subject then exhales rapidly. The four-way valve is adjusted by the investigator to enable the subject to breathe normal air and exhale maximally to normal air (A), inspire from the bag (B), expire to space surrounding the bag (C, 1 litre wash-out) and to ensure 1 litre collection of alveolar air in the sampling bag (D).

Figure 3.11 Conventional manual system for DL_{COsb}. (Modified from Ferris, 1978.)

5. The following values are recorded: (1) breath-hold time from mid-inspiration to beginning of the alveolar sampling (Figure 3.12), (2) the inspired volume (ATPS), (3) the final He concentration in the sampling bag and (4) the final CO concentration in the sampling bag.

It is important to note that a number of factors affect the calculation of DL_{COsb} such as the Valsalva manoeuvre, the method of measuring the breath-hold time, the actual breath-hold time and other factors. For more detail of these factors refer to the American Thoracic

Society Epidemiology Standardization Project compiled by Ferris (1978). It is possible to reduce the breath-hold time to as low as 3 s with a minimum loss of accuracy during strenuous exercise (Turcotte *et al.*, 1992).

3.14.4 GAS ANALYSIS

The analysers for CO and He are connected in series, preceded by an H_2O absorber, CO_2 absorber, dust filter and a flow meter. A small pump should draw air through at a rate of 400 ml min^{-1} and a stable reading for CO and He is obtained in 30–40 s.

Figure 3.12 Standardized measurements from the spirographic tracing obtained during the single breath diffusing capacity maneouvre. The inspired volume is measured from the maximal expiration to the fullest inspiration. The breath-holding time is measured from the time when one-half of the inspiration is made to the time when washout has been completed and collection of alveolar gas has begun.

Example calculation of DL_{COsb}
  Equation:

$$DL_{COsb} = V_{A(STPD)} \times \frac{60}{\text{breath holding time}} \times \frac{1}{P_B - 47} \times \frac{CO_A}{CO_E}$$

where:
  DL_{COsb} = single breath diffusing capacity for CO
  P_B = barometric pressure
  CO_A = initial concentration of CO
  CO_E = expired concentration of CO
  V_A = alveolar volume (STPD) at which the breath was held

$$V_A = V_I (ATPS) \times (He_I / He_E) \times 1.05 \times \text{STPD correction factor}$$

where:
  V_I = inspired volume (ATPS)
  He_I = inspired He
  He_E = expired He
$$CO_A = CO_I \times \frac{He_E}{He_I}$$

Sample data
  P_B = 754 mmHg He_E = 12.0%
  CO_I = 0.3%   T = 21°
  He_I = 10.0 %   STPD cf = 0.895
  V_I (ATPS) = 5000ml CO_E = 0.2%
  Breath-hold time = 10 s

Stage 1 (Solve for V$_{A(STPD)}$)

$$V_{A(STPD)} = 5000 \text{ ml} \times \frac{0.10}{0.12} \times 1.05 \times 0.895$$

$$V_{A(STPD)} = 3915 \text{ ml}$$

Stage 2 (Solve for CO$_A$)

$$CO_A = 0.003 \times \frac{0.12}{0.10} = 0.0036$$

Stage 3 (Solve for DL_{COsb})

$$DL_{COsb} = 3915 \text{ ml} \times \frac{60 \text{ s}}{10 \text{ s}} \times \frac{1}{754 - 47} \times \frac{0.0036}{0.0020}$$

$$DL_{COsb} = 33.8 \text{ ml CO min}^{-1} \text{ mm Hg}^{-1}$$

3.15 PRACTICAL 4: MEASUREMENT OF OXYGEN UPTAKE BY CLOSED-CIRCUIT SPIROMETRY

3.15.1 PURPOSE

Although the closed-circuit, indirect spirometry system is rarely used today, it can be used to exemplify some of the basic principles of measurement of oxygen consumption at rest and during exercise. Estimations of energy expenditure may be calculated using caloric equivalents for oxygen uptake for an RER of 0.83, i.e. 20.2 kJ l^{-1} (4.8 kcal l^{-1}). The following procedure should be used to produce the spirometry tracings as exemplified in Figure 3.13.

3.15.2 PROCEDURE FOR CLOSED-CIRCUIT OXYGEN UPTAKE

1. The spirometer is rinsed with 100% oxygen and then filled with 100% oxygen.
2. The subject is seated on the arm ergometer and connected to the spirometer and breathes atmospheric air for a few minutes to acclimatize to the mouthpiece and the resistance of the spirometer.
3. Expired air is directed through soda lime to remove CO_2.
4. The kymograph speed is set at 25 mm min^{-1}.
5. The subject then inspires oxygen from the spirometer. Initially, the expired air should be directed to the atmosphere. The spirometer should then be then closed so that oxygen is breathed from and back into the spirometer. Recordings can be made for several minutes, after which time the subject should breathe normal air.
6. After a warm-up the subject should then commence arm ergometry at 50 W for 3 minutes. Oxygen is inspired from the spirometer for the last minute. The spirometer is then refilled with oxygen.
7. After a 20 minute rest period the mode of ergometry is switched to cycling at 50 W and the above procedure is repeated.

8. Oxygen uptake at STPD may be calculated using the following formulae. The correction factor for converting ATPS to STPD volumes can be calculated from the formulae in Practical 2 or from Chapter 6, Table 6.2.

Calculation of $\dot{V}O_2$ at STPD (ml min^{-1})

$$\frac{y\,(mm) \times 30\,(ml\ mm^{-1}) \times correction\ factor\,(CF) \times 60\,(s)}{x\,(mm) \times 2.4\,(s\ mm^{-1})}$$

Sitting at rest $\quad$ $(20 \times 30 \times 0.919 \times 60) / (45 \times 2.4) = 306$ ml min^{-1}
Arm ergometry $\quad$ (50 W) $\quad$ $(50 \times 30 \times 0.919 \times 60) / (30 \times 2.4) = 1149$ ml min^{-1}
Cycling (50 W) $\quad$ $(48 \times 30 \times 0.919 \times 60) / (45 \times 2.4) = 735$ ml min^{-1}
NB: Paper speed = 25 mm min^{-1} or 1 mm = 2.4 s

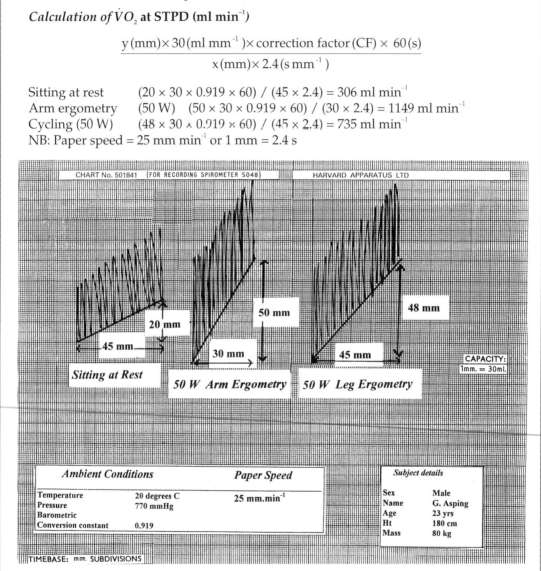

Figure 3.13 Closed circuit spirograph showing oxygen uptake at rest and during arm and leg exercise for a healthy, fit male student.

REFERENCES

Akabas, S.R., Bazzyar, A., Dimauro, S. and Haddad, G.G. (1989). Metabolic and functional adaptation of the diaphragm to training with resistive loads. *Journal of Applied Physiology*, **66**, 529–35.

Allen, S.M., Hunt, B. and Green, M. (1985). Fall in vital capacity with posture. *British Journal of Diseases of the Chest*, **79**, 267–71.

American Thoracic Society (1991). Lung function testing: selection of reference values and interpretation strategies. *American Review of Respiratory Disease*, **144**, 1202–18.

Åstrand, P.O. (1952). *Experimental Studies of Physical Work Capacity in Relation to Sex and Age*. (E. Munksgaard, Copenhagen).

Åstrand, P.O. (1954). The respiratory activity in man exposed to prolonged hypoxia. *Acta Physiologica Scandinavica*, **30**, 343–68.

Åstrand, P.O. and Rodahl, K. (1986). *Textbook of Work Physiology*. (McGraw-Hill, New York).

Becklake, M.R. (1986). Concepts of normality applied to the measurement of lung function. *American Journal of Medicine*, **80**, 1158–64.

Bevegard, S., Freyschuss, U. and Strandell, T. (1966). Circulatory adaptation to arm and leg exercise in supine and sitting position. *Journal of Applied Physiology*, **21**, 37–46.

Blair, E. and Hickam, J.B. (1955). The effect of change in body position on lung volume and intrapulmonary gas mixing in normal subjects. *Journal of Clinical Investigations*, **34**, 383–9.

Boren, H.G., Kory, R.C. and Syner, J.C. (1966). The Veterans Administration Army cooperative study of pulmonary function. *American Journal of Medicine*, **41**, 96–114.

Buono, M.J., Constable, S.A., Morton, A.R., *et al.* (1981). The effect of an acute bout of exercise on selected pulmonary function measurements. *Medicine and Science in Sports and Exercise*, **13**, 290–3.

Carey, C.R., Schaefer, K.E. and Alvis, H.J. (1956). Effect of skin diving on lung volume. *Journal of Applied Physiology*, **8**, 519–23.

Cookson, J.B., Blake, G.T.W. and Faranisi, C. (1976). Normal values for ventilatory function in Rhodesian Africans. *British Journal of Diseases of the Chest*, **70**, 107–11.

Cotes, J.E. (1979). *Lung Function: Assessment and Application in Medicine*. (Blackwell Scientific, Oxford).

Cotes, J.E., Dabbs, J.M., Hall, A.M., *et al.* (1979). Sitting height, fat-free mass and body fat as reference variables for lung function in healthy British children: comparison with stature. *Annals of Human Biology*, **6**, 307–14.

Crapo, R.O., Morris, A.H. and Gardner, R.M. (1981). Reference spirometric values using techniques and equipment that meet ATS recommendations. *American Review of Respiratory Disease*, **123**, 659–64.

Crapo, R.O., Morris, A.H., Clayton, P.D. and Nixon, C.R. (1982). Lung volumes in healthy non-smoking adults. *Bulletin European de Physiopathologie Respiratoire*, **18**, 419–25.

Damon, A. (1966). Negro–white differences in pulmonary function (vital capacity, timed vital capacity and expiratory flow rate). *Human Biology*, **38**, 381–93.

Datta, S.R. and Ramanathan, N.L. (1969). Energy expenditure in work predicted from heart rate and pulmonary ventilation. *Journal of Applied Physiology*, **26**, 297–302.

Davies, C.T., Few, J., Foster, K.G. and Sargeant, T. (1974). Plasma catecholamine concentration during dynamic exercise involving different muscle groups. *European Journal of Applied Physiology*, **32**, 195–206.

DeGroodt, E.G., Quanjer, P.H., Wise, J.E. and Van Zomeren, B.C. (1986). Changing relationships between stature and lung volumes during puberty. *Respiration Physiology*, **65**, 139–53.

DeGroodt, E.G., van Pelt, W., Quanjer, P.H., *et al.* (1988). Growth of lung and thorax dimensions during the pubertal growth spurt. *European Respiratory Journal*, **1**, 102–8.

Ekblom, B. and Hermansen, L. (1968). Cardiac output in athletes. *Journal of Applied Physiology*, **25**, 619–25.

Eston, R.G. and Brodie, D.A. (1986). Responses to arm and leg ergometry. *British Journal of Sports Medicine*, **20**, 4–7.

Ferris, A. (1978). Epidemiology standardization project (Part III), *American Review of Respiratory Disease*, **118**, 55–89.

Ferris, B.G. and Stoudt, H.E. (1971). Correlation of anthropometry and simple tests of pulmonary function. *Archives of Environmental Health*, **22**, 672–6.

Fringer, M.N. and Stull, G.A. (1974). Changes in cardiorespiratory parameters during periods of training and detraining in young adult females. *Medicine and Science in Sports*, **6**, 20–5.

Frisancho, A.R. (1975). Functional adaptation to high-altitude hypoxia. *Science*, **187**, 313–19.

Gimeno, F., Berg, W.C., Sluiter, H.J. and Tammeling, G.J. (1972). Spirometry-induced bronchial obstruction. *American Review of Respiratory Disease*, **105**, 68–74.

Guberan, E., Williams, M.K., Walford, J. and Smith, M.M. (1969). Circadian variation of FEV in shift workers. *British Journal of Industrial Medicine*, **26**, 121–5.

Hagberg, J.M., Yerg, J.E. and Seals, D.R. (1988). Pulmonary function in young and older athletes and untrained men. *Journal of Applied Physiology*, **65**, 101–5.

Hagberg, J.M., Coyle, E.F., Carroll, J.E., *et al.* (1982). Exercise hyperventilation in patients with McArdle's disease. *Journal of Applied Physiology*, **52**, 991–4.

Hall, A.M., Heywood, C., and Cotes, J.E. (1979). Lung function in healthy British women. *Thorax*, **34**, 359–65.

Hanson, J.S. (1973). Maximal exercise performance in members of the US Nordic Ski Team. *Journal of Applied Physiology*, **35**, 592–5.

Hetzel, M.R. (1981). The pulmonary clock. *Thorax*, **36**, 481–6.

Hetzel, M.R. and Clark, T.J.H. (1980). Comparison of normal and asthmatic circadian rhythms in peak expiratory flow rate. *Thorax*, **35**, 732–8.

Hibbert, M.E., Lanigan, A., Raven, J. and Phelan, P.D. (1988). Relation of armspan to height and the prediction of lung function. *Thorax*, **43**, 657–9.

Hong, S.K., Moore, T.O., Seto, G., *et al.* (1970). Lung volumes and apneic bradycardia in divers. *Journal of Applied Physiology*, **29**, 172–6.

Jacobs, D.R., Nelson, E.T., Dontas, A.S., *et al.* (1992). Are race and sex differences in lung function explained by frame size? *American Review of Respiratory Disease*, **146**, 644–9.

Jirka, Z. and Adamus, M. (1965). Changes of ventilation equivalents in young people in the course of three years of training. *Journal of Sports Medicine and Physical Fitness*, **5**, 1–6.

Johannsen, Z.M. and Erasmus, L.D. (1968). Clinical spirometry in normal Bantu. *American Review of Respiratory Disease*, **97**, 585–97.

Jones, N.L. (1984). Dyspnea in exercise. *Medicine and Science in Sports and Exercise*, **16**, 14–9.

Knudson, R.J., Lebowitz, M.D., Holberg, C.J. and Burrows, B. (1983). Changes in normal maximal expiratory flow–volume curve with growth and aging. *American Review of Respiratory Disease*, **127**, 725–34.

Krogh, M. (1915). Diffusion of gases through the lungs of man. *Journal of Physiology*, **49**, 271–300.

Krowka, M.J., Enright, P.L., Rodarte, J.R. and Hyatt, R.E. (1987). Effect of effort on forced expiratory effort in one second. *American Review of Respiratory Disease*, **136**, 829–33.

Lapp, N.L., Amandus, H.E., Hall, R. and Morgan, W.K.C. (1974). Lung volumes and flow rates in black and white subjects. *Thorax*, **29**, 185–8.

Levison, H. and Cherniack, R.M. (1968). Ventilatory cost of exercise in chronic obstructive pulmonary disease. *Journal of Applied Physiology*, **25**, 21–7.

McArdle, W., Katch, F.I. and Katch, V.L. (1991). *Exercise Physiology: Energy, Nutrition and Human Performance*. (Williams and Wilkins, Baltimore, MD).

Mangum, M. (1984). Research methods: application to arm crank ergometry. *Journal of Sports Sciences*, **2**, 257–63.

Melissinos, C.G. and Mead, J. (1977). Maximum expiratory flow changes induced by longitudinal tension on trachea in normal subjects. *Journal of Applied Physiology*, **43**, 537–44.

Miles, D.S., Cox, M.H., Bomze, J.P. and Gotshall, R.W. (1991). Acute recovery profile of lung volumes and function after running 5 miles. *Journal of Sports Medicine and Physical Fitness*, **31**, 243–8.

Minors, D.S. (1985). Abnormal pressure. In *Variations in Human Physiology*. ed. R.M. Case (Manchester University Press, Manchester, UK), pp. 78–110.

Morris, J.F., Koski, A. and Johnson, L.C. (1971). Spirometric standards for healthy non-smoking adults. *American Review of Respiratory Disease*, **103**, 57–67.

Newman, F., Smalley, B.F. and Thomson, M.L. (1962). Effect of exercise, body and lung size on CO diffusing capacity in athletes and non-athletes. *Journal of Applied Physiology*, **17**, 649–55.

Ogilvie, C.M., Forster, R.E., Blakemore, W.S. and Morton, J.W. (1957). A standardized breath holding technique for the clinical measurement of the diffusing capacity of the lung for carbon monoxide. *Journal of Clinical Investigations*, **36**, 1–17.

Polgar, G. and Promadhat, V. (1971). *Pulmonary Function Testing in Children: Techniques and Standards*. (W.B. Saunders, Philadelphia, PA), p. 272.

Rasmussen, B., Klausen, K., Clausen, J.P. and Trap-Jensen, J. (1975). Pulmonary ventilation, blood gases and pH after training of the arms and legs. *Journal of Applied Physiology*, **38**, 250–6.

Rasmussen, R.S., Elkjaer, P. and Juhl, B. (1988). Impaired pulmonary and cardiac function after maximal exercise. *Journal of Sports Sciences*, **6**, 219–28.

Reilly, T. (1990). Human circadian rhythms and

exercise. *Critical Reviews in Biomedical Engineering*, **18**, 165–80.

Saltin, B. and Åstrand P.O. (1967). Maximal oxygen uptake in athletes. *Journal of Applied Physiology*, **23**, 353–8.

Schwartz, J.D., Katz, S.A., Fegley, R.W. and Tockman, M.S. (1988). Analysis of spirometric data from a national sample of healthy 6–24-year-olds (NHANES II). *American Review of Respiratory Disease*, **138**, 1405–14.

Song, S.H., Kang, D.H., Kang, B.S. and Hong, S.K. (1963). Lung volumes and ventilatory responses to high CO_2 and low O_2 in the ama. *Journal of Applied Physiology*, **18**, 466–70.

Sonne, L.J. and Davis, J.A. (1982). Increased exercise performance in patients with severe COPD following inspiratory resistive training. *Chest*, **81**, 436–9.

Stenberg, J., Åstrand, P.O., Ekblom, B. *et al.* (1967). Hemodynamic response to work with different muscle groups, sitting and supine. *Journal of Applied Physiology*, **22**, 61–70.

Thurlbeck, W.M. (1982). Postnatal human lung growth. *Thorax*, **37**, 564–71.

Townsend, M.C. (1984). Spirometric forced expiratory volumes measured in the standing versus the sitting posture. *American Review of Respiratory Disease*, **130**, 123–4.

Turcotte, R.A., Perrault, H., Marcotte, J.E. and Beland, M. (1992). A test for the measurement of pulmonary diffusing capacity during high intensity exercise. *Journal of Sports Sciences*, **10**, 229–35.

Turino, G.M., Bergofsky, E.H., Goldring, R.M. and Fishman A.P. (1963). Effect of exercise on pulmonary diffusing capacity. *Journal of Applied Physiology*, **18**, 447–56.

Turner, J.M., Mead, J. and Wohl, M.E. (1968). Elasticity of human lungs in relation to age. *Journal of Applied Physiology*, **25**, 664–71.

Tzankoff, S.P., Robinson, S., Pyke, F.S. and Brown, C.A. (1972). Physiological adjustments to work in older men as affected by physical training. *Journal of Applied Physiology*, **33**, 346–50.

Van de Wal, B.W., Erasmus, L.D. and Hechter, R. (1971). Sitting and standing heights in Bantu and white South Africans – The significance in relation to pulmonary function values. *South African Medical Journal*, **45 (Suppl)**, 568–70.

Wasserman, K., Hansen, J.E., Sue, D.Y. and Whipp, B.J. (1987). *Principles of Exercise Testing and Interpretation*, (Lea and Febiger, Philadelphia, PA), pp. 33–6.

HAEMATOLOGY

4

Ron Maughan, John Leiper and Mike Greaves

4.1 AIMS

The aims of this chapter are to:
- describe practical issues and procedures relevant to blood sampling and handling,
- explain the rationale for haematology measurement procedures most widely used in the exercise science laboratory,
- describe some of the factors that influence haematological variables and their physiological significance.

4.2 INTRODUCTION

A high aerobic capacity is a prerequisite for success in all endurance-based sports, and many different factors contribute to the body's ability to derive energy from oxidative metabolism. Although maximum cardiac output is often considered to be the limiting factor to oxygen transport, this is true only in the absence of another limitation. For different individuals and in different situations, any of the steps in the chain of oxygen transport and use, from pulmonary function to mitochondrial enzyme activity, may determine this limit. This includes the transport of oxygen in the circulation, which in turn depends on the blood haemoglobin concentration and the total red blood cell mass. For this reason, athletes are often concerned to know their circulating haemoglobin concentration, as this is the most widely understood measure of adequacy or otherwise of an individual's iron status and is also the marker that is most closely related to

exercise performance. Although it can be argued that other markers may be of more diagnostic use, it is generally accepted that some form of haematological assessment is an important part of any routine screening of athletes being carried out as part of a sports science or sports medicine athlete support programme.

A high circulating haemoglobin concentration can confer performance advantages, and abuse of erythropoietin, the hormone that stimulates red blood cell formation, is thought to be common in some groups of sportsmen and women. For this reason, the Governing Bodies of some sports have established an upper limit to the acceptable level of circulating red cells. In cycling, a rider with a haematocrit level of 52% or more is deemed to have committed a doping offence, and is liable to disqualification and suspension, even though this value is within the normal range for men (Table 4.1). Haematological assessment is thus also an essential part of doping control in many sports.

In the exercise laboratory, an individual's haematological profile can be seen as an important descriptor alongside other variables such as age, height, weight or body fat content. Measurement of changes in blood volume or plasma volume can also be important in assessing the significance of changes in the circulating concentration of a variety of hormones, substrates, metabolites and other organic and inorganic components. Haemoconcentration or haemodilution may cause or obscure changes in the

Kinanthropometry and Exercise Physiology Laboratory Manual: Tests, Procedures and Data. 2nd Edition, Volume 2: Exercise Physiology Edited by RG Eston and T Reilly. Published by Routledge, London, June 2001

Table 4.1   Normal values

	Units	Men	Women
Haemoglobin	g l^{-1}	13.5–17.5	11.5–15.5
Red cell count	× 10^{12} l^{-1}	4.5–6.5	3.9–5.6
Haematocrit (Hct, PCV)	l^{-1}, %	40–52	36–48
Mean cell volume	fl	80–95	80–95
Plasma volume	ml kg^{-1} body mass	45±5	45±5
Serum iron	μmol l^{-1}	10–30	10–30
Serum transferrin	g^{-1}	2.0–4.0	2.0–4.0
Total iron binding capacity	μmol l^{-1}	40–75	40–75
Serum ferritin	μg^{-1}	40–340	14–150

circulating concentration of the entity of interest (Kargotich *et al.*, 1998). Whether or not one should correct measured concentrations for changes in the volume of distribution depends on the question that is being asked.

This chapter will focus on a detailed description of the practical issues relevant to blood sampling and handling, and on those haematology measurement procedures most widely used in the exercise science laboratory. More sophisticated measures used in the clinical assessment of iron status and in the physiology research laboratory will be described more briefly as a full description of the methodology is outwith the scope of a single chapter.

4.3 BLOOD SAMPLING AND HANDLING

There are several different methods and sites of blood sampling that can be used in the collection of samples for analysis, and the results obtained will be affected by both sampling site and the procedures used in sample collection. The chosen procedures will be determined by the needs of the investigator and the facilities available. Whatever the method used, the safety of the subject and the investigator is paramount, and appropriate sterile or antiseptic precautions must be observed. Strict safety precautions must be followed at all times in the sampling and handling of blood. It is wise to assume that all samples are infected and to treat them accordingly. This means wearing gloves and appropriate protective clothing and following guidelines for handling of samples and disposal of waste material. Used needles, cannulae and lancets must be disposed of immediately in a suitable sharps bin: re-sheathing of used needles must never be attempted. Sharps – whether contaminated or not – must always be disposed of in an approved container and must never be mixed with other waste. All other contaminated materials must be disposed of using appropriate and clearly identified waste containers. Any spillage of blood must be treated immediately.

The main sampling procedures involve collection of arterial, venous, arterialized venous or capillary blood. In most routine laboratory investigations of interest to the sports scientist, arterial blood sampling is impractical and unnecessarily invasive, and will not be considered in detail here. Where arterial blood is required, arterial puncture may be used, but in most situations, collection of arterialized venous blood as described below gives an adequate representation of arterial blood.

4.3.1 VENOUS BLOOD

Venous blood sampling is probably the method of choice for most routine purposes: sampling from a superficial forearm or ante-cubital vein is simple, painless and relatively free from risk of complications. Sampling may be by venous puncture or by an indwelling cannula. Where repeated sampling is necessary at short time intervals, introduction of a cannula is obviously preferred to avoid repeated venous punctures. Either a plastic cannula or a butterfly-type cannula can be used. The latter has obvious limitations if introduced into an ante-cubital vein, as movement of the elbow is severely restricted. However, because it is smaller and therefore less painful for the subject, as well as being very much less expensive, the butterfly cannula is often preferable if used in a forearm vein, provided that long-term access is not required. A 21 G cannula is adequate for most purposes, and only where large volumes of blood are required will a larger size be necessary. In most situations where vigorous movements are likely, the forearm site is preferred to the elbow (Figure 4.1). A disadvantage of

Figure 4.1 (a) Venous sampling from a superficial forearm vein is conveniently accomplished using an indwelling plastic cannula. (b) The cannula is inserted into the vein. If slight tension is applied to the skin, this should be completely painless. (c) The needle is withdrawn, leaving the plastic sheath in place. This is then advanced into the vein. (d) A three-way tap is attached to the end of the cannula, allowing samples to be withdrawn and the cannula to be flushed with saline as necessary.

venous cannulation is the need to ensure that clotting of blood in the cannula does not occur. This is easily avoided by flushing with sterile isotonic saline, but this in turn requires stringent hygiene procedures. Where intermittent sampling is performed, the cannula may be flushed with a bolus of saline to which heparin (10–50 IU ml^{-1} of saline) is added, allowing the subject freedom to move around between samples. Alternatively where the subject is to remain static, as in a cycle or treadmill exercise test, a continuous slow infusion (about 0.3 ml min^{-1}) of isotonic saline may be used, avoiding the need to add heparin. Collection of samples by venous puncture is not practical in most exercise situations, and increases the risk that samples will be affected by venous occlusion applied during puncture. If repeated venous puncture is used, care must be taken to minimize the duration of any occlusion of blood flow and to ensure that sufficient time is allowed for recovery from interruption of blood flow before samples are collected. The use of a butterfly cannula rather than a needle facilitates the collection of samples without the problems that arise from occlusion of the circulation, even when repeated sampling is not required.

The dead space of a 21 G butterfly cannula is small (about 0.4 ml), and even with the addition of a three-way tap does not exceed about 0.5 ml. It is, however, essential to ensure that the deadspace is completely cleared when taking samples. It is recommended that about 1–1.5 ml be withdrawn through the cannula before each sample is collected.

A disadvantage of the use of a superficial forearm vein is that flow through these veins is very much influenced by skin blood flow, which in turn depends on ambient temperature and the thermoregulatory strain imposed on the individual. In cold conditions, flow to the limbs and to the skin will be low, and venous blood will be highly desaturated. It is easy to observe that, where samples are taken progressively throughout an exercise task, the oxygen content of the venous blood increases progressively, reflecting the increased peripheral blood flow, especially the skin blood flow. Where sampling occurs over time, therefore, and where the degree of arterialization of the venous blood will influence the measures to be made, this may cause major problems. A good example of such a situation is where a tracer – deuterium oxide – is added to an ingested beverage, and the rate of rise of the blood deuterium concentration is used as an index of the combined rates of gastric emptying and intestinal absorption. Deuterium enters the vascular compartment as the blood passes through the gut, and leaves as it equilibrates with body water. The rate of equilibration with body water will depend on a number of factors, but it is clear that the arterial deuterium concentration will always be higher than the venous concentration, at least until all the ingested beverage has been absorbed and complete equilibration among all body water compartments has occurred. If peripheral venous blood sampling is used, and if these measurements are made during exercise or in a situation where ambient temperature changes, the degree of arterialization of the venous blood will change, and the values for deuterium accumulation will be meaningless. For some metabolites which are routinely measured, the difference between arterial and venous concentrations is relatively small and in many cases it may be ignored. Where a difference does occur and is of importance, the effect of a change in arterialization of the blood at the sampling site may be critical.

4.3.2 ARTERIALIZED VENOUS BLOOD

Where arterial blood is required, there is no alternative to arterial puncture, but for most practical purposes, blood collected from a superficial vein on the dorsal surface of a heated hand is indistinguishable from arterial blood. This reflects both the very high flow rate and the opening of arterio-venous shunts in the hand. Sampling can conveniently be achieved by introduction of a butterfly cannula into a suitable vein (Figure 4.2). The hand is

a

b

c

d

Figure 4.2 (a) A butterfly style cannula is convenient for sampling of arterialised venous blood from a dorsal vein in a hand that has been warmed by immersion for 10 minutes in warm (42°C) water. (b) Blood samples are withdrawn from the cannula as necessary via a syringe connected to the cannula by way of a three-way tap. (c) After sampling, the cannula is flushed with saline, which should be heparinized if there is more than a short time (1–2 minutes) between samples. (d) The cannula is taped in place, allowing the subject free use of the hand between sample collections.

first heated, either by immersion up to the forearm for at least 10 minutes in hot (about 42°C) water (Forster *et al.*, 1972) or by insertion into a hot air box (McGuire *et al.*, 1976). If hot water immersion is used prior to exercise, arterialization – as indicated by oxygen saturation – can be maintained for some considerable time by wearing a glove, allowing this technique to be used during exercise studies. This procedure allows large volumes of blood to be collected without problems. Capillary sampling by the 'finger prick' method cannot guarantee adequate volumes for many procedures.

4.3.3 CAPILLARY BLOOD

Where only small samples of blood are required, capillary blood samples can readily be obtained from a fingertip or ear lobe. The use of micromethods for analysis means that the limited sample volume that can be obtained should not necessarily be a problem in metabolic studies. It is possible to make duplicate measurements of the concentrations of glucose, lactate, pyruvate, alanine, free fatty acids, glycerol, acetoacetate and 3-hydroxybutyrate, as well as a number of other metabolites on a single 20 µl blood sample using routine laboratory methods (Maughan, 1982).

The sampling site should be arterialized, by immersion of the whole hand in hot (42°C) water in the case of the fingertip, and by the use of a rubefacient in the case of the ear lobe. Samples can be obtained without stimulating vasodilatation, but bleeding is slower, the volumes that can be reliably collected are smaller, and the composition of the sample is more variable. It is essential that a free-flowing sample is obtained. If pressure is applied, an excess of plasma over red cells will be obtained. Samples are most conveniently collected into calibrated glass capillaries where only small volumes are required (typically 10–100 µl). The blood must never be expelled from these tubes by mouth, because of the obvious risks involved.

Where larger volumes are required, a clean plastic or glass vessel may be used for collection and the blood then pipetted in the normal way using an automatic pipette. Use of suitable analytical methods allows most of the metabolites of interest to be measured on samples collected in this way. More difficulty arises when larger volumes are required. Nonetheless, a volume sufficient for the measurement of haematocrit, which is normally measured in triplicate and requires a blood volume of about 150 µl, and haemoglobin (2 × 20 µl) in addition to the metabolites referred to above is usually possible. Volumes greater than about 0.5 ml present real difficulties.

4.3.4 PROCEDURES FOR CAPILLARY BLOOD SAMPLING

As indicated above, capillary samples are commonly obtained from the ear lobe or from a digit. In most situations, the fingertip site is to be preferred. In order to ensure that a free-flowing sample can be obtained, it is helpful to immerse the hand to the wrist in hot (42°C) water or in a heated box for 10–15 minutes before the sample is collected. If necessary, the hand can be kept warm by continued immersion between samples where this is

practicable. Where this is not possible, some degree of arterialization can be maintained by wearing a glove. The degree of arterialization can be verified by measurement of blood gases.

A clean laboratory coat and disposable gloves must be worn during collection and handling of samples. The sampling kit – prepared in advance – will consist of:

- Lancets (a Lancer (B.D. Ltd., Dublin, Ireland) may be preferred)
- Sterile alcohol swabs
- Tissues
- Rubber gloves
- Disposal facility: sharps bin for used lancets and clear autoclavable bags for contaminated waste

For handling blood, collection into graduated glass capillaries is preferred. Larger volumes may be collected directly into disposable plastic beakers, but such volumes are difficult to collect reliably using the 'finger prick' technique, and there is a real danger that clotting will occur before sufficient volume is obtained. Suitably prepared and labelled tubes for sample reception should be prepared in advance if required. For most metabolite analysis where spectrophotometric or fluorimetric analysis is used, collection of 20 µl of blood into 200 µl of deproteinizing agent is appropriate. This may be facilitated by the use of heparinized capillary tubes, which will hold about 50 µl of blood. The blood can be ejected from the capillary and 20 µl aliquots transferred using a pipette.

Subjects should be instructed to wash their hands before the procedure begins. The sampling site should be swabbed with alcohol and wiped dry with a tissue, and the cleaned area stabbed with a single prick. It is essential to ensure a free-flowing sample: the puncture wound should not be squeezed. If pressure is applied, extracellular fluid will contaminate the sample collected, and some haemolysis is also inevitable. The results will therefore be invalid. The extent to which contamination with extracellular fluid will invalidate the results depends on the measurements to be made. The first drop of blood to appear should be wiped away with a clean tissue. The capillary should be filled to about 1 cm beyond the graduation mark: the outside of the capillary should then be wiped clean, and the end touched against a tissue until the bottom of the blood meniscus is aligned with the graduation mark. Transfer into the deproteinization agent is achieved by use of a rubber blow-bulb, with repeated aspiration and dispensing until all the residual blood is washed out of the capillary. Samples should always be collected in duplicate.

The site of the puncture wound should be wiped clean. If bleeding continues, a waterproof dressing should be applied. A new puncture must be made when repeated sampling is required, unless the time interval between samples is short. It is unwise to rely on continued bleeding from the same site.

4.4 BLOOD TREATMENT AFTER COLLECTION

Analysis of most metabolites can be carried out using either whole blood, plasma or serum. This requires a recognition of the differential distribution of most metabolites and substrates between the plasma and the intracellular space. It is important to recognize also that changes in the plasma volume during exercise or other situations may be quite different from the changes in the whole blood volume, and the effects of changes in the distribution space may require consideration. For most practical purposes, it is convenient to use whole blood for the measurement of most metabolites. The obvious exception is the free fatty acid concentration, which should be measured using plasma or serum. Glucose, glycerol and lactate are commonly measured on either plasma or whole blood. Most of the other metabolites of interest to the exercise physiologist are normally measured on whole blood. The differences become significant where there is a concentration difference between the intracellular and extracellular compartments, or where there is a change in

this distribution over the time course of an experiment.

If plasma is to be obtained by centrifugation of the sample, a suitable anticoagulant must be added. A variety of agents can be used, depending on the measurements to be made. The potassium salt of EDTA is a convenient anticoagulant, but is clearly inappropriate when plasma potassium is to be measured. Heparin is a suitable alternative in this situation. For serum collection, blood should be added to a plain tube and left for at least one hour before centrifugation: clotting will take place more rapidly if the sample is left in a warm place. If there is a need to stop glycolysis in serum or plasma samples (for example, where the concentration of glucose, lactate or other glycolytic intermediates is to be measured), fluoride should be added.

Where metabolites are to be measured on whole blood, the most convenient method is immediate deproteinization of the sample. The primary reason for deproteinization of whole blood is to inactivate the enzymes that would otherwise alter the concentrations of substances of interest after the sample has been withdrawn. A variety of agents can be used to achieve this: perchloric acid or trichloroacetic acid are equally effective. A 2.5% (0.3 N) solution of perchloric acid is recommended for general use. This can be prepared by adding 36 ml of the 70% acid to 964 ml of water.

Where blood samples are to be collected for analysis of glucose and lactate, it is convenient to add 100 µl of whole blood to 1 ml of 2.5% perchloric acid. Smaller volumes can be used, but pipetting and other measurement errors are reduced if the larger volume is used. The use of a 10:1 dilution reduces volumetric errors due to the presence of a substantial volume of precipitate. The tubes containing the acid should be prepared in advance and kept in iced water. Deproteinization should take place immediately upon collection of the sample. It is, however, recommended that an anticoagulant should be used. Blood should be transferred using an automatic pipette as described below. The deproteinized sample should be kept on ice until it can be centrifuged. A note of caution: glucose is not stable in this acid medium, even when frozen at $-20°C$. Lactate, pyruvate and other metabolites can be stored frozen, but glucose and ammonia should be analysed within a few hours of collection. If frozen samples are to be analysed, they must be centrifuged again after thawing.

4.5 MEASUREMENT OF CIRCULATING HAEMOGLOBIN CONCENTRATION

Haemoglobin is the porphyrin-iron-protein compound that binds with oxygen and gives blood its characteristic red colour. Many different methods have been developed to determine the concentration of haemoglobin and its derivatives in circulating and occult blood. The techniques usually depend on reactions involving the iron component of haemoglobin or the pseudoperoxidase activity of the haem. The two most common methods currently used are the oxyhaemoglobin and the cyanmethaemoglobin techniques. The oxyhaemoglobin method is currently mainly used in conjunction with automated or semi-automated haemoglobinometers, while the cyanmethaemoglobin method is the technique of choice for manual procedures.

4.5.1 THE CYANMETHAEMOGLOBIN METHOD

In 1966 the International Congress of Haematology recommended this method be the accepted routine manual procedure for measurement of haemoglobin in blood. The main reasons for adopting this as the standard technique were:

1. The method requires dilution of blood with a single reagent.
2. All forms of haemoglobin likely to occur in the circulation are determined.
3. The colour produced is suitable for measurement in filter photometers and narrow-band spectrophotometers because its absorption band at 540 nm is broad and relatively flat.

4. Standards prepared from either crystalline haemoglobin or washed erythrocytes when stored in brown glass containers and in sterile conditions are stable for at least 9 months (<2% change in absorbance).

(a) Principle

The iron of haem in haemoglobin, oxyhaemoglobin and carboxyhaemoglobin is oxidized to the ferric state by ferricyanide to form methaemoglobin. Methaemoglobin then combines with ionized cyanide to produce the stable, red cyanmethaemoglobin which is measured photometrically at 540 nm.

Cyanmethaemoglobin solutions generally obey Beer's Law within the concentration range of interest at a wavelength of 540 nm, and a calibration curve can therefore be constructed using a reagent blank as a zero standard and a single additional standard of known concentration. Secondary standards, prepared from blood and Drabkin's reagent, can be calibrated against the commercial standard and then used for construction of the calibration curve.

The method outlined below uses a sample volume of 10 µl and a reagent volume of 2.5 ml, and the reaction is always carried out in duplicate. Smaller sample volumes can be used, but the precision of the assay, which has a coefficient of variation of about 1–2% in the hands of an experienced operator, declines with very small volumes of blood. Larger volumes are wasteful of reagent.

(b) Procedure

Drabkin's Reagent: This reagent is stable for several months when stored in a brown bottle. As cyanide is a constituent of Drabkin's solution care must be taken in preparing and storing this reagent.

    1.0 g $NaHCO_3$
    0.2 g $K_3Fe(CN)_6$
    0.05 g KCN

Make up to 1 litre of solution.

Standard: 180 g l^{-1} human methaemoglobin

(available from Sigma Ltd (Poole, UK) or BDH (Poole, UK))

Calibrate: The calibration curve is prepared by measuring the optical density of the Drabkin's reagent (zero standard) and of the 180 g l^{-1} Sigma standard at 540 nm without dilution. Addition of other standards will only confirm the linearity of the calibration curve.

Sample assay: In duplicate, add 10 μl sample to 2.5 ml of Drabkin's reagent and mix thoroughly; incubate at room temperature for at least 10 minutes. Read samples at 540 nm. The colour is stable for several hours if kept in the dark. Standards should be exposed to the same conditions as the samples.

4.5.2 FACTORS AFFECTING MEASURED HAEMOGLOBIN CONCENTRATION

Many different factors – independent of the analytical method used – will affect the measured haemoglobin concentration. The sampling site and method can affect the haemoglobin concentration, as arterial, capillary and venous samples differ in a number of respects due to fluid exchange between the vascular and extravascular spaces and to differences in the distribution of red blood cells (Harrison, 1985). The venous plasma to red cell ratio is higher than that of arterial blood.

The measured haemoglobin concentration is also markedly influenced by the physical activity, hydration status and posture of the subject prior to sample collection, although the total body haemoglobin content is clearly not acutely affected by these factors. Posture is particularly important and should be standardized for a period of at least 15 minutes prior to sampling as plasma volumes will change significantly over this time (Figure 4.3a) (Harrison, 1985). This effect can be demonstrated reproducibly as a simple student laboratory class. Haemoglobin concentration is rather stable while a subject remains standing at rest, but increases promptly on assuming a seated or supine position. The time course of change is exponential and is largely complete within 15–20 minutes: it is then reversed with a similar time course on returning to the original posture.

Haemodynamic changes caused by postural shifts will alter the fluid exchange across the capillary bed, leading to plasma volume changes that will cause changes in the circulating haemoglobin concentration. On going from a supine position to standing, plasma volume falls by about 10% and whole blood volume by about 5% (Harrison, 1985). This corresponds to a change in the measured haemoglobin concentration of about 7 g l^{-1}. These

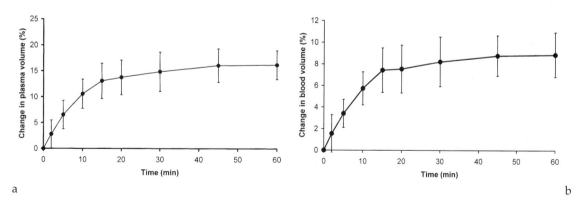

a   b

Figure 4.3 Calculated plasma volume (a) and blood volume (b) change on going from an upright to a supine position. The plasma volume change is relatively much greater than the change in blood volume: the entire blood volume change is accounted for by the changing plasma volume.

changes are reversed on going from an upright to a seated or supine position. These changes make it imperative that posture is controlled in studies where haemoglobin changes are to be used as an index of changes in blood and plasma volume over the time course of an experiment. It is, however, common to see studies reported in the literature where samples were collected from subjects resting in a supine position prior to exercise in a seated (cycling or rowing) or upright (treadmill walking or running) position. The changing blood volume not only invalidates any haematological measures made in the early stages of exercise; it also confounds cardiovascular measures, as the stroke volume and heart rate will also be affected by the blood volume.

Normal haemoglobin values for men are higher by about $20–40$ g l^{-1} than those typically found in women, although it should be recognized that there is some overlap in the normal ranges for men and women. Many factors will affect the measured haemoglobin concentration. Many published reports, and most textbooks, describe a haemodilution as one of the characteristics of endurance-trained athletes. This is ascribed to a disproportionate expansion of the plasma volume relative to the red cell mass. In a comprehensive review of the published data, and of the methodology used in these studies, however, Sawka and Coyle (1999) concluded that the evidence is not as convincing as might be thought. There are also problems with sample collection from athletes in daily training because of the short-term changes that occur during and after a single exercise bout.

The circulating haemoglobin concentration generally increases during exercise, but the magnitude of the increase depends very much on the exercise intensity (Figure 4.4). At high exercise intensities, there is a marked fall in plasma volume due to the movement of water into the active muscle. Intracellular osmolality rises sharply due to the increased concentration of glycolytic intermediates. In prolonged exercise, at intensities of about 60–75% of maximum

Figure 4.4 Effect of exercise intensity on measured haemoglobin (Hb) concentration. The circulating Hb concentration increases as a consequence of the plasma volume decrease: the rapid decrease in plasma volume at the onset of high-intensity exercise results from a redistribution of body water rather than a loss of water from the body.

oxygen uptake ($\dot{V}O_2$max) the initial fall in plasma volume that occurs within the first few minutes of exercise is smaller in magnitude and is often reversed with time as exercise progresses (Figures 4.5a and 4.5b; Maughan, Bethell and Leiper, 1996). After prolonged hard exercise, the haemoglobin concentration is likely to be elevated, and this will return to the pre-exercise level over the few hours following exercise, with the rate and magnitude of this change being influenced primarily by the volume and composition of fluids ingested, but also by activity, posture and other factors. If sampling continues beyond this time, however, a haemodilution will be observed, and this may persist for 2–3 days (Robertson *et al.*, 1988).

Hydration status clearly affects blood volume and therefore the concentration of all circulating variables, including haemoglobin concentration. The significance of this effect is clearly seen when comparing responses to exercise with and without fluid ingestion (Figure 4.5). The rise in haemoglobin concentration is smaller

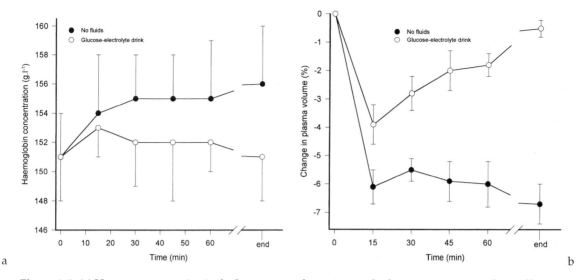

Figure 4. 5 (a) Haemoconcentration in the later stages of exercise results from an interaction of two effects: a loss of body water due to sweat loss and a redistribution of fluid between the vascular and extravascular spaces. (b) Ingestion of fluids attenuates the change in plasma volume that occurs. These results are from a trial where fluid was ingested immediately before exercise and at intervals throughout the exercise period.

when fluid is ingested because of the better maintenance of blood volume. The dehydrated individual will have an elevated haemoglobin concentration, and care must therefore be taken to ensure euhydration if 'normal' values are to be obtained. These issues have been extensively debated in relation to the possibility that cyclists who have a high haematocrit level may find that this is further increased if they allow themselves to become dehydrated, leading to ejection from competition if the value exceeds 52%.

Other factors affecting the normal values include cigarette smoking, which causes a chronic elevation of the circulating haemoglobin concentration in part due to tissue hypoxia secondary to increased carbon monoxide levels and carboxyhaemoglobin formation. Ascent to high altitude also results in an increase in haemoglobin concentration. There is an initial fluid retention followed by diuresis. The latter may be sufficient to cause a reduction in plasma volume and a consequent increase in haemoglobin concentration and haematocrit through haemoconcentration. This is followed after a period of days to weeks by an erythropoietin-driven increase in

the rate of erythropoiesis in response to hypoxia, and a true erythrocytosis with a raised haemoglobin concentration (polycythaemia). This adaptation confers a potentially increased oxygen-carrying capacity on return to sea level, but the evidence that it is this which translates to an improved exercise performance is not strong. Indigenous populations resident at an altitude of more than 1500 m have a chronic true polycythaemia.

Polycythaemia is occasionally constitutional, as a familial condition. This can arise through synthesis of a haemoglobin variant with increased oxygen affinity, through increased sensitivity to erythropoietin or through a genetically determined abnormality of the erythropoietin receptor which results in a loss of the 'off switch' for erythropoiesis. These erythropoietin-related familial polycythaemic conditions might be expected to confer increased oxygen-carrying capacity and a relative increase in endurance capacity in affected individuals. More commonly, in clinical practice, polycythaemia results from cardiac, respiratory or bone marrow disorders.

4.6 MEASUREMENT OF RED CELL PARAMETERS

4.6.1 PACKED CELL VOLUME (PCV) OR SPUN HAEMATOCRIT (HCT)

Packed cell volume is the measurement of the volume occupied by the erythrocytes compared with the overall volume of a column of the whole blood. Anticoagulated blood is spun at about 12000 g for 3–5 minutes in a glass capillary tube. The measured length of the column of packed erythrocytes is compared with that of the total length of the column of blood in the tube. Plain or heparinized micro-haematocrit capillary tubes can be used, but they must conform to the British Standard 4316 (1968) that stipulates that the capillary bore must be less than ±2% of the mean throughout the tube. Heparinized or EDTA-treated blood should be spun in plain capillary tubes, and heparinized tubes are used to collect capillary blood directly. Plain tubes may be used provided the sample is to be processed immediately, but the use of an anticoagulant is recommended in most situations to ensure that no clotting occurs. If there is any clotting of the sample, it must be discarded.

Method: Well-mixed blood is drawn into the tube by capillary attraction without the introduction of any air bubbles. The tube should be filled to approximately $^2/_3$ to $^3/_4$ of its length. Each blood sample should be measured in triplicate. The capillary end not dipped in blood is sealed by inserting that end into a block of 'Cristaseal' (clay-type sealant) (BDH Laboratories, Poole, UK) and twisting the tube into the clay. These tubes are fragile, so care must be taken to avoid breakages with the associated loss of sample and risk of injury. Haematocrit is normally measured in triplicate. After wiping the outside of the tube, place the capillary in the rotor of the micro-haematocrit centrifuge. The tube must lie in one of the channels in the rotor with the sealed end of the tube resting against the rubber rim. The safety cover is gently screwed down. The centrifuge lid is closed and the tubes spun for 5 minutes.

The spun tube is placed into the channel of the reader. The upper edge of the sealant plug is aligned with the black base line, and the meniscus of the column of blood plasma is aligned with the angled black upper line. The silver line of the movable slide on the reader is set at the level of the top of the packed erythrocyte column and the PCV reading is taken where the silver line cuts the scale on the right hand side of the instrument. It is not easy to measure more precisely than to the nearest 0.5%, and the three measurements should normally agree to within 1%. The mean of the three values should be used.

The PCV was traditionally expressed as a percentage of the whole blood volume (e.g. 45.3%), but it is now recommended that this value be expressed as litres of red cells per litre of whole blood (e.g. 0.453 1 l^{-1}).

Determination of the true proportions of red cells and plasma in the blood requires suitable correction for plasma trapped between the red cells. Corrections of 2–4% are widely used, but Dacie and Lewis (1968) suggested that 1–1.5% is a more realistic figure when the standard microhaematocrit method is used. There are also differences between the central and peripheral haematocrit due to differential distribution of the red blood cells in the circulation. This can cause practical difficulties if, for example, peripheral venous blood is sampled and the degree of arterialization changes due to changes in the distribution of cardiac output (see Harrison (1985) for a discussion of this).

4.6.2 ERYTHROCYTE (RED CELL) COUNT

The red cell count is seldom measured outwith a clinical setting, where it has diagnostic significance. Counting of red and white blood cells was, until recently, a standard laboratory practical class in most undergraduate physiology courses, but this seems now to be rare. Manual methods for cell counting involve counting individual cells in a known volume of diluted blood on a graduated microscope slide, and are tedious and time-consuming. These methods have also all but disappeared from the clinical laboratory, where they have been replaced by automatic cell counters.

The Coulter counter is the most widely known of the automated systems, and operates by passing diluted blood through a small aperture where electrical conductivity is measured. The cell membrane is an effective electrical insulator while the diluent is an electrolyte solution. Each particle displaces electrolyte, giving an electrical pulse proportional in amplitude to the cell volume: counting these signals gives a measure of cell number in the measured volume of sample and of the volume of each of the cells counted. These automated procedures are more reliable than the manual methods. A measure of total red cell volume is obtained from the mean cell volume and the total red cell count.

The modern Coulter counter incorporates an autosampler and spectrophotometer which permits automated measurement of haemoglobin concentration. While this automation has considerable attractions, including a high level of accuracy in the measures of red cell count and haemoglobin concentration, care must be taken in the interpretation of the measures of cell volume. The diluent commonly used in the preparation of samples for analysis is not isotonic with normal human blood plasma: Isoton II (Beckman Coulter Co., High Wycombe, UK) has an osmolality of about 340 mosmol kg^{-1}, compared with an osmolality of human plasma of about 285–290 mosmol kg^{-1}. Because the red cell membrane is freely permeable to water, a rapid equilibration will take place on mixing of blood with the diluent, leading to a change (in the case of Isoton II there will be a decrease) in the red cell volume. The measured volume is therefore different, by an amount proportional to the difference in osmolality between the plasma and the diluent, from the volume of the cells while in the circulation. In situations where the plasma osmolality changes substantially, as during intense or prolonged exercise, this will invalidate measures made using automated cell-counting procedures.

4.7 ANAEMIA AND THE MEASUREMENT OF IRON STATUS

Athletes are often concerned about the possibility of anaemia, which will adversely affect exercise performance, and the usual measure used to assess this is the circulating haemoglobin concentration. This has some value, as iron deficiency does not adversely affect performance until it is sufficiently severe to cause a fall in the circulating haemoglobin level (Weight *et al.*, 1988). Haemoglobin concentration, however, is a poor index of an individual's iron status and more reliable measures should be used in any screening where there is reason to suspect that iron status might be suboptimal. The prevalence of iron deficiency anaemia is not different between the athletic population and the general population, but whereas mild anaemia may be of little consequence to the sedentary individual, it will have a negative effect on all exercise situations where oxygen transport is a factor.

4.7.1 ASSESSMENT OF IRON STATUS

When anaemia is due to iron deficiency, erythropoiesis is microcytic, and the mean cell volume (MCV) is therefore low. The adequacy or otherwise of the body's iron stores is most commonly assessed clinically by measurement of the serum concentration of ferritin. Ferritin is tissue storage iron and the small proportion present in blood generally reflects total body iron stores. A low serum ferritin concentration is therefore diagnostic of tissue iron deficiency and this reduction precedes any fall in MCV and haemoglobin concentration. This early warning of impending anaemia is clearly advantageous in any routine monitoring of athletes. However the serum ferritin concentration rises as a response to inflammatory and malignant conditions, and in such circumstances the serum concentration of ferritin may be misleadingly normal, or even raised, in the face of iron deficiency. This is not a significant problem in otherwise healthy subjects.

The serum iron concentration is also reduced in iron deficiency and this is accompanied by a rise in the total iron binding capacity, which represents transferrin, the principal iron transport protein in blood. Transferrin is normally around one-third saturated with iron, and a saturation of <15% is insufficient to support normal erythropoiesis, which becomes iron-deficient. Although low serum iron, low transferrin saturation and increased iron-binding capacity are typical of iron deficiency, the serum iron is also reduced in systemic disease even in the face of normal iron stores. This fall is usually accompanied by a reduced iron-binding capacity, in contrast to the typical increase in iron deficiency.

4.7.2 RED CELL TURNOVER AND CELL AGE

Erythropoiesis takes place in the red bone marrow in post-natal life. In adults, red marrow is restricted to the cavities of the flat and proximal long bones, especially the skull, sternum, ribs, vertebrae, pelvis and proximal ends of the femora. The released red cells circulate for 120 days and senescent cells are removed by macrophages of the reticuloendothelial system in liver, spleen and bone marrow. For the first 48 hours after this release, red cells contain residual ribonucleic acid (RNA) which gives these immature red cells a purple tinge on a stained blood film. These reticulocytes can be more readily identified and counted by staining of a spread blood film using a supravital stain. An absolute increase in reticulocytes, which normally represent less than 1% of red cells, is indicative of increased erythropoietic activity, typically in response to acute blood loss or shortened red cell life span due to haemolysis. A more accurate assessment of total erythropoiesis is best achieved through measurement of iron turnover. This can be measured using an isotope of iron, ^{52}Fe or ^{59}Fe, which binds to transferrin *in vivo*

and is cleared from plasma with a half-time of 60 to 120 minutes when erythropoiesis is in steady state and normal.

4.8 ALTITUDE TRAINING, BLOOD DOPING AND ERYTHROPOIETIN

Most endurance athletes are aware of the benefits of an elevated haemoglobin concentration, and can set about trying to achieve this in a number of ways. As indicated earlier, residence at high altitude results in a measurable increase in haemoglobin concentration due to an increase in body red cell mass in response to increased secretion of erythropoietin. This may be one mechanism for the perceived benefit of training at altitude. Historically, transfusion of red cells has been used to achieve an increase in body red cell mass, improved oxygen carriage and endurance performance. Transfusion of homologous blood (from a donor) carries many risks, including transfusion reactions and transmission of infections such as hepatitis. The same ends have been achieved more safely by transfusion of pre-donated autologous red cells. Because a donor who is iron-replete can replenish the red cells in a donated unit (around 400 ml of blood) in one week, and because the shelf life of blood or separated red cells under appropriate conditions is up to 5 weeks, it is possible to increase the haemoglobin concentration by up to 50 g l^{-1} from normal by transfusion of pre-donated autologous cells. Transfusion of as little as the equivalent of two units has been shown to improve aerobic work capacity and endurance performance under laboratory conditions. More recently erythropoietin has been employed to achieve the same ends as blood doping by transfusion. Erythropoietin manufactured by recombinant techniques has been and is readily available for clinical use, principally to treat the anaemia of chronic renal failure. When administered parenterally, along with intensive iron supplementation, to healthy individuals, it causes a predictable increase in body red cell mass, haemoglobin concentration and haematocrit which is likely to be performance-enhancing in endurance events. Should the haemoglobin be allowed to rise excessively, blood hyperviscosity results with reduced capillary perfusion. This situation, compounded by a further rise in haematocrit due to dehydration during competition, probably accounts for some cases of sudden death amongst competitive sportsmen using erythropoietin. Blood doping, by transfusion or pharmacological means, is banned under the International Olympic Committee (IOC) regulations. However, neither method can be detected by urine-testing and increased haematocrit can occur in other situations, as described earlier. This represents a difficult challenge for governing bodies in a range of sports.

4.9 BLOOD AND PLASMA VOLUME CHANGES

4.9.1 MEASUREMENT OF BLOOD AND PLASMA VOLUME

Many studies require the measurement of the blood and/or plasma volume. Blood and plasma volumes can be determined using a number of different dilution methods, but all of these are relatively invasive. They also require sophisticated labelling facilities and suffer from the problem of not being amenable to repeated measurements at short time intervals.

In many investigations, it is more important to know how these measurements change over the time course of a study than to know their absolute magnitude. Because of the practical difficulties, the indirect estimation of plasma or blood volume changes is more widely used in exercise physiology laboratories and will be discussed in greater detail here. First, however, a brief description of the methods for determination of blood and plasma volumes will be given.

Detailed descriptions of methods for measurement of red cell volume and plasma volume can be found in Dacie and Lewis (1984). In principle, a small volume of tracer material is injected intravenously and its dilution measured after allowing time for mixing in the circulation. The plasma volume can thus be measured using human albumin labelled with radioactive iodine (^{131}I or ^{125}I), although it should be noted that this has limitations as there is some interchange between albumin in plasma and that in extravascular extracellular fluids. There is also some concern regarding the small risk of contamination with infective agents, especially prions, of any product prepared from donor blood. Red cells can be easily labelled with radioactive chromium, technetium or indium (^{51}Cr, ^{99m}Tc, ^{111}In) and from the dilution of labelled injected autologous red cells and the haematocrit the total blood volume and red cell volume can be calculated.

4.9.2 ESTIMATION OF BLOOD AND PLASMA VOLUME CHANGES

Because of the difficulties outlined in the previous section, changes in blood volume are usually estimated without direct measurement of the absolute volume. Changes in the concentration of an endogenous marker can be used as an index of blood volume changes. Total plasma protein and plasma albumin have been used for this purpose, but some exchange of protein across the vascular endothelium does occur in exercise, making these markers unsuitable (Dill and Costill, 1974). Haemoglobin (Hb) is generally accepted as the most appropriate marker: Hb is contained within the red blood cell, and neither enters nor leaves the circulation in significant amounts over the timescale on which most exercise studies are conducted. Haemoglobin also has the added advantage of being easy and inexpensive to measure. It should be noted that the method is not suitable for use over long timescales where significant changes in the circulating Hb mass may occur or in experimental situations where there is a significant blood loss.

A change in haemoglobin concentration reflects, and can be used to calculate, a change in blood volume. Although the absolute plasma volume cannot be determined other than by dilution methods, changes in plasma volume can be calculated if both the Hb concentration and the haematocrit are known: various descriptions of the method have been published, but the most appropriate is that of Dill and Costill (1974). Use of changes in other circulating variables, such as total plasma protein, have been shown to be unreliable: proteins can enter and leave the vascular compartment during exercise (Harrison, 1985). Haemoglobin, which is trapped within the red cells, does not leave the circulation.

As mentioned above, it is not appropriate to use haematocrit (Hct) values derived from automated analysers (such as the widely used Coulter counter) to calculate changes in blood or plasma volume: these analysers rely on dilution of the blood in a medium with a constant osmolality prior to analysis. The osmolality of these solutions is often very different from plasma osmolality: Isoton II has an osmolality of about 340 mosmol kg^{-1}. Because plasma and intracellular osmolality are not the same as that of the diluent, the measured Hct will not reflect the true *in vivo* Hct due to changes in cell volume on being mixed with the diluent after collection. A more serious error arises if the osmolality of the plasma changes, as it almost invariably does when the plasma volume changes. In this situation, calculation of changes in plasma volume based on repeat measures of haematocrit have no validity, although there are many publications in the literature in which Coulter-derived values have been used inappropriately in this way.

4.9.3 CALCULATION OF VOLUME CHANGES

Changes in blood volume (BV), plasma volume (PV) and red cell volume (RCV) can be calculated from the changes in Hb and Hct. The subscripts B and A are used to denote the first (before) and second (after) samples in the following calculations.

$$BV_A = BV_B \times (Hb_B / Hb_A)$$
$$RCV_A = BV_A \times Hct_A$$
$$PV_A = BV_A - RCV_A$$

Percentage changes in BV, PV and RCV can be calculated even though the absolute values in the above equations remain unknown.

$$\Delta BV = 100 \, (BV_A - BV_B) / BV_B$$
$$\Delta RCV = 100 \, (RCV_A - RCV_B) / RCV_B$$
$$\Delta PV = 100 \, (PV_A - PV_B) / PV_B$$

Sample calculation: The calculations described above are demonstrated by a worked example based on the following data obtained before and after exercise:

Before: Hb = 151, Hct = 0.437

After: Hb = 167, Hct = 0.453

If the initial blood volume is assumed to be 100 ml, the blood volume after exercise is given by:

$$BV_A = 100 \, (151/167) \text{ ml} = 90.4 \text{ ml}$$

The decrease in blood volume (ΔBV) is therefore:

$$\Delta BV = ((90.4 - 100) / 100) \times 100 = -9.6\%$$

The red cell volume before exercise is 43.7 ml (Hct = 0.437): after exercise the red cell volume is given by:

$$RCV_A = 0.453 \times 90.4 \text{ ml} = 41.0 \text{ ml}$$

The decrease in red cell volume is therefore:

$$((41.0 - 43.7) / 43.7) \times 100 = -6.2\%$$

The plasma volume before exercise was (1 - Hct) × 100 ml, or 56.3 ml. After exercise, the plasma volume was (90.4 - 41.0) ml, or 49.4 ml. The decrease in plasma volume was therefore 6.9 ml, or:

$$((49.4 - 56.3) / 56.3) \times 100 = -12.3\%$$

Where some indication of the absolute magnitude of the volume shifts is required, an estimate of blood volume based on anthropometric data may be made. Several data sets are available, and a reasonable estimate may be that blood volume equals 75 ml kg^{-1} body mass in men and 65 ml kg^{-1} body mass in women (Åstrand and Rodahl, 1986).

REFERENCES

Åstrand, P.O. and Rodahl, K. (1986). *Textbook of Work Physiology*, 3rd edn. (McGraw Hill, New York).

Dacie, J.V. and Lewis, S.M. (1968). *Practical Haematology*. 4th edn. (Churchill, London). pp. 45–9.

Dacie, J.V. and Lewis, S.M. (1984). Blood volume, Chapter 9. In *Practical Haematology*, 6th edn. (Churchill Livingstone, London).

Dill, B.D. and Costill, D.L. (1974). Calculation of percentage changes in volumes of blood, plasma, and red cells in dehydration. *Journal of Applied Physiology*, **37**, 247–8.

Forster, H.V. and Dempsey, J.A., Thomson J., *et al.* (1972). Estimation of arterial PO_2, PCO_2, pH and lactate from arterialized venous blood. *Journal of Applied Physiology* **32**, 134–7.

Harrison, M. (1985). Effects of thermal stress and exercise on blood volume in humans. *Physiological Reviews*, **65**, 149–209.

Kargotich, S., Goodman. C., Keast, D. and Morton, A.R. (1998). The influence of exercise-induced plasma volume changes on the interpretation of biochemical parameters used for monitoring exercise, training and sport. *Sports Medicine*, **26**, 101–17.

McGuire, E.A.H., Helderman, J.H., Tobin, J.D., *et al.* (1976). Effects of arterial versus venous sampling on analysis of glucose kinetics in man. *Journal of Applied Physiology*, **41**, 565–73.

Maughan, R.J. (1982). A simple rapid method for the determination of glucose, lactate, pyruvate, alanine, 3-hydroxybutyrate and acetoacetate on a single 20μl blood sample. *Clinica Chimica Acta*, **122**, 232–40.

Maughan, R.J., Bethell, L.R. and Leiper, J.B. (1996). Effects of ingested fluids on exercise capacity and on cardiovascular and metabolic responses to prolonged exercise in man. *Experimental Physiology*, **81**, 847–59.

Robertson, J.D., Maughan, R.J. and Davidson, R.J.L. (1988). Changes in red cell density and related parameters in response to long distance running. *European Journal of Applied Physiology*, **57**, 264–9.

Sawka, M.N. and Coyle, E.F. (1999). Influence of body water and blood volume on thermoregulation and exercise performance in the heat. *Exercise and Sports Sciences Reviews*, **27**, 167–218.

Weight, L.M., Myburgh, K.H. and Noakes, T.D. (1988). Vitamin and mineral supplementation: effect on running performance of trained athletes. *American Journal of Clinical Nutrition*, **47**, 192–5.

Nigel T. Cable

5.1 AIMS

The aims of this chapter are to:
- provide students with an understanding of human cardiovascular control mechanisms during exercise,
- discuss techniques that are used for the measurement of blood pressure and peripheral blood flow,
- outline practical exercises that demonstrate the cardiovascular response to exercise, the reflexes involved in the cardiovascular response and the measurement of skin blood flow.

5.2 INTRODUCTION

During physical activity, several organs share the demand for increased perfusion. The heart must supply adequate blood to its own contracting muscle as well as to the contractile apparatus of skeletal muscle. Blood flow to the central nervous system must be maintained and skin perfusion augmented to allow for the dissipation of metabolic heat. During exercise, cardiac output, heart rate, oxygen consumption and systolic blood pressure are linearly related to the intensity of the activity performed. Indeed, during isotonic exercise in a thermally controlled environment, blood flow to skeletal muscle may be increased twenty-five-fold. Such an increase is mediated by means of an increase in cardiac output, a redistribution of the cardiac output and a reduction in muscle vascular resistance. According to the Fick principle ($\dot{V}O_2$ = cardiac output (Q) × arteriovenous difference for oxygen (a–vO_2 diff)), oxygen consumption is also elevated by increasing oxygen extraction in the muscle (during exercise).

5.3 CARDIOVASCULAR ADJUSTMENTS DURING EXERCISE

5.3.1 HEART RATE

Cardiac output is a function of heart rate and stroke volume. During exercise, heart rate may increase 300% above that at rest; the actual increase being dependent upon the exercise intensity. At low workloads, this increase in heart rate is mediated through a withdrawal of vagal tone (Ekblom *et al.*, 1972). As exercise intensity is increased above a workload of 50% $\dot{V}O_2$max, the gradual rise in heart rate is mediated by both neural and humoral adrenergic activity, stimulating β_1 adrenoceptors. Evidence for such reciprocal control comes from studies in which atropine and propranolol have been infused (Ekblom *et al.*, 1972). Atropine is a competitive antagonist of acetylcholine and can therefore be used to block the action of the parasympathetic system. On the other hand, propranolol, which is a β_1 and β_2 receptor blocker, can be used to block sympathetic nervous activity to the heart. These drugs can therefore be used to examine the relative importance of parasympathetic and

Kinanthropometry and Exercise Physiology Laboratory Manual: Tests, Procedures and Data. 2nd Edition, Volume 2: Exercise Physiology
Edited by RG Eston and T Reilly. Published by Routledge, London, June 2001

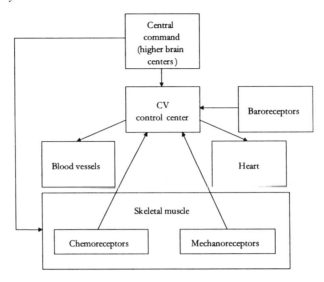

Figure 5.1 Reflexes responsible for cardiovascular control mechanisms.

sympathetic control of heart rate. Only at higher heart rates is the influence of vagal tone totally diminished. However, with β adrenergic blockade during exercise, the maximal heart rate achieved is some 40 beats min^{-1} below that normally attained. Adrenergic activity is therefore a prerequisite for the increase in heart rate during heavy exercise. The withdrawal of vagal tone and the initiation of sympathetic noradrenergic activity seen rapidly after the onset of exercise are probably mediated by central command, a resetting of the operating point of arterial blood pressure and a neural reflex mechanism originating in muscle and joint receptors (Group III fibre receptors). During longer-term exercise, heart rate responses are probably adjusted by means of a pressure 'error' signal and the stimulation of peripheral chemoreceptors (Group IV fibre receptors) following chemical changes in the extracellular fluid of active muscles (see Figure 5.1).

5.3.2 STROKE VOLUME

Stroke volume increases two-fold during dynamic exercise, with maximum stroke volume reached at an intensity of 50% $\dot{V}O_2$max

(Higginbotham *et al.*, 1986). The mechanisms that contribute to the increase in stroke volume include the Frank–Starling law of the heart and sympathetic neuronal activity. The Frank–Starling law of the heart states that the force of contraction is proportional to the initial length of the cardiac muscle fibres. Thus, the more blood that enters the ventricle during diastole, the greater the degree of stretch on the cardiac fibre and the greater the strength of contraction. The relationship only holds for work-rates up to 50% $\dot{V}O_2$max. Above this threshold, end diastolic volume (EDV) is reduced due to the increase in heart rate, which reduces cardiac filling time. Nevertheless, stroke volume is maintained in spite of the decreased EDV by a greater force of contraction of cardiac fibres mediated by stimulation of β$_1$ adrenoceptors arising from sympathetic noradrenergic activity. Such stimulation increases the contractility of the cardiac muscle as evidenced by a reduction in end systolic volume (ESV).

During exercise the stimulus that mediates the increased sympathoadrenal activity remains equivocal. There have been two major hypotheses (central command vs. peripheral command) generated to explain the control of the sympathoadrenal response to exercise. These hypotheses are not mutually exclusive and must be considered to be integrated in some manner. At the onset of exercise, it is thought that impulses from motor centres in the brain, as well as afferent impulses from inside the working skeletal muscle, are integrated to produce an increase in both noradrenergic and sympathoadrenal activity, which is dependent on work-rate. Throughout exercise the degree of this autonomic activity is continually adjusted by metabolic signals, and also by non-metabolic signals arising from the stimulation of pressure, volume, osmolality and temperature receptors (Galbo *et al.*, 1987).

During static isometric exercise there is a rapid pressor effect, an increase in mean arterial pressure (MAP) and an associated increase in heart rate. During dynamic exercise, there is a more gradual (depending upon intensity) increase in mean arterial pressure and heart rate, although the change in pressure is far less than that observed during static exercise. It has long been thought that these responses occur to maintain the close match necessary between blood flow and tissue metabolism.

5.3.3 CENTRAL COMMAND

Evidence that these haemodynamic responses are initiated by centrally generated motor command signals arises from studies in humans and animals that have used motor paralysis and partial neuromuscular blockade. In humans with the muscles of the forearm fully blocked by succinylcholine, an attempt to contract the paralysed muscle group was accompanied by approximately 50% of the increase in arterial pressure and heart rate reported under normal unblocked conditions (Freyschuss, 1970). Therefore in the absence of peripheral feedback (i.e. from immobile muscle) the cardiovascular responses must have been mediated by central command. This suggestion is complemented by studies employing partial neuromuscular blockade using tubocurarine. This drug causes muscle weakness, and therefore in order to produce

the same absolute force of muscle contraction after blockade as that of before, a greater motor command signal is required. In studies in which maximum voluntary contraction (MVC) has been reduced by 50% with tubocurarine, arterial pressure rose more markedly at the same absolute force (Leonard *et al.*, 1985). However, at the same relative force before and after blockade (i.e. the same percent of pre-MVC and post-MVC, and presumably therefore the same degree of motor command) pressure changes were of a similar degree (Leonard *et al.*, 1985).

Mitchell (1990) suggested that the peripheral chemoreflex is also an important mediator of the exercise pressor reflex. This suggestion arose from studies using epidural anaesthesia, which not only reduces muscle strength by partial motoneuron blockade but also inhibits afferent feedback from the contracting muscle. When repeating the same experimental model described above, it was observed that at the same absolute force the pressor effect was similar. However, at the same relative force cardiovascular responses were less. In attempting to exert the same absolute force, which requires a greater central command signal, the expected elevation of cardiovascular response was not observed. Similarly at the same relative intensity, when central command and therefore the pressor response should have been similar, a reduced cardiovascular response was observed. Given that sensory afferents were inhibited, these studies indicate that the peripheral chemoreflex as well as central command have a role to play in generating the cardiovascular response to exercise.

In response to a powerful isometric contraction there is an immediate increase in arterial pressure and heart rate. The increase in arterial pressure is attributable to an immediate increase in cardiac output resulting from a rapid elevation of heart rate (Martin *et al.*, 1974). This tachycardia is governed by the removal of vagal tone rather than an increase in sympathetic activity, as the response is blocked by atropine and not propranolol

(Maciel *et al.*, 1987). In addition Maciel *et al.* (1987) found that the blockade of parasympathetic activity only influenced the first 10 s of very forceful isometric contractions at 50–70% MVC, whereas sympathetic blockade modified the heart rate response after 10 s.

It is clear, therefore, that central command governs the immediate cardiovascular response to exercise by the removal of vagal inhibition of heart rate. Following the initial 10 s of moderate to intense exercise, this response is increasingly controlled by augmented sympathetic nervous activity. Thus, it appears that central command plays a role in the removal of parasympathetic activity but not in the activation of the sympathetic nervous system (SNS).

5.3.4 PERIPHERAL COMMAND

The chemoreceptors located in muscle have been proposed as possible mediators of the increased activity of the sympathetic nervous system. These receptors are thought to be stimulated by the release of metabolites from exercising muscle in response to a mismatch between blood flow and metabolism. This response can be demonstrated during isometric muscle contraction by occluding the circulation to the muscle during and after exercise. The resultant post-exercise ischaemia maintains both the level of MAP (Alam and Smirk, 1937) and muscle sympathetic nerve activity (MSNA) (Seals *et al.*, 1988) that is observed during exercise. As this response persists, even during passive recovery (and therefore in the absence of any central command), it must be mediated by metabolite activation of muscle chemoreceptors, the leading candidates of which are lactate and changes in pH. The increase in MSNA observed during exercise is delayed for 0.5 to 2 minutes after the initiation of contraction, a time period required for the accumulation of metabolites needed to activate the chemoreflex. Thus, the current thinking is that cardiovascular responses to isometric exercise are governed by a central command-mediated withdrawal of vagal tone and a peripheral chemoreflex initiation of sympathetic activity.

It was indicated earlier that sympathetic nervous activity (as measured by MSNA and increased concentrations of circulating noradrenaline) begins to increase at a heart rate of approximately 100 beats min^{-1}. In sedentary populations, lactate accumulation is not evident until work-rates of about 50% $\dot{V}O_2max$ are reached. In endurance-trained athletes this threshold may be 80% $\dot{V}O_2max$. These thresholds correspond to heart rates of approximately 140 and 170 beats min^{-1} respectively. Clearly at heart rates of 100 beats min^{-1} when SNS becomes active, sufficient lactate to stimulate the muscle chemoreceptors will not be present. It is therefore unlikely that the increase in sympathetic nervous activity observed during exercise of a moderate intensity is controlled by such chemoreceptor stimulation.

In summary, central command appears to govern the cardiovascular response to dynamic exercise at heart rates below 100 beats min^{-1} by the withdrawal of vagal tone. At higher work-rates, the haemodynamic response is mediated by the stimulation of peripheral chemoreceptors. The signal that initiates the increase in MSNA at moderate work-rates remains to be established.

5.3.5 RESETTING OF THE CAROTID SINUS BAROREFLEX

The rapid rise in arterial blood pressure and heart rate at the onset of exercise, has led to the conclusion that the arterial baroreflex is inactivated during exercise. This would therefore allow blood pressure to increase, without the baroreflex attempting to return it to a regulated value. Papelier *et al.* (1994) reported that the sensitivity of the baroreflex was unaltered during dynamic exercise in humans, but that the operating point (the value around which pressure is regulated) was shifted upwards in an intensity-dependent manner. That blood pressure may be regulated at a higher level immediately at the onset of exercise is supported by indirect evidence, showing that when the arterial baroreflex is denervated in exercising dogs, blood pressure falls (Melcher and Donald, 1981).

Rowell (1993) suggested that the resetting of the arterial baroreflex to a higher operating point during exercise is responsible for the increased activity seen in the sympathetic nervous system. Immediately at the onset of exercise, central command shifts the operating point of blood pressure to a higher level and withdraws vagal inhibition of heart rate. During mild exercise, the removal of vagal tone is sufficient to allow cardiac output to increase to a level that raises arterial pressure to the new regulated value, and there is therefore no perceived pressure 'error'. During more intense exercise, the vagally-induced increase in cardiac output is not sufficient to counteract the sudden vasodilation occurring in active muscle (i.e. a sudden fall in total peripheral resistance) and therefore according to the equation, MAP = Q × TPR (where MAP = mean arterial pressure (mmHg), Q = cardiac output ($l\ min^{-1}$) and TPR = total peripheral resistance ($mmHg\ l^{-1}$)), there is a mismatch between the new operating point of arterial pressure and the pressure detected. This pressure 'error' must be corrected by increased sympathetic nervous activity to the heart and vasculature, resulting in increased cardiac output and increased vasoconstrictor tone. Thus above a heart rate of 100 beats min^{-1} (when most vagal activity has been withdrawn), increased sympathetic activity is promoted in response to an arterial pressure error, rather than in response to metabolic changes occurring in the active muscle. At higher work-rates as lactate begins to accumulate, the muscle chemoreflex may become tonically active and increase sympathetic activity further (there is a close correlation between muscle sympathetic nerve activity and lactate accumulation). Rowell (1993) therefore proposed that cardiovascular adjustments observed during dynamic exercise resulted from pressure-raising reflexes secondary to the detection of arterial pressure errors, rather than a mismatch between blood flow and metabolism.

5.4 CONTROL OF BLOOD FLOW AT REST AND DURING EXERCISE

Regional blood flow is adjusted according to functional requirements of the tissue by changes in the resistance to flow through blood vessels. The resistance to flow through a given blood vessel varies inversely with the fourth power of the radius of the vessel, and therefore a relatively small change in the diameter of a resistance vessel initiates a dramatic fluctuation in blood flow through that tissue.

Depending on their functional requirements, tissues have varying ranges of blood flow. The rate of flow through organs such as the brain and liver remains relatively constant even when there are pronounced changes in both arterial blood pressure and cardiac output. In more compliant vascular beds such as skeletal muscle, skin and splanchnic regions, perfusion rates can vary markedly depending on the physiological conditions experienced.

5.4.1 LOCAL REGULATING MECHANISMS

There are various substances that are either required for cellular metabolism or are produced as a consequence of it, and that have a direct effect on the vasculature of muscle and therefore constitute the metabolic autoregulation of peripheral blood flow. This autoregulatory control is of great significance as it allows the matching of local blood flow to momentary nutritional requirements of the tissue. These local responses can completely override neurogenic constrictor effects which are mediated centrally.

Vasodilatation is evoked by a fall in partial pressure of oxygen in the local vascular bed. Thus, when arterial partial pressure of oxygen decreases as metabolic activity in the region is accelerated, vasodilatation occurs. Various mechanisms have been proposed to explain this process, including a direct effect of oxygen on vascular smooth muscle (Detar, 1980). In addition, as regional metabolism increases, there are local increases in the partial pressure of CO_2 and the concentration of H^+ which are also thought to cause vasodilatation. The accumulation of lactate in a vascular bed is associated with vasodilatation, but this effect is thought to be mediated indirectly by changes in plasma pH. It is unclear how these metabolites promote vasodilatation, but their release during contraction of muscle has a similar time course to the release of adenosine and its nucleotides, which are known to be potent vasodilator substances (Ballard *et al.*, 1985). Potassium is also a potent vasodilatory substance. Wilson *et al.* (1994) have reported a strong correlation between forearm vascular resistance and venous potassium concentration during potassium infusion into the brachial artery. The same authors reported relatively small changes in venous potassium during forearm exercise despite large decreases in forearm vascular resistance. During maximal whole-body exercise there were large changes in systemic potassium which might be expected to increase exercise hyperaemia (Wilson *et al.*, 1994).

It is now recognized that a substance released from the endothelium acts upon smooth muscle cells to produce relaxation. This substance was originally termed endothelium derived relaxing factor, but has since been identified as nitric oxide (Palmer *et al.*, 1987). It is produced from arginine in endothelial cells and stimulates cGMP (an intracellular second messenger signal) in smooth muscle cells to bring about relaxation (Collier and Vallance, 1989). Nitric oxide is now thought to be released continually from the vascular endothelium to exert a profound hypotensive effect.

In addition to a tonic release of nitric oxide from the endothelial cells at rest, blood flow through the lumen of blood vessels has been shown to stimulate the release of nitric oxide (Green *et al.*, 1996). This phenomenon is thought to be caused by shear stress on the endothelial cells, the stimulus for release being proportional to the magnitude of blood flow. With microvascular perfusion coupled to muscle fibre activity, muscle blood flow can be matched to metabolic demands. It has recently been observed, in an isolated electrically stimulated *in vitro* muscle preparation, that nitric oxide is released from muscle tissue itself. Thus, the possibility exists that, in response to exercise, the muscle cell produces endogenous nitric oxide which diffuses into the smooth muscle of the vasculature and decreases resistance. The resultant hyperaemia would presumably stimulate greater nitric oxide release via shear stress, thereby increasing blood flow further.

5.4.2 NEURAL REGULATION

The sympathetic nervous system influences vasomotor tone in a number of vascular beds. All blood vessels except capillaries are innervated, the result of stimulation dependent upon the distribution and density of the subclasses of adrenoceptors. The small arteries and arterioles of the skin, kidney and splanchnic regions receive a dense supply of sympathetic noradrenergic vasoconstrictor fibres, whereas those of skeletal muscle and the brain have a relatively sparse supply of these fibres. When stimulated, noradrenaline is released from postganglionic fibres which combines with α adrenoceptors to initiate constriction of the smooth muscle surrounding the lumen of the vessel, leading to increased resistance to blood flow and thereby reduced tissue perfusion.

As previously stated, the skeletal muscular, splanchnic, renal and cutaneous vascular beds are the major determinants of changes in systemic vascular resistance, which is under sympathetic noradrenergic control. If sympathetic activity to resting limb muscles is completely abolished there is a two- to three-fold increase in blood flow, and conversely when noradrenergic activity is maximal, resting blood flow is reduced by 75%. Although these changes only account for a small proportion of those observed during exercise, they nevertheless function to mediate important changes in total systemic vascular resistance due to the large proportion of muscle as a percentage of total body mass. The action of noradrenaline on α adrenoceptors may actually be modulated by the release of local factors from active skeletal muscle. Adenosine, adenine nucleotides, potassium, hydrogen ions and extracellular osmolarity may directly inhibit smooth muscle cell contraction by interrupting vasoconstrictor impulses of sympathetic nerves. Thus, during exercise muscle blood flow may be partially increased by the withdrawal of noradrenergic tone.

The resistance vessels in the arterial circulation of skeletal muscle possess β_2 adrenoceptors which have a high affinity for circulating adrenaline. As the exercise effort increases in duration and intensity, adrenaline concentration increases. This increase leads to stimulation of β_2 receptors, causing relaxation of the smooth muscle and a reduction of vascular resistance in skeletal muscle and therefore an increase in flow.

Controversy still exists as to the contribution of the cholinergic vasodilator pathway in exercise hyperaemia. Although reflex cholinergic vasodilator responses have been observed in humans during severe mental stress, it remains unclear whether such a mechanism exerts any influence on muscle blood flow during exercise. Cholinergic activity is thought to increase muscle blood flow during the initial 10 s of exercise, existing primarily as an anticipatory response to exercise initiated by the cholinergic vasodilatory pathway in the motor cortex.

5.5 CONTROL OF SKIN BLOOD FLOW DURING EXERCISE

Direct heating of the body or exercising, particularly in a warm environment, raises core temperature and results in a rapid increase in skin blood flow (SkBf) in an attempt to transfer this internal heat convectively away from the body. Such changes in SkBf are thought to be mediated by competition between vasoconstrictor and vasodilatory systems (Johnson, 1992). These systems are in turn regulated by a number of thermoregulatory and non-thermoregulatory reflexes.

All cutaneous resistance vessels receive a rich supply of sympathetic fibres, and therefore usually display tonic vasoconstriction. Additionally skin of the limbs and body trunk possesses an active vasodilator system. Therefore any increases in SkBf can be mediated by the removal of vasoconstrictor tone, an increase in active vasodilator activity, or both. Indeed, humans are the only species known to be dependent upon active vasodilation and sweating for their heat loss mechanisms. It is still not known whether vasodilation is mediated by specific vasodilator nerve fibres or is secondary to the effects of a neurohumoral compound co-released from sympathetic cholinergic nerve terminals which innervates sweat glands. The close association between active vasodilation and sweating is evident from studies indicating an inability to vasodilate in subjects that have a congenital absence of sweat glands (Brengelmann *et al.*, 1981). It has been proposed that sympathetic cholinergic nerves supplying the sweat gland co-release a potent vasodilator, along with acetylcholine. The identity and precise mode of action of this vasodilatory substance remain unknown, but possible candidates include vasoactive intestinal polypeptide and nitric oxide. Although the increases in sweating and SkBf are generally considered to be coincident, the temperature threshold at which both occur has been uncoupled (Kenney and Johnson, 1992), indicating that the control of sudomotor and vasodilator activity are independent of each other.

There are many complex interactions between thermoregulatory and non-thermoregulatory reflexes in the control of SkBf. The thermoregulatory reflexes are activated by an increase in both core and skin temperature, leading to the inhibition of vasoconstrictor tone and possibly the initiation of the active vasodilator system. Non-thermoregulatory reflexes include baroreceptor control of blood pressure and exercise reflexes associated with exercise itself (Rowell, 1993).

The cutaneous vascular response to exercise is as follows. Immediately at the onset of exercise there is a vasoconstrictor activity that causes SkBf to decrease below resting baseline values. Having reached its lowest value SkBf returns to pre-exercise values and increases markedly until a core temperature of 38°C is reached. Beyond this temperature SkBf attains a plateau or increases only by a small amount during prolonged endurance exercise (Kenney and Johnson, 1992). In addition, during exercise the threshold core temperature at which SkBf begins to increase is much greater than that observed in a warm environment at rest. Therefore, during exercise, SkBf at any given core temperature is much lower than at rest. The rate of increase in core temperature, once the threshold for vasodilation has been reached, is unaffected by exercise (see Figure 5.2).

Rowell (1983) hypothesized that the rightward shift of the SkBf–body temperature relationship is caused by a increased sympathetic vasoconstrictor activity during exercise, in response to a fall in resistance to blood flow in skeletal muscle (and therefore in order to maintain MAP, resistance in non-active circulation must be increased). Thus, SkBf was presumed to be limited by increased vasoconstrictor activity rather than a reduction in vasodilator activity, due to the fact that the vasodilator system was thought to be independent of non-thermal control systems (i.e. the baroreflex).

Kellogg *et al.* (1990) have shown that the baroreflex can decrease SkBf by the withdrawal of vasodilator activity. This phenomenon was demonstrated by blocking the release of noradrenaline and therefore vasoconstriction, whilst leaving the active vasodilator mechanism intact. Using this model, Kellogg *et al.* (1991) observed that the usual decrease in SkBf associated with the onset of exercise was mediated by sympathetic noradrenergic activity and not by the withdrawal of active

Figure 5.2 Skin blood flow (expressed as forearm blood flow) during passive whole-body heating and during upright exercise (adapted from Rowell, 1993).

vasodilation. In addition, it was observed that the delayed increase in SkBf during exercise, compared with heating at rest, was unaffected by adrenergic inhibition, and was therefore caused by a delayed onset in vasodilation outflow to the skin. Furthermore, Kenney and Johnson (1992) reported that the plateau in SkBf observed during prolonged exercise is not mediated by augmented vasoconstriction, but rather by a withdrawal of vasodilator activity. Kenney and Johnson (1992) therefore concluded that the control of SkBf is dominated by active vasodilation and that this system may be under non-thermal baroreflex control in an attempt to preserve arterial blood pressure.

5.6 MEASUREMENT OF BLOOD PRESSURE

Arterial blood pressures are most accurately measured through the use of rapidly responding pressure transducers located in the arterial circulation. Due to the invasive nature of this technique, its use is limited to a clinical environment. For this reason, blood pressure is not usually measured directly, but estimated using the auscultatory technique. This technique requires the use of a sphygmomanometer and stethoscope, and is dependent upon the observer detecting the characteristic 'Korotkoff sounds' that are produced following occlusion of the circulation to the forearm.

A cuff is inflated to supra-systolic pressure around the upper arm and then slowly deflated whilst simultaneously listening for the 'Korotkoff sounds' through a stethoscope which is placed over the brachial artery in the region of the antecubital fossa. At supra-systolic pressures, blood flow to the forearm is completely occluded. When the pressure in the occluding cuff is equal to systolic pressure in the cardiovascular system, blood forces its way back into the artery, creating turbulent flow and producing the so-called 'First Korotkoff sound'. The pressure cuff is connected to a mercury or aneroid manometer, allowing for the estimation of systolic blood pressure at this point. As pressure in the cuff is reduced further, blood flow entering the artery remains turbulent, until the diameter of the artery reaches its normal patency. This point reflects diastolic pressure and is indicated by the disappearance of the 'Korotkoff sounds' as the blood flow in the artery is now non-turbulent. When resting environmental conditions and measurement protocol are standardized, this indirect method gives reliable estimations of blood pressures, particularly when used by experienced personnel. In addition, this technique can be used during static and dynamic exercise in steady-state conditions. Indeed, when used to predict mean arterial pressure (diastolic pressure + $^1/_3$ (systolic − diastolic pressure)), this technique has been shown to provide a good estimation of blood pressure measured directly in the brachial artery during exercise (MacDougall *et al.*, 1999).

Until recently, beat-to-beat monitoring of blood pressure was only possible using the invasive technique of an intra-arterial catheter. Since the development of the photoelectric principle, it is now possible to demonstrate the full blood pressure waveform non-invasively from the finger during each cardiac cycle.

This measurement can be performed using the photoplethysmographic technique for measurement of the finger arterial pressure. The instrument (Ohmeda Finapres 2300, Englewood, Colorado, USA) comprises an electropneumatic transducer and an infrared plethysmograph within a small finger cuff. The transducer measures the absorption of light and links the plethysmograph to an air pressure source through a fast-reacting servomechanism. Air pressure in the finger cuff is then rapidly regulated to maintain the finger blood volume and plethysmographic light level equivalent to that detected at zero transmural pressure of the digital artery (unloaded arterial wall), thus reflecting the finger arterial pressure waveform. Measurement of blood pressure is fully automated using the Finapres device and the equipment is self-calibrating. A volume clamp level is established within 10 heart beats. Thereafter, blood pressure is continuously monitored except for a small interruption every 10 beats initially followed by 70-beat intervals. Such a device allows the immediate assessment of changes in blood pressure in response to various interventions (for example, upright posture, recovery from exercise), and provides an indication of the real-time change in pressure.

5.7 MEASUREMENT OF PERIPHERAL BLOOD FLOW

5.7.1 STRAIN GAUGE PLETHYSMOGRAPHY

Limb blood flow may be determined non-invasively by measurement of the volume change in a limb segment. Occlusion of the veins draining a limb to a pressure between venous and diastolic blood pressure allows continued arterial flow into the limb segment resulting in increased venous volume and limb volume. Changes in limb volume during venous occlusion may be determined by the displacement of water or air from a jacket secured around the limb or by the measurement of limb circumference changes using a mercury strain gauge. Whitney (1953) pioneered the mercury strain gauge technique

Figure 5.3 Mercury in silastic strain gauge connected to plethysmograph.

Figure 5.4 Measurement of forearm blood flow using strain gauge plethysmograph.

which is based on Ohm's law of electrical conductance (voltage = current × resistance). The principle of operation is related to the effect of changes in gauge length and diameter on the electrical resistance offered by the mercury thread within a silastic rubber tube (Whitney, 1953). This mercury thread forms one arm of a balanced Wheatstone bridge circuit which is housed within a plethysmograph device (Parks Medical Electronics Inc., OR, USA). Owing to the good linear correlation between voltage output from the bridge circuit and a change in strain gauge length (Whitney, 1953), the change in voltage may be used to reflect the change in limb circumference during venous occlusion (see Figure 5.3).

(a) Limb blood flow measurement protocol

The strain gauge is secured around the greatest circumference of the limb. In order to encourage rapid venous drainage during cuff deflation, the elbow and wrist or knee and ankle are comfortably elevated on foam supports to heights of 10 cm and 15 cm respectively. Circulation to the hand or foot is then occluded at a pressure of 200 mmHg for 1 minute before each venous occlusion cycle commences. Venous occlusion is achieved by inflating a collecting cuff, placed around the upper limb (e.g. immediately above the elbow or knee) to a pressure of 50 mmHg in a cycle of 10 s inflation – 5 s deflation for a total of 3 minutes using a rapid cuff inflator (see Figure 5.4).

(b) Calculation of limb blood flow

From the geometry of the circle and cylinder ($2\pi r$, πr^2, $\pi r^2 h$, where h = cylinder length), a percentage change in the volume of a cylinder is twice the percentage change in its circumference. Although limbs are not cylindrical, their length does not increase upon expansion with blood. The mathematical relationship between percentage changes in circumference and volume therefore holds (Whitney, 1953). Following calculation of the slope relating the changes between voltage and time during venous occlusion, the increase in gauge length is determined using the linear regression equation for each individually calibrated strain gauge. The change in gauge length is then expressed as a percentage of limb circumference according to the equation:

$$\text{Bloodflow} = \frac{\Delta \text{gauge length (mm)} \times 60(s) \times 100 \times 2}{\text{girth (mm)} \times 10(s)}$$

For example, for a change in gauge length of 1 mm in a forearm of girth 20 cm,

$$\text{Bloodflow} = \frac{1 \times 60 \times 100 \times 2}{200 \times 10}$$

$$= 6 \text{ ml } 100 \text{ ml tissue}^{-1} \text{ min}^{-1}$$

The percentage change in limb volume over time is then a direct indication of the rate of blood flow, expressed as ml 100 ml tissue^{-1} min^{-1}.

5.7.2 SKIN BLOOD FLOW

There is no method currently available to quantify total blood flow through the skin. The various techniques that have been utilized estimate skin blood flow indirectly from variables that are related to flow (Rowell, 1993). When blood flow to deeper structures is considered, venous occlusion plethysmography offers a useful indication of skin blood flow (Johnson, 1992). Measurements are confined to whole limbs at maximum intervals of 3–4 evaluations per minute. Laser Doppler flowmetry is a new method of skin blood flow measurement with an excellent frequency response that has the capability of continuous, non-invasive monitoring of perfusion to any region of skin or exposed tissue.

Figure 5.5 Laser Doppler equipment for the measurement of skin blood flow.

(a) Theory of laser Doppler flowmetry

The use of the laser Doppler technique to measure flow is based on the principle that the frequency shift of laser light reflected from the skin is linearly related to red blood cell flux and thus tissue blood flow. A narrow 2 mW beam of laser-generated monochromatic light is directed at a wavelength of 780 nm through a 2 m optical fibre to a probe (3 mm in diameter) which rests against the skin. Blood cell movement below the illuminated area of skin scatters the light causing a change in wavelength and frequency known as Doppler shift. Since the measurement depth is only 0.5–1.0 mm, there should be no contribution from blood flow in deeper tissues to the laser Doppler signal. Some of the reflected light is returned along another optical fibre to a photodetector in the instrument which converts the frequency differences (Doppler shift) into an electrical signal. Thus, the greater the movement velocity of the blood cells within the measurement area, the greater the Doppler shift. The basic arbitrary unit of laser Doppler measurement is the perfusion unit (PU) which is equivalent to an analogue output of 10 mV (see Figure 5.5).

(b) Performance of the laser Doppler flowmeter

During whole-body heating the changes in skin blood flow in the forearm, measured simultaneously using laser Doppler flowmetry and venous occlusion plethysmography, are linearly related. This relationship (correlation coefficient = 0.94 to 0.98) holds over a range of forearm blood flows. Thus, changes in skin blood flow can be reliably and continuously monitored by means of the laser Doppler method. The between-subject variability in laser Doppler values at a given forearm blood flow, however, appears to prevent any possible calibration of the instrument output voltage into conventional blood flow units. This source of error is considered to be most likely related to the variable number of capillaries within the illuminated area of the laser Doppler probe.

The changes in skin blood flow throughout the cardiac cycle may be detected by the laser Doppler flowmeter. With this degree of sensitivity, skin blood flow changes during rapid challenges to arterial pressure may be followed continuously.

(c) Skin blood flow measurement protocol

Skin blood flow can be monitored from any skin surface, the most common being the lateral calf and the anterior aspect of the forearm. It is usually necessary to shave a small area on the leg to gain a good contact. Each probe is secured in a plastic holder and attached onto the limb, using an adhesive disc, so that the probe tip just touched the skin surface.

5.8 PRACTICAL EXERCISES

It is easier to demonstrate cardiovascular responses using single-case studies as examples. Experiments require quiet and controlled laboratory conditions. In addition, Practical 1 requires some modification of environmental temperature.

5.9 PRACTICAL 1: SKIN BLOOD FLOW RESPONSE TO REACTIVE HYPERAEMIA AND EXERCISE

This practical involves measuring maximal skin blood flow, and the skin blood flow response following exercise in normal and warm conditions.

5.9.1 AIM

To measure maximal skin blood flow and express skin blood flow measured after exercise in different environments as a percentage of this maximum.

5.9.2 EQUIPMENT

Sphygmomanometer, stethoscope, pressure cuff, laser Doppler flowmeter, cycle ergometer.

5.9.3 PROTOCOL

The subject lies supine and rests during the placement of the laser Doppler probe on the anterior surface of the forearm. Resting skin blood flow and blood pressures are measured. The subject exercises on cycle ergometer at 70% of the maximal heart rate for 20 minutes. (If the arm is kept very still during exercise it is possible to measure skin blood flow). Immediately on cessation of exercise, the subject adopts a supine position for the measurement of skin blood flow and blood pressures for 10 minutes of recovery. Following this recovery, blood flow to the forearm is occluded by inflating the pressure cuff to supra-systolic pressure for 5 minutes. The cuff is released and maximal reactive hyperaemic skin blood flow measured (i.e. peak value for blood flow following cuff release). This protocol can be repeated at varying environmental temperatures (e.g. 16°C and 30°C).

5.9.4 RESULTS

Table 5.1 displays skin blood flow results expressed in absolute units and as vascular resistance (blood pressure / flow) that can be expected following exercise in normothermic and hyperthermic conditions. These values are also expressed as a percentage of maximal skin blood flow. This is derived by dividing SkBf by maximum blood flow measured following circulatory occlusion and multiplying by 100 (e.g. at rest 16°C; (10 / 100) × 100 = 10). Results are also expressed graphically in Figures 5.6 and 5.7 to demonstrate how skin blood flow increases following exercise, and in particular following exercise in the heat.

Table 5.1 Skin blood flow data at 16°C

	Rest	Recovery (min)		
		2	5	10
SkBf (PU)	10	25	20	12
MAP (mmHg)	90	90	90	90
Skin vascular resistance (SkVR)	9	3.6	4.5	7.5
% of max SkBf	10	25	20	12

The percentage of maximum Skin blood flow assumes that peak reactive hyperaemic blood flow = 100 PU (PU = Perfusion unit).

Skin blood flow data at 30°C

	Rest	Recovery (min)		
		2	5	10
SkBf (PU)	20	60	40	30
MAP (mmHg)	80	80	80	80
Skin vascular resistance (SkVR)	4	1.3	2	2.6
% of max SkBf	20	60	40	30

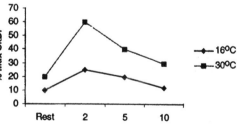

Figure 5.6 Changes in skin vascular resistance following exercise in different environmental temperatures.

Figure 5.7 Skin blood flow expressed as a percentage of maximum flow following exercise in different environmental temperatures.

5.10 PRACTICAL 2: ACUTE EFFECTS OF EXERCISE ON CARDIOVASCULAR FUNCTION

5.10.1 AIM

To assess the effects of body position and dynamic and static exercise on heart rate, blood pressure, myocardial oxygen demand (an index of cardiac workload), cardiac output, oxygen pulse, total peripheral resistance and oxygen uptake.

5.10.2 EQUIPMENT

Sphygmomanometer, stethoscope, means of measuring oxygen consumption (Douglas bags or on-line system), handgrip dynamometer, cycle ergometer.

5.10.3 PROTOCOL

1. Resting and static exercise measurements
   (a) Using a data sheet similar to that shown in Table 5.2, record the heart rate, systolic, diastolic and mean arterial blood pressures, and oxygen consumption measurements after:

       Sitting quietly for 2–3 minutes
       Lying quietly for 2–3 minutes
       Standing quietly for 2–3 minutes
   (b) Repeat the standing measurement whilst the subject performs a 50% MVC using a handgrip dynamometer for 1 minute. BP (blood pressure) is measured on the contralateral arm.

2. Dynamic exercise with and without static contraction
   (a) The subject exercises for 4 minutes at 50, 100 and 150 W. Measure the $\dot{V}O_2$ and haemodynamic parameters in the fourth minute.
   (b) The subject exercises as above, BUT during the fourth minute simultaneously performs a 50% MVC on the handgrip dynamometer.
   Assume a–vO_2 diff values indicated in Table 5.2.

5.10.4 SOME FORMULAE TO HELP

$$\dot{V}O_2 = Q\,(1\ \text{min}^{-1}) \times \text{a–v}O_2\,\text{diff}\quad (\text{litres of oxygen per litre of blood flow, } 1\,1^{-1})\ (\text{Fick principle})$$

Myocardial oxygen demand (RPP) = HR (beats min^{-1}) × SBP (mmHg)
Oxygen pulse (ml beat^{-1}) = $\dot{V}O_2$ (ml) / HR
MAP (mmHg) = DBP + (0.33 × (SBP – DBP))
Q = HR × SV
MAP = Q × TPR

Where: SBP is the systolic blood pressure, HR is the heart rate, DBP is the diastolic blood pressure and TPR is the total peripheral resistance.

Table 5.2 displays expected values for cardiovascular variables during postural change and imposition of exercise stress. Notice that in the upright position MAP and TPR fall. During exercise HR and MAP increase, placing greater demands on the heart (myocardial work). These changes are even greater when handgrip exercise is superimposed on cycling. Notice also, that TPR falls as exercise intensity increases. In this practical the arterial–venous oxygen difference was not measured. The values were assumed to exemplify the relationships between the variables.

Table 5.2 Typical values of cardiovascular function at rest and during dynamic and static exercise

Power (W)	HR	SBP mmHg	DBP mmHg	MAP mmHg	RPP	$\dot{V}O_2$ l min^{-1}	Q l min^{-1}	TPR mmHg l^{-1} min^{-1}	O_2 pulse	a–vO$_2$ dif assumed l l^{-1}	SV ml
Sit	60	120	80	93	7 200	0.25	5.0	18.6	4.2	0.05	83
Lying	50	125	80	95	6 250	0.25	5.0	19.0	4.2	0.05	100
Stand	70	110	70	83	7 700	0.30	6.0	13.8	4.3	0.05	85
50% HG static stand	85	145	85	105	12 325	0.30	6.0	17.5	3.5	0.05	71
50 W	95	130	80	97	12 350	0.9	10.0	9.7	9.5	0.09	105
50 W with 50% HG	115	140	90	107	16 100	0.9	10.0	10.7	7.8	0.09	87
100 W	120	135	80	98	16 200	1.5	12.5	7.8	12.5	0.12	104
100 W with 50% HG	135	150	90	110	20 250	1.5	12.5	8.8	11.1	0.12	93
150 W	140	140	80	100	19 600	2.1	15.0	6.7	15.0	0.14	107
150 W with 50% HG	150	160	90	113	24 000	2.1	15.0	7.5	14.0	0.14	100
5 min post ex	100	110	60	77	11 000	0.6	8.6	9.0	6.0	0.07	86

5.11 PRACTICAL 3: EXERCISE PRESSOR RESPONSE

This practical measures blood pressure during isometric muscle contraction with and without occlusion of blood flow to the exercising limb.

5.11.1 AIM

• To demonstrate the importance of peripheral chemoreceptor action in cardiovascular regulation

5.11.2 EQUIPMENT

Sphygmomanometer, stethoscope, pressure cuff, handgrip dynamometer

5.11.3 PROTOCOL

The subject performs a maximal handgrip exercise to establish maximum voluntary contraction (MVC). Resting blood pressures are then measured, following which the subject performs rhythmical dynamic handgrip exercise at 50% MVC for 2 minutes. Blood pressures are measured in the contralateral limb during the last minute of exercise and at 2 minute intervals during a recovery period of 6 minutes.

After blood pressure has returned to baseline values, the above protocol is repeated but with blood flow to the exercising limb occluded using supra-systolic pressures (220 mmHg) immediately prior to exercise and for the duration of recovery. Such occlusion, whilst uncomfortable, can be maintained safely for at least 10 minutes.

5.11.4 RESULTS

Figure 5.8 displays an example of blood pressure response with and without occlusion. This clearly highlights the stimulation of peripheral chemoreceptors by trapped metabolites and the maintained or even increased cardiovascular response compared with exercise.

Figure 5.8 Mean arterial pressure during and after dynamic exercise of one forearm with and without circulatory arrest (adapted from Alam and Smirk, 1937).

REFERENCES

Alam, M. and Smirk, F.H. (1937). Observations in man upon a blood pressure raising reflex from the voluntary muscles. *Journal of Physiology (London)*, **89**, 372–83.

Ballard, H.J., Cotterrell, D. and Karini, F. (1985). The effect of stimulation of the gracilis muscle on venous adenosine content and vascular responses in dogs. *Journal of Physiology*, **365**, 97P.

Brengelmann, G.L., Freund, P.L., Rowell, L.B., *et al.* (1981). Absence of active cutaneous vasodilation associated with congenital absence of sweat glands in man. *American Journal of Physiology*, **240**, H571-5.

Collier, J. and Vallance, P. (1989). Second messenger role of NO widens to nervous and immune systems. *Trends in Pharmacological Sciences*, **10**, 427–31.

Detar, R. (1980). Mechanism of physiological hypoxia-induced depression of vascular smooth muscle contraction. *American Journal of Physiology*, **238**, H761–9.

Ekblom, B., Goldbarg, A.N., Kilbom, A. and Astrand, P.O. (1972). Effects of atropine and propranolol on the oxygen transport system during exercise in man. *Scandinavian Journal of Clinical Laboratory Investigation*, **30**, 35–42.

Freyschuss, U. (1970). Cardiovascular adjustment of somatomotor activation. *Acta Scandinavica Physiologica*, **342 (Suppl. 1)**, 1–63.

Galbo, H., Kjaer, M. and Secher, N.H. (1987). Cardiovascular, ventilatory and catecholamine response to maximal dynamic exercise in partially curarised man. *Journal of Physiology (London)*, **389**, 557–68.

Green, D.J., O'Driscoll, G., Blanksby, B.A. and Taylor R.R. (1996). Control of skeletal muscle blood flow during dynamic exercise: contribution of endothelium-derived nitric oxide. *Sports Medicine*, **21**, 119–46.

Higginbotham, M.B., Morris, K.G., Williams, R.S., *et al.* (1986). Physiologic basis for the age-related decline in aerobic work capacity. *American Journal of Cardiology*, **57**, 1374–9.

Johnson, J.M. (1992). Exercise and the cutaneous circulation. *Exercise and Sport Sciences Reviews*, **20**, 59–97.

Kellogg, D.M., Johnson, J.M. and Kosiba, W.A. (1990). Baroreflex control of the cutaneous active vasodilator system in humans. *Circulation Research*, **66**, 1420–6.

Kellogg, D.M., Johnson, J.M. and Kosiba, W.A. (1991). Competition between the cutaneous active vasoconstrictor and vasodilator systems during exercise in man. *American Journal of Physiology*, **216**, H1184–9.

Kenney, W.L. and Johnson, J.M. (1992). Control of skin blood flow during exercise. *Medicine and Science in Sports and Exercise*, **24**, 303–12.

Leonard, B., Mitchell, J.H., Mizuno, M., *et al.* (1985). Partial neuromuscular blockade and cardio-vascular responses to static exercise in man. *Journal of Physiology (London)*, **359**, 365–79.

MacDougall, J.D., Brittain, M., MacDonald, J.R., *et al.* (1999). Validity of predicting mean arterial blood pressure during exercise. *Medicine and Science in Sports and Exercise*, **31**, 1876–9.

Maciel, B.C., Gallo, L., Marin Neto, J.A. and Martins, L.E.B. (1987). Autonomic nervous control of the heart rate during isometric exercise in normal man. *Pflugers Archives*, **408**, 173–7.

Martin, C.E., Shaver, J.A., Leon, D.F., *et al.* (1974). Autonomic mechanisms in haemodynamic responses to isometric exercise. *Journal of Clinical Investigation*, **54**, 104–15.

Melcher, A. and Donald, D.E. (1981). Maintained ability of the carotid baroreflex to regulate arterial pressure during exercise. *American Journal of Physiology*, **241**, H838–49.

Mitchell, J.H. (1990). Neural control of the circulation during exercise. *Medicine and Science in Sports and Exercise*, **22**, 141–54.

Palmer, R.M.J., Ferridge, A.G. and Moncada, S. (1987). Nitric oxide accounts for the biological activity of endothelium-derived relaxing factor. *Nature*, **327**, 524–6.

Papelier, Y., Escourrou, P., Gauthier, J.P. and Rowell, L.B. (1994). Carotid baroreflex control of blood pressure and heart rate in men during dynamic exercise. *Journal of Applied Physiology*, **77**, 502–6.

Rowell, L.B. (1983). Cardiovascular aspects of human thermoregulation. *Circulation Research*, **52**, 367–79.

Rowell, L.B. (1993). *Human Cardiovascular Control*. (Oxford University Press, New York), pp. 441–83.

Seals, D.R., Victor, R.G. and Mark, A.L. (1988). Plasma norepinephrine and muscle sympathetic discharge during rhythmic exercise in humans. *Journal of Applied Physiology*, **65**, 940–4.

Whitney, R.J. (1953). The measurement of volume changes in human limbs. *Journal of Physiology*, **121**, 1–27.

Wilson, J.R., Kapoor, S.C. and Krishna, G.G. (1994). Contribution of potassium to exercise-induced vasodilation in humans. *Journal of Applied Physiology*, **77**, 2552–7.

PART THREE

ASSESSMENT OF ENERGY AND EFFICIENCY

METABOLIC RATE AND ENERGY BALANCE

6

Carlton B. Cooke

6.1 AIMS

The aims in this chapter are to:
- describe methods of measuring metabolic rate and energy balance,
- describe methods of predicting resting metabolic rate,
- describe methods of measuring energy expenditure using expired air analysis,
- provide examples of the measurement of metabolic rate and energy balance.

6.2 BASAL METABOLIC RATE (BMR)

The main component of daily energy expenditure in the average person is the energy expenditure for maintenance processes, usually called basal metabolic rate (BMR). The BMR is the energy expended for the ongoing processes in the body in the resting state, when no food is digested and no energy is needed for temperature regulation. The BMR reflects the body's heat production and can be determined indirectly by measuring oxygen uptake under strict laboratory conditions. No food is eaten for at least 12 hours prior to the measurement so there will be no increase in the energy required for the digestion and absorption of foods in the digestive system. This fast ensures that measurement of BMR occurs with the subject in the postabsorptive state. In addition, no undue muscular exertion should have occurred for at least 12 hours prior to the measurement of BMR.

Normally, a good time to make a measurement of BMR is after waking from a night's sleep, and in a hospital situation BMR is typically measured at this time. In laboratory practicals and exercise physiology experiments involving volunteer subjects, it is often impossible to obtain the correct conditions for a true measure of BMR. It is likely that in a laboratory practical the subject will have eaten a meal in the preceding 12 hours, which will increase metabolism in certain tissues and organs such as the liver. This is known as the specific dynamic effect. Any measurement not made under the strict laboratory conditions already described is referred to as resting metabolic rate (RMR).

However, if the subject has only eaten a light meal some 3–4 hours prior to the experiment, and is allowed to rest in a supine position for at least 30 minutes, then the measurement of RMR will be elevated only slightly above the true BMR value. A description of the procedures for the measurement of RMR using the Douglas bag technique is given in Section 6.8. Although the Système International (SI) unit for rate of energy expenditure is the watt (W), RMR and BMR values are typically quoted in kcal min^{-1}. A calorie is defined as the amount of heat necessary to raise the temperature of 1 kg of water 1°C, from 14.5 to 15.5°C. The calorie is therefore typically referred to as the kilocalorie (kcal). To convert kcal into kilojoules (kJ) (the joule (J) is the SI unit of energy), multiply the kcal value by 4.2. To convert kcal min^{-1} into kilowatts (kW) multiply the kcal min^{-1} by 0.07.

Kinanthropometry and Exercise Physiology Laboratory Manual: Tests, Procedures and Data. 2nd Edition, Volume 2: Exercise Physiology
Edited by RG Eston and T Reilly. Published by Routledge, London, June 2001

(See the Appendix for a full list of conversion factors between different units of measurement.)

Estimates of BMR values can be used to establish an energy baseline for constructing programmes for weight control by means of diet, exercise, or the more effective and healthier option of combining both diet and exercise prescriptions. The measurement of BMR on subjects drawn from a variety of populations provides a basis for studying the relationships between metabolic rate and body size, sex and age.

6.2.1 BODY SIZE, SEX AND AGE EFFECTS ON BMR AND RMR

Since the time of Galileo, scientists have believed that BMR and RMR are related to body surface area. Rubner (1883) showed that the rate of heat production divided by body surface area was more or less constant in dogs that varied in size. He offered the explanation that metabolically produced heat was limited by ability to lose heat, and was therefore related to body surface area. This relationship between body surface area and basal and resting metabolic rate has since been verified for animals ranging in size from the mouse up to the elephant (Kleiber, 1975; McMahon, 1984; Schmidt-Nielsen, 1984) and is an important consideration when comparing children and adults. The 'surface area law' therefore states that metabolic rates of animals of different size can be made similar when BMR or RMR is expressed per unit of body surface area.

Table 6.1 shows that, related to body surface area, BMR is at its greatest in early childhood and declines thereafter (Altman and Dittmer, 1968; Knoebel, 1963). When RMR is based on oxygen uptake values the differences between a 10-year-old boy and a middle-aged man are of the order of 1–2 ml kg^{-1} min^{-1}, which amounts to a 25–35% greater metabolic rate in the child (MacDougall *et al.*, 1979). As can be seen from Table 6.1, BMR values are about 5% lower in women than in men. This does not reflect a true sex difference in the metabolic rate of specific tissues, but is largely due to the

differences in body composition (McArdle *et al.*, 1996). Women generally have a higher percentage of body fat than men of a similar size, and stored fat is essentially metabolically inert.

If the BMR values are expressed per unit of lean body mass (or fat-free mass) then the sex differences are essentially eliminated. Differences in body composition also largely explain the 2% decrease in BMR per decade observed through adulthood.

6.2.2 ESTIMATION OF BODY SURFACE AREA AND RESTING METABOLIC RATE

Using the mean BMR values (kJ m^{-2} h^{-1}) for age and sex from Altman and Dittmer (1968) shown in Table 6.1 it is possible to predict an individual's BMR value using an estimate of body surface area. The procedure is outlined in Section 6.4.

Table 6.1 Basal metabolic rate (kJ m^{-2} h^{-1}) as a function of age and sex (data from Altman and Dittmer, 1968)

Age (years)	Females	Males
5	196.7	205.1
10	178.0	183.3
15	163.2	177.9
20	152.4	165.8
25	151.5	162.0
30	151.1	157.4
35	151.1	155.7
40	151.1	156.1
45	150.3	155.3
50	146.5	154.5
55	142.7	152.4
60	139.4	149.4
65	136.9	146.5
70	135.6	144.0
75	134.8	141.5
80	133.5	139.0

6.3 MEASUREMENT OF ENERGY EXPENDITURE

Energy expenditure can be measured using either direct or indirect calorimetry. Both methods depend on the principle that all the energy used by the body is ultimately degraded into heat. Therefore the measurement of heat produced by the body is also a measure of energy expenditure (direct calorimetry). Direct measures of energy expenditure are made when a subject remains inside a chamber with walls specifically designed to absorb and measure the heat produced. This method is both technically difficult and costly. Since the energy provided from food can only be used as a result of oxidations utilizing oxygen obtained from air, measurement of steady-state oxygen uptake by the body is also used as a measurement of energy expenditure (indirect calorimetry). Detailed procedures for the measurement of oxygen uptake by means of the Douglas bag technique are given in Section 6.6.

6.4 PRACTICAL 1: ESTIMATION OF BODY SURFACE AREA AND RESTING METABOLIC RATE

With the mean BMR values (kJ m^{-2} h^{-1}) for age and sex from Altman and Dittmer (1968) shown in Table 6.1, it is possible to predict an individual's BMR value using an estimate of body surface area. The most commonly used formula is that of DuBois and DuBois (1916) which requires measures of stature and body mass only.

Subjects should remove their shoes for both the stature and body mass measures. Stature is measured to the nearest millimetre using a stadiometer. The subject should stand up as tall as he or she can, keeping the heels on the floor and maintaining the head position in the Frankfurt plane (i.e. the straight line through the lower bony orbital margin and the external auditory meatus should be horizontal). Mass should be measured on calibrated weighing scales to the nearest 0.1 kg. The subject should be wearing minimal clothing.

The formula for estimation of body surface area according to DuBois and DuBois (1916) is:

$$BSA = M^{0.425} \times H^{0.725} \times 71.84 \times 10^{-4}$$

where: BSA is body surface area in m^2, M is body mass in kg and H is stature in cm.

For example, a subject with a mass of 70 kg and stature of 177 cm will have a body surface area of

$$BSA = 70^{0.425} \times 177^{0.725} \times 71.84 \times 10^{-4}$$

$$= 6.0837 \times 42.6364 \times 71.84 \times 10^{-4}$$

$$= 1.86 \text{ m}^2$$

If the subject is male aged 20 then according to the average values of BMR (kJ m^{-2} h^{-1}) of Altman and Dittmer (1968) (Table 6.1) he would have an approximate BMR value of 165.8 kJ m^{-2} h^{-1} (±10%). This would compute to a resting energy expenditure of 165.8 kJ m^{-2} h^{-1} × 1.86 m^2 = 308.4 kJ h^{-1}. Over a 24-hour period this would result in an estimated resting energy expenditure of 308.4 kJ h^{-1} × 24 h = 7401 kJ (1762 kcal).

Other sex-specific formulae based on body mass, stature and age have also been widely used for the estimation of BMR:

Harris and Benedict (1919)

$$103 \text{ lean females BMR} = 655 + 9.6(M) + 1.85(ht) - 4.68(age)$$

$$136 \text{ lean males BMR} = 66 + 13.8(M) + 5.0(ht) - 6.8(age)$$

Owen *et al.* (1986)

$$32 \text{ non-athletic females RMR} = 795 + 7.2(M)$$

Owen *et al.* (1987)

$$60 \text{ lean to obese males RMR} = 879 + 10.2(M)$$

Mifflin *et al.* (1990)

$$247 \text{ lean to obese females RMR} = -161 + 10(M) + 6.25(ht) - 5(age)$$

$$247 \text{ lean to obese males RMR} = 5 + 10(M) + 6.25(ht) - 5(age)$$

where: M = body mass (kg), ht = stature (cm), age = age (years), RMR and BMR are expressed in kcal day^{-1}.

Mifflin *et al.* (1990) provided the most general equations for age and weight. The equations of Harris and Benedict (1919) are shown to predict within 5% of RMR values, with the equations of Owen *et al.* (1986, 1987) performing even better (Cunningham, 1991).

6.5 PRACTICAL 2: ESTIMATION OF RESTING METABOLIC RATE FROM FAT-FREE MASS

The resting metabolic rate (RMR) can be estimated from fat-free mass (FFM) according to the following regression equation from Cunningham (1991):

$$\text{RMR (kcal day}^{-1}) = 370 + 21.6 \times \text{FFM}$$

This equation was derived from a review by Cunningham (1991) where all studies measured FFM according to the whole-body potassium K^{40} method and RMR, BMR and resting energy expenditure (REE) were considered to be physiologically equivalent. An equation was also presented for FFM estimated from triceps skinfold thickness:

$$\text{RMR (kcal day}^{-1}) = 261 + 22.6 \times \text{FFM}$$

Number of subjects = 77 and variance accounted for E (r^2) = 0.65.

Unfortunately, no reference to the specific source of the estimation of FFM from triceps skinfold thickness was given. However, values of fat-free mass from a variety of methods can be used in the estimation of RMR.

6.6 PRACTICAL 3: MEASUREMENT OF OXYGEN UPTAKE USING THE DOUGLAS BAG TECHNIQUE

Oxygen uptake can be measured using the open circuit Douglas bag technique. With this method the subject breathes from normal air into a Douglas bag, while wearing a nose clip. (All valve boxes, valves, tubing and Douglas bags should be routinely checked for wear and tear and leaks.) If subjects are exercising it is preferable to use a lightweight, low-resistance, low dead space valve box such as that described by Jakeman and Davies (1979). This is attached to lightweight tubing which is at least 30 mm internal diameter (e.g. Falconia tubing; Baxter, Woodhouse and Taylor Ltd., Macclesfield, UK), as these provide for some movement of the head and do not require fixed support, or the wearing of a headset. During gas collection the subject must also wear a nose clip (Figure 6.1).

Mouth pieces, valve boxes and tubing should be sterilized and dried prior to use by the next subject. Douglas bags must be completely empty before a collection of expired air is made. Ideally, they should be flushed out with a sample of the subject's expired air prior to data collection. For ease of data collection and long life, the Douglas bags should be hung on suitable racks and evacuated by means of vacuum cleaners, rather than rolling them out.

Naive subjects need habituating to breathing through a mouthpiece prior to data collection. At first, this should be done at rest, and then included in the habituation to ergometry prior to any exercise testing. For steady-state protocols, with 3-minute or 4-minute stages,

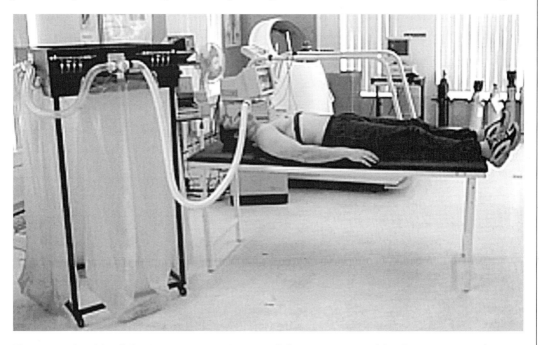

Figure 6.1 A subject lying in a supine position in a laboratory practical for the estimation of resting metabolic rate (RMR). Expired air collection is through a mouthpiece attached to a Salford valve (Cranlea and Company, Birmingham, UK) and lightweight tubing, which is connected to a Douglas bag. The subject is wearing a nose clip, and heart rate data are being recorded by a short-range radio telemeter (Polar, Finland).

the subject need only exercise with the mouthpiece in for 15–20 s before gas collection, as this gives ample time to clear any dead space in the tubing. In ramp protocols and in maximal testing during the latter stages it is necessary to keep the mouthpiece in all the time (Figure 6.2).

Prior to any measurements of gas concentration or volume of expired air, the O_2 and CO_2 analysers should be calibrated and the dry gas meters checked. Gas meters should be calibrated with a minimum of a three-point calibration. This is most conveniently achieved by using 100% nitrogen to set the zero for both analysers, and two known concentrations of O_2 and CO_2 which span the working range. If Haldane or Micro-Scholander apparatus (Rudolf Holker, Swathmore, PA, USA) is available then this can be used to check new standard gases before they are used for routine calibration

Figure 6.2 A subject on a standard Monark cycle ergometer (Monark Crescent AB, Varberg, Sweden), with expired air collection to a Douglas bag, and heart rate monitored by a short-range radio telemeter (Polar, Finland).

purposes. Room air can be used as a span gas for setting oxygen to 20.93%, but caution should be used in the site of collection of room air to ensure it will be valid as 20.93% (i.e. avoid any area where room air could be contaminated). Gas volume meters can be checked with a suitable calibration syringe or with a Tissot Spirometer (Collins Med Inc., Braintree, MA, USA).

6.6.1 SIMPLIFIED ESTIMATION OF OXYGEN UPTAKE

The most straightforward estimation of oxygen uptake ($\dot{V}O_2$) only requires the following measures to be made:

- Volume of expired air collected in the Douglas bag VE (litres)
- Temperature of air as volume is measured (°C)
- Barometric pressure (mmHg)
- Fraction of oxygen in expired air (F_EO_2 or $\%O_{2E}$)
- Time taken for collection of expired air in Douglas bag (s)

Oxygen uptake ($\dot{V}O_2$) is the volume of oxygen inspired minus the volume of oxygen expired, i.e.: $\dot{V}O_2 = (\dot{V}I \times F_IO_2) - (\dot{V}E \times F_EO_2)$
where:
$\dot{V}O_2$ = oxygen uptake (l min^{-1})
$\dot{V}I$ = volume of air inspired (l min^{-1})
F_IO_2 = fraction of oxygen in inspired air = constant value of 0.2093 (i.e. 20.93%)
$\dot{V}E$ = volume of air expired (l min^{-1})
F_EO_2 = fraction of oxygen in expired air

6.6.2 TIMING GAS COLLECTIONS AND CORRECTION OF GAS VOLUMES

It should be noted that V stands for volume, whereas $\dot{V}$ stands for volume per unit of time, usually per minute.

$$VE = \text{volume of air expired in the Douglas bag}$$

$$\dot{V}E = \text{volume of expired air per minute (l min}^{-1})$$

$$\dot{V}O_2 = \text{volume of oxygen consumed per minute (l min}^{-1})$$

Expired air collections should always be timed accurately over a complete number of respiratory cycles, from end expiration to end expiration. Collection times are therefore rarely equal to 30 s or 1 minutes, but can be easily converted into minute ventilation values by the following general calculation:

$$\dot{V}E \text{ (l min}^{-1}) = \text{(volume of expired air collection / 60 s)}$$

End expiration can be judged by the following:
1. Watching for the closure of the expiratory valve in the valve box.
2. Feeling the air flow stop at the tap before turning it to fill the Douglas bag.
3. In strenuous exercise, listening for each breath of expired air rushing down the tubing into the Douglas bag.
A stop-watch should be used to time collections.

Gas volumes obtained in laboratory experiments are typically expressed in one of three ways.

$$ATPS = \text{ambient temperature, pressure and saturated}$$

$$STPD = \text{standard temperature, pressure and dry}$$

$$BTPS = \text{body temperature, ambient pressure and saturated}$$

The conditions at the time of the measurement of the volume of expired air in the Douglas bag are reflected in ATPS. It should be noted that the volume of gas varies with temperature and pressure, and its water content, even though the number of molecules in the gas does not change. More specifically, as the temperature of gas increases the volume increases proportionately and vice versa (i.e. if the pressure is constant then a doubling of the temperature will result in a doubling of the volume). This is known as Charles' Law. However, gas volumes vary inversely with pressure. Thus, an increase in pressure causes a proportionate decrease in volume, and vice versa (i.e. if temperature is constant then a doubling of pressure will cause a halving of volume). This is known as Boyle's Law. Finally, the volume of a gas increases with the amount of water content.

To compare measures of volume taken under different environmental conditions, there is a need for a standard set of conditions which are defined by STPD and BTPS. Standard temperature and pressure dry (STPD) refers to a gas volume expressed under *Standard Temperature* (273K or 0°C), *Pressure* (760 mmHg) and *Dry* (no water vapour). Volumes corrected to STPD conditions therefore allow comparison between values collected at different temperatures, altitudes and degrees of saturation. Values of $\dot{V}E$, $\dot{V}O_2$, and $\dot{V}CO_2$ are always expressed at STPD.

The formula for conversion of a volume of moist gas to STPD such as $\dot{V}_E$ is:

$$\dot{V}E_{STPD} = \dot{V}E_{ATPS} \times \frac{273}{273 + T°C} \times \frac{P_B - P_{H_2O}}{760}$$

where T°C is the temperature of the expired air; P_B is barometric pressure; and P_{H_2O} is the water vapour pressure of the sample at the time volume is measured. The P_{H_2O} is not measured directly because conversion factors are tabulated for the normal range of temperatures of moist gas samples. Furthermore, none of the correction factors for volumes need to be calculated since tables for converting moist gas volumes into STPD conditions are readily available for the range of values of temperature and pressure normally experienced in most laboratories (Carpenter, 1964; McArdle *et al.*, 1996).

Body temperature and pressure saturated (BTPS) refers to a gas volume expressed at *Body Temperature* (273K + 37K), *Ambient* pressure and *Saturated* with water vapour with a partial pressure of 47 mmHg at 37°C. This is the conventional standard used for assessing lung function volumes (see Chapter 3 by Eston).

As with correction from ATPS to STPD, corrections from BTPS to STPD can be achieved by use of tabulated values of correction factors for a broad range of temperatures, or by using the formula:

$$\dot{V}E_{STPD} = \dot{V}E_{BTPS} \times (1 \, / \, \text{factor to convert ATPS to BTPS}) \times (\text{factor to convert ATPS to STPD}).$$

When using the simplified estimation of $\dot{V}O_2$ the composition of expired air remains relatively constant ($F_IO_2 = 0.2093$, $\%O_2I = 20.93\%$; $F_ICO_2 = 0.0003$, $\%CO_2I = 0.03\%$ and $F_IN_2 = 0.7904$, $\%N_2I = 79.04\%$).

Substituting the value for the fraction of O_2 in inspired air of F_IO_2 the expression becomes:

$$\dot{V}O_{2\,STPD} \, (l \, min^{-1}) = \dot{V}E_{STPD} \, (0.2093 - F_EO_2)$$

For example, given $\dot{V}E_{ATPS} = 60 \, l \, min^{-1}$ (volume measured in Douglas bag), barometric pressure = 754 mmHg (measured by barometer), temperature of gas = 22°C (measured by thermometer as volume is measured), $F_EO_2 = 0.1675$ (measured by oxygen analyser), then

$$\dot{V}E_{STPD} = \dot{V}E_{ATPS} \times 0.891 \text{ (correction factor taken from Table 6.2)}$$

$$\dot{V}E_{STPD} = 60 \times 0.891 = 53.46 \, l \, min^{-1}$$

$$\dot{V}O_{2\,STPD} \, (l \, min^{-1}) = 53.46 \, (0.2093 - 0.1675) = 2.23 \, l \, min^{-1}$$

In summary, there are two steps to the calculation.

1. Correct the $\dot{V}E$ value from ATPS to STPD by multiplying by a correction factor from the appropriate table of values (Table 6.2).
2. Calculate the difference between the concentration of O_2 in inspired and expired air. Then all variables on the right of the equation are known and $\dot{V}O_2$ can be calculated.

6.6.3 CALCULATION OF OXYGEN UPTAKE ($\dot{V}O_2$) USING THE HALDANE TRANSFORMATION

In addition to the measurements required for the simplified calculation of $\dot{V}O_2$ a value for the fraction of carbon dioxide in expired air is also required (F_ECO_2).

Table 6.2 Conversion of gas volumes from ATPS to STPD (data from Carpenter, 1964; McArdle *et al.*, 1996)

Barometric reading	Temperature (°C)																	
	15	16	17	18	19	20	21	22	23	24	25	26	27	28	29	30	31	32
700	0.855	851	847	842	838	834	829	825	821	816	812	807	802	797	793	788	783	778
702	857	853	849	845	840	836	832	827	823	818	814	809	805	800	795	790	785	780
704	860	856	852	847	843	839	834	830	825	821	816	812	807	802	797	792	787	783
706	862	858	854	850	845	841	837	832	828	823	819	814	810	804	800	795	790	785
708	865	861	856	852	848	843	839	834	830	825	821	816	812	807	802	797	792	787
710	867	863	859	855	850	846	842	837	833	828	824	819	814	809	804	799	795	790
712	870	866	861	857	853	848	844	839	836	830	826	821	817	812	807	802	797	792
714	872	868	864	859	855	851	846	842	837	833	828	824	819	814	809	804	799	794
716	875	871	866	862	858	853	849	844	840	835	831	826	822	816	812	807	802	797
718	877	873	869	864	860	856	851	847	842	838	833	828	824	819	814	809	804	799
720	880	876	871	867	863	858	854	849	845	840	836	831	826	821	816	812	807	802
722	882	878	874	869	865	861	856	852	847	843	838	833	829	824	819	814	809	804
724	885	880	876	872	867	863	858	854	849	845	840	835	831	826	821	816	811	806
726	887	883	879	874	870	866	861	856	852	847	843	838	833	829	824	818	813	808
728	890	886	881	877	872	868	863	859	854	850	845	840	836	831	826	821	816	811
730	892	888	884	879	875	871	866	861	857	852	847	843	838	833	828	823	818	813
732	895	890	886	882	877	873	868	864	859	854	850	845	840	836	831	825	820	815
734	897	893	889	884	880	875	871	866	862	857	852	847	843	838	833	828	823	818
736	900	895	891	887	882	878	873	869	864	859	855	850	845	840	835	830	825	820
738	902	898	894	889	885	880	876	871	866	862	857	852	848	843	838	833	828	822
740	905	900	896	892	887	883	878	874	869	864	860	855	850	845	840	835	830	825
742	907	903	898	894	890	885	881	876	871	867	862	857	852	847	842	837	832	827
744	910	906	901	897	892	888	883	878	874	869	864	859	855	850	845	840	834	829
746	912	908	903	899	895	890	886	881	876	872	867	862	857	852	847	842	837	832
748	915	910	906	901	897	892	888	883	879	874	869	864	860	854	850	845	839	834

continued on next page

Table 6.2 Conversion of gas volumes from ATPS to STPD (data from Carpenter, 1964; McArdle et al., 1996) (cont.)

Barometric reading	Temperature (°C)																	
	15	16	17	18	19	20	21	22	23	24	25	26	27	28	29	30	31	32
750	917	913	908	904	900	895	890	886	881	876	872	867	862	857	852	847	842	837
752	920	915	911	906	902	897	893	888	883	879	874	869	864	859	854	849	844	839
754	922	918	913	909	904	900	895	891	886	881	876	872	867	862	857	852	846	841
756	925	920	916	911	907	902	898	893	888	883	879	874	869	864	859	854	849	844
758	927	923	918	914	909	905	900	896	891	886	881	876	872	866	861	856	851	846
760	930	925	921	916	912	907	902	898	893	888	883	879	874	869	864	859	854	848
762	932	928	923	919	914	910	905	900	896	891	886	881	876	871	866	861	856	851
764	936	930	926	921	916	912	907	903	898	893	888	884	879	874	869	864	858	853
766	937	933	928	924	919	915	910	905	900	896	891	886	881	876	871	886	861	855
768	940	935	931	926	922	917	912	908	903	898	893	888	883	878	873	868	863	858
770	942	938	933	928	924	919	915	910	905	901	896	891	886	881	876	871	865	860

Although the concentrations of oxygen (O_2), carbon dioxide (CO_2) and nitrogen (N_2) are constant for inspired air, the values recorded for expired air fractions will vary. The value for F_EO_2 will be less than F_IO_2 as some of the O_2 is extracted from the lungs into the blood capillaries. The F_EO_2 will range between approximately 0.15 and 0.185. The F_ECO_2 will increase in expired air since the body excretes CO_2 with the lungs from the blood by gas exchange. The F_ECO_2 will range from approximately 0.025 to 0.05. Although nitrogen is inert, i.e. the same number of molecules of N_2 exist in both the inspired and expired air, its concentration will change if the number of O_2 molecules removed from inspired air is not equal to the number of CO_2 molecules excreted in expired air. In simple terms, when the molecules of O_2 removed do not equal the molecules of CO_2 added, then the volume of inspired air (VI) will not equal the volume of air expired (VE), and the constant number of N_2 molecules will represent a different fraction or percentage of the inspired and expired volumes.

For example: inspired air constant fractions:

$$F_IO_2 = 0.2093, \text{ or } \%O_{2I} = 20.93\%;$$
$$F_ICO_2 = 0.003, \text{ or } \% CO_{2I} = 0.03\%;$$
$$\text{and } F_IN_2 = 0.7904, \text{ or } \%N_{2I} = 79.04\%$$

$$\%O_{2I} + \%CO_{2I} + \%N_{2I} = 100\%; (20.93 + 0.03 + 79.04 = 100)$$

Given expired air measured values from experiment:

$$\%O_{2E} = 16.75\%; \%CO_{2E} = 3.55$$
$$\%O_{2E} + \%CO_{2E} + \%N_{2E} = 100$$
$$\%N_{2E} = 100 - (\%O_{2E} + \%CO_{2E})$$
$$\%N_{2E} = 100 - (16.75 + 3.55)$$
$$\%N_{2E} = 79.7\%$$

Here the fraction of oxygen in inspired air has decreased from a value of 0.2093 to 0.1675 in expired air, whereas the concentration of carbon dioxide in inspired air has increased from a value of 0.0003 to 0.0355 in expired air. The decrease in oxygen concentration is therefore greater than the increase in carbon dioxide concentration in expired air. Therefore the fraction of nitrogen in inspired air ($F_IN_2 = 0.7904$) rises to a value of 0.7970 in expired air (the same number of molecules but increased in concentration).

The constant number of N_2 molecules representing a different percentage or concentration of inspired and expired volumes can be used to calculate VI from VE or vice versa. This is possible because the change in volume from inspired to expired is directly proportional to the change in nitrogen concentration:

$$\text{Mass of N}_2 \text{ inspired} = \text{Mass of N}_2 \text{ expired}$$

$$\text{As concentration} = \frac{\text{Mass}}{\text{Volume}}$$

$$\%N_{2I} = \frac{\text{Mass of N}_2}{\dot{V}I} \quad \text{and} \quad \%N_{2E} = \frac{\text{Mass of N}_2}{\dot{V}E}$$

$$\dot{V}I_{STPD} = \frac{\dot{V}E_{STPD} \times \%N_{2E}}{\%N_{2I}}$$

Given the same values as for the simplified calculation, i.e. $\dot{V}E_{ATPS} = 60 \, l \, min^{-1}$, temperature = 22°C, barometric pressure = 754 mmHg, correction factor from ATPS to STPD = 0.891, then $\dot{V}E_{STPD}$ will also be the same: $\dot{V}E_{STPD} = 53.46 \, l \, min^{-1}$

Given that $\%N_{2E}$ was calculated from expired $\%O_{2E}$ and $\%CO_{2E}$ as 79.7% and $\%N_{2I}$ is constant at 79.04%, all the values on the right of the equation are known and can be used to calculate $\dot{V}O_{2\,STPD}$.

Oxygen uptake ($\dot{V}O_2 \, l \, min^{-1}$) can now be calculated as the volume of oxygen removed from expired air per minute:

$$\dot{V}O_2 = \frac{[(\dot{V}E \times \%N_{2E} \times \%O_{2I}) - (\dot{V}E \times \%O_{2E})]}{\%N_{2I}} \div 100 \, O_2 = [(\dot{V}I \times \%O_{2I}) - (\dot{V}E \times \%O_{2E})] \div 100$$

Substituting using the Haldane transformation $\dot{V}I = \dot{V}E \times \dfrac{\%N_{2E}}{\%N_I}$ we can replace $\dot{V}I$ by our known expression $\dot{V}E \times \dfrac{\%N_{2E}}{\%N_I}$

$$\dot{V}O_2 = \frac{[(\dot{V}E \times \%N_{2E} \times \%O_{2I}) - (\dot{V}E \times \%O_{2E})]}{\%N_{2I}} \div 100$$

Substituting in constants for inspired air and simplifying the expression:

$$\dot{V}O_2 = \frac{[(\dot{V}E \times \%N_{2E} \times 20.93\%) - \%O_{2E})]}{79.04\%} \div 100$$

With the most simple form of the equation for computation being:

$$\dot{V}O_2 = \dot{V}E \times [(\%N_{2E} \times 0.265) - \%O_{2E}] \div 100$$

where $\dot{V}E$ is measured under ATPS conditions and corrected to STPD conditions before substitution into this equation, $\%O_{2E}$ is measured from O_2 analyser and $\%N_{2E} = 100 - \%O_{2E} - \%CO_{2E}$ ($\%CO_{2E}$ is measured from CO_2 gas analyser).

Inserting the example values into the simplified equation gives:

$$\dot{V}O_2 \, (l \, min^{-1}) = 53.46 \, [(79.7 \times 0.265) - 16.75\%] \div 100 = 53.46 \, (4.3705) \div 100 = 2.34 \, l \, min^{-1}$$

6.6.4 CALCULATION OF CARBON DIOXIDE PRODUCTION ($\dot{V}CO_2$)

The volume of carbon dioxide produced is calculated according to the following equation:

$$\dot{V}CO_2 = [\dot{V}E \, (\%CO_{2E} - \%CO_{2I})] \times 100$$

Where $\dot{V}E$ is measured and corrected to STPD conditions, $\%CO_{2I} = 0.03\%$ (constant for inspired air) and $\%CO_{2E}$ is measured from CO_2 gas analyser.

Since the fraction of CO_2 in inspired air is negligible, the Haldane transformation is unimportant in the calculation of $\dot{V}CO_2$. In many cases the fraction of CO_2 in inspired air is ignored altogether.

6.7 PRACTICAL 4: THE RESPIRATORY QUOTIENT

The respiratory quotient (RQ) is calculated as the ratio of metabolic gas exchange:

$$RQ = \frac{\dot{V}CO_2 \text{ (volume of carbon dioxide produced)}}{\dot{V}O_2 \text{ (volume of oxygen consumed)}}$$

The RQ gives an indication of what combination of carbohydrates, fats and proteins are metabolized in steady-state submaximal exercise or at rest. The specific equation associated with the RQ for oxidation of pure carbohydrates, fats and proteins is as follows:

(a) RQ for carbohydrates (glucose)

$$C_6H_{12}O_6 + 6O_2 + 6CO_2 + 6H_2O$$

Consequently, during the oxidation of a glucose molecule, six molecules of oxygen are consumed and six molecules of carbon dioxide are produced, therefore:

$$RQ = \frac{6CO_2}{6O_2} = 1$$

The RQ value for carbohydrate is therefore 1.

(b) RQ for fat (palmitic acid)

$$C_{16}H_{32}O_2 = 16CO_2 + 16H_2O$$

$$RQ = \frac{16CO_2}{23O_2} = 0.696$$

Generally, the RQ value for fat is taken to be 0.7.

(c) RQ for protein

The process is more complex for protein to provide energy as proteins are not simply oxidized to carbon dioxide and water, during energy metabolism. Generally, the RQ value for protein is taken to be 0.82.

McLean and Tobin (1987) published equations for the calculation of calorific factors from elemental composition, which included the following equation for respiratory quotient (RQ):

$$RQ = 1 / (1 + 2.9789 f_H / f_C - 0.3754 f_O / f_C)$$

where 1 g of a substance contains f_C, f_H and f_O g of carbon, hydrogen and oxygen respectively.

Given the formula for the chemical composition of carbohydrate, fat or protein, together with the atomic weights for carbon, hydrogen and oxygen ($a_C = 12.011$, $a_H = 1.008$ and $a_O = 15.999$) it is then possible to calculate f_C, f_H and f_O and solve the equation for RQ.

If we use the example of glucose ($C_6H_{12}O_6$):

$$C_6 \text{ gives } a_C \times 6 = 72.1$$

$$H_{12} \text{ gives } a_H \times 12 = 12.1$$

$$O_6 \text{ gives } a_O \times 6 = 96.0$$

The total is therefore 180.2, which gives fractions for each of 0.4, 0.067 and 0.533 for carbon, hydrogen and oxygen respectively. Substitution of these values in the equation above gives an RQ of 1 as previously derived.

As previously stated, the RQ calculated as the ratio of $\dot{V}CO_2$ and $\dot{V}O_2$ will reflect a combination of carbohydrates, fats and proteins currently being metabolized to provide energy. However, the precise contribution of each of the nutrients can be obtained from the calculation of the non-protein RQ.

(d) Non-protein RQ

This calculation of the non-protein RQ is based upon McArdle *et al.* (1996), where the procedures are discussed in more detail. Although this calculation is typical of the approach in most text books, Durnin and Passmore (1967) described the non-protein RQ as 'an abstraction which has no physiological meaning, as protein metabolism is never zero'. Durnin and Passmore (1967) preferred the four equations set out by Consolazio *et al.* (1963) which are used to define the metabolic mixture and calculate energy expenditure. The four equations are also based on oxidation of carbohydrates, fats and proteins and require the measurement of $\dot{V}CO_2$, $\dot{V}O_2$ and urinary nitrogen. Furthermore, they give the same answer as the classical method using non-protein RQ.

Approximately 1 g of nitrogen is excreted in the urine for every 6.25 g of protein metabolized for energy. Each gram of excreted nitrogen represents a carbon dioxide production of approximately 4.8 litres and an oxygen consumption of about 6.8 litres.

Example calculation:
A subject consumes 3.8 litres of oxygen and produces 3.1 litres of carbon dioxide during 15 minutes of rest, during which 0.11 g of nitrogen are excreted into the urine.

1. CO_2 produced in the catabolism of protein is given by $4.8 \, l \, CO_2 \, g^{-1} \times 0.11 \, g = 0.53 \, l \, CO_2$.
2. O_2 consumed in the catabolism of protein is given by $6.0 \, l \, O_2 \, g^{-1}$ protein $\times 0.11 \, g = 0.66 \, l \, O_2$.
3. Non-protein CO_2 produced $= 3.1 - 0.53 = 2.57 \, l \, CO_2$
4. Non-protein O_2 consumed $= 3.8 - 0.66 = 3.14 \, l \, O_2$
5. Non-protein RQ $= 2.57 \, / \, 3.14 = 0.818$

Table 6.3 shows the energy equivalents per litre of oxygen consumed for the range of non-protein RQ values and the percentage of fat and carbohydrates utilized for energy. As Table 6.3 shows 20.20 kJ per litre of oxygen are liberated for a non-protein RQ of 0.82 as calculated above. Thus, 59.7% of the energy is derived from carbohydrate and 40.3% from fat. The non-protein energy production from carbohydrate and fat for the 15 minute period is 63.42 kJ (20.20 kJ $l^{-1} \times 3.14 \, l \, O_2$), whereas the energy derived from protein is 12.71 kJ (19.26 kJ $l^{-1} \times 0.66 \, l \, O_2$). Therefore, the total energy for the 15 minute period is 76.13 kJ (63.42 kJ non-protein + 12.71 kJ protein).

In terms of carbohydrate and fat metabolism, for the non-protein RQ of 0.818, 0.454 g of carbohydrate and 0.313 g of fat were metabolized per litre of O_2 respectively (Table 6.3). This amounts to 1.43 g of carbohydrate (3.14 $l \, O_2 \times 0.455$) and 0.98 g of fat (3.14 $l \, O_2 \times 0.313$) in the 15 minute rest period.

Table 6.3 Thermal equivalent of O_2 for non-protein respiratory quotient, including percentage energy and grams derived from carbohydrate and fat

Non-protein RQ	Energy (kJ) per litre oxygen used	Percentage energy derived from		Grams per litre O_2 consumed	
		Carbohydrate	Fat	Carbohydrate	Fat
0.707	19.62	0	100	0.000	0.496
0.71	19.63	1.1	98.9	0.012	0.491
0.72	19.68	4.8	95.2	0.051	0.476
0.73	19.73	8.4	91.6	0.090	0.460
0.74	19.79	12.0	88.0	0.130	0.444
0.75	19.84	15.6	84.4	0.170	0.428
0.76	19.89	19.2	80.8	0.211	0.412
0.77	19.94	22.8	77.2	0.250	0.396
0.78	19.99	26.3	73.7	0.290	0.380
0.79	20.04	29.9	70.1	0.330	0.363
0.80	20.10	33.4	66.6	0.371	0.347
0.81	20.15	36.9	63.1	0.413	0.330
0.82	20.20	40.3	59.7	0.454	0.313
0.83	20.25	43.8	56.2	0.496	0.297
0.84	20.30	47.2	52.8	0.537	0.280
0.85	20.35	50.7	49.3	0.579	0.263
0.86	20.41	54.1	45.9	0.621	0.247
0.87	20.46	57.5	42.5	0.663	0.230
0.88	20.51	60.8	39.2	0.705	0.213
0.89	20.57	64.2	35.8	0.749	0.195
0.90	20.61	67.5	32.5	0.791	0.178
0.91	20.66	70.8	29.2	0.834	0.160
0.92	20.71	74.1	25.9	0.875	0.143
0.93	20.77	77.4	22.6	0.921	0.125
0.94	20.82	80.7	19.3	0.981	0.108
0.95	20.87	84.0	16.0	1.008	0.080
0.96	20.92	87.2	12.8	1.052	0.072
0.97	20.97	90.4	9.58	1.097	0.054
0.98	21.02	93.6	6.37	1.142	0.036
0.99	21.08	96.8	3.18	1.186	0.018
1.00	21.13	100.0	0	1.231	0.000

During rest or steady-state exercise such as walking or running slowly, the RQ does not reflect the oxidation of pure carbohydrate or fat, but a mixture of the two, producing RQ values which range between 0.7 and 1.00. As shown by the sample calculation of non-protein RQ, protein contributes only a minor amount of the total energy expenditure. For this reason the specific contribution of protein is often ignored, avoiding the monitoring of N_2 excretion together with the more complex and lengthy calculations. In most instances an RQ of 0.82 can be assumed (40% carbohydrate and 60% fat) and the energy equivalent of 20.2 kJ (5.6 kcal) per litre of oxygen can be used in energy expenditure calculations. The maximum error associated with this simplification in estimating energy expenditure from $\dot{V}O_2$ is only of the order of 4% (McArdle *et al.*, 1996).

Durnin and Passmore (1967) stated that in most studies of energy expenditure there is no need to find out how much carbohydrate, fat or protein is used. Furthermore, they advocated the use of Weir's (1949) formula for estimation of energy expenditure which negates the need for CO_2 measurement.

$$\text{Energy (kcal min}^{-1}) = \frac{4.92}{100} \dot{V}E_{\text{STPD}} (20.93 - \%O_{2E})$$

The advice of Durnin and Passmore (1967) is worth serious consideration, given the possible sources of error associated with the Douglas bag technique, gas analysis and volume measurement in unskilled hands.

6.7.1 RESPIRATORY QUOTIENT (RQ) AND RESPIRATORY EXCHANGE RATIO (RER)

Under steady-state conditions of exercise, the assumption that gas exchange at the lungs reflects gas exchange from metabolism in the cells is reasonably valid. When conditions are other than steady state, such as in severe exercise, or with hyperventilation, the assumption is no longer valid. Under such conditions the ratio of carbon dioxide production to oxygen consumption is known as RER even though it is calculated in exactly the same way.

6.8 PRACTICAL 5: ESTIMATION OF RMR USING THE DOUGLAS BAG TECHNIQUE

Under ideal conditions RMR should be estimated as soon as the person wakes up from an overnight sleep. This is not possible in most practical situations, but provided that the subject can rest in a supine position for a reasonable period of time a good estimate of RMR can be obtained. During the test the subject lies quietly in a supine position (Figure 6.1), preferably in a temperature-controlled room, thus ensuring a thermoneutral environment. After 30–60 minutes, the subject's oxygen uptake is measured for a minimum of 6–10 minutes, preferably 15 minutes. If O_2 and CO_2 concentrations are measured in expired air then the RQ, energy expenditure, and substrate utilization can be estimated according to the procedures outlined above. Values for oxygen uptake used as an estimate of BMR range between 160 and 290 ml min^{-1} (3.85–6.89 kJ min^{-1}), depending upon a variety of factors, but particularly on body size (McArdle *et al.*, 1996).

6.9 PRACTICAL 6: ENERGY BALANCE

This practical introduces the procedures for the measurement of energy balance, incorporating a simplified assessment of energy expenditure and food intake. In simple terms, if the total energy intake is repeatedly greater than the daily energy expenditure, the excess energy is stored as fat. In contrast, if daily energy expenditure is greater than energy intake the subject will lose weight. The aim of the laboratory practical is to calculate the energy expenditure and energy intake for a typical day. An understanding of key concepts in energy expenditure and intake is important for several areas of exercise physiology, such as the use of diet and exercise to alter body composition, thermoregulation and mechanical efficiency. Energy expenditure is calculated by a combination of measurements, using the Douglas bag technique or an automated gas analysis system (Figure 6.3), and estimations using generalized predictive equations and tables for a range of activities. Alternatively, if available, energy expenditure can be recorded for a range of activities using a portable gas analysis system, an example of which is shown in Figure 6.4 (this is a MetaMax II, Cortex GmbH, Leipzig, Germany). The estimation of energy intake is based on the energy value of food using standard reference tables. The subject should keep a diary of activities (duration and intensity) and food consumed (quantity and preparation) for a 24-hour period. Energy intake and expenditure can then be calculated from standard tables and from direct measures of energy expenditure completed in the laboratory.

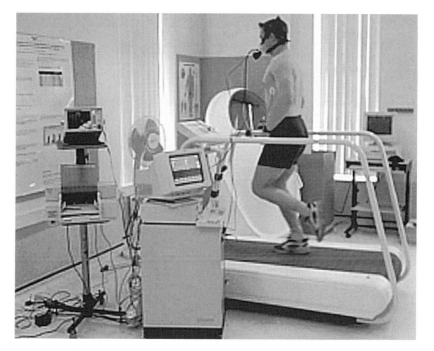

Figure 6.3 A subject running on a motorized treadmill, with expired air analysis through a face mask (Hans Rudolph Inc., KS, USA) connected to an on-line automated breath-by-breath gas analysis system (Oxycon Champion, Mijnhardt, Bunnik, Netherlands; Jaeger, Hoechberg, Germany) and a three-lead ECG through an ECG Oscillograph (CR7 Cardiorater, Cardiac Recorders, Enfield, UK).

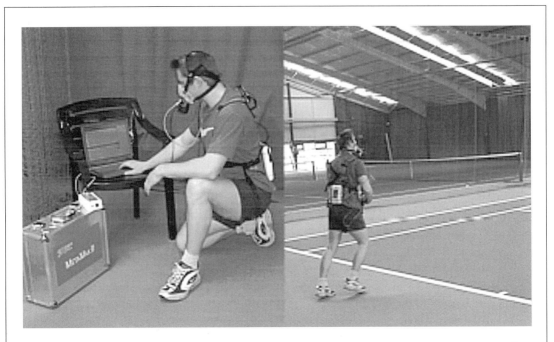

Figure 6.4 A portable gas analysis system (MetaMax II, Cortex, Germany) to collect individual energy expenditure values for tennis. The left-hand photograph shows the system being initialised to work via telemetry, sending the signals from the device whilst the subject is playing tennis (right-hand photograph). Alternatively, the device can be used in data logging mode, with the data downloaded to the computer after the game has finished.

6.9.1 ENERGY EXPENDITURE

It is possible to measure oxygen uptake for a range of everyday activities, which should be ordered such that the least demanding are completed first. Oxygen uptake should be measured for RMR, and compared with RMR from the predictive formulae in Section 6.4. Oxygen uptake values can then be obtained for sitting, standing, self-paced walking, stair climbing and an appropriate form of exercise for the subject, such as running or cycling. If time permits, duplicate gas collections should be made. Most of the measurements can be made in the laboratory, but some may necessitate access to other buildings, such as stair climbing and descending, and self-paced walking. In such cases, the Douglas bag should be supported in some way. This is where purpose-designed portable gas analysis systems are most useful (Figure 6.4). All gas collections should be made under steady-state conditions for an appropriate length of time to analyse the expired air accurately (minimum of 10 minutes for RMR, dropping to 1 minute for the most strenuous exercise to ensure an accurately quantifiable volume).

Energy expenditure can then be calculated using the $\dot{V}O_2$, $\dot{V}CO_2$ and RQ values and their energy equivalents shown in Table 6.3 or Weir's formula presented in Section 6.7. A comparison of the two forms of calculation will indicate whether the extra precision associated with the measurement of carbon dioxide concentration and the calculation of RQ is warranted if the aim is to calculate energy expenditure.

The directly measured energy expenditure values can then be used in the calculation of the daily energy expenditure from the information recorded in the diary of activities. Where direct measurement was not possible, values for energy expenditure can be estimated from objective measures of physical activity such as heart rate. Heart rate telemetry systems, typically consisting of a chest strap, or electrodes, to detect heart rate and transmit the signal to a wrist-watch receiver with data storage (e.g. Polar, Finland), can be worn throughout the day, with data downloaded through an interface onto a computer for subsequent analysis. To use such heart rate data to estimate energy expenditure requires the relationship between heart rate and oxygen uptake to be established for the subject in the laboratory in a similar fashion to that described above for a range of everyday activities typical for the subject. Oxygen uptake and heart rate are related by a robust linear relationship which holds true throughout the submaximal range, especially when measured under controlled conditions. The heart rate values recorded throughout a typical day can be affected by a number of other factors, such as state of arousal, emotion, fatigue, stress, fever and other environmental factors such as temperature and humidity, which limits the validity of using heart rate for assessing energy expenditure and physical activity (Rowlands *et al.*, 1997). The nature of the linear relationship between heart rate and oxygen uptake will, however, be dependent upon the state of training of the subject. Remember that changes in heart rate response to a given workload or energy expenditure constitute a physiological response to endurance training. Heart rate recordings are therefore indicative of the individual, provided they are interpreted in terms of an equation relating heart rate and energy expenditure for that subject. Energy expenditure can then be estimated from the activity diary for the day using energy expenditure values estimated from the appropriate HR–VO$_2$ relationship and summed over the time period for which the particular activity was recorded.

Other objective measures of activity are also available, such as movement sensors based on mercury switches or accelerometers. These devices include a large range of relatively inexpensive pedometers to more sophisticated accelerometers that are capable of storing multidimensional data for subsequent computer analysis. Many devices will display a cumulative value for energy expenditure, most typically in kcal. However, it should not be assumed that such values are credible. These values are based on equations that link the direct measurement of steps, for example, to an estimate of energy expenditure based on an equation developed and validated on a particular population. It is not always possible to find out the equation used and therefore to understand the limitations of such values produced by the device. It is possible to use the raw data in the form of movement counts or steps, by calibration of the device with subjects prior to use, as exemplified in the study of habitual physical activity in children by Rowlands *et al.* (1999). These and other methods of estimating physical activity are described in more detail in Chapter 6 by Rowlands in Volume 1.

When either directly determined oxygen uptake or estimated oxygen uptake values are not available, estimates can be taken from mean values of energy expenditure published in the literature (e.g. Durnin and Passmore, 1967; Bannister and Brown, 1968; Ainsworth *et al.*, 1993; McArdle *et al.*, 1996). (Table 6.4 gives some examples of common activities.) The disadvantage of using mean values of energy expenditure taken from the literature is that they will not be specific to the individual, in terms of efficiency, and often are not very sensitive to the intensity of the activity.

Table 6.4   Energy expenditure values for selected activities

Activity	kcal kg^{-1} min^{-1} [a]	METS [b]
Badminton	0.097	4.5 (general)
		7.0 (competitive)
Basketball	0.138	6.0 (general)
		8.0 (competitive)
Cycling	0.100 (15 km h^{-1})	6.0 (16–19 km h^{-1})
	0.169 (racing)	16.0 (racing >32 km h^{-1})
Dancing (aerobics)	0.135 (intense)	7.0 (high impact)
		5.0 (low impact)
		6.0 (general)
Home (cleaning general)	0.060	3.5 (general)
Home (play with child)		5.0 (run/walk – vigorous)
		2.5 (sitting)
Home (inactivity – quiet)	0.022 (lying)	1.0 (sitting)
Running	0.163 (cross-country)	9.0 (cross-country)
	0.193 (10.4 km h^{-1})	10.0 (9.6 km h^{-1})
	0.252 (16.0 km h^{-1})	16.0 (16 km h^{-1})
Squash	0.212	12.0
Swimming (crawl)	0.156 (fast)	11.0 (fast)
	0.128 (slow)	8.0 (slow)
Volleyball	0.050	4.0 (competitive)
	3.0 (non-competitive)	
Walking	0.080 (normal pace)	3.5 (4.8 km h^{-1})
		4.5 (6.4 km h^{-1})
		6.0 (backpacking)
		3.0 (downstairs)
		8.0 (upstairs)

a Values in kcal kg^{-1} min^{-1} are from McArdle *et al.* (1996).
b Values in METS are from Ainsworth *et al.* (1993).

Ainsworth *et al.* (1993) have presented a comprehensive compendium of physical activities classified in terms of intensity according to the number of METS of energy required. A MET is defined as the energy requirement for RMR. The most accurate way to compute the energy expenditure values for a given individual using their compendium is to measure the RMR and multiply it by the MET value associated with the physical activity of interest. For example, if the oxygen uptake measured as an estimate of RMR for a person of mass 70 kg was 270 ml min^{-1} with an RQ of 0.87 this would equate to an RMR value of 0.27 × 20.46 kJ l^{-1}, which equals 5.52 kJ min^{-1} (331 kJ h^{-1} or 7954 kJ day^{-1}) (1900 kcal day^{-1}). This value of RMR would represent one MET and could be multiplied by the appropriate MET value for a given physical activity. According to Ainsworth *et al.* (1993), fencing requires an energy expenditure equivalent to 6 METS. For the 70 kg individual this equates with an energy expenditure value of 6 × 5.52 kJ min^{-1}, which equals 33.1 kJ min^{-1} (7.91 kcal min^{-1}).

Table 6.5 Proforma for recording activity over a 24–hour period

Hour	15–minute time periods			
	1	2	3	4
1	Sleep	Sleep	Sleep	Sleep
2	Sleep	Sleep	Sleep	Sleep
3	Sleep	Sleep	Sleep	Sleep
4	Sleep	Sleep	Sleep	Sleep
5	Sleep	Sleep	Sleep	Sleep
6	Sleep	Sleep	Sleep	Sleep
7	Sleep	Sleep	Sitting	Eating
8	Walking	Walking	Walking	Typing
9	Typing	Typing	Typing	Typing
10	Sitting	Sitting	Sitting	Sitting
11	Typing	Typing	Typing	Typing
12	Typing	Typing	Typing	Typing
13	Walking	Eating	Eating	Typing
14	Typing	Typing	Typing	Typing
15	Typing	Typing	Walking	Walking
16	Walking	Sitting	Play child	Play child
17	Cooking	Cooking	Cleaning	Cleaning
18	Eating	Sitting	Walking	Sitting
19	Aerobics (general)	Aerobics	Aerobics	Aerobics
20	Walking	Sitting	Eating	Sitting
21	Sitting	Sitting	Sitting	Sitting
22	Sleep	Sleep	Sleep	Sleep
23	Sleep	Sleep	Sleep	Sleep
24	Sleep	Sleep	Sleep	Sleep

(Short intensive activity should be noted separately)

In the absence of a measure or prediction of RMR, diaries of self-reported physical activity can be conveniently assessed for energy expenditure based on a mean estimate of RMR of 1 kcal kg^{-1} h^{-1}. For a body mass of 70 kg this value would produce an energy expenditure value of (6 METS × 70 kg × 1 kcal kg^{-1} h^{-1} / 60 min = 7.00 kcal min^{-1} (29.3 kJ min^{-1})) for fencing. This value represents 88% of the value calculated from the measured RMR value.

The diary of physical activities for the day should be broken down into periods of the order of 10–15 minutes, with high intensity activities of a short duration, such as stair climbing, also recorded as these events can have a significant cumulative effect on the total energy expenditure for the day. Table 6.5 shows an example of such a diary which has been completed by a young female (age 24 years; mass 57 kg) who has a sedentary desk job. The data indicate that this person spends much of her time sitting, but walks to work, walks the children home from school, and attends an aerobics class in the evening. Using the appropriate MET values from Ainsworth *et al.* (1993), the daily energy expenditure can be estimated using a mean estimated RMR of 1 kcal kg^{-1} h^{-1}. For a body mass of 57 kg, this value would produce the following estimates of energy expenditure for Table 6.5:

Sleep = (57 kg × 0.9 MET × 1 kcal kg^{-1} h^{-1} × 38 (15 min periods))/4 = 487 kcal

Walking = (57 × 3.5 × 1 × 9)/4 = 449 kcal

Typing = (57 × 1.5 × 1 × 20)/4 = 428 kcal

Sitting = (57 × 1 × 1 × 14)/4 = 200 kcal

Play = (57 × 5 × 1 × 2)/4 = 143 kcal

Eating E = (57 × 1.5 × 1 × 5)/4 = 107 kcal

Cooking = (57 × 2.5 × 1 × 2)/4 = 71 kcal

Cleaning = (57 × 3.5 × 1 × 2)/4 = 100 kcal

Aerobics = (57 × 6 × 1 × 4)/4 = 342 kcal

Total = 2327 kcal (9773 kJ)

This fictitious young female subject therefore expended 2327 kcal of energy on this particular day. Table 6.6 shows an example of an alternative data collection form for recording physical activity (Ainsworth *et al.*, 1993) for a few activities for the same person (57 kg).

Table 6.6 Example of recording form for physical activities (Ainsworth *et al.*, 1993)

	Type of activity	*METS*	*Duration (h:min)*	*Energy expended (kcal kg^{-1}h^{-1})*
1	Sitting	1.0	8:0	456
2	Walking	3.5	2:0	399
3	Swimming fast	11.0	0:30	313
			Total	1 168 (in a 10.5 h period)

6.9.2 MEASURING ENERGY INTAKE

A set of calibrated kitchen weighing scales should be used to weigh all food that is consumed in the 24-hour period under examination. The weight of the food, its form of preparation (e.g. fried, boiled) and the amount and type of fluid drinks should be recorded in the 24-hour food diary. An example of a 24-hour diet for the young female subject for whom a 24-hour activity diary was analysed is shown in Table 6.7. The diet can then be analysed for energy intake using standard tables for common foods (e.g. McArdle *et al.*, 1996; Holland *et al.*, 1992). For the example shown in Table 6.7, using COMPEAT software (Nutrition Systems, Grantham, UK), the total energy intake is calculated to be 8346 kJ (1994 kcal).

This means that for this particular day the young female subject would be in negative energy balance, expending 1629 kJ (389 kcal) more energy than she consumes. The dietary analysis can easily be extended to a seven-day weighed food intake, with a more accurate dietary analysis of nutrients and percentages of recommended daily allowances of fat, carbohydrate and protein which can be performed using commercially available software (e.g. COMPEAT, based on Holland *et al.*, 1992).

Table 6.7 Example of a 24-hour diet record sheet

Food description	Mass (g)
Special K	50.0
Skimmed milk	150.0
Water	1 700.0
Indian tea	520.0
Meat paste	30.0
Wholemeal bread	76.0
Tomatoes (raw)	65.0
Eating apples (Cox's Pippin)	100.0
Crisps	25.0
Chocolate digestive biscuits	51.0
Cheese and tomato pizza	365.0
Hot cross bun	50.0
Ribena (undiluted)	30.0

6.10 SUMMARY

This chapter has set out a small selection of laboratory practicals which will give an introduction to the measurement of metabolic rate and energy balance. These procedures form the basis of many aspects of experimental work in a variety of areas of study, such as kinanthropometry, nutrition and exercise physiology, and can easily be adapted to the specific requirements of a large number of experiments using different items of equipment.

REFERENCES

Ainsworth, B.E., Haskell, W.L., Leon, A.S., *et al.* (1993). Compendium of physical activities: classification of energy costs of human physical activities. *Medicine and Science in Sports and Exercise*, **25**, 71–80.

Altman, P.L. and Dittmer, D.S. (1968). *Metabolism*. (FASBEB, Bethesda, MD).

Bannister, E.W. and Brown, S.R. (1968). The relative energy requirements of physical activity. In *Exercise Physiology*. ed. H.B. Falls (Academic Press, New York).

Carpenter, T.M. (1964). *Tables, Functions, and Formulas for Computing Respiratory Exchange and Biological Transformation of Energy*, 4th edn. (Carnegie Institution of Washington, Publication 303C, Washington, DC).

Consolazio, C.F., Johnson, R.E. and Pecora, L.J. (1963). *Physiological Measurements of Metabolic Functions in Man.* (McGraw-Hill, New York).

Cunningham, J.J. (1991). Body composition as a determinant of energy expenditure: a synthetic review and a proposed general prediction equation. *American Journal of Clinical Nutrition*, **54**, 963–9.

DuBois, D. and DuBois, E.F. (1916). Clinical calorimetry. A formula to estimate the approximate surface area if stature and weight are known. *Archives of Internal Medicine*, **17**, 863–71.

Durnin, J.V.G.A. and Passmore, R. (1967). *Energy, Work and Leisure.* (Heinemann, London.)

Harris, J. and Benedict, F. (1919). *A Biometric Study of Basal Metabolism in Man.* (Carnegic Institution, Publication 279, Washington, DC).

Holland, B., Welch, A.A., Unwin, I.D., *et al.* (1992). *McCance and Widdowson's The Composition of Foods*, 5th edn. (The Royal Society of Chemistry and Ministry of Agriculture, Fisheries and Food, Richard Clay Ltd, UK).

Jakeman, P. and Davies, B. (1979). The characteristics of a low resistance breathing valve designed for measurement of high aerobic capacity. *British Journal of Sports Medicine*, **13**, 81–3.

Kleiber, M. (1975). *The Fire of Life. An Introduction to Animal Energetics.* (Kreiger, New York).

Knoebel, L.K. (1963). *Energy metabolism, in Physiology.* ed. E.E. Selkurt. (Little, Brown, Boston, MA), pp. 564–79.

McArdle, W.D., Katch, F.I. and Katch, V.L. (1996). *Exercise Physiology, Energy Nutrition and Human Performance*, 4th edn. (Williams and Wilkins, Baltimore, MD).

MacDougall, J.D., Roche, P.D., Bar-Or, O. and Moroz, J.R. (1979). Oxygen cost of running in children of different ages; maximal aerobic power of Canadian school children. *Canadian Journal of Applied Sports Sciences*, **4**, 237–41.

McLean, J.A. and Tobin, G. (1987). *Animal and Human Calorimetry.* (Cambridge University Press, Cambridge).

McMahon, T.A. (1984). *Muscles, Reflexes and Locomotion.* (Princeton University Press, Princeton, NJ).

Mifflin, M.D., St Jeor, S.T., Hill, L.A., *et al.* (1990). A new predictive equation for resting energy expenditure in healthy individuals. *American Journal of Clinical Nutrition*, **51**, 241–7.

Owen, O.E., Kavle, E. and Owen, R.S. (1986). A re-appraisal of the caloric requirements in healthy women. *American Journal of Clinical Nutrition*, **44**, 1 19.

Owen, O.E., Holup, J.L. and D'Allessio, D.A. (1987). A re-appraisal of the caloric requirements of healthy men. *American Journal of Clinical Nutrition*, **46**, 875–85.

Rowlands, A.V., Eston, R.G. and Ingledew, D.K. (1997). Measurement of physical activity in children with particular reference to the use of heart rate and pedometry. *Sports Medicine*, **24**, 258–72.

Rowlands, A.V., Eston, R.G. and Ingledew, D.K. (1999). The relationship between activity levels, aerobic fitness, and body fat in 8- to 10-yr-old children. *Journal of Applied Physiology*, **86**, 1428–35.

Rubner, M. (1883). Über den Einfluss der Körpergrösse auf Stoff- und Kraftwechsel. *Z. Biology.* Munich, **19**, 535–62.

Schmidt-Nielsen, K. (1984). *Scaling: Why is Animal Size so Important?* (Cambridge University Press, Cambridge).

Weir, J. B. De V. (1949). New methods for calculating metabolic rate with special reference to protein metabolism. *Journal of Physiology*, **109**, 1–9.

MAXIMAL OXYGEN UPTAKE, ECONOMY AND EFFICIENCY

Carlton B. Cooke

7.1 AIMS

The aims in this chapter are to:
- define the measurements of maximal oxygen uptake, economy and efficiency,
- describe procedures for the direct determination of maximal oxygen uptake,
- consider methods and limitations of predicting maximal oxygen uptake,
- describe procedures for assessing the economy of movement,
- discuss the concept of 'efficiency' and describe the limitations of various measurements for assessing the efficiency of human movement,
- describe the effects of load carriage on the economy, posture and kinematics of walking.

7.2 INTRODUCTION

Measurements of maximal oxygen uptake, economy and efficiency of different forms of exercise are important in gaining an understanding of the differences between groups of athletes, and the requirements of sporting, recreational and occupational activities. They also serve to help highlight effects of sex, age and size differences.

Maximal oxygen uptake and economy are commonly measured in studies in which the aerobic performances of different individuals or groups of athletes are compared. Defining the current training status of an elite runner, or comparing the physiological profiles of different standards of athlete are examples. Efficiency

measures, other than average values for estimating oxygen uptake from external work done, are less often quoted in the literature due to problems of measurement which are often exacerbated by the use and abuse of different definitions (Cavanagh and Kram, 1985).

Load carriage is an activity that provides an appropriate focus for the study of economy, including the need to consider energy expenditure, posture and kinematics. Load carriage is of interest from both occupational and recreational perspectives. The efficacy of rucksacks as a means of load carriage is important for trekkers as well as soldiers, both of which may have to carry relatively heavy loads for prolonged periods of time.

7.3 DIRECT DETERMINATION OF MAXIMAL OXYGEN UPTAKE

7.3.1 RELEVANCE

There is an upper limit to the oxygen that is consumed during exercise requiring maximal effort. This upper limit is defined as maximal oxygen uptake ($\dot{V}O_2$max), which is the maximum rate at which an individual can take up and utilize oxygen while breathing air at sea level (Åstrand and Rodahl, 1986). It has traditionally been used as the criterial standard of cardiorespiratory fitness, as it is considered to be the single physiological variable that best defines the functional capacity of the cardio-vascular and respiratory systems. However, it is more accurate to consider it as an indicator of both potential for endurance performance and, to a lesser extent, training status. Even though the physiological basis of $\dot{V}O_2$max has been established for a considerable time, there has recently been some robust debate based on a challenge of A.V. Hill's paradigm by Noakes (1997, 1998) which has been refuted by Bassett and Howley (1997) and others.

At any given time the $\dot{V}O_2$max of an individual is fixed and specific for a given task, e.g. running, cycling, rowing and so on. The $\dot{V}O_2$max can be increased with training or decreased with a period of enforced inactivity, such as bed rest. Changes of up to 100% in $\dot{V}O_2$max have been reported after a period of training following prolonged bed rest (Saltin *et al.*, 1968). Pollock (1973) published a review in which the effect of endurance training is reported to have produced changes in $\dot{V}O_2$max which ranged from 0 to 93%. The initial level of fitness (a reflection of an individual combination of endowment and habitual activity), intensity, frequency and duration of training are factors that will influence the effects of endurance training on $\dot{V}O_2$max. The age and sex of the individual are relevant considerations also. It is, therefore, not surprising that training studies carried out on habitually active endurance athletes have produced non-significant changes in $\dot{V}O_2$max, of the order of only 2–3%, whereas endurance performance has dramatically increased. Training programmes carried out on previously sedentary subjects can produce significant changes in $\dot{V}O_2$max values, usually of the order of 20–30%.

Measurements of $\dot{V}O_2$max indicate aerobic potential and to a lesser extent, training status. The sensitivity of $\dot{V}O_2$max to changes in training or the establishment of regular habitual physical activity is strongly related to the degree of development in $\dot{V}O_2$max that may be ultimately realized, which reflects a combination of endowment and habitual physical activity. Although it is generally agreed that

genetic factors play an important role in defining the potential for development of physiological variables such as $\dot{V}O_2$max, the extent to which $\dot{V}O_2$max is determined by endowment has been adjusted downwards in more recent studies from 90% to something of the order of 40–70% (Bouchard and Malina, 1983).

The maximal oxygen uptake ($\dot{V}O_2$max) is also important as a baseline measure to be used with other measures of endurance performance, such as fractional utilization (%$\dot{V}O_2$max that can be sustained for prolonged periods), onset of blood lactate accumulation (OBLA) and running economy (see Chapter 10 by Jones and Doust). A high $\dot{V}O_2$max may be considered to be a prerequisite for elite performance in endurance sport, but does not guarantee achievement at the highest level of sport. Technique, state of training and psychological factors also have positive and negative modifying effects on performance. It is for these reasons that measures of $\dot{V}O_2$max do not allow an accurate prediction of an individual's performance potential in aerobic power events. Shephard (1984) reviewed 37 studies reporting correlation coefficients between all-out running performance and measured $\dot{V}O_2$max, and found coefficients ranging from 0.04 to 0.90.

(a) Age, sex and $\dot{V}O_2$max

A combination of cross-sectional and longitudinal studies provides a reasonably clear picture of the development of $\dot{V}O_2$max during childhood and adolescence and its decline during adulthood (Bar-Or, 1983; Krahenbuhl *et al.*, 1985; Åstrand and Rodahl, 1986; Allied Dunbar National Fitness Survey, 1992). Absolute $\dot{V}O_2$max values increase steadily prior to puberty with the growth of the pulmonary, cardiovascular and musculoskeletal systems. At the onset of puberty the curves relating age and $\dot{V}O_2$max values for males and females begin to diverge and continue to do so during adolescence. After the acceleration of $\dot{V}O_2$max values in males at puberty which reflects the increased muscle mass, and given that $\dot{V}O_2$max in females remains virtually unchanged after early teens, females' $\dot{V}O_2$max values are on average 65–75% of those of males.

In both sexes there is a peak in $\dot{V}O_2$max values at 18–20 years of age followed by a gradual decline with increasing age. The results of the Allied Dunbar National Fitness Survey (1992), where $\dot{V}O_2$max was estimated for over 1700 men and women, produced average values of 55 and 40 ml kg^{-1} min^{-1} for men and women aged 16–24 years, respectively. After this time, $\dot{V}O_2$max declined steadily with increasing age, resulting in average values of about 30 and 25 ml kg^{-1} min^{-1} for men and women aged 65–74 years, respectively. In contrast, $\dot{V}O_2$max values for elite endurance athletes may exceed 80 ml kg^{-1} min^{-1}. Data from a variety of population studies indicate that at the age of 65 the average $\dot{V}O_2$max value is approximately 70% of that of a 25-year-old of the same sex.

(b) Body size and $\dot{V}O_2$max

Comparisons of physiological measurements between subjects of different size are commonplace, especially in the case of children versus adults. These comparisons are made in both cross-sectional and longitudinal studies, which in the latter case include comparisons of the same subjects during the growing years.

In the case of $\dot{V}O_2$max there is a strong positive relationship between body size and absolute $\dot{V}O_2$max (l min^{-1}). Generally speaking, the larger the subject the larger the $\dot{V}O_2$max in absolute terms (l min^{-1}). In an attempt to overcome the effects of differences in body mass when comparing $\dot{V}O_2$max values, the latter are often divided by body mass prior to comparison. The $\dot{V}O_2$max (ml kg^{-1} min^{-1}) is therefore considered to be a weight-adjusted expression of $\dot{V}O_2$max where the effects of differences in body mass have been factored out.

However, $\dot{V}O_2$max expressed in ml kg^{-1} min^{-1} correlates negatively with body mass. Far from eliminating the effect of body mass, this form of expression converts a positive relationship

between $\dot{V}O_2$max (l min^{-1}) and body mass into a negative one between $\dot{V}O_2$max (ml kg^{-1} min^{-1}) and body mass. Therefore, this common form of weight correction does not eliminate the effects of body mass or weight at all.

Nevertheless, $\dot{V}O_2$max has probably continued to be related to body mass in the form ml kg^{-1} min^{-1} because body mass is easily obtained. It also correlates well with most measures of cardiorespiratory function. There is also a strong positive relationship with performance in weight-bearing activities such as running, so expressing the power output per kilogram of body mass would seem appropriate where the body mass has to be carried in the activity.

If dividing $\dot{V}O_2$max by body mass does not factor out the effects of body mass on $\dot{V}O_2$max (l min^{-1}), then the question arises as to what form of expression of $\dot{V}O_2$max is independent of body mass and can therefore allow meaningful comparisons among individuals differing in body size?

Theoretically, since maximal force in muscle is dependent on cross-sectional area, muscle force will be proportional to length^2 (L^2), the squared function representing an area. Similarly, work or energy is based on force × distance, therefore work done or energy expended is proportional to $F \times L$ or L^3 (on a cubic function). As $\dot{V}O_2$max is an expression of energy expenditure per unit of time or power output, which is $(F \times L) / t$, and time is proportional to L then $\dot{V}O_2$max (l min^{-1}) is proportional to $L^3 L^{-1}$ or L^2.

Since mass (M) is proportional to volume which is proportional to L^3, then $\dot{V}O_2$max (l min^{-1}) should be proportional to $M^{2/3}$ (since M is proportional to L^3, $\dot{V}O_2$max is proportional to L^2 and $M^{2/3} = L^2$). A more detailed discussion of the scaling effects of body size and dimensional analysis can be found in Schmidt-Nielson (1984), McMahon (1984) and Åstrand and Rodahl (1986).

The theoretical expectation that $\dot{V}O_2$max (l min^{-1}) should be proportional to L^2 or $M^{2/3}$ is true for well-trained adult athletes (Åstrand and Rodahl, 1986) and recreationally active adult males and females (Nevill *et al.*, 1992). However, longitudinal studies of children's $\dot{V}O_2$max (l min^{-1}) have identified exponents of L which range from 1.51 to 3.21 (or M from 0.503 to 1.07) (Bar-Or, 1983).

In the case of active adults and athletes, expressing $\dot{V}O_2$max in ml kg$^{-2/3}$ min^{-1} would appear to eliminate the confounding effects of body mass on $\dot{V}O_2$max (l min^{-1}). It therefore provides a more meaningful index than the more conventional expression of $\dot{V}O_2$max in ml kg^{-1} min^{-1}, which disadvantages heavier individuals.

Besides demonstrating the superiority of the expression of $\dot{V}O_2$max in ml kg$^{-2/3}$ min^{-1}, in adjusting for differences in body mass, Nevill *et al.* (1992) also showed that the more conventional expression of $\dot{V}O_2$max in ml kg^{-1} min^{-1} held true in terms of predicting ability to run 5 km expressed as a function of average running speed. This supports the use of the conventional expression of $\dot{V}O_2$max in ml kg^{-1} min^{-1} for weight-bearing activities, which are highly dependent on body size. It is therefore important to be clear on the aim of comparing different forms of expression, since performance and physiological function do not always use the same criteria. Further discussion on the principles of scaling physiological and anthropometric data is presented in Volume 1, Chapter 11 by Winter and Nevill.

7.3.2 PROTOCOLS

There is a large number of protocols reported in the literature for the direct determination of $\dot{V}O_2$max. These range from short, single-load protocols performed at so-called 'supra-maximal' workloads, lasting no longer than 6 minutes, to relatively long discontinuous protocols where the subject exercises for anything from 3 to 6 minutes at each workload and then rests for about 3 minutes between increments (Åstrand and Rodahl, 1986).

One of the general recommendations for the assessment of $\dot{V}O_2$max is that subjects should perform rhythmic exercise which requires a large muscle mass. This ensures that the cardiorespiratory system is taxed and the test is not limited by local muscular endurance. The muscle mass engaged explains why simulated cross-country skiing produces the highest $\dot{V}O_2$max values, followed by graded treadmill running, flat treadmill running and cycle ergometry. The specificity of the activity of the subject undergoing assessment should take precedence if the aim is to produce meaningful values for interpretation of aerobic potential or current training status. For example, canoeists should be tested on a canoe ergometer, but will generally produce lower $\dot{V}O_2$max values than if they were running on a treadmill. It has been known, in exceptional cases, for a subject only used to strenuous exercise in canoeing to produce a higher $\dot{V}O_2$max value than when running on a treadmill.

Given the plethora of protocols for the direct determination of $\dot{V}O_2$max, it is worthwhile to consider attempts at standardization through guidelines such as those published by the British Association of Sports Sciences (1992) in its 'Position Statement on the Physiological Assessment of the Elite Competitor'. These guidelines contain tables for establishing the appropriate exercise intensities for the direct determination of $\dot{V}O_2$max using leg and arm cycling and graded treadmill running (Tables 7.1 and 7.2).

The British Association of Sports and Exercise Sciences (BASES) (1997) have recommended the following criteria for establishing maximal oxygen uptake in adult subjects:

1. A plateau in the oxygen uptake–exercise intensity relationship. This has been defined as an increase in oxygen uptake of less than 2 ml kg^{-1} min^{-1} or 3% with an increase in exercise intensity. If this plateau is not achieved, then the term $\dot{V}O_2$peak is preferred.
2. A final respiratory exchange ratio of 1.15 or above.
3. A final heart rate of within 10 beats min^{-1} of the predicted age-related maximum. (Maximum heart rate can be estimated from the

Table 7.1 Guidelines for establishing exercise intensity for the determination of maximal oxygen uptake during leg or arm cycling in adults

	Warm-up (W)	*Initial work-rate (W)*	*Work-rate increment (W)*
Leg cycling (pedal frequency 60 min^{-1})			
Male	120	180–240	30
Female	60	150–200	30
Arm cycling (pedal frequency 60 min^{-1})	60	90	30
Elite cyclists (pedal frequency 90 min^{-1})			
Male	150	200–250	35
Female	100	150	35

Table 7.2 Guidelines for establishing exercise intensity for the determination of maximal oxygen uptake during treadmill running in adults

	Warm-up speed (m s^{-1})	*Test speed (m s^{-1})*	*Initial grade (%)*	*Grade increment*
Endurance athletes				
Male	3.13	4.47	0	2.5
Female	2.68	4.02	0	2.5
Games players				
Male	3.13	3.58	0	2.5
Female	2.68	3.13	0	2.5

formula: Maximal heart rate = 220 − age (years) if the maximum value is unknown.)

4. A post-exercise (4–5 minutes) blood lactate concentration of 8 mmol l^{-1} or more.
5. Subjective fatigue and volitional exhaustion.
6. A rating of perceived exertion (RPE) of 19 or 20 on the Borg 6 to 20 rating of perceived exertion scale.

The third edition of the BASES guidelines has been considerably developed and includes much more useful information than the second edition, including sport-specific testing guidelines and considerations for testing children. Nevertheless, the tables presented above still provide useful guidance for testing maximal oxygen uptake in adult subjects. Considerations for testing children are presented in Volume 1, Chapter 8 by Boreham and Van Praagh.

(a) Example treadmill protocol (continuous protocol)

The protocol in Table 7.2 is based on that of Taylor *et al.* (1955) and is suitable for the habitually active and sports participants. The recommended exercise intensities should produce volitional exhaustion in 9–15 minutes of continuous exercise, following a 5 minute warm-up. Thus, unless steady-state values are required, 2-minute increments are recommended.

(b) Example cycle ergometer protocol (discontinuous protocol)

A detailed description of such a protocol and associated procedures is given in Section 7.8.

7.3.3 RESULTS

Table 7.3 shows a completed pro forma for the discontinuous cycle ergometer protocol. It can be used for most protocols involving expired air collection and analysis using the Douglas bag technique, but is easily adapted for variations in data collection or experimental protocols. Figure 7.1 shows the results from a $\dot{V}O_2$max test performed on the treadmill by a trained male runner aged 21. Data for the

Figure 7.1 Results of a $\dot{V}O_2$max test performed by a 21-year-old male runner on a motorized treadmill.

Table 7.3 Douglas bag data collection during an intermittent cycle ergometer protocol

Subject: J. Bloggs	Date: 30–9–1993	Time: 2.00	Mass (kg): 81
Age: 21	DoB: 7.12.71	PB (mmHg): 753.5	Ht (cm): 180
Temp. (°C): 21	Humidity (%) 65	Protocol: Discontinuous	Ergometer: Cycle (3 min work, 3 min rest)

Bag no.	1	2	3	4	5
Work-rate (W)	200	250	300	350	400
Exercise time (min)	2–3	5–6	8–9	11–12	14–15
Collection time (s)	60	60	60	60	60
Temperature of expired air (°C)	24.0	24.0	23.8	24.0	24.0
Volume (l) (ATPS)	68.60	93.75	125.5	162.1	170.3
Volume of sample (l)	2.0	2.0	2.0	2.0	2.0
$\dot{V}E$ ATPS (l)	70.60	95.75	127.5	164.1	172.3
$\dot{V}E$ STPD (l min^{-1})	62.44	84.68	113.1	145.1	152.4
F_EO_2 (%)	16.13	17.03	17.37	17.71	17.82
F_ECO_2 (%)	4.30	3.46	3.34	3.25	3.22
$\dot{V}O_2$ (l min^{-1})	3.09	3.41	4.10	4.69	4.73
$\dot{V}CO_2$ (l min^{-1})	2.66	2.91	3.74	4.69	4.86
RER	0.863	0.852	0.913	1.00	1.03
Borg RPE	13	15	16	19	20
Heart rate (beats min^{-1})	154	168	183	197	198

treadmill test were collected using an Oxycon 5 automated gas analysis system (Mijnhardt Oxycon Champion, Bunnik, Netherlands). The test was continuous until volitional exhaustion, after which the subject attempted two further workloads to demonstrate a plateau in oxygen uptake.

7.4 PREDICTION OF MAXIMAL OXYGEN UPTAKE

Although a direct determination of maximal oxygen uptake is feasible with well-conditioned and highly motivated individuals, provided there is access to appropriate laboratory facilities, it is often only possible to conduct either a submaximal exercise test, or a maximum performance test in the field. The results from many such tests are then used to estimate maximal oxygen uptake (Åstrand and Ryhming, 1954; Siconolfi *et al.*, 1982; Åstrand and Rodahl, 1986).

Probably the most widely used procedure for predicting maximal oxygen uptake is the Åstrand–Ryhming (1954) nomogram. Use of the nomogram in submaximal field tests is based on measuring the heart rate response to a quantifiable form of external work for which the mechanical efficiency is known. Thus, the oxygen uptake elicited by the external work can be estimated (i.e. cycle ergometry, treadmill walking and running, stepping). The nomogram consists of scales for work-rate in cycle ergometry, and steps of 33 cm and 40 cm in height, which are located alongside a scale for oxygen uptake. Therefore, if the appropriate step height or cycle ergometry is used, then a prediction of maximal oxygen uptake can be obtained from the measured heart rate response. The value can then be age-adjusted based on empirically derived age-correction factors. Shephard (1970) produced an algorithm for a computer solution of the Åstrand–Ryhming nomogram which is easily programmed in most computer languages.

Åstrand and Rodahl (1986) described a simple submaximal cycle ergometer test which when used in conjunction with the nomogram will provide an estimate of maximal oxygen uptake. For women a work-rate of 75–100 W has been suggested, and for men 100–150 W. If the heart rate exceeds 130 beats min^{-1} the test is stopped after 6 minutes. If the heart rate is lower than 130 beats min^{-1} after a couple of minutes of exercise, the work-rate should be increased by 50 W. The steady-state heart rate response, taken as the mean of the value at 5 and 6 minutes, together with the work-rate, can then be used to predict the maximal oxygen uptake. There is error associated with the prediction of $\dot{V}O_2$max using the Åstrand–Ryhming nomogram and associated submaximal test procedures. Some of the reasons for this are: assumptions of linearity in the heart rate–oxygen uptake relationship for all subjects, decline and variation in maximum heart rate with increasing age and variations in mechanical efficiency. In addition, there are factors which affect the heart rate response to a given exercise intensity, but not maximal oxygen uptake, such as anxiety, dehydration, prolonged heavy exercise, exercise with a small muscle mass and exercise after consumption of alcohol.

The standard error for predicting maximal oxygen uptake from the studies used to validate the nomogram is 10% in relatively well-trained individuals of the same age as the original sample, but up to 15% in moderately trained individuals of different ages when the age correction factors are used. Values for untrained subjects are often underestimated, whereas elite athletes are often overestimated (Åstrand and Rodahl, 1986). This limitation in accuracy for estimation of maximal oxygen uptake is an important consideration, especially when dealing with repeated measures of subjects participating in a training study. The authors concluded that 'this drawback (in accuracy) holds true for any submaximal cardiopulmonary test'.

Another common form of submaximal test using a step or a cycle ergometer is to exercise the subject at four different exercise intensities and measure the heart rate (HR) and oxygen uptake at each work-rate (Wyndham *et al.*, 1966; Harrison *et al.*, 1980). Using linear regression, the HR–$\dot{V}O_2$ relationship is extrapolated to a predicted maximum heart rate value (e.g. maximum heart rate = 220 – age in years) to obtain an estimate of maximal oxygen uptake.

The Physical Work Capacity (PWC) test is also a popular form of submaximal exercise test, and was adopted as the cycle ergometer test for use with children in the Eurofit initiative (Council of Europe, 1988). The relationship between heart rate and work-rate is established using three or four submaximal work-rates and the PWC is calculated by extrapolation to a specific heart rate, which is most commonly 170 beats min^{-1}; hence the score is called a PWC$_{170}$. However, if the oxygen uptake can be measured directly, then it is preferable to do so, as the PWC procedure takes no account of individual variations in mechanical efficiency. This test has also been used with adults in an adjusted form where the target heart rate for the final workload was 85% of predicted maximum heart rate. Whether or not this heart rate value is achieved during the test, it is used as the criterion value for the extrapolation or interpolation of the PWC value.

There are also a large number of field tests which include an equation for the prediction of maximal oxygen uptake, such as a one-mile-walk test (Kline *et al.*, 1987), a 20 m multistage shuttle test (Léger and Lambert, 1982; Paliczka *et al.*, 1987; Boreham *et al.*, 1990), and Cooper's 12 minute walk–run test (Cooper, 1968). All these tests are maximal in that the subjects have to go as fast as possible in the walk and run tests, and for as long as possible in the multistage shuttle test. They are therefore dependent on subjects being well motivated and used to strenuous exercise. However, they are acceptable as indicators of current training status as they are all performance tests, irrespective of their accuracy in the prediction of maximal oxygen uptake. The reliability and validity of run–walk tests have been reviewed by Eston and Brodie (1985).

In conclusion, whatever form of submaximal test is adopted, whether it is based on either the work-rate–heart rate relationship or the oxygen uptake–heart rate relationship, extreme caution should be used in the interpretation of predicted maximal oxygen uptake values.

7.5 ECONOMY

7.5.1 INTRODUCTION

Economy of energy expenditure is important in any endurance event which makes demands on aerobic energy supply. If a lower oxygen uptake can be achieved through the optimization of skill and technique for a given exercise intensity, be it cross-country skiing, kayaking or running, then, all other things being equal, performance can be maintained for a longer period of time at a given exercise intensity, or at a slightly increased exercise intensity for the same period of time. Although the measurement of economy of energy expenditure described here is that of running economy, similar principles, procedures and protocols also apply to other activities. One such activity that is also considered is that of load carriage, which may have an effect on economy, kinematics and efficiency of movement.

Running economy can be defined as the metabolic cost, measured as oxygen uptake per kilogram per minute for a given treadmill speed and slope. A lower oxygen uptake for a given running speed is therefore interpreted as a better running economy.

There is a strong correlation between $\dot{V}O_2$max and distance running performance in studies based on a wide range of running capabilities (Cooper, 1968; Costill *et al.*, 1973). This relationship is not evident in a homogeneous sample of elite runners (Conley and Krahenbuhl, 1980). However, running economy is correlated significantly with distance running performance (Costill, 1972; Costill *et al.*, 1973; Conley and Krahenbuhl, 1980) and therefore may, in part, account for why $\dot{V}O_2$max is not a good predictor.

7.5.2 METHODOLOGY

Running economy is measured by means of establishing the oxygen cost to running speed (or speed and gradient) relationship. Many of the studies in the literature have entailed comparisons of measures of running economy for a single running speed (e.g. equivalent to race pace and/or training pace). Nevertheless, there is value in measuring oxygen uptake over a range of running speeds, especially if comparing the performance of children and adults.

In order to obtain a 'true' measure of running economy at a range of running speeds the oxygen uptake must be measured under steady-state conditions. The subject should be exercising in the aerobic range (i.e. no significant contribution to metabolic energy from anaerobic sources). Åstrand and Rodahl (1986) suggested that $\dot{V}O_2$max protocols based on work-rates where a steady state of oxygen uptake is achieved have the advantage of simultaneously establishing relationships between submaximal oxygen cost and speed of performance. Similarly, measures of running economy can be made at the same time as the establishment of blood lactate responses (see Chapter 10 by Jones and Doust). When the $\dot{V}O_2$max of the subject is known, it is common practice to select four running speeds which are predicted to elicit 60%, 70%, 80% and 90% of $\dot{V}O_2$max.

(a) Protocol

A protocol for measurement of running economy is described in section 7.9. This protocol and associated procedures can easily be adapted for other forms of ergometry.

7.5.3 RESULTS

Figure 7.2 shows the relationships between oxygen cost and running speed for three groups of adult male runners: 10 elite, 10 club and 10 recreational runners. There was a significant increase ($p < 0.001$) in the oxygen cost of running over the range of speeds analysed

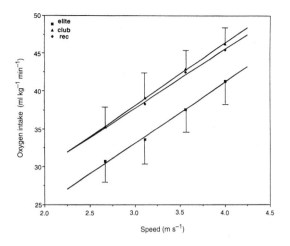

Figure 7.2 Oxygen cost to running speed relationship for three groups of ten adult male runners: elite, club and recreational.

(2.67–4.00 m s^{-1}) in all three groups. Linear regression equations for the three groups are:

Elite $\dot{V}O_2$ (ml kg^{-1} min^{-1}) = 8.07 × SPEED (m s^{-1}) + 8.87

$$(r = 0.99; r^2 = 0.98)$$

Club $\dot{V}O_2$ (ml kg^{-1} min^{-1}) = 8.27 × SPEED (m s^{-1}) + 13.27

$$(r = 0.99; r^2 = 0.98)$$

Rec $\dot{V}O_2$ (ml kg^{-1} min^{-1}) = 7.80 × SPEED (m s^{-1}) + 14.35

$$(r = 0.99; r^2 = 0.98)$$

There was a significant difference ($p < 0.001$) in the oxygen cost of running in the three groups. The elite group required significantly lower ($p < 0.001$) oxygen uptakes than either the club or recreational runners (mean difference of 4.7 ml kg^{-1} min^{-1}; 11.5%). The recreational runners appeared to have slightly better running economy at the higher running speeds than the club runners (Figure 7.2). Blood lactate values revealed that not all the recreational runners were meeting the energy requirements by aerobic sources alone, which would account for the less steep slope of their regression line. It is therefore important to ensure that comparisons of running economy are made on subjects who are exercising aerobically so that steady-state oxygen uptake values reflect the energy requirements of the exercise.

Figure 7.3 shows the relationships between oxygen cost and running speed for two groups of male runners: adults aged 21.3 ± 2.3 years and children aged 11.9 ± 1.0 years (Cooke *et al.*, 1991). There was a significant increase ($p <$ 0.001) in the oxygen cost of running over the range of speeds studied (2.67, 3.11, 3.56 and 4.0 m s^{-1}) in both the children and adults. The children required a significantly greater ($p <$ 0.001) $\dot{V}O_2$, on average 7 ml kg^{-1} min^{-1} (18.5%), for any given running speed. The divergence of the two regression lines shows the significant difference (ANCOVA; $p < 0.05$) in the $\dot{V}O_2$ response of the children and the adults over the range of speeds. Slopes of 10.87 for the children and 9.05 for the adults equate to a difference of 5.8 ml kg^{-1} min^{-1} at 2.67 m s^{-1} and 8.6 ml kg^{-1} min^{-1} at 4.0 m s^{-1}.

As the correlation between oxygen uptake and body mass is non-significant when oxygen uptake is expressed in ml kg$^{-0.75}$ min^{-1} (Kleiber, 1975), the ANCOVA was repeated with $\dot{V}O_2$ expressed in ml kg$^{-0.75}$ min^{-1} to establish whether the group differences in the oxygen cost of unloaded running could be accounted for by differences in body mass. Figure 7.4 shows that there was no significant difference between the groups, as the regression lines became similar. For an explanation of the analysis of covariance procedure and its application, see Volume 1, Chapter 11 by Winter and Nevill).

7.5.4 DISCUSSION

(a) Adult running economy values

The running economy results for the three groups of adult male runners reflect that elite runners have trained themselves in the technique of running, optimizing their running style to produce significantly lower oxygen uptake values for any given running speed. This finding is in agreement with other cross-sectional studies which have generally reported that highly-trained distance runners have better running economy than runners of club and recreational standard, but there is variation in economy within each standard of running (Costill and Fox, 1969; Costill, 1972; Pollock, 1973; Bransford and Howley, 1977; Conley and Krahenbuhl, 1980; Morgan *et al.*, 1995). Longitudinal studies have also shown that running economy can

Figure 7.3 Oxygen cost (ml kg^{-1} min^{-1}) to running speed relationship for two groups of well-trained male runners: 8 boys and 8 men (Cooke *et al.*, 1991).

Figure 7.4 Oxygen cost (ml kg$^{-0.75}$ min^{-1}) to running speed relationships for two groups of well-trained male runners: 8 boys and 8 men (Cooke *et al.*, 1991).

be improved with training (Conley *et al.*, 1981).

It is fairly well established that there is a U-shaped relationship between stride length or stride frequency and energy cost at a given unloaded walking or running speed (Cavanagh and Williams, 1982). Moreover, it appears that the curve is relatively flat near to the optimum stride length / stride frequency combination (Cavanagh and Williams, 1982). As a result small deviations from the normal pattern have little or no effect on energy cost. Freely chosen stride length / stride frequency combinations are known to be close to optimum (Cavanagh and Williams, 1982). However, variations in stride length and stride frequency have been shown to increase the oxygen uptake for a given running speed, thereby making the movement less economical. This has been found in experiments where runners have made acute adjustments to their running technique by either deliberately overstriding or understriding. Both forms of adjustment therefore decrease economy, which led researchers to the conclusion that runners adopt a stride length / stride frequency combination that best suits them in terms of running economy. However, the research that has led to this viewpoint is based on experiments that incorporate acute rather than chronic changes to running kinematics. In the case of competitive athletes, the stride length / stride frequency combination has developed as a result of long-term training. The effect of stride manipulation on running economy can be demonstrated easily in the laboratory.

The effect of posture on running economy can be assessed by altering head position. In one study, runners were required to run with their eyes focussed on a target 2 m in front of them at eye level, to produce an upright posture, or 1 m in front of them at floor level to induce a bent-over posture. Running economy was lower in the bent-over position (Jordan and Cooke, 1998). The protocol outlined in Section 7.9 can be used to evaluate the effects of the adjustments of either head position or stride length. When altering stride length it is necessary to measure stride frequency using a stopwatch to time a set number of stride cycles. Changes in stride length (SL) can then be calculated from the stride frequency (SF) and speed of the treadmill, using the formula SL (m) = SPEED (m s^{-1}) / SF (str s^{-1}). If required, a video camera can be set up perpendicular to the line of running to record the runner. This allows the changes in posture to be checked by simple measurements taken from the video images.

One criticism of comparing weight-corrected oxygen uptake values between individuals or groups is that oxygen uptake per kilogram body mass is not itself independent of body mass. Since the elite subjects had a lower mean body mass, the differences between the elite, club and recreational runners would be increased only slightly if oxygen uptake was expressed in ml kg$^{-0.75}$ min^{-1}.

(b) Child and adult running economy values

The mass-specific equations relating oxygen uptake to running speed for both children and adults shown in Figure 7.3 are similar to others reported in the literature (Åstrand, 1952; Margaria *et al.*, 1963; Davies, 1980). Some variation in equations due to population bias, treadmill type, and measurement techniques is to be expected. However, the mean difference between children and adults of 8 ml kg^{-1} min^{-1} in oxygen uptake is similar to that of other studies.

Smaller animals are metabolically more active than larger ones. This difference is also apparent in a comparison of mass-specific resting metabolic rates of children and adults. If the estimated resting metabolic rate is subtracted from the gross oxygen cost of running shown in Figure 7.3 then the difference between the regression lines decreases by 1.8 ml kg^{-1} min^{-1} (25%). Resting metabolic rate was estimated from the data of Altman and Dittmer (1968) using the formula of DuBois and DuBois (1916) for estimating body surface area.

The correlation between metabolic rate per

unit of body size and body mass is non-significant when metabolic rate is divided by body mass to the power of 0.75 (Kleiber, 1975). The data for boys and men shown in Figure 7.4 are consistent with this established comparative measure of metabolic body size.

The data also agree closely with a power function developed to predict the mass-specific oxygen cost of running from body mass and running speed in over 50 animal species (Taylor *et al.*, 1982). The power function was indicated by:

$$\frac{\dot{V}O_2}{M} = 0.533 \times M^{-0.316} \times V + 0.300 \times M^{-0.303}$$

where $\dfrac{\dot{V}O_2}{M}$ = oxygen cost $(ml\ kg^{-1}s^{-1})$

V = velocity $(m\ s^{-1})$

M = body mass (kg)

The analogy between animals of different mass (from the flying squirrel with a mass of 0.063 kg to zebu cattle with a mass of 254 kg) would appear to suggest that differences in the relationship between oxygen cost and running speed in children and adults might be expected. However, Eston *et al.* (1993) showed that when body mass was used as a covariate (i.e. the dependent variable of oxygen uptake was linearly adjusted such that comparisons were made as if all subjects had the same body mass) differences between the oxygen uptake of boys and men running at the same speeds were non-significant. The use of scaling techniques to partition out the effects of size is currently an area of renewed interest and investigation, and is discussed in greater detail in Volume 1, Chapter 11 by Winter and Nevill.

Rowland (1990) has suggested a number of factors that might explain the differences in running economy between children and adults:

1. Ratio of surface area to mass: as discussed previously, differences in BMR may account for something of the order of 25% of the greater oxygen cost of running in children compared with adults. This difference in BMR is based on the surface area law as described in Chapter 6 of this text.

2. Stride frequency: the higher oxygen uptake for a given running speed in children may be partly explained by the necessarily higher stride frequency, resulting in the more frequent braking and acceleration of the centre of mass of the body, and the increased metabolic cost of producing more muscle contractions (Unnithan and Eston, 1990).

3. Immature running mechanics: the running styles of children are different from those of adults, with changes occurring through the growing years to adulthood (Wickstrom, 1983). However, the extent to which variations in running style with age might explain the differences between adults and children in the relationship between oxygen uptake and running speed is as yet unknown.

4. Speed–mass mismatch: the speed at which a muscle contracts is inversely related to the force generated. Thus, as muscles contract more quickly they produce less force (Hill, 1939). Davies (1980) suggested that an imbalance of these two factors might help to explain the differences between children and adults in running economy. This suggestion was based on observations that when children were loaded with a weight jacket their oxygen uptake per kilogram total mass decreased, and approached adult values. However, similar experiments have revealed different results, suggesting that children and adults may be equally efficient at running with different forms of loading (Thorstensson, 1986; Cooke *et al.*, 1991).

5. Differences in anaerobic energy: it is well established that children are unable to produce anaerobic energy as effectively as adults. It is therefore important that subjects are exercising aerobically to prevent any inflation of child–adult differences in running economy values due to anaerobic energy contributions in the adult subjects.

6. Less efficient ventilation: children need to ventilate more than adults for each litre of oxygen consumed (i.e. $\dot{V}E/\dot{V}O_2$, the ventilatory equivalent for oxygen is greater in children). These differences in ventilation patterns in children and adults may contribute to the differences in economy, since during maximal exercise the oxygen cost of ventilation may reach 14–19% of total oxygen uptake.

Sex differences in the running economy of six-year-old children have been reported in terms of absolute and mass-specific oxygen uptake values, but oxygen uptake values expressed relative to fat-free mass were not different. The conclusion was that the sex differences in running economy may reflect an increase in aerobic energy demands associated with the greater muscle mass of the boys (Morgan *et al.*, 1999). For anyone interested in running economy it is worthwhile to read the collection of papers from a symposium on this topic that are introduced by Morgan (1992).

7.6 EFFICIENCY

7.6.1 INTRODUCTION

Efficiency is defined as:

$$\%\text{Efficiency} = \frac{\text{output}}{\text{input}} \times 100$$

In order to produce an efficiency ratio, both the numerator and the denominator have to be measured. With regard to activities such as walking, running and load carriage, there are several definitions of efficiency which are based on different forms of numerator and denominator in the efficiency equation (Whipp and Wasserman, 1969; Gaesser and Brooks, 1975). However, the numerator is always based on some measure of work done (either internal, external or both) and the denominator is based on some measure of metabolic rate (oxygen uptake).

These efficiency ratios are defined as:
Gross efficiency

$$\%\text{Efficiency} = \frac{\text{Work accomplished} \times 100}{\text{Energy expended}}$$
$$= \frac{W \times 100}{E}$$

Net efficiency

$$\%\text{Efficiency} = \frac{\text{Work accomplished} \times 100}{\text{Energy expended above that at rest}}$$
$$= \frac{W \times 100}{E-e}$$

Apparent or work efficiency

$$\%\text{Efficiency} = \frac{\text{Work accomplished} \times 100}{\text{Energy expended above unloaded}}$$
$$= \frac{W \times 100}{EL - EU}$$

Delta efficiency

$$\%\text{Efficiency} = \frac{\text{Delta work accomplished}}{\text{Delta energy}}$$
$$= \frac{DW \times 100}{DE}$$

where:
W = caloric equivalent of mechanical work done
E = gross caloric output
e = resting caloric output
EL = caloric output loaded condition
EU = caloric output unloaded condition
DW = caloric equivalent of increment in work performed above previous work-rate
DE = increment in caloric output above that at previous work-rate.

These definitions of efficiency are not a complete set and have received criticism by several authors (e.g. Stainsby *et al.*, 1980; Cavanagh and Kram, 1985).

Muscle efficiency is the efficiency of the conversion of chemical energy into mechanical energy at the cross-bridges and is based on phosphorylative coupling and contraction coupling, which are essentially linked in series. Phosphorylative coupling efficiency, which is defined as:

$$\frac{\text{Free energy conserved as ATP}}{\text{Free energy of oxidized food}} \times 100$$

has been estimated to be between 40 and 60% (Krebs and Kornberg, 1957). Contraction coupling, the conversion of energy stored as phosphates into tension in the muscle, is of the order of 50% efficient, giving an overall theoretical maximum muscle efficiency of 30% (Whipp and Wasserman, 1969; Wilkie, 1974; Gaesser and Brooks, 1975). Given a maximum value of only 30% for muscle efficiency, it is of interest to examine why gross efficiency values quoted in the literature for activities such as running are often considerably higher, and can even exceed 100% using certain forms of calculation in the estimation of mechanical work done (Norman *et al.*, 1976).

Measures of whole-body efficiency or implied changes based on the different $\dot{V}O_2$ responses of children and adults to unloaded running (Davies, 1980) do not indicate the efficiency of muscle. The different definitions of efficiency quoted above are therefore important when trying to compare values from various sources.

The efficiency experiment which will be described in detail is that originally proposed by Lloyd and Zacks (1972). It was designed to measure the mechanical efficiency of running against a horizontal impeding force.

7.6.2 METHODOLOGY

The problem of accurately measuring external work in horizontal running was overcome, to a large extent, by Lloyd and Zacks (1972), who reported an experimental procedure in which they used a quantifiable external workload in the form of a horizontal impeding force, on adult subjects running on the treadmill. Loaded running efficiency (LRE) was then calculated for a given running speed from the linear relationship between metabolic rate (oxygen uptake) and external work-rate. The

value of LRE is therefore consistent with apparent or work efficiency as defined by Whipp and Wasserman (1969). This method was also used by Cooke *et al.* (1991) to test the hypothesis that there are differences in LRE between children and adults.

Protocol

The protocol and procedures for the LRE experiment are described in detail in Section 7.10.

7.6.3 RESULTS

The results presented here are from a comparison of LRE values between a group of well-trained boys and men (Cooke *et al.*, 1991). Figure 7.5 shows that no significant differences were found between the two groups in terms of LRE and the effects of speed. The mean LRE was 43.8% for the boys and 42.9% for the men.

7.6.4 DISCUSSION

The major finding from the horizontal impeding force experiment on boys and men is that there is no significant difference between the LRE values. The mean LRE values quoted in the results fall between the small number of values published in the literature (36%, Lloyd

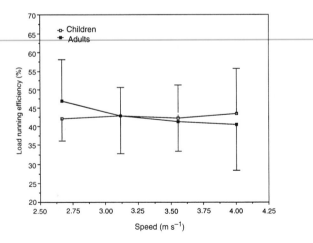

Figure 7.5 Loaded running efficiency values (means ±SD) for two groups of well-trained male runners: 8 boys and 8 men (Cooke *et al.*, 1991).

and Zacks, 1972; 39.1%, Zacks, 1973; 53.8%, Asmussen and Bonde-Peterson, 1974). These data support the hypothesis that there is no significant difference in efficiency between children and adults in the performance of external work.

Measures of mechanical efficiency for other forms of ergometry such as the cycle or the step are necessary for the estimation of energy expenditure from mechanical work done when $\dot{V}O_2$ is not measured. For example, such values form the basis of the Åstrand–Ryhming (1954) nomogram, when only the mechanical work done is known. Oxygen uptake is estimated from the work performed in stepping or cycling, which together with the heart rate response can be used to estimate $\dot{V}O_2$max. A description of how to measure mechanical efficiency in both stepping and cycle ergometry is given in Section 7.11.

7.7 LOAD CARRIAGE

7.7.1 EFFECTS ON ECONOMY

Load carriage is an activity that provides an appropriate focus for the study of economy, including the need to consider energy expenditure, posture and kinematics. Load carriage is of interest from both an occupational and recreational perspective, where relatively heavy loads are carried for prolonged periods of time. The physiology of load carriage has been extensively studied, with the effect of the position of the carried load on energy expenditure receiving particular attention. Carrying loads on the head is a common method of load carriage in both Africa and Asia (Datta and Ramanathan, 1970; Maloiy *et al.*, 1986). Maloiy *et al.* (1986) found that African women could carry loads of up to 20% body weight with no increase in energy cost and that thereafter oxygen uptake rose proportionately with added load, i.e. an added load of 30% body weight produced a 10% increase in oxygen uptake, an added load of 40% body weight produced an increase in oxygen uptake of 20%.

It would seem then that the energy cost of carrying loads is not fixed but can be affected by the position of the load. This fact may have implications for different load carriage systems. Again many comparative studies have been undertaken. Datta and Ramanathan (1971) compared seven modes of carrying loads. The results indicated the best economy for a double pack system, where the load was shared between the back and front of the trunk. The order in terms of energy cost from lowest to highest was: double pack, load carried on basket on head, rucksack, load supported by strap on forehead, rice bag, yoke and finally load in canvas bags carried by hands. The oxygen uptake associated with the double pack was significantly lower than that associated with all of the other methods except for the load carried in a basket on the head. Legg and Mahanty (1985) compared five modes of carrying loads close to the trunk. No significant differences were found between any of the load carriage systems but there was a consistent trend for the double pack to be associated with the lowest physiological cost. Lloyd and Cooke (2000) also observed that the economy of level and inclined walking was greater when wearing a rucksack which distributed the weight around the front and back of the trunk, compared to a traditional rucksack (Figure 7.6).

Kirk and Schneider (1992) compared the performance of internal and external frame packs. The results indicated no significant difference in economy between the two packs, although there was a consistent trend for the internal frame pack to elicit lower oxygen uptake values than the external frame pack. The postulated advantage for the internal frame pack is that the load can be carried closer to the body.

7.7.2 EFFECTS ON STRIDE PATTERN

The majority of previous studies relating to the kinematics of load carriage have been concerned with alterations to stride length and frequency. Theoretically, changes in stride length / stride frequency associated with acute responses to load carriage may lead to an increased energy cost, therefore changing both economy and efficiency. The studies reported, however, all deal with acute perturbations to the walking gait. The effect of chronic changes are less well known, but given the long term changes in stride length / stride frequency achieved by athletes it is possible that adaptation may take place.

There is no consensus concerning the effect of load carriage on stride length / stride frequency. Martin and Nelson (1986) observed an increase in stride frequency, 2% for men and a 5% for women, when carrying a load of 36 kg, made up of military clothing, waist belt and rucksack, at 6.34 km h^{-1}. Cooke *et al.* (1991) reported a significant difference in stride frequency when loads of 5 and 10% body weight were carried around the trunk. The magnitudes of the increases were 1.5 and 5% above the unloaded condition. Thorstensson (1986) found significant differences in stride frequency for both boys and men when carrying a load of 10% body weight around the trunk at 10 km h^{-1} for the boys and 11 km h^{-1} for the men. The percentage increases were 1.5% and 1.9% for the men and boys respectively. Kram *et al.* (1987) reported a significant increase in stride frequency when 60% body weight was carried at 10.8 km h^{-1} using a method in which the load is attached to either end of a bamboo pole which is carried across the shoulders. They found no significant difference in stride frequency when the same load was carried in a traditional rucksack. A number of other studies, covering a wide range of loading conditions and speeds, have reported no significant changes in stride frequency. These include Robertson *et al.* (1982) (loads of 0–15% body weight carried at speeds between 3.2 and 8.1 km h^{-1}), Maloiy *et al.* (1986) (34 kg carried on the head) and Kinoshita (1985) (loads of 20 and 40% body weight carried at 4.5 km h^{-1} in a traditional rucksack and a double pack system).

7.7.3 EFFECTS ON TRUNK ANGLE

It would seem that the alterations to stride length / stride frequency elicited by load carriage are relatively small and, on their own, unlikely to have a significant effect on energy cost. It is possible, however, that these small alterations may either contribute to, or combine with, changes in other variables and thus have a significant effect on the economy of load carriage. One of the most important changes in kinematics associated with load carriage is an alteration in trunk angle. This is an aspect of load carriage that has received scant attention.

Kinoshita (1985) found that both back and front/back load carriage systems were associated with increased forward lean but that the forward lean associated with the back system, (11°), was considerably greater than for the double pack system. Bloom and Woodhull-McNeal (1987) observed increased forward lean whilst standing for both an internal and an external frame pack loaded with 27% body weight, but did not quantify it. Martin and Nelson (1986) showed that forward lean increased when a load was carried on the back but not when distributed about the waist. When carrying a total of 36 kg (19 kg on the back) forward lean was increased by approximately 10°. Gordon *et al.* (1983) also noted that forward lean increased with the addition of load but did not quantify this.

Another form of measurement that has been used to make comparisons between different load carriage systems, loads, speeds and gradients is the extra load index (ELI) (Taylor *et al.*, 1980). This is a measure of relative economy, which is calculated by dividing the oxygen consumption when carrying a load (ml kg total mass^{-1} min^{-1}) by the oxygen consumption for no load (ml kg body mass^{-1} min^{-1}). An ELI of 1 indicates that the energy cost of carrying 1 kg of extra load is the same as that of 1 kg of live mass; a value >1 indicates a reduction in the economy of load carriage; a value <1 indicates an increased economy. Using this technique, the results of Lloyd and Cooke (2000) suggested that the energy cost of carrying a kilogram of extra load is greater than that of carrying a kilogram of live mass.

7.7.4 METHODOLOGY

Numerous protocols have been used to assess the effects of load carriage on economy and efficiency. Various treadmill walking and running speeds and both uphill and downhill gradients have been used to compare a variety of different forms of load carriage. The methodology for assessing the effects of load carriage on economy is very similar to that described for running economy in section 7.9. The protocols typically consist of steady state exercise, walking or running at each speed and gradient combination for a period of a minimum of three minutes.

Protocol

A protocol for investigating the effects of load carriage on economy is described in detail in Section 7.10.

The experimental protocol and results presented here are based on the work of Lloyd and Cooke (2000). The protocol involved walking downhill at a speed of 3 km h^{-1} for 3 minutes at gradients of 27%, 22%, 17%, 12% and 5%. Subjects were then given a rest of 20 minutes, after which they walked uphill at a speed of 3 km h^{-1} for 3 minutes at gradients of 0%, 5%, 10%, 15% and 20%. Expired air was collected throughout both the downhill and uphill sections. The protocol was completed three times. On each occasion the subjects completed one of three conditions in random order: unloaded, loaded with a traditional rucksack and loaded with a rucksack that incorporated front pockets. This distributed the load around the front and back of the trunk. The mass of both 65 litre packs and contents was 25.6 kg. All the treadmill tests were filmed with a video camera.

7.7.5 RESULTS

(a) Economy

Statistical analysis (3 × 10 repeated measures ANOVA) of the data indicated that unloaded walking requiring a significantly lower ($p < 0.05$)

Figure 7.6 Oxygen uptake values (means ±SD) for walking with rucksack with front and back pockets (■), traditional rucksack (□) and unloaded conditions (▨)(* denotes $p < 0.05$ between the two rucksacks).

$\dot{V}O_2$ than either of the loaded conditions. On average the extra oxygen cost, above that for unloaded walking, associated with the front and back loading rucksack was 5.4 ml kg^{-1} min^{-1} (45.1%), whilst that associated with the traditional rucksack was 6.3 ml kg^{-1} min^{-1} (52.8%). The $\dot{V}O_2$ was also about 8% lower ($p < 0.05$) for the front and back loading rucksack on the uphill gradients (Figure 7.6).

(b) Stride length

Mean values of stride length (m) and percentage changes from the unloaded condition at each gradient are shown in Table 7.4. Changes in stride length were greater in the loaded condition ($p < 0.05$). Across the whole protocol, the traditional rucksack and the front and back loading rucksack were associated with, on average, 3.2 cm (3%) and 5.1 cm (5%) shorter stride lengths, respectively, although there was no significant difference ($p > 0.05$) in stride length for the two conditions. The reduction in stride length associated with both rucksacks was slightly more marked during the uphill section than the downhill section.

Table 7.4 Mean stride length (m) (±SD) and meanpercentage change (±SD) from the unloaded condition at each gradient

	Gradient									
	−27%	−22%	−17%	−12%	−5%	0%	5%	10%	15%	20%
Front and back Mean stride length (±s)	0.86	0.88	0.89	0.95	1.04	1.12	1.13	1.14	1.11	1.08
	0.07	0.06	0.07	0.08	0.08	0.08	0.09	0.12	0.11	0.11
Mean	−5.4	−5.4	−5.8	−4.0	0.1	0.5	−5.7	−5.0	−5.7	−7.8
% change (±s)	5.8	5.4	5.9	5.8	4.6	4.2	5.5	4.1	5.7	5.6
Traditional Mean stride length (±s)	0.86	0.89	0.91	0.99	1.06	1.14	1.17	1.15	1.12	1.08
	0.07	0.07	0.06	0.12	0.10	0.11	0.15	0.14	0.13	0.13
Mean	−5.1	−4.3	−3.7	−0.4	1.9	1.6	−2.0	−3.6	−4.8	−7.6
% change (±s)	6.5	4.5	4.4	4.8	7.1	7.2	6.0	8.3	8.0	5.9
Unloaded Mean stride length (±s)	0.91	0.93	0.95	0.99	1.04	1.12	1.19	1.20	1.18	1.18
	0.07	0.08	0.08	0.11	0.11	0.09	0.13	0.13	0.13	0.13

(c) Trunk angle

The increase in forward lean was greater whilst wearing the traditional rucksack when standing still and walking ($p < 0.001$). The increases amounted to about 4° and 14° for the front and back loading and traditional rucksacks, respectively. The extra forward lean induced by the traditional rucksack also tended to increase as the slope increased, whereas it remained relatively constant in the front- and back-loaded condition.

7.8 PRACTICAL 1: DIRECT DETERMINATION OF $\dot{V}O_2$ USING A DISCONTINUOUS CYCLE ERGOMETER PROTOCOL

7.8.1 PROTOCOL

1. Warm-up: cycle for 3 minutes at 50 W for females or 100 W for males.
2. Rest: 2 minutes.
3. Initial work-rate: 50–150 W for females, 100–200 W for males, depending on type of subject, e.g. lighter less active subjects would be set lower work-rates (heart rate response during warm-up is a good guide to selection of appropriate work-rate). Record heart rate every 30 s. Collect expired air for last 30 s of work-rate.
4. Rest: 3 minutes (during which time team members can analyse expired air).
5. Increase work-rate by 50 W and repeat stages 3 and 4 of the protocol.
6. At higher workloads increments of 25 W may be used. If the subject cannot complete a 3- minute workload then a gas collection can be made on a signal from the subject (minimum 30 s, preferably 1 minute).
7. Recovery: at the end of the test the subject should continue to pedal gently at a low work-rate of the order of 25–50 W.

The subject should be closely monitored at all times, both during the test and recovery, since the probability of some sort of cardiac episode occurring is higher at exercise intensities above 80% of age-related maximum heart rate and during the 20 minutes or so following the cessation of the test. The subject may need verbal encouragement to complete the latter stages of the test in order to attain a maximal oxygen consumption.

Although heart rate can be monitored effectively by radio telemetry, it is preferable to use chest electrodes linked to an oscilloscope and/or chart recorder. This enables the shape of the electrocardiogram (ECG) to be observed. In the event of a gross abnormality or arrhythmia occurring, the test can be stopped and the hard copy of the ECG examined by a qualified person. Clearly the more sophisticated the ECG equipment used, the more objective will be the ECG analysis. It is possible to see arrhythmias such as ventricular ectopics with a simple three-lead system, which is available in most laboratories.

7.8.2 PROCEDURES

The procedures for the cycle ergometer protocol are as described, but they can be generalized in most cases to any direct determination of $\dot{V}O_2$max using the Douglas bag technique.

1. The procedures and protocol should be explained to the subject, and should include a statement that he or she can stop the test at any time.

2.   The subject should sign an informed consent form.
3.   The name, age and sex of the subject should be recorded.
4.   The stature (m) and body mass (kg) of the subject should be measured.
5.   The heart rate measuring device or ECG electrodes should be attached and a check made that a good signal is being recorded or displayed.
6.   The handlebar and saddle positions should be adjusted to suit the size of the subject, especially as subjects can become uncomfortable during the latter stages of the test, resulting in the premature cessation of the test. If the saddle is too low, the subject may experience undue fatigue in the quadriceps muscles and possibly pain in the knee joint. If the saddle is too high, the subject will have to raise and lower his/her left and right hips repeatedly in order to maintain effective contact with the pedals. The recommended position is obtained by placing the middle of the foot on the pedal at the bottom of its travel. If the saddle height is correct the leg will be very slightly flexed. More sophisticated guidelines are available in the literature, but the simple procedure described here works well in most cases. Competitive cyclists will have their own measures for obtaining an optimal saddle height and handlebar position. They also prefer their own bicycles mounted on turbo-trainers. More sophisticated examples, such as the King Cycle (High Wycombe, UK) have gained wider acceptance in exercise physiology laboratories.
7.   The respiratory value and mouthpiece should be connected to allow room air to be inspired and then expired into the Douglas bag.
8.   The nose clip should be placed on the subject's nose so that all the expired air passes into the Douglas bag.
9.   The warm-up and the test proper should be completed according to the protocol described above.

With respect to the control of cycle ergometers, the following points should be considered.

1.   All cycle ergometers should be calibrated regularly according to the manufacturer's instructions.
2.   Recommended pedalling frequencies for mechanically-braked cycle ergometers are traditionally of the order of 50–60 rev min^{-1}. Although a frequency of 60 rev min^{-1} is comfortable and efficient for low work-rates, it is recommended that the pedalling frequency be increased above work-rates of the order of 200 W to 70–80 rev min^{-1}. This will decrease the force required per pedal revolution, thus decreasing the strength component of the pedalling action and the probability of cessation of the test due to fatigue in the quadriceps.
3.   It is always important to inform the subject in advance of alterations in work-rate in continuous protocols. This is especially important in the use of electronically-braked cycle ergometers, which automatically alter the resistance at the pedals to accommodate changes in pedalling frequency, thus keeping the power output constant. A tired subject pedalling at 200 W with an unexpected increase of 50 W, and who is already pedalling at the lower end of the pedalling frequency range (approximately 50 rev min^{-1}) may well let the cadence drop still further with the increase in load. This will result in a further increase in resistance offered at the pedals. The result could then be that the

subject terminates the test, so a warning of pending increases in workload should always be given, together with encouragement to pedal faster to accommodate the increase in work-rate on an electronically-braked cycle ergometer.

4. Mechanically-braked cycle ergometers of the type used in most laboratories require the subject to pedal at a constant frequency in order to maintain a constant power output. To help maintain a constant pedalling frequency the subject may pedal in time to a metronome and/or use the digital display of pedalling frequency which is now fitted to most new cycle ergometers. Another alternative is to mount small mechanical cams or optoelectric devices on the flywheel to count the number of revolutions during each workload. Use of these suggestions should help ensure that quantification of external power output is as objective as possible.

7.8.3 CALCULATIONS

Gas analysis, volume measurement, $\dot{V}O_2$, $\dot{V}CO_2$ and respiratory exchange ratio calculations should be performed in accordance with the procedures outlined in Chapter 6 of this text.

7.8.4 RESULTS

Table 7.3 shows a completed pro forma for the discontinuous cycle ergometer test described above.

Some questions to consider for the measurement of maximum oxygen uptake:

• What day-to-day variability might you expect in repeated measures of maximum oxygen uptake and what might be the factors that contribute to this variability?
• What are the ethical implications and methodological limitations of using direct measurements of maximal oxygen uptake on subjects who are not well accustomed to strenuous exertion?
• What are the apparent contradictions in considering the general principles of testing for maximal oxygen uptake, such as using a large muscle mass in a rhythmic movement pattern, and testing sports performers from a particular sport?
• Should maximal oxygen uptake be considered the criterion standard measure of aerobic or endurance fitness?
• What are the practical and theoretical factors that might effect whether a plateau in oxygen consumption is measurable or not?

7.9 PRACTICAL 2: MEASUREMENT OF RUNNING ECONOMY

7.9.1 PROTOCOL

The protocol outlined here is recommended by The British Association of Sport and Exercise Sciences. Where the $\dot{V}O_2$max of the subject is known, an appropriate generalized equation relating $\dot{V}O_2$ to running speed can be used to predict the running speeds that should elicit 50–90% of $\dot{V}O_2$. For example, PE Students (British Association of Sport Sciences, 1992):

Males	$n = 58$	$Y = 11.6\,X + 0.72$
Females	$n = 44$	$Y = 10.7\,X + 3.30$

where:

$Y = \dot{V}O_2$ (ml kg^{-1} min^{-1}) and X = running speed (m s^{-1})

or those cited in Section 7.5.3. However, the selection of the running speeds should take into account the state of training of the subjects, since only well-conditioned athletes can cope with running speeds that elicit 90% of $\dot{V}O_2$max

1. Warm-up: no warm-up other than gentle jogging and stretching is required, since the first workload represents a running speed approximately equivalent to 60% $\dot{V}O_2$max. Ideally, naive subjects should be habituated to treadmill running on a previous occasion so $\dot{V}O_2$ values will be a true reflection of running economy.
2. Test: the protocol consists of 16 minutes of running on a level treadmill during which running speed is increased every 4 minutes. For children aged less than 15 years, a 3-minute interval is recommended.
3. Expired air should be collected for the 4th, 8th, 12th and 16th minute for adults, and for the 3rd, 6th, 9th and 12th minute for children.

7.9.2 DATA COLLECTION, GAS ANALYSIS AND CALCULATIONS

Follow the procedures outlined in Chapter 6 for the collection and analysis of expired air using the Douglas bag technique, and the calculation of oxygen uptake. Alternatively an automated gas analysis system can be used to collect and analyse the expired air (as in Figure 6.3).

7.9.3 RESULTS

The results from the experiment should be plotted with oxygen uptake on the y axis and running speed on the x axis. The method of least squares can then be used to establish the extent to which the data conform to the expected linear relationship, with the production of a linear regression equation, correlation coefficient (r) and coefficient of determination ($r^2 =$ variance accounted for) (see Volume 1, Chapter 10 by Nevill and Atkinson). Group data can then be compared using appropriate statistical techniques such as ANOVA or ANCOVA. Examples of group comparisons for both equations and graphs appear in Sections 7.5.3 and 7.5.4.

Some questions to consider on running economy and related areas of study include:

- Is it appropriate to be totally confident in extrapolating forwards or backwards using an individual subject's equation that allows you to predict oxygen uptake from running speed?
- What applications might make use of extrapolations from such equations?
- What happens to the oxygen uptake / speed relationship when the subject walks instead runs?

7.10 PRACTICAL 3: MEASUREMENT OF LOADED RUNNING EFFICIENCY (LRE)

7.10.1 PROTOCOL

For each running speed the subject should run unloaded for 3 minutes. A horizontal imped-ing force is then exerted via weights attached to the subject by a cord running over a pulley (Figure 7.7). A total of three increasing loads can then be added to the system, one every 3 minutes (a total of 12 minutes continuous running including the 3 minutes unloaded), fol-lowed by 5 minutes rest. Weights should be individually selected such that the maximum external load applied to the system does not elicit a $\dot{V}O_2$ greater than 85% of $\dot{V}O_2$max in well-trained subjects (this value would have to be adjusted down for less active individuals as it is important that the energy expenditure is derived from aerobic metabolism and therefore reflected in the measured $\dot{V}O_2$ values). Even increments in $\dot{V}O_2$ can be achieved by predict-ing the increase in $\dot{V}O_2$ per kilogram of mass added to the pulley, on the basis of a mean LRE value from the literature of approximately 40%. Running speeds and weight increments can then be individually tailored to the subject in terms of $\dot{V}O_2$max and running economy. Where subjects represent a homogeneous sample it is better in terms of experimental design to have all subjects run at the same speeds with the same increments. Typical values for weights to be added to the pulley would be 1, 2 and 3 kg for adults and 0.5, 1 and 1.5 kg for children.

7.10.2 PROCEDURES

Collection and analysis of expired air can be performed either according to the proce-dures outlined for the Douglas bag tech-nique in Chapter 6, or using an automated gas analysis system. The data presented in Figure 7.5 and discussed in Section 7.6.4 were collected using an Oxycon 5 system). A full description of the experimental pro-cedures can be found in Cooke *et al.* (1991).

Figure 7.7 Diagram of the horizontal imped-ing force experiment used to calculate loaded running efficiency (Lloyd and Zacks, 1972).

7.10.3 CALCULATION OF LRE

Metabolic work-rate is calculated from steady-state $\dot{V}O_2$ for each load condition. A value of 20.9 kJ min^{-1} (5.0 kcal min^{-1}, 348.8 W) can be used as the energy equivalent for one litre of oxygen since this will cause no more than a 4% variation based on observed respiratory exchange ratios.

    External work-rate is calculated as the product of the force exerted by the weight over the pulley and the distance moved per unit of time by the treadmill belt. A linear regression equation is then fitted to the data, with metabolic rate as the dependent variable and exter-nal work-rate as the independent variable. Apparent efficiency of running against a hori-zontal load, or LRE, is then calculated for each speed of running by taking the inverse of the slope of the regression equation, as shown in Figure 7.8. For example, given the raw data that form the basis for Figure 7.8, the calculations are as follows:

Running speed constant at 11.2 km h^{-1} = 3.11 m s^{-1}

The calculation of metabolic work-rate (MWR) in watts is given by:

$$MWR (W) = \dot{V}O_2 (l\ min^{-1}) \times 348.8$$

where: $\dot{V}O_2$ = measured oxygen uptake for each load condition = 20.9 kJ min^{-1} = 348.8 W = 5 kcal min^{-1} = 1 litre of oxygen

The calculation of external work-rate (EWR) in watts is given by:

$$EWR (W) = M \times g \times D$$

where: M is mass (kg) applied to runner acting over pulley, g is acceleration due to gravity (m s^{-2}), D is distance moved by treadmill belt in 1 s = velocity of treadmill (m s^{-1}).

Given the following oxygen uptake values for each of four external loads measured as mass applied to the pulley the metabolic work-rate and external work-rate can be calculated according to the formulae above. These are shown in Table 7.5.

The EWR and MWR values are plotted in Figure 7.8, which also shows the linear regression equation fitted by the method of least squares. Given that EWR is the independent variable it has to be plotted on the x axis, and the dependent variable, MWR, is plotted on

Table 7.5 Example of metabolic work-rate and external work-rate results

Mass on pulley (kg)	EWR (W)	$\dot{V}O_2$ (l min^{-1})	MWR (W)
0	0.00	2.01	701.1
1	30.51	2.22	774.3
2	61.02	2.43	847.6
3	91.53	2.63	917.3

Figure 7.8 Calculation of loaded running efficiency (LRE) in the horizontal impeding force experiment for a subject running at 11.2 km h^{-1}. Values are means ± SD for data collected in two experiments completed by the same subject on different days (Cooke *et al.*, 1991).

the y axis. Loaded running efficiency expressed as a percentage is therefore given by the reciprocal of the gradient of the linear regression equation multiplied by 100:

$$\text{\% Loaded running efficiency} = (1 / 2.4) \times 100 = 41.7 \%$$

- What are the limitations involved in the measurement of loaded running efficiency?
- The example discussed in the text for this practical is concerned with a comparison of children and adults. What other applications and research questions can this procedure be used to investigate?

7.10.4 RESULTS

The results can be reported in terms of individual LRE values for each speed of running, and combined in a variety of ways depending on the aim of the experiment (e.g. either to investigate the effects of running speed on LRE or to compare the apparent efficiency of horizontal treadmill running against other forms of ergometry).

7.11 PRACTICAL 4: MEASUREMENT OF THE EFFICIENCY OF CYCLING AND STEPPING

7.11.1 CYCLE ERGOMETRY

In mechanical cycle ergometry the external power output (W) or mechanical work-rate is quantified as the product of the frictional force (N) or resistance applied to the flywheel and the distance travelled (m) by one point on the circumference of the flywheel, which gives the work done (J), divided by the time to do the work (s):

$$\text{External power output (W)} = \frac{\text{Force (N)} \times \text{Distance (m)}}{\text{Time (s)}}$$

Most cycle ergometers allow the work-rate to be set in watts, whether they are mechanically or electronically braked.

As with the LRE experiment, metabolic work-rate is calculated from steady-state $\dot{V}O_2$:

$$\text{Metabolic work-rate (W)} = (\dot{V}O_2 \, \text{l min}^{-1}) \times 348.8$$

A gross measure of efficiency can then be calculated by dividing the external power output by the metabolic power output:

$$\text{\%Gross efficiency} = \frac{\left[(\text{Force} \times \text{Distance}) \, \text{Time}\right]}{\dot{V}O_2 \, (\text{l min}^{-1}) \times 348.8} \times 100$$

Net efficiency can be calculated by dividing the external power output by net metabolic power, the latter being obtained by subtracting an estimate of resting $\dot{V}O_2$ (see Chapter 6) from the gross measured value. Provided that both the numerator and denominator are in the same units (watts, kJ min^{-1} or kcal min^{-1}) the correct ratio will be calculated and when multiplied by 100 will give percentage net efficiency.

7.11.2 STEPPING

For stepping, the external work-rate (W) is calculated as a function of the vertical height that the centre of mass of the body is raised (m). This is estimated by multiplying the step height (m) by the number of complete step cycles performed. The total vertical height is then multiplied by the force (body weight (N)), and divided by the duration (s) of the stepping exercise:

$$\text{External power output (W)} = \frac{\text{Step height (m)} \times \text{No. steps} \times \text{Weight (N)}}{\text{Time (s)}}$$

The gross and net efficiency ratios can then be calculated using the external work-rate and metabolic work-rate as for cycle ergometry

The net efficiency of stepping is of the order of 16% (Shephard *et al.*, 1968).

7.11.3 EXPERIMENTAL PROCEDURES AND PROTOCOLS

Gross and net efficiency ratios can be calculated over the submaximal range of exercise intensities, provided that the energy demands of the exercise are matched by a steady state of oxygen uptake. Efficiency values calculated for high-intensity exercise, where anaerobic sources make a significant contribution to the energy demands, will be higher than expected since under such conditions oxygen uptake will not reflect the energy demands of the exercise.

For stepping on a double 'nine-inch' step (total vertical height 45 cm) the oxygen uptake can be estimated to be:

$$\dot{V}O_2 \text{ (ml kg}^{-1} \text{ min}^{-1}) = 1.34 \times n$$

where n = number of step cycles per minute.

For example, stepping on a double step requires a six-beat cadence. Therefore stepping to a metronome set at 120 beats per minute would result in the completion of 20 step cycles per minute, giving an estimated oxygen uptake of 26.8 ml kg^{-1} min^{-1}.

A suitable submaximal range of work-rates for the above step would consist of four by three minute work-rates with metronome cadences set at 60, 90, 120 and 150 beats min^{-1}. Expired air can be collected during the third minute of each work-rate and analysed according to the methods described in Chapter 6.

Although stepping is considered to be a simple inexpensive form of ergometry, every effort must be made to ensure that the subject keeps in time with the metronome and that he/she stands up straight on a flat foot with full knee extension.

For cycle ergometry a suitable range of submaximal exercise intensities would consist of 50–150 W depending on the age, sex and condition of the subjects. As a guide, heart rate response should not exceed 85% of age-related maximum heart rate during a submaximal test. Traditionally a pedal frequency of 50 rev min^{-1} has been used in submaximal exercise tests using mechanically-braked cycle ergometers. However, 60 rev min^{-1} is often a more comfortable pedalling frequency.

Shephard *et al.* (1968) showed that over a range of submaximal loads the mean net mechanical efficiency for stepping and cycle ergometry was 16% and 23% respectively.

7.11.4 DISCUSSION

The values quoted from Shephard *et al.* (1968) represent group means for subjects performing repeated experiments in both stepping and cycling to a random design. There was more variability in stepping (coefficient of variation approximately 10%) than cycling (coefficient of variation approximately 7%). There was also some variation in mechanical efficiency values associated with loading.

Individual values for mechanical efficiency can be used as calibration factors for estimating oxygen uptake from work done, rather than having to use estimates from the literature. There are several experiments that can be conducted with either stepping or cycle ergometry to investigate variations in mechanical efficiency values. For example, the effects of pedalling frequency, stepping frequency, work-rate, saddle height, single or double step, step height and leg length in relation to step height can all be investigated.

Consider the effects that the variability in efficiency across subjects might have on estimating energy expenditure for a given task, predicting fitness (e.g. maximum oxygen uptake) and predicting performance without reference to measures of economy, based on assumptions of constant mechanical efficiency.

7.12 PRACTICAL 5: THE EFFECTS OF LOAD CARRIAGE ON THE ECONOMY OF WALKING

7.12.1 PROTOCOL

The experimental protocol involves walking at a speed of 3 km h^{-1} for 3 minutes at each selected gradient. The gradients used in the study discussed above were downhill at 27%, 22%, 17%, 12%, and 5%, which was completed first. Subjects were then given a rest of 20 minutes. After the rest subjects walked uphill at a speed of 3 km h^{-1} for 3 minutes at gradients of 0%, 5%, 10%, 15% and 20%. This gives a total test time of 50 minutes (30 minutes walking and 20 minutes resting) per subject per load condition, but allows the data to be compared directly to the results presented above. In terms of a single practical, reasonable results could be obtained for one subject using one downhill gradient of 20%, level walking and one uphill gradient of 20%. For the purpose of comparing unloaded and loaded walking it is only necessary to use two conditions, one without a rucksack and one carrying a loaded rucksack. Clearly, different rucksacks, load carriage systems or loads can be used, but this would only be practical for project work. The practical could also be adapted by looking at different walking speeds, or running with a daysack.

7.12.2 MEASUREMENTS

Follow the procedures outlined in Chapter 6 for the collection and analysis of expired air using the Douglas bag technique, and the calculation of oxygen uptake. Alternatively use an automated gas analysis system, making sure that you calibrate each system carefully before you start your testing. If you are using an automated gas analysis system it is worthwhile ensuring that you include minute ventilation, breathing frequency and tidal volume in your configuration of the system as well as oxygen consumption and carbon dioxide production.

Although not essential for the comparison of economy between unloaded and loaded walking, it is also worthwhile timing a set number of stride cycles at each workload using a stopwatch to assess whether there is any difference in stride length and frequency between the two conditions. If you have a video camera available, it is also worthwhile setting up one with the axis of the lens perpendicular to the plane of walking (about 5–6m away from the side of the treadmill should suffice). This will facilitate measurement of the forward lean of the trunk (touch-down, toe-off and mid-stance are good points for comparison) in both conditions, as well as allowing checks on the stride length and stride frequency calculations. Rating of perceived exertion and heart rate can also be recorded for each stage of the protocol.

7.12.3 RESULTS

1. Draw a graph of the results for the following variables for every stage of the protocol for each of the two (or more) loading conditions (use mean and standard deviations if you have more than one subject): oxygen consumption, minute ventilation, breathing frequency, tidal volume, heart rate, stride length, stride frequency, stride length and forward lean. Use values from the Douglas bag collected in the third minute, or the last two 30 s values from the automated gas analysis system for expired air variables.
2. Calculate ELI values for your data and compare them with the mean values presented above.
3. Compare all of your results with those presented above and, more importantly, evaluate the differences between the results for the two loading conditions. It may be worthwhile to consider whether there are any associations between changes in certain variables with loading, which might suggest some explanation of some of the physiological effects of load carriage.
4. Consider the implications, in terms of different types of validity and reliability, for designing an appropriate protocol to be used in comparing different load carriage systems. What would you need to add to the experiment in order to measure the efficiency of different load carriage systems? How might you go about doing this?

REFERENCES

Allied Dunbar National Fitness Survey (1992). *Main Findings*. Sports Council and Health Education Authority.

Altman, P.L. and Dittmer, D.S. (1968). *Metabolism* (FASBEB, Bethesda, MD).

Asmussen, E. and Bonde-Peterson, F. (1974). Apparent efficiency and storage of elastic energy in human muscles during exercise. *Acta Physiologica Scandanavica*, **92**, 537–45.

Åstrand, P.O. (1952). *Experimental Studies of Physical Working Capacity in Relation to Sex and Age*. (Munksgaard, Copenhagen).

Åstrand, P.O. and Ryhming, I. (1954). A nomogram for the calculation of aerobic capacity (physical fitness) from pulse rate during submaximal work. *Journal of Applied Physiology*, **7**, 218.

Åstrand, P.O. and Rodahl, K. (1986). *Textbook of Work Physiology, Physiological Bases of Exercise*, 3rd edn. (McGraw-Hill, New York).

Bar-Or, O. (1983). Pediatric sports medicine for the practitioner. In *Physiological Principles to Clinical Application*. (Springer, New York).

Bassett. D.R., and Howley, E.T. (1997). Maximal oxygen uptake: 'classical' versus 'contemporary' viewpoints. *Medicine and Science in Sport and Exercise*, **29**, 591–603.

Bloom, D. and Woodhull-McNeal, A.P. (1987). Postural adjustments while standing with two types of loaded backpack. *Ergonomics,* **30,** 1425–30.

Boreham, C.A.G., Paliczka, V.J. and Nichols, A.K. (1990). A comparison of PWC_{170} and 20-MST tests of aerobic fitness in adolescent schoolchildren. *Journal of Sports Medicine and Physical Fitness,* **30,** 19–23.

Bouchard, C. and Malina, R.M. (1983). Genetics of physiological fitness and motor performance. *Exercise and Sport Sciences Reviews,* **11,** 306–39.

Bransford, D.R. and Howley, E.T. (1977). Oxygen cost of running in trained and untrained men and women. *Medicine and Science in Sports and Exercise,* **9,** 41–4.

British Association of Sport and Exercise Sciences (1997). *Guidelines for the Physiological Testing of Athletes.* eds. S. Bird and R. Davison (British Association of Sport and Exercise Sciences, Leeds, UK).

British Association of Sports Sciences (1992). *Position Statement on the Physiological Assessment of the Elite Athlete.* (British Association of Sports Sciences. Physiology Section).

Cavanagh, P.R. and Williams, K.R. (1982). The effect of stride length variation on oxygen uptake during distance running. *Medicine and Science in Sports and Exercise,* **14,** 30–5.

Cavanagh, P.R. and Kram, R. (1985). The efficiency of human movement – a statement of the problem. *Medicine and Science in Sports and Exercise,* **17,** 304–8.

Conley, D.L. and Krahenbuhl, G. (1980). Running economy and distance running performance of highly trained athlete. *Medicine and Science in Sports and Exercise,* **12,** 357–60.

Conley, D.L., Krahenbuhl, G. and Burkett, L. (1981). Training for aerobic capacity and running economy. *Physician and Sportsmedicine,* **9 (4),** 107–15.

Cooke, C.B., McDonagh, M.J.N., Nevill, A.M. and Davies, C.T.M. (1991). Effects of load on oxygen intake in trained boys and men during treadmill running. *Journal of Applied Physiology,* **71,** 1237–44.

Cooper, K.H. (1968). A means of assessing maximal oxygen intake, correlation between field and treadmill testing. *Journal of American Medical Association,* **203,** 201–4.

Costill, D.L. (1972). Physiology of marathon running. *Journal of the American Medical Association,* **221,** 1024–9.

Costill, D.L. and Fox, E.L. (1969). Energetics of marathon running. *Medicine and Science in Sports,* **1,** 81–6.

Costill, D.L., Thomson, H. and Roberts, E. (1973). Fractional utilisation of the aerobic capacity during distance running. *Medicine and Science in Sports and Exercise,* **5,** 248–52.

Council of Europe (1988). *Testing Physical Fitness.* (Eurofit, Strasbourg).

Datta, S.R. and Ramanathan, N.L. (1970). Ergonomical studies on load carrying up staircases. Part 1 – effect of external load on energy cost and heart rate. *Indian Journal of Medical Research,* **58,** 1629–35.

Datta, S.R. and Ramanathan, N.L. (1971). Ergonomic comparison of seven modes of carrying loads on the horizontal plane. *Ergonomics,* **14,** 269–78.

Davies, C.T.M. (1980). Metabolic cost of exercise and physical performance in children with some observations on external loading. *European Journal of Applied Physiology,* **45,** 95–102.

DuBois, D. and DuBois, E.F. (1916). Clinical calorimetry. A formula to estimate the approximate surface area if height and weight are known. *Archives of Internal Medicine,* **17,** 863–71.

Eston, R.E. and Brodie, D.A. (1985). The assessment of maximal oxygen uptake from running tests. *Physical Education Review,* **8(1),** 26–34.

Eston, R.G., Robson, S. and Winter, E. (1993). A comparison of oxygen uptake during running in children and adults, in *Kinanthropometry IV.* eds. W. Duquet and J.A.P. Day (E & FN Spon, London), pp. 236–41.

Gaesser, G.A. and Brooks, G.A. (1975). Muscular efficiency during steady-rate exercise: effects of speed and work rate. *Journal of Applied Physiology,* **38,** 1132–9.

Gordon, M.J., Goslin, B.R., Graham, T. and Hoare, J. (1983). Comparison between load carriage and grade walking on a treadmill. *Ergonomics,* **26,** 289–98.

Harrison, M.H., Bruce, D.L., Brown, G.A. and Cochrane, L.A. (1980). A comparison of some indirect methods of predicting maximal oxygen uptake. *Aviation Space and Environmental Medicine,* **51,** 1128.

Hill, A.V. (1939). The mechanical efficiency of frog's muscle. *Proceedings of the Royal Society of London,* **127,** 434–51.

Jordan, C.D. and Cooke, C.B. (1998). The effects of upper posture on horizontal running economy. *Journal of Sports Sciences,* **16,** 53–4P.

Kinoshita, H. (1985). Effects of different loads and carrying systems on selected biomechanical parameters describing walking gait. *Ergonomics*, **28**, 1347–62.

Kirk, J. and Schneider, D.A. (1992). Physiological and perceptual responses to load carrying in female subjects using internal and external frame backpacks. *Ergonomics*, **35**, 445–55.

Kleiber, M. (1975). *The Fire of Life. An Introduction to Animal Energetics*. (Kreiger, New York).

Kline, G.M., Porcari, J.P., Hintermeister, R., *et al.* (1987). Estimation of $\dot{V}O_2$ max from a one-mile track walk, gender, age, and body weight. *Medicine and Science in Sports and Exercise*, **19**, 253–9.

Krähenbuhl, G.S., Skinner, J.S. and Kohrt, W.M. (1985). Developmental aspects of maximal aerobic power in children. *Exercise and Sport Sciences Reviews*, **13**, 503–38.

Kram, R., McMahon, T.A. and Taylor, C.R. (1987). Load carriage with compliant poles – Physiological and/or biomechanical advantages. *Journal of Biomechanics*, **20**, 893.

Krebs, H.A. and Kornberg, H.L. (1957). *Energy Transformations in Living Matter*. (Springer, Berlin).

Léger, L. and Lambert, J. (1982). A maximal multistage 20 m shuttle run test to predict $\dot{V}O_2$ max. *European Journal of Applied Physiology*, **49**, 1–12.

Legg, S.J. and Mahanty, A. (1985). Comparison of five modes of carrying a load close to the trunk. *Ergonomics*, **28**, 1653–60.

Lloyd, B.B. and Zacks, R.M. (1972). The mechanical efficiency of treadmill running against a horizontal impeding force. *Journal of Physiology (London)*, **223**, 355–63.

Lloyd, R. and Cooke, C.B. (2000). The oxygen consumption associated with unloaded walking and load carriage using two different backpack designs. *European Journal of Applied Physiology*, **81**, 486–92.

McMahon, T.A. (1984). *Muscles, Reflexes and Locomotion*. (Princeton University Press, Princeton, NJ).

Maloiy, G.M.O., Heglund, N.C., Prager, L.M., *et al.* (1986). Energetic cost of carrying loads: have African women discovered an economic way? *Nature*, **319**, 668–9.

Margaria, R., Cerretelli, P., Aghemo, P. and Sassi, G. (1963). Energy cost of running. *Journal of Applied Physiology*, **18**, 367–70.

Martin, P.E. and Nelson, R.C. (1986). The effects of carried loads on the walking patterns of men and women. *Ergonomics*, **29**, 1191–202.

Morgan, D.W. (1992). Introduction: economy of running: a multidisciplinary perspective. *Medicine and Science in Sports and Exercise*, **24**, 454–5.

Morgan, D.W., Tseh, W., Caputo, J.L., *et al.* (1999). Sex differences in running economy of young children. *Pediatric Exercise Science*, **11**, 122–8.

Morgan, D.W., Bransford, D.R., Costill, D.L., *et al.* (1995). Variation in the aerobic demand of running among trained and untrained subjects. *Medicine and Science in Sports and Exercise*, **27**, 404–9.

Nevill, A.M., Ramsbottom, R. and Williams, C. (1992). Scaling physiological measurements for individuals of different body size. *European Journal of Applied Physiology*, **65**, 110–17.

Noakes, T.D. (1997). Challenging beliefs: ex Africa semper aliquid novi. *Medicine and Science in Sport and Exercise*, **29**, 571–90.

Noakes, T.D. (1998). Maximal oxygen uptake: 'classical' versus 'contemporary' viewpoints: a rebuttal. *Medicine and Science in Sport and Exercise*, **30**, 1381–98.

Norman, R., Sharrat, M., Pezzack, J. and Noble, E. (1976). Re-examination of the mechanical efficiency of horizontal treadmill running. *Biomechanics*, **7**, 87–98.

Paliczka, V.J., Nichols, A.K. and Boreham, C.A.G. (1987). A multi-stage shuttle run test as a predictor of running performance and maximal oxygen uptake in adults. *British Journal of Sports Medicine*, **21**, 163–5.

Pollock, M.L. (1973). The quantification of endurance training programmes. In *Exercise and Sport Sciences Reviews*. ed. J.H. Wilmore (Academic Press, New York), pp. 155–88.

Robertson, R.J., Caspersen, C.J., Allison, T.G., *et al.* (1982). Differentiated perceptions of exertion and energy cost of young women while carrying loads. *European Journal of Applied Physiology and Occupational Physiology*, **49**, 69–78.

Rowland, T.W. (1990). *Exercise and Childrens Health*. (Human Kinetics, Champaign, IL).

Saltin, B., Blomquist, G., Mitchell, J.H., *et al.* (1968). Response to exercise after bed rest and after training. *Circulation*, **38 (suppl. 7)**, 1–78.

Schmidt-Nielsen, K. (1984). *Scaling: Why is Animal Size so Important?* (Cambridge University Press, Cambridge).

Shephard, R.J. (1970). Computer programs for solution of the Åstrand nomogram and calculation of body surface area. *Journal of Sports Medicine and Physical Fitness*, **10**, 206–12.

Shephard, R.J. (1984). Tests of maximum oxygen intake: a critical review. *Sports Medicine*, **1**, 99–124.

Shephard, R.J., Allen, C., Benade, A.J.S., *et al.* (1968). Standardization of submaximal exercise tests. *Bulletin of the World Health Organization*, **38**, 765–75.

Siconolfi, J.F., Cullinane, E. M., Carleton, R.A. and Thompson, P.D. (1982). Assessing in epidemiologic studies: modifications of the Astrand–Ryhming test. *Medicine and Science in Sports and Exercise*, **14**, 335–8.

Stainsby, W.N., Gladden, L.B., Barclay, J.K. and Wilson, B.A. (1980). Exercise efficiency: validity of baseline subtractions. *Journal of Applied Physiology*, **48**, 518–22.

Taylor, C.R., Heglund, N.C. and Maloiy, G.M.O. (1982). Energetics and mechanics of terrestrial locomotion I. Metabolic energy consumption as a function of speed and body size in birds and mammals. *Journal of Experimental Biology*, **97**, 1–22.

Taylor, C.R., Heglund, N.C., McMahon, T.A. and Looney, T.R. (1980). Energetic cost of generating muscular force during running. *Journal of Experimental Biology*, **86**, 9–18.

Taylor, H.L., Buskirk, E. and Henschel, A. (1955). Maximal oxygen uptake as an objective measure of cardiorespiratory performance. *Journal of Applied Physiology*, **8**, 73–7.

Thorstensson, A. (1986). Effects of moderate external loading on the aerobic demand of submaximal running in men and 10-year-old boys. *European Journal of Applied Physiology and Occupational Physiology* , **55**, 569–74.

Unnithan, V.B. and Eston, R.G. (1990). Stride frequency and submaximal treadmill running economy in adults and children. *Pediatric Exercise Science*, **2**, 149–55.

Whipp, B.J. and Wasserman, K. (1969). Efficiency of muscular work. *Journal of Applied Physiology*, **26**, 644–8.

Wickstrom, R.L. (1983). *Fundamental Motor Patterns.* (Lea and Febiger, Philadelphia).

Wilkie, D.R. (1974). The efficiency of muscular contraction. *Journal of Mechanochemistry and Cell Motility*, **2**, 257–67.

Wyndham, C.H., Strydom, N.B., Leary, W.P. and Williams, C.G. (1966). Studies of the maximum capacity of men for physical effort. *Internationale Zeitschrift für Angewandte Physiologie*, **22**, 285–95.

Zacks, R.M. (1973). The mechanical efficiencies of running and bicycling against a horizontal impeding force. *Internationale Zeitschrift für Angewandte Physiologie*, **31**, 249–58.

THERMOREGULATION

8

Thomas Reilly and Nigel T. Cable

8.1 AIMS

The aims of this chapter are to:
- provide students with an understanding of human thermoregulation, at rest and during exercise,
- describe the relevance of anthropometric factors in maintaining heat balance,
- outline practical exercises for the acquisition of techniques to monitor physiological responses to heat loads.

8.2 INTRODUCTION

The human is homoeothermic, meaning that body temperature is maintained within narrow limits independently of fluctuations in environmental temperature. For thermoregulatory purposes the body can be regarded as consisting of a core within which the temperature is 37°C and an outer shell where the ideal average temperature is 33°C, although this value is largely dependent on environmental factors. The precise temperature gradient from core to skin depends on the body part, but generally speaking the size of the gradient that exists between the skin and the environment will determine the amount of heat that is lost or gained by the body.

8.3 PROCESSES OF HEAT LOSS / HEAT GAIN

Normally the body is maintained in thermo-equilibrium or heat balance. Heat is produced by metabolism and the level of heat production can be increased dramatically by physical exercise. The processes of conduction, convection and radiation allow for either heat loss or heat gain (depending on environmental conditions) with evaporation being a major avenue of heat loss when body temperature is rising.

The heat of basal metabolism is about 1 kcal kg^{-1} h^{-1}. One kcal (4.186 kJ) is the energy required to raise 1 kg of water through 1°C. The specific heat of human tissue is less than this figure, 0.83 kcal of energy being needed to raise 1 kg of tissue through 1°C. Thus if there were no avenue of heat loss, the temperature of the body would rise by 1°C per hour in an individual with body mass of about 72 kg, and within 4–6 hours death from overheating would follow. The process would be accelerated during exercise, when energy expenditure might approach 25 kcal min^{-1} (105 kJ min^{-1}). This value might include 1 kcal min^{-1} for basal metabolism and 6 kcal min^{-1} for producing muscular work. The remaining 18 kcal is dissipated as heat which builds up within the body. In this instance the theoretical rise in body temperature would be 20°C in just over one hour. Obviously maintaining life depends on the ability to exchange heat with the environment.

A number of factors contribute to heat production and heat loss (Figure 8.1). The maintenance of a relatively constant core temperature is frequently expressed in the form of a heat balance equation:

8

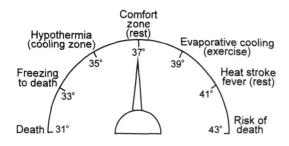

Figure 8.1 The body temperature range.

$$Heat\ stored = Metabolic\ rate - Evaporation$$
$$\pm\ Radiation \pm Convection \pm Conduction$$
$$- Work\ done$$

Heat may be gained from terrestrial sources of radiation or from solar radiation, while the body radiates heat to its immediate environment. In physical terms the human body can be regarded as a black box, the body surface being a good absorber of radiant heat and also a good radiator.

Convection refers to transfer of heat by movement of gas or fluid. The barriers to convective heat exchange include subcutaneous adipose tissue, clothing and films of stationary air or water in immediate contact with clothing.

Conduction describes heat transfer from core through body fluids to the surface of the body and exchange with the environment by direct contact of the skin with objects, materials or surfaces.

Evaporative heat loss includes vaporization of water from moist mucous membrane of the upper respiratory tract with breathing, insensible perspiration through the skin and evaporation of sweat from the surface of the body. When water evaporates from any surface, that surface is cooled. When sweat droplets fall from the skin, no heat is exchanged. At rest in a room temperature of 21°C the heat lost by a nude human would be about 60% from radiation, 25% evaporation from lungs and skin, 12% by means of convective air currents and 3% by means of conduction from the feet. During exercise the main mechanism for heat loss is evaporation of sweat. This mechanism will be less effective when the air is highly humid, 100% relative humidity meaning that the air is already totally saturated with water vapour and can take up no more at the prevailing temperature.

The rate of evaporative heat loss is dependent on the vapour pressure gradient across the film of stationary air surrounding the skin and on the thickness of the stationary film. It is influenced also by air movement over the skin surface. Evaporative loss from the lungs depends on minute ventilation, dryness of the atmosphere and the barometric pressure. Consequently, dry nose and throat are experienced at altitude, where the atmospheric pressure is lower than at sea level.

8.4 CONTROL OF BODY TEMPERATURE

Body temperature is regulated by temperature-sensitive neurons located in the anterior and posterior hypothalamus. These cells detect the temperature of the circulating blood, with the cells in the anterior hypothalamus responding to an increase in body temperature and those in the posterior portion triggering the effector response to a decrease. These areas also receive afferent input from peripheral warm and cold receptors located in the skin and therefore receive information about changes in the body's immediate environment. Warm receptors in the skin are stimulated in the temperature range of 28–45°C. Paradoxically, above this level the cold receptors begin to fire, particularly if the skin is subjected to a rapid increase. This is called paradoxical inhibition and gives the sensation of cold in very hot surroundings (e.g. in a shower).

During exposure to cold, or when body temperature decreases, the posterior hypothalamus initiates a number of responses. This activity will be neurally mediated via the sympathetic nervous system, and will result in a generalized vasoconstriction of the cutaneous circulation. Blood will be displaced centrally away from the peripheral circulation, promoting a fall in skin temperature which will ultimately increase the temperature gradient between the core and the skin. Importantly, however, this reduction in skin temperature will decrease the gradient that exists between the skin and the environment, and therefore reduce the potential for heat loss from the body. Superficial veins are also affected such that blood returning from the limbs is diverted from them to the vena comitantes that overlie the main arteries. The result is that arterial blood is cooled by the venous return almost immediately it enters the limb by means of the countercurrent heat exchange mechanism.

The reduction in blood flow is not uniform throughout the body, its effects being most pronounced in the extremities. Severe cold may decrease blood flow to the fingers to 2.5% of its normal value whereas, in contrast, blood flow to the head remains unaltered. There are no vasoconstrictor fibres to the vessels of the scalp, which seem to be slow in responding to the direct effect of cooling (Webb, 1982). As heat loss from the head can account for up to 25% of the total heat production, the importance of covering the head to protect against the cold is clear. This would equally apply to the underwater swimmer and to the winter jogger or skier. Froese and Burton (1957) showed that there is a linear relationship between heat loss through the head and ambient temperature within the range –20°C to +32°C, emphasizing the need to insulate the top of the head in extreme cold.

Paradoxically, if the environment is extremely cold, there may be a delayed vasodilation of the blood vessels in the skin which alternates with intense vasoconstriction in cycles of 15–30 minutes and leads to excessive heat loss. This has been described as a hunting reaction in the quest for an appropriate skin temperature to achieve the best combination of gradients between core, shell and environment. The vasodilation may be the result of accumulated vasoactive metabolites arising from increased anaerobic metabolism in local tissues which is associated with the reduced blood flow. The explanation by Keatinge (1969) is that the smooth muscle in the walls of peripheral blood vessels is paralysed at temperatures of 10°C; as the muscles cannot then respond to noradrenaline released by vasoconstrictor nerves, the muscles relax to allow a return of blood flow through the vessels, thus completing the cycle. This alternation of high and low blood flow to local tissue produced by ice-pack application is exploited in the treatment of sports injuries by physiotherapists. The phenomenon is also well recognized by runners and cyclists if they train in cold conditions without wearing gloves; the fingers are initially white but become a ruddy colour as blood enters the digits in increased volumes. Blood flow to the skin may also be influenced by alcohol, which has a vasodilator effect. Though alcohol can make a person feel more comfortable when exposed to cold, it will increase heat loss and so may endanger the individual. Consequently, drinking alcohol is not recommended when staying outdoors overnight in inclement weather conditions and the customary hip-flask of whiskey serves no useful protective function for recreational skiers or mountaineers.

Shivering represents a response of the autonomic nervous system to cold. It constitutes involuntary activity of skeletal muscles and the resultant heat production may be as large as three times the basal metabolic rate. Indeed, metabolic rates five times that at rest have been reported (Horvath, 1981), though such values are rare. Shivering tends to be intermittent and persists during exercise until the exercise intensity is sufficient on its own to maintain core temperature. The piloerection response to cold that is found in animals is less useful to the human who lacks the furry overcoat to the skin that cold-dwelling animals possess. Contraction of the small muscles attached to hair roots causes air to be trapped in the fur and this impedes heat loss. The pilomotor reflex in humans has little thermal impact but is reflected in the appearance of goose pimples. Paradoxically, the 'gooseflesh syndrome' is sometimes found in marathon runners during heat stress when heat loss mechanisms begin to fail, the condition being accompanied by a sensation of coldness (Pugh, 1972).

Elevation of basal heat production may be brought about by the neuroendocrine system in conditions of long-term cold exposure. The hypothalamus stimulates the pituitary gland to release hormones that affect other target organs, notably the thyroid and adrenal glands. Thyroxine causes an increase in metabolic rate within 5–6 hours of cold exposure. This elevation will persist throughout a sojourn, the metabolic rate at rest being greater in cold than in temperate climates and elevated over that of tropical residents. Adrenaline and adrenocortical hormones may also cause a slight increase in metabolism, though the combined hormonal effects are still relatively modest. Brown fat, so-called because of its iron-containing cytochromes active in oxidative processes, is a potential source of thermogenesis. This form of fat is located primarily in and around the kidneys and adjacent to the great vessels, beneath the shoulder blades and along the spine. It is evident in abundance in infants but its stores decline during growth and development. Its high metabolic rate has been presented as an explanation of why some individuals fail to increase body weight despite appearing to overeat, though this point is highly contentious.

The anterior hypothalamus initiates vasodilation of the cutaneous circulation in response to an increase in body temperature. This results in an expansion of the core and ultimately increases the temperature gradient between the skin and the environment, allowing for greater heat exchange. Cutaneous vasodilation is initiated by a removal of vasoconstrictor tone in the skin, and enhanced by the release of vasodilator substances (bradykinin and vasoactive intestinal polypeptide) from the sweat glands following stimulation via sympathetic cholinergic fibres. These substances are thought to cause the smooth muscle of the cutaneous blood vessels to relax and allow total peripheral resistance to decrease, thereby increasing

blood flow. Evidence for this response comes from individuals with a congenital lack of sweat glands, who are not able to increase skin blood flow when body temperature increases.

It is, therefore, evident that the process of thermoregulation is subserved by the cardiovascular system. That is to say, heat is gained or lost by changes in blood flow. Such changes in blood flow must obviously have ramifications for the control of blood pressure. If total peripheral resistance is increased (i.e. when body temperature falls and skin blood flow is restricted), blood pressure will increase. Conversely with peripheral vasodilation skin blood flow is enhanced and blood pressure may fall. Thus thermoregulatory responses can initiate changes in non-thermal control mechanisms. Examples of this include the increased diuresis seen in cold weather. As total peripheral resistance increases, antidiuretic hormone secretion is reduced and therefore less fluid is reabsorbed from the kidney; ultimately some blood volume is lost, which returns blood pressure to normal. Conversely, the soldier who stands on parade for a number of hours in the heat will, following increases in skin blood flow, no longer be able to maintain blood pressure sufficiently to perfuse the cerebral circulation, and therefore may faint to allow blood flow to return to normal.

8.5 THERMOREGULATION AND OTHER CONTROL SYSTEMS

During exercise, particularly in the heat, sweating becomes the main mechanism for losing heat. Sweat is secreted by corkscrew-shaped glands within the skin and it contains a range of electrolytes as well as substances such as urea and lactic acid. Its concentration is less than in plasma and so sweat is described as hypotonic. Altogether there are about 2 million eccrine sweat glands in the human body, though the number varies between individuals; the other type, apocrine sweat glands, are found mainly in the axilla and groin and are not important in thermoregulation in the human.

Table 8.1 The 24-hour water balance in a sedentary individual

Intake (ml)		Output (ml)	
Solid and semi-solid food	1 200	Skin	350
Water released in metabolism	300	Expired air	500
Drinks (water, tea, fruit juice, coffee, milk and so on)	1 000	Urine	1 500
		Faeces	150
Total	2 500		2 500

While exercising hard in hot conditions, the amount of fluid lost in sweat may exceed $2 l h^{-1}$ so athletes may lose 5–6% of body weight as water within 2 hours of heavy exercise. This loss would amount to over 8% of body water stores and represent a serious level of dehydration. The normal body water balance is illustrated in Table 8.1.

As thermoregulatory needs tend to override the physiological controls over body water, sweat secretion will continue and exacerbate the effects of dehydration until heat injury is manifest. Costill (1981) demonstrated how losses are distributed among body water pools during prolonged exercise. Muscle biopsies were taken before, during and after exercise in active and non-active muscles, and blood samples were also obtained. It was calculated that extracellular and intracellular and total body water values decreased by 9, 3 and 7.5%, respectively. The conclusion was that electrolyte losses in sweat did not alter the calculated membrane potential of active and inactive muscles sufficiently to be the cause of cramp suffered in such conditions.

Effects of dehydration are manifest at a water deficit of 1% of body weight in a sensation of thirst. This is due to a change in cellular osmolarity and to dryness in the mucous membrane of the mouth and throat. The sensation can be satisfied long before the fluid is replaced so that thirst is an imperfect indication of the body's needs. As fluid may be lost at a greater rate than it can be absorbed, regular intakes of water, say 150 ml every 10–15 minutes, are recommended in events such as marathon running. This can halt the rise in heart rate and body temperature towards hyperthermic levels that might otherwise have resulted. Energy drinks have no added value for thermoregulatory purposes, though hypotonic solutions have marginal benefits in terms of the speed at which the ingested fluid is absorbed. Indeed, in hot conditions, it is sound practice to start contests well stocked up with body water and then take small amounts of fluid frequently en route. However, in prolonged endurance events care must be taken not to over-hydrate as this can lead to the development of hyponatraemia or water toxicity, which if severe may need hospitalization. This condition usually only presents itself in avid water drinkers, but is becoming more common during events such as 'ironman' triathlons and 'ultramarathons'.

Boxers and wrestlers are known to use dehydrating practices to lose weight before their events and stay within the limit of their particular weight categories. In many cases the use of diuretics for the purpose of body water loss has been suspected. The practice is dangerous, especially if the impending contest is to be held in hot conditions and severe levels of dehydration have been induced prior to weighing-in. It was soundly condemned in a position statement of the American College of Sports Medicine in 1976 which was updated in 1984.

Effects of dehydration on performance vary with the amount of fluid lost and the nature of the activity being performed. These are compounded when accompanied by imminent hyperthermia due to a combination of high humidity and high ambient temperature. Throughout the history of sport there are many dramatic examples of competitors suffering from heat stress. Television audiences witnessing transmission of the first Women's Olympic Marathon in 1984 empathized with the struggle of the Swiss competitor to complete the course. The Irish professional boxer, Barry McGuigan, lost his world title in the heat of Las Vegas, having had difficulty in making the scheduled weight limit before the fight. Examples of less fortunate victims of heat stress were the deaths of a Danish cyclist (Knud Jensen) at the Rome Olympics in 1960 and later that of the British professional cyclist, Tommy Simpson. In both cases the use of amphetamines was allegedly implicated, these having an enhanced effect on performance but a deleterious effect on thermoregulatory mechanisms.

The fact that body water content is variable should be taken into account when body composition is assessed from measurements of body water. This applies to chemical methods for measuring body water and predicting body fat values from the measurements. It applies also to the use of bioelectric impedance analysis (BIA) methods, which record conductance or resistance of the whole body in response to a low-voltage electrical signal administered to the subjects. The resistance is dependent on water content, and estimates of body fat will be affected by the state of the subject's hydration (Brodie *et al.*, 1991, Lemmey *et al.*, 2000).

Women are often reputed to have inferior thermoregulatory functions to men during exercise in the heat. It seems that the early studies reporting women to be less tolerant of exercise in the heat ignored the low fitness levels of the women who were studied. Though women tend to have more body fat than men and so greater insulation properties, their larger surface area relative to mass gives them an advantage in losing heat. There appears to be no sex difference in acclimatization to heat, and the frequency of heat illness in road races in the USA is approximately the same for each sex (Haymes, 1984).

There are, however, differences between the sexes that should be considered when body temperature is concerned. The greater subcutaneous tissue layers in females should provide them with better insulation against the cold. In females the set point is not fixed at 37°C but varies with the menstrual cycle. In mid-cycle there is a sharp rise of about 0.5°C which is due to the influence of progesterone and this elevation is indicative of ovulation.

There is also a circadian rhythm in body temperature that is independent of the environmental conditions (Reilly, 1990). Core temperature is at a low point during sleep and is at its peak at about 18:00 hours (Figure 8.2). The peak-to-trough variation is about 0.6°C and this applies to both males and females. The amplitude is less than this in aged individuals (Reilly *et al.*, 1997). There is a wealth of evidence intimating that many types of sports performance follow a curve during the day that is closely linked to the rhythm in body temperature (Reilly *et al.*, 2000).

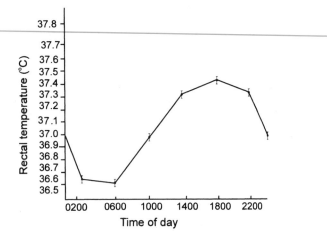

Figure 8.2 Circadian variation in core temperature.

8.6 MEASUREMENT OF BODY TEMPERATURE

Core temperature refers to the thermal state of essential internal organs such as heart, liver, viscera and brain. Although it is normally considered that core temperature is regulated about an internal temperature of 37°C, this value varies depending on the site of measurement. There are also rhythmic changes in the temperature set point, which varies during exercise and in fever.

Rectal temperature is the most commonly used site for indicating core temperature in athletes. The probe should be inserted to a depth of 10 cm beyond the external anal sphincter if reliable measures are to be obtained. Care is also necessary that probes are sterilized and treated with HIV risk in mind. Rectal temperature is not the best measure of core temperature in situations where temperature is changing rapidly. For this reason oesophageal temperature is preferred in some exercise experiments. This entails inserting a probe through the nose and threading it into the oesophagus.

An alternative is tympanic temperature where a sensor is placed adjacent to the tympanic membrane. Caution is necessary as it is easy to damage the membrane and also the ear must be completely insulated to avoid environmental influences. External auditory meatus temperatures can also be measured by inserting a probe 1 cm inside the ear canal and insulating the ear. However, with this measurement and those of rectal and oesophageal temperatures, it is best to represent data as a change from a baseline, since a temperature gradient exists down these tissues.

Oral or sublingual temperatures, typically measured with a mercury thermometer, are used in clinical rather than exercise contexts and give values about 0.4°C lower than rectal temperature. Oral temperature is of little use in swimmers, for example, whose mouths are affected by surrounding water and high ventilation rates. Similarly measurement of axilla or groin temperatures in athletic subjects gives a poor indication of their thermal status. A temperature-sensitive pill which can be swallowed and then monitored by radio-telemetry has been used in occupational contexts. Difficulties include the necessity for accurate calibration, differences in temperature between the internal organs adjacent to the passage of the pill, the influences of recently digested food on core temperature and the possible unsavoury task of its retrieval once the pill has traversed the full course of the digestive tract. A more acceptable alternative is to measure the temperature of mid-stream urine which gives a reasonable indication of internal body temperature.

Skin temperature has conventionally been measured by thermistors and thermocouples. Optoelectronic devices are now also available. The common method is to place thermistors over the surface of the skin and tape over them. From measurements of a number of designated skin sites, a mean skin temperature may be calculated. The formulae that require the least number of observations are;

$$MST = 0.5\ T_c + 0.36\ T_l + 0.14\ T_a$$
(Burton, 1935)

$$MST = 0.3\ T_c + 0.3\ T_a + 0.2\ T_t + 0.2\ T_l$$
(Ramanathan, 1964)

where: MST is mean skin temperature, T_c is temperature of the chest, juxta-nipple, T_l is leg temperature measured over the lateral side of the calf muscle, T_a is lower arm temperature and T_t is anterior thigh temperature. Mean body temperature (MBT) may then be calculated by weighting rectal temperature (T_r) and MST in the ratio 4:1. In other words: $MBT = 0.8\ T_r + 0.2\ MST$.

8.7 THERMOREGULATORY RESPONSES TO EXERCISE

Exercise implies activity of skeletal muscle and this demands energy. Most of the energy utilized is dissipated as heat, a small amount contributing towards mechanical work. The muscular efficiency represents the work performed as a percentage of the total energy expenditure. For cycle ergometry this value is about 22%, depending on whether or not the resting energy expenditure is taken into consideration. In swimming, this figure is much lower; in weight lifting, it has been calculated to be about 12% (Reilly, 1983). It is acknowledged that the mechanical efficiency is difficult to estimate in activities such as running.

During sustained exercise the cardiac output supplies oxygen to the active muscles but also distributes blood to the skin to cool the body. In cases where cardiac output is maximal, the exercise performance is impaired by thermoregulatory needs. Since the maximal cardiac output determines how well blood can be distributed for peripheral cooling, the heat load induced by exercise is a function of the percentage of maximal oxygen uptake rather than the absolute work rate engaged.

The body acts as a heat sink in the early minutes of exercise and blood is shunted from viscera and other organs to the exercising muscles. Blood flow to the brain remains intact although there seems to be differential distribution to areas within the brain. If exercise imparts a severe heat load, the sweat glands are activated and droplets appear on the skin surface after about 7 minutes. The extent to which body temperature rises then depends on the exercise intensity and the environmental conditions.

8.8 ENVIRONMENTAL FACTORS

Heat exchange with the environment is influenced by a number of environmental variables as well as individual characteristics. The clothing and equipment used also affect heat exchange. Thus some background is provided on relevant interactions with the environment in this section before progressing to anthropometric considerations in the next.

Athletic contests are sometimes held in conditions that challenge the body's thermoregulatory system. Cold is less of a problem than heat since athletes usually choose to avoid extremes of cold. Exceptions are winter sports such as mountaineering, where it is imperative to protect the individuals against the cold. Outdoor games, such as American football, are also sometimes played in freezing conditions.

Experiments in cold air close to freezing have not consistently shown a significant effect on the maximal oxygen uptake. The effects are more marked in the periphery of the body, where the drop in temperature of tissues is more pronounced. Normally the mean skin temperature is about 33°C and extreme discomfort is felt when this drops below 25°C. As skin temperature of the hand falls below 23°C, movements of the limb begin to get clumsy, and finger dexterity is severely affected at skin temperatures between 13°C and 16°C. This is especially critical in winter sport activities that require fine manipulative actions of the fingers, which are impaired because of numbness in those digits. Tactile sensitivity of the fingers is also affected for the worse to the extent that an impact on the skin at 20°C has to be about six times greater than normal for usual sensations to be felt. The skeletal muscles function at an optimal internal temperature and when this drops to about 27°C, the muscle's contractile force is much impaired. This can be demonstrated by the progressive decline in grip strength with increased cooling of the arm. In sports such as downhill skiing, the performer could be cooled during the chair lift to the top of the ski run and must therefore take steps to keep the limb muscles warm prior to skiing. Synovial fluid in the joints also becomes colder and more viscous, thus increasing the stiffness of the joints. The fatigue curve of muscle also deteriorates due to a combination of factors such as impaired strength, lower blood flow, increased resistance of connective tissue and increased discomfort.

One of the most important consequences of sports participation outdoors in the cold is the poorer neuromuscular co-ordination that may result. As temperature in nervous tissue falls, conduction velocity of nerve impulses is retarded and this slows reaction time. If the slide in temperature is not reversed, eventually complete neural block occurs. Co-ordination is also impaired by the effect of cold on the muscle spindles which, at 27°C, respond to only 50% of normal to a standardized stimulus. Consequently, the stumbling and poor locomotion of climbers in the cold may be due to impairments in peripheral nerves.

Such an effect is particularly evident during cold water immersion. When swimming in water temperatures below 10°C there is a progressive reduction in swimming efficiency that appears to be related to local cooling in the arm muscles, rather than whole-body hypothermia. Arm cooling tends to result in local muscle weakness and even paralysis, which results in increasing drag and risk of sinking. This coupled with the hyperventilation often seen during cold immersion makes a co-ordinated swimming stroke virtually impossible, and may be a reason why many drowning deaths occur in cold water, even in cases where the victim is very close to land and safety (Tipton *et al.*, 1999).

Some protection against this risk is offered by a greater subcutaneous fat layer around the arm muscles to restrict heat loss. In addition, lean individuals acutely exposed to cold water immersion should restrict body movement in order to prevent hypothermia. Whilst this manoeuvre may limit heat production, it will allow heat loss to be markedly restricted. This is because both fat and inactive muscle act as good insulators. However, when muscle becomes active, blood flow is dramatically increased, which ultimately changes a good insulator under resting conditions into a very effective heat conductor.

Frostbite is one of the risks of recreational activities in extreme cold. This can occur when the temperature in the fingers or toes falls below freezing and at –1°C ice crystals are formed in those tissues. The results can be a gangrenous extremity, often experienced by mountaineers in icy conditions when their gloves or boots fail to provide adequate thermal insulation. Recent clinical experience is that amputation of damaged tissue is not a necessary consequence of frostbite and prognosis tends to be more optimistic than thought in previous decades. Of more serious consequence is a fall in the body's core temperature. The cold stress is progressively manifested by an enlargement of the area of the shell while the area of the core becomes smaller until its temperature ultimately begins to fall dangerously. A core temperature of 34.5°C is usually taken as indicative of grave hypothermic risk, though there is no absolute consensus of a critical end point. Some researchers assume that a rectal temperature of 32–33°C is a critical end point, though the exact value of hypothalamic temperature for fatality is subject to controversy.

Scientists have used metaphorical models to predict survival time by extrapolating from initial rates of decline in core temperature to an arbitrary value of 30°C (Ross *et al.*, 1980). This avoids the need to take subjects too close to a risk of hypothermia. Researchers in Nazi concentration camps were not so considerate to their prisoners, who were cooled to death at core temperatures of about 27°C. An example was given by Holdcroft (1980) of an alcoholic woman exposed overnight in Chicago to sub-freezing temperatures and whose rectal temperature was reported to be 18°C when she was found in a stupor. In hindsight it is doubtful if this was representative of core temperature in these conditions. Happily, she survived after being re-warmed in a hospital room temperature of 20°C. Death usually occurs at a much higher core temperature than that reported for the fortunate Chicago woman, shivering being usually replaced by permanent muscle rigidity, then loss of consciousness at core temperatures of 32°C and heart failure may follow. The range of clinical symptoms associated with hypothermia is presented in texts such as Holdcroft (1980).

Behavioural strategies and proper clothing can safeguard individuals in cold environments. Enormous strides have been made in the provision of protective equipment against the cold for sports participants. Major advances have been made in clothing design and in the reliability and durability of tents. A similar systematic improvement is noted in the provision of first-aid and rescue services for most outdoor pursuits. The specially treated sheets of foil paper readily availed of by recreational marathon runners to safeguard against rapid heat loss on cessation of activity are an example.

Existence of good rescue facilities is no excuse for climbing parties to take risks in inclement weather. Early warning systems used by rangers on mountainsides must be heeded if they are to be effective, and this inevitably means consumer education. Otherwise, the safety of the rescue team in addition to that of the climbing party may be jeopardized if weather conditions further deteriorate. Assessment of the risk involves some calculations of the magnitude of cold stress. On the mountainside the wind velocity may be the most influential factor in cooling the body, so that the ambient temperature alone would grossly underestimate the prevailing risk. The windchill index designed by Siple and Passel (1945), and widely used by mountaineers and skiers, provides a method of comparing different combinations of temperature and wind speed. The values calculated correspond to a caloric scale for rate of heat loss per unit body surface area; they are then converted in to a sensation scale ranging from hot (about 80) through cool (400) to bitterly cold (1200) and on to a value where exposed flesh freezes within 60 s. The cooling effects of combinations of certain temperatures and wind speeds are expressed as 'temperature equivalents' and are estimated with a nomogram. Use of the wind-chill index enables sojourners to evaluate the magnitude of cold stress and take appropriate precautions. Wet conditions can exacerbate cold stress, especially if the clothing worn begins to lose its insulation. Attention to safety may be even more important in water sports since, apart from the risk of drowning, body heat is lost much more rapidly in water than in air.

The formula of Siple and Passel (1945) for calculating heat loss is:

$$K_o = \left(\sqrt{100V} + 10.5 - V\right)\left(33 - T\right)$$

where: K_o = heat loss in kcal m^{-2} h^{-1}; V = wind velocity in m s^{-1}; T = environmental temperature in °C; 10.5 = a constant; 33 = assumed normal skin temperature in °C

For example, if wind velocity is 14 m s^{-1} and the ambient temperature is 2°C, the rate of heat loss is:

$$K_o = \left(\sqrt{100 \times 14} + 10.5 - 14\right)\left(33 - 2\right) = (33.9)(31)$$
$$= 1051 \text{ kcal m}^{-2} \text{ h}^{-1}$$

Water has a much greater heat conduction capacity than air, and so heat is readily exchanged with the environment when the human body is immersed. Though mean skin temperature is normally about 33°C, a bath at that temperature feels cold, yet if the water temperature is elevated by 2°C, the temperature of the body will begin to rise. This suggests that the human is poorly equipped for spending long spells in the water. Finding the appropriate water temperature is important for swimming pool managers who have to cater for different levels of ability. The preferred water temperature for inactive individuals is 33°C, for learners it is about 30°C, for active swimmers it is in the range of 27–29°C, whereas competitive swimmers are more content with temperatures around 25°C. Generally the water is regulated to suit the active users. Indeed, the whole environment of the swimming pool must be engineered for the comfort of users. Condensation in the arena may not be welcomed by spectators, but the high humidity in the swimming pool militates against heat loss when the swimmer is out of the water. Engineering may involve double glazing of the surround to avoid losing radiant heat outwards from the building as well as provision of supplementary radiant heating. Permissible indoor dew points can be calculated from temperature differences between outdoors and inside the pool to avoid high condensation risks, these being the points where moisture is deposited. Air ventilation rates inside the building may reduce the moisture content of indoor areas to decrease the discomfort of spectators, but this will cool the bather and call for increased heating costs. A practical compromise is to have air temperatures in the region of 28–30°C, which are much warmer than normal office room temperatures.

In hot conditions, heat stroke is a major risk and should be classed as an emergency. It reflects failure of normal thermoregulatory mechanisms. It is characterized by a body temperature of 41°C or higher, cessation of sweating and total confusion. Once sweating stops, the body temperature will rise quickly and soon cause irreversible damage to liver, kidney and brain cells. In such an emergency immediate treatment is essential.

Calculating the risk of heat injury requires accurate assessment of environmental conditions. The main factors to consider are dry bulb temperature, air velocity and cloud cover. Dry bulb temperature can be measured with a mercury glass thermometer, whereas relative humidity can be calculated from data obtained from a wet bulb thermometer used in either a sling psychrometer or a Stevenson screen. The dew point temperature, the point at which the air becomes saturated, is a measure of absolute humidity and it can be measured with a whirling hygrometer. Radiant temperature is measured by a globe thermometer inserted into a hollow metal sphere coated with black matt paint. Air velocity can be measured by means of a vane anemometer or an alcohol thermometer coated with polished silver. Cloud cover will protect against solar radiation and may provide some intermittent relief to the athlete. More details of the measuring devices and their operations are contained in the classic publication by Bedford (1946).

A problem for the sports scientist is to find the proper combination of factors to reach an integrated assessment of the environmental heat load. Many equations have been derived

for this purpose and three-quarters of a century of research to this end were reviewed by Lee (1980). Most of the formulae incorporate composites of the environmental measures, whereas some, such as the predicted 4-hour sweat rate (P4SR), predict physiological responses from such measures. Probably the most widely used equation in industrial and military establishments has been the WBGT Index, WBGT standing for wet bulb and globe temperature. The US National Institute of Occupational Safety and Health recommended it as the standard heat stress index in 1972. The weightings (beta weights) underline the importance of considering relative humidity:

$$WBGT = 0.7\ WBT + 0.2\ GT + 0.1\ DBT$$

where: WB represents wet bulb; G indicates globe; DB represents dry bulb; T indicates temperature.

A comprehensive selection of indices derived in the United Kingdom and the USA was given by Lee (1980). A later development is the Botsball which was validated by Beshir *et al.* (1982). It combines the effects of air temperature, humidity, wind speed and radiation into a single reading. It got its name from its designer, Botsford, and the WBGT can be reliably predicted from it if necessary.

Heat stress indices provide a framework for evaluating the risk of competing in hot conditions and for predicting the casualties. The American College of Sports Medicine (1984) set down guidelines for distance races, recommending that events longer than 16 km should not be conducted when the WBGT Index exceeds 28°C. This value is often exceeded in distance races in Europe and in the USA during the summer months, and in many marathon races in Asia and Africa. It is, however, imperative in all cases that the risks are understood and that symptoms of distress are recognized and promptly attended to. The plentiful provision of fluids en route and facilities for cooling participants are important precautionary steps.

8.9 ANTHROPOMETRY AND HEAT EXCHANGE

The exchange of heat between the human and the environment is affected by both body size and weight composition. Age, sex and physique of the individual are relevant considerations also.

The exchange of heat is a function of the body surface area relative to body mass. The dimensional exponent for this relation is 0.67. The smaller the individual, the easier it is to exchange heat with the environment. Consequently children gain and lose heat more quickly than do adults, and marathon runners on average tend to be smaller than those specialising in shorter running events. It is important to recognize that children are more vulnerable than adults in extremes of environmental conditions.

It is thought that elderly people living alone prefer warmer environments than younger individuals due to their lower metabolic rate. This is countered by a decrease in insensible perspiration due to a change in the vapour diffusion resistance of the skin with age. There is a higher incidence of death from hypothermia in old people living alone in the European winter than in the general population. These deaths are more likely to be due to socio-economic conditions and physical immobility than to thermoregulatory changes with age.

Physiological thermoregulatory responses, notably skin blood flow and sweat rates, to heat stress tend to diminish with increasing age. This is probably due to age-related changes in the skin. Nevertheless, changes in core temperature and heat storage often show only marginal age-related effects if healthy men and women preserve a high degree of aerobic fitness. The ability to exercise in hot conditions is more a function of the status of the oxygen transport system (especially maximal oxygen uptake and cardiac output) than of chronological age.

Differences between the sexes in heat exchange are largely explained by body composition, physique and surface-to-volume ratios. These predominate once differences in fitness levels are taken into account.

Adipose tissue layers beneath the skin act to insulate the body and are protective in cold conditions. The degree of muscularity or mesomorphy can add to this. Ross *et al.* (1980) demonstrated that prediction of survival time in accidental immersion in water should take both endomorphy and mesomorphy into consideration, and the best prediction was when the entire somatotype was taken into account. Pugh and Edholm (1955), in their classical studies of English Channel swimmers, showed that the leaner individuals suffered from the cold much earlier than did those with high proportions of body adiposity. They compared responses of two ultra-distance swimmers in water of 15°C. The larger and fatter individual showed no decrease in rectal temperature for 7 hours, after which his radial pulse was impalpable for 50 minutes. The lighter and leaner swimmer was taken from the water after half an hour when his rectal temperature had dropped from 37°C to 34.5°C. In their studies in a swimming flume, Holmer and Bergh (1974) found that oesophageal temperature was constant at a water temperature of 26°C in subjects operating at 50% $\dot{V}O_2$ max, except for a decrease in those with low body fat. They would be at an even greater disadvantage in colder water.

Racial differences in thermoregulatory response to heat seem to reflect physiological adjustments to environmental conditions more than genetic factors. Acclimatization to heat occurs relatively rapidly, a good degree of adaptation being achieved within two weeks. Sweating capacity is increased, concentrations of electrolytes in sweat are reduced due to an influence of aldosterone and there is an expansion of plasma volume. The sensitivity of the sweat glands is altered so that more sweat is produced for a given rise in core temperature. It is less clear how genetic and acclimatization factors are separated for cold exposure, since diet, activity, living conditions and so on are confounding factors. Studies of the ama, professional pearl divers of Korea and Japan, suggest a mild adjustment to chronic cold water exposure occurs (Rahn and Yokoyama, 1965). Thermal conductance in a given water temperature was found to be lower for diving than for non-diving women matched for skin-fold thickness. These divers were also reported to have higher resting metabolic rates, which would help them to preserve heat. A similar vasoconstriction to reduce thermal conductance of tissues was reported by Skreslet and Aarefjord (1968) in subjects diving with self-contained underwater breathing apparatus (SCUBA) in the Arctic for 45 days.

The elevation of metabolic rate is also found in Eskimos when their thermal values are compared to Europeans. To what extent this can be attributed to diet and the specific dynamic activity of food is not clear. Adaptive vasoconstriction is most pronounced in Aborigines sleeping semi-naked in near-freezing temperatures in the Australian outback. By restricting peripheral circulation, they can tolerate cold conditions that would cause grave danger to sojourners similarly exposed. This circulatory adjustment occurs without an increase in metabolic rate.

8.10 PRACTICAL EXERCISES

It is easier to demonstrate thermoregulatory factors using single-case studies as examples. Experiments require controlled laboratory conditions and usually prolonged exercise is involved. In the absence of an environmental chamber, three different laboratory demonstrations are suggested.

8.11 PRACTICAL 1: MUSCULAR EFFICIENCY

This practical entails exercise under steady-rate conditions on a cycle ergometer with work-rate being controlled and metabolic responses measured. From these measurements the muscular efficiency of exercise can be calculated.

8.11.1 AIM

To examine the efficiency of various cycling cadences

8.11.2 EQUIPMENT

- Electronically-braked cycle ergometer
- Oxygen consumption measuring device (e.g. on-line system or Douglas bags and oxygen and carbon dioxide analysers)

8.11.3 PROTOCOL

An electronically-braked ergometer maintains work-rate (power output) independent of changes in pedal cadence. In this instance the work-rate chosen was 120 W. The subject has $\dot{V}O_2$ measured whilst sitting still, then commences exercise pedalling at a frequency of 50 rev min^{-1} for 20 minutes with $\dot{V}O_2$ measured during the last 2 minutes. This is followed by a 10 minute rest period and then this regimen is performed twice more using exactly the same work-rate but with new pedalling frequencies of 70 and 100 rev min^{-1}.

8.11.4 CALCULATIONS

$$\text{Work efficiency} = \frac{\text{work done (kJ min}^{-1})}{\text{energy expended (kJ min}^{-1})}$$

where: 1 watt = 0.06 kJ min^{-1}

Energy expended = $\dot{V}O_2$ (l min^{-1}) × caloric equivalent (see Table 6.3)

Net efficiency; as above, except that resting $\dot{V}O_2$ must be subtracted from the exercise value. (Note: If an electronically-braked cycle ergometer is not available, use a mechanically-braked ergometer and exercise entailing a steady-state protocol.)

8.11.5 EXAMPLES OF CALCULATIONS

Efficiency
e.g. Work-rate = 120 W = 7.2 kJ min^{-1}
Resting $\dot{V}O_2$ = 0.25 l min^{-1}
Exercise $\dot{V}O_2$ = 2.0 l min^{-1}
RER = 0.85
Energy equivalent for 2.0 l min^{-1} at RER = 0.85 = 20.3 kJ min^{-1}

$$\text{Therefore: Gross efficiency} = \frac{72}{2.0 \times 20.3} \times 100 = 17.74\%$$

$$\text{Net efficiency} = \frac{72}{(2.0 - 0.25) \times 20.3} \times 100 = 20.3\%$$

8.12 PRACTICAL 2: THERMOREGULATORY RESPONSES TO EXERCISE

The laboratory exercise involves recordings of rectal and skin temperatures at regular intervals during sustained performance. Exercise may be undertaken on either a motor-driven treadmill or a cycle ergometer. The purpose is to demonstrate physiological responses to exercise using thermoregulatory variables.

An example is shown in Figure 8.3. The exercise intensity was 210 W sustained for 60 minutes. Rectal temperature and skin temperatures were measured. The rectal temperature rose by 2°C during the experiment.

8.12.1 AIM

To investigate the thermoregulatory response to steady state and incremental exercise

8.12.2 EQUIPMENT

- Cycle ergometer
- Weighing scales
- Rectal thermistor (e.g. Grant Instruments, Royston, UK)
- Analogue or digital temperature monitor
- Electrocardiogram or short-range radio telemetry (e.g. Sport Tester, Polar Electro, Kempele, Finland)

8.12.3 PROTOCOL

Two subjects are required for this test. The subjects should place the rectal thermistor 10 cm beyond the external anal sphincter and attach skin thermistors on the sternum, on the medial forearm midway between elbow and wrist, on the anterior surface of the thigh midway between hip and knee and on the lateral surface of the lower leg between knee and ankle. Measure the subject's body mass immediately prior to exercise. One subject exercises at 70% maximum heart rate for 60 minutes with measurements of all variables taken at 3 minute intervals. The other subject exercises at 60 W for 5 minutes with the work-rate increased by 30 W each subsequent 5 minutes until exhaustion. Variables should be measured every minute. At the completion of exercise subjects should be weighed immediately (without drying the skin) to obtain an index of sweat evaporation rate.

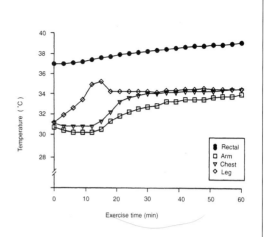

Figure 8.3 Temperature changes during exercise at 70% maximal heart rate.

8.12.4 CLEANING OF PROBES

Rectal probes should be washed in warm soapy water and then immersed in a 1:20 concentration of sterilization fluid for at least 30 minutes. On removal from the solution, the probes should be left to dry completely in room air before further use. Skin probes can be washed and immersed in a 1:40 solution of sterilization fluid for 10 minutes and left to dry.

8.13 PRACTICAL 3: ESTIMATION OF PARTITIONAL HEAT EXCHANGE

8.13.1 AIM

To examine the effect of different environmental conditions on evaporative and partitional heat exchange during exercise

8.13.2 EQUIPMENT

- Cycle ergometer
- Weighing scales
- Oxygen consumption measuring device (e.g. on-line system or Douglas bag method)
- Rectal thermistor
- Four skin thermistors
- Analogue or digital temperature monitor

8.13.3 PROTOCOL

One of the subjects exercises on two separate occasions, once in normal ambient conditions (21°C) and again in a hotter environment at the same work-rate. Immediately prior to exercise the individual is weighed (with all probes and clothes) and then completes 30–60 minutes of exercise followed by rapid re-weighing. All temperatures are measured every 5 minutes and $\dot{V}O_2$ is measured at 20-minute intervals.

8.13.4 CALCULATIONS

Heat balance equation

$$HS = M \pm (R \pm C \pm K) - E - W$$

Where:

$$\text{Metabolic Rate (M)} = \frac{\dot{V}O_2(\text{l min}^{-1}) \times \text{caloric equivalent} \times 60}{\text{Body Surface Area } (BSA)}$$

$$\text{Metabolic Rate (M)} = \frac{(\text{pre} - \text{exercise mass} - \text{post} - \text{exercise mass})(\text{kg}) \times 2430 \, (\text{kJ l}^{-1} \text{ sweat loss})}{\text{Time of exercise (h)} \times \text{BSA}}$$

$$Work(W) = \frac{\text{Work - rate (kJ min}^{-1} \times 60)}{\text{BSA}}$$

$$\text{Stored heat} = \frac{(\text{post} - \text{exercise T}_B - \text{pre} - \text{exercise T}_B) \times 3.47 (\text{kJ kg}^{-1} \text{ h}^{-1} \times \text{mass})}{\text{Time (h)} \times \text{BSA}}$$

All units are kJ m^{-2} h^{-1}

Examples of calculations using the following data:

$\dot{V}O_2 = 2.0 \, \text{l min}^{-1}$

RER = 0.85

Pre-exercise rectal temperature = 36.5°C

Post-exercise rectal temperature = 38.0°C

Pre-exercise skin temperature = 33.0°C

Post-exercise skin temperature = 33.9°C

Pre-exercise body mass = 72.0 kg

Post-exercise body mass = 71.5 kg

Body surface area = 1.8 m^2

Work-rate = 120 W

Duration of exercise = 60 minutes

$$\text{Metabolic rate (M)} = \frac{\dot{V}O_2 \times \text{caloric equivalent} \times 60}{\text{BSA}} = \frac{2 \times 20.3 \times 60}{1.8} = 1353.33 \text{ kJ m}^{-2} \text{ h}^{-1}$$

$$\text{Evaporation (E)} = \frac{\text{weight loss} \times 2430}{\text{time} \times \text{BSA}} = \frac{(72.0 - 71.5) \times 2430}{1 \times 1.8} = 675 \text{ kJ m}^{-2} \text{ h}^{-1}$$

$$\text{Work (W)} = \frac{72 \times 60}{1.8} = 240 \text{ kJ m}^{-2} \text{ h}^{-1}$$

$$\text{Stored heat} = \frac{(\text{post-exercise } T_B - \text{pre-exercise } T_B) \times 3.47 \times 72}{\text{Time (h)} \times \text{BSA}}$$

Where $T_B = (0.65 \text{ rectal}) + (0.35 \text{ skin})$

$$= \frac{(36.57 - 35.28) \times 3.47 \times 72}{1 \times 1.8} = 179.1 \text{ kJ m}^{-2} \text{h}^{-1}$$

Heat balance HS = M – E ± (R ± C ± K) – W
Therefore rearranging:
Partitional heat exchange = HS – M + E + W
$$= 179.1 - 1353.3 + 675 + 240$$
$$= -259.2 \text{ kJ m}^{-2} \text{ h}^{-1}$$

Therefore in the above example 259.2 kJ m^{-2} h^{-1} is lost from the body by the combined processes of radiation, conduction and convection.

REFERENCES

American College of Sports Medicine (1984). Position Statement. Prevention of thermal injuries during distance running. *Physician and Sportsmedicine*, **12** (7), 43–51.

Bedford, T. (1946). Environmental warmth and its measurement. *Medical Research Council War Memorandum no. 17.* (HMSO, London).

Beshir, M.Y., Ramsey, J.D. and Burford, C.L. (1982). Threshold values for the Botsball: a field study of occupational heat. *Ergonomics*, **25**, 247–54.

Brodie, D.A., Eston, R.G., Coxon, A., *et al.* (1991). The effect of changes of water and electrolytes on the validity of conventional methods of measuring fat-free mass. *Annals of Nutrition and Metabolism*, **35**, 89–97.

Burton, A.L. (1935). Human calorimetry. *Journal of Nutrition*, **9**, 261–79.

Costill, D.L. (1981). Muscle water and electrolyte distribution during prolonged exercise. *International Journal of Sports Medicine*, **2**, 130–4.

Froese, G. and Burton, A.C. (1957). Heat loss from the human head. *Journal of Applied Physiology*, **10**, 235–41.

Haymes, E.M. (1984). Physiological responses of female athletes to heat stress: a review. *Physician and Sportsmedicine*, **12**, no.3, March, 45–50.

Holdcroft, P. (1980). *Body Temperature Control.* (Baillière Tindall, London).

Holmer, I. and Bergh, U. (1974). Metabolic and thermal responses to swimming in water at varying temperatures. *Journal of Applied Physiology*, **37**, 702–5.

Horvath, S.M. (1981). Exercise in a cold environment. *Exercise and Sport Science Reviews*, 9, 221–63.

Keatinge, W.R. (1969). *Survival in Cold Water.* (Blackwell, Oxford).

Lee, D.H.K. (1980). Seventy five years of searching for a heat index. *Environmental Research*, 22, 331–56.

Lemmey, A., Eston, R.G., Moloney, S. and Yeomans, J. (2000). The effects of hydration state and rehydration method on bioelectrical impedance analysis. *South African Journal of Sports Medicine*, **7**, 8–12.

Pugh, G. (1972). The gooseflesh syndrome in long distance runners. *British Journal of Physical Education*, March, ix-xii.

Pugh, L.G.C. and Edholm, O.G. (1955). The physiology of channel swimmers. *Lancet*, **ii**, 761–8.

Rahn, H. and Yokoyama, T. eds. (1965). *Physiology of Breathold Diving and the Ama of Japan.* (National Academy of Sciences, Washington, DC).

Ramanathan, N.L. (1964). A new weighting system for mean temperature of the human body. *Journal of Applied Physiology*, **19**, 531–3.

Reilly, T. (1983). The energy cost and mechanical efficiency of circuit weight training. *Journal of Human Movement Studies*, **9**, 39–45.

Reilly, T. (1990). Human circadian rhythms and exercise. *Critical Reviews in Biomedical Engineering*, **18**, 165–80.

Reilly, T., Waterhouse, J. and Atkinson, G. (1997). Ageing, rhythms of physical performance, and adjustment to changes in the sleep-activity cycle. *Occupational and Environmental Studies*, **54**, 812–6.

Reilly, T., Atkinson, G. and Waterhouse, J. (2000). Chronobiology and physical performance, in *Exercise and Sport Science*. eds. W.E. Garrett Jr. and D.T. Kirkendall (Lippincott, Williams and Wilkins, Philadelphia, PA), pp. 351–72.

Ross, W.R., Drinkwater, D.T., Bailey, D.A. *et al.* (1980). Kinanthropometry; traditions and new perspectives. In *Kinanthropometry II*. eds. M. Ostyn, G. Beunen and J. Simons (University Park Press, Baltimore, MD), pp. 3–27.

Siple, P.A. and Passel, C.F. (1945). Measurement of dry atmospheric cooling in sub-freezing temperatures. *Proceedings of the American Philosophical Society*, **89**, 177–99.

Skreslet, S. and Aarefjord, F. (1968). Acclimatisation to cold in man induced by frequent scuba diving in cold water. *Journal of Applied Physiology*, **24**, 177–81.

Tipton, M., Eglin, C., Gennser, M. and Golden, F. (1999). Immersion deaths and deterioration in swimming performance in cold water. *Lancet*, **354**, 626–9.

Webb, P. (1982). Thermal problems. In *The Physiology and Medicine of Diving*. eds. O.G. Edholm and J.S. Weiner (Baillière Tindall, London), pp. 297–318.

PART FOUR

ASSESSMENT AND REGULATION OF ENERGY EXPENDITURE AND EXERCISE INTENSITY

CONTROL OF EXERCISE INTENSITY USING HEART RATE, PERCEIVED EXERTION AND OTHER NON-INVASIVE PROCEDURES

9

Roger G. Eston and John G. Williams

9.1 AIMS

The aims of this chapter are to:
- review and apply common non-invasive methods of determining exercise intensity,
- review relationships between heart rate, rating of perceived exertion, oxygen uptake and exercise intensity,
- assess the reliability of ratings of perceived exertion and evaluate the validity of such methods in controlling exercise intensity.

9.2 INTRODUCTION

People participate in physical exercise to improve general health, to improve performance-related fitness for a particular sport, and/or for recreation and relaxation. Improved fitness results from adaptation and improvement of cardiovascular, respiratory, and metabolic function as well as local responses in the muscle groups engaged. The nature and magnitude of any training effect are influenced by the frequency, duration, and intensity of exercise. The process of determining and controlling appropriate exercise intensity presents a challenge, which has implications related to both physiological changes and to individual compliance within an exercise programme.

9.3 NON-INVASIVE METHODS OF DETERMINING EXERCISE INTENSITY

An important principle to be assimilated at the outset is that intensity is interpreted by the person engaged in the exercise. No matter how sophisticated the physiological measurements, the psychological interpretation of cardiorespiratory, metabolic, and musculoskeletal functions will play a major role in this process. The psychological component of how 'hard' or 'easy' people perceive their physical efforts to be has been emphasized by Gunnar Borg for exercise testing and prescription since the 1960s (e.g. Borg, 1962). It is now included in mainstream guidelines for the conduct of exercise testing and prescription (American College of Sports Medicine, ACSM, 1995; British Association of Sport and Exercise Sciences, BASES, 1997).

However perceptive an individual's judgements of exercise intensity may be, accurate determination is enhanced by assessment of functional capacity and monitoring to ensure that optimal intensity is not exceeded. The acquisition of such data is only possible in a fully equipped exercise physiology laboratory using trained personnel. Plainly, this requirement invokes considerable practical limitations for many categories of participant. The

Kinanthropometry and Exercise Physiology Laboratory Manual: Tests, Procedures and Data. 2nd Edition, Volume 2: Exercise Physiology
Edited by RG Eston and T Reilly. Published by Routledge, London, June 2001

ACSM (1995) and BASES (1997) have provided concise guidelines for the conduct of such assessments.

9.4 PHYSIOLOGICAL INFORMATION

Several measurements for gauging exercise intensity for various exercise modalities have been devised and applied. These include proportion of maximal oxygen uptake (%$\dot{V}O_2$ max), proportion of maximal heart rate (%HR_{max}), proportion of maximal heart rate reserve (%HRR_{max}), and blood lactate indices. The following will cover the main principles of predicting and controlling exercise intensity by extrapolation from the relationships between oxygen uptake, heart rate, power output and running speed. For a detailed review of the application of metabolic and ventilatory measures for controlling exercise intensity, refer to Chapter 10 by Jones and Doust.

9.4.1 USING OXYGEN CONSUMPTION ($\dot{V}O_2$) TO PRESCRIBE EXERCISE INTENSITY

Exercising at a high (or moderate) intensity for a sustained period of time requires the ability to deliver oxygen to the active muscles. The most frequently cited criterion of maximal functional capacity for sustained exercise is the maximal oxygen uptake ($\dot{V}O_2$ max). Acquisition of this information requires appropriately equipped facilities and expert personnel as well as a high degree of compliance on the part of the participant. The method is explained in Chapter 7 by Cooke. Ideally, proportions of the $\dot{V}O_2$ max are used to specify exercise intensity levels. The recommended intensity range is normally between 40% and 85% depending on the health and training status of the individual (ACSM, 1995).

(a) Prediction of oxygen consumption levels using a multi-stage test

Although the measurement of $\dot{V}O_2$ is preferred, it is possible to predict $\dot{V}O_2$ max using the equations suggested by the ACSM (1995) for cycling, running, walking, stepping and rowing. Oxygen uptake can be predicted for any speed of walking and running on the level and uphill, as well as for cycling, stepping and rowing at specific work rates. In this way, the submaximal, predicted oxygen uptake values can be compared against the subject's heart rate and extrapolated to the maximal heart rate to predict $\dot{V}O_2$ max. With knowledge of the subject's $\dot{V}O_2$ max, it is then possible to prescribe speeds/work-rates that correspond to a given exercise intensity (%$\dot{V}O_2$ max values), using the ACSM formulae. The following examples are for running and cycling.

The formula used to predict $\dot{V}O_2$ at any given speed and gradient is:

$$\dot{V}O_2 \text{ (ml kg}^{-1}\text{ min}^{-1}) = \text{horizontal component} + \text{vertical component} + \text{resting component}$$

For running

$$\dot{V}O_2 \text{ (ml kg}^{-1}\text{ min}^{-1}) = (\text{speed (m min}^{-1})$$
$$\times 0.2 \text{ ml kg}^{-1}\text{ min}^{-1}) + (\text{gradient} \times \text{m min}^{-1}$$
$$\times 0.9 \text{ ml kg}^{-1}\text{ min}^{-1}) + 3.5 \text{ ml kg}^{-1}\text{ min}^{-1}$$

For cycling

$$\dot{V}O_2 \text{ (ml min}^{-1}) = (\text{work rate (kg m min}^{-1})$$
$$\times 2 \text{ ml kg}^{-1}\text{ min}^{-1}) + (\text{mass} \times 3.5 \text{ ml kg}^{-1}\text{ min}^{-1})$$

(Note: $1 W = 6.12 \text{ kg m min}^{-1}$; an alternative and simpler formula is: $\dot{V}O_2$ (ml min^{-1}) = $(12 \times W) + 300$)

In a multi-stage test the subject runs or cycles at two levels. When two submaximal $\dot{V}O_2$ values are calculated, the slope of the $\dot{V}O_2$ regression line is obtained and this is used to predict the $\dot{V}O_2$ max by extrapolation of one of the multi-stage $\dot{V}O_2$: HR values.

Calculation of the 'slope' of the $\dot{V}O_2$: HR relationship is determined by:

$$\text{Slope (b)} = \frac{(\dot{V}O_2 \text{ stage 2} - \dot{V}O_2 \text{ stage 1})}{(\text{HR stage 2} - \text{HR stage 1})}$$

$$\dot{V}O_2 \text{ max} = \dot{V}O_2 \text{ stage 2} + b\,[(220 - \text{age}) - \text{HR stage 2}]$$

It is important to note that HR values must be at steady state. Thus, the subject must exercise for at least 3 minutes. If the HR is not at steady state (i.e. it is still increasing) it will predict an unrealistic overestimation of the $\dot{V}O_2$ max and be inaccurate for prescription of subsequent exercise intensity. What follows is an example of the method used to predict $\dot{V}O_2$ max using actual data derived from an exercise test on one of the authors (RGE, age 38, mass 86 kg) a few years ago!

Prediction of $\dot{V}O_2$ max (treadmill protocol)

Treadmill data of the example are shown in Table 9.1.

Table 9.1 Treadmill data

	Stage 1	Stage 2
Speed (mph)	6	8
Gradient (%)	4	8
HR	134	172

Calculation of submaximal $\dot{V}O_2$
Stage 1:

$$\dot{V}O_2 \text{ (ml kg}^{-1}\text{ min}^{-1}) = (160.8 \text{ m min}^{-1} \times 0.2 \text{ ml kg}^{-1}\text{ min}^{-1} + (0.04 \times 160.8 \text{ m min}^{-1} \times 0.9 \text{ ml kg}^{-1}\text{ min}^{-1}) + 3.5 \text{ ml kg}^{-1}\text{ min}^{-1} = 41.4 \text{ ml kg}^{-1}\text{ min}^{-1}$$

Stage 2:

$$\dot{V}O_2 \text{ (ml kg}^{-1}\text{ min}^{-1}) = (214.4 \text{ m min}^{-1} \times 0.2 \text{ ml kg}^{-1}\text{ min}^{-1}) + (0.08 \times 214.4 \text{ m min}^{-1} \times 0.9 \text{ ml kg}^{-1}\text{ min}^{-1})$$

$$+ 3.5 \text{ ml kg}^{-1}\text{ min}^{-1} = 61.8 \text{ ml kg}^{-1}\text{ min}^{-1}$$

(Note: 1 mph $= 26.8 \text{ m min}^{-1} = 0.45 \text{ m s}^{-1}$)

Calculation of slope (b)

$$b = (61.8 - 41.4) / (172 - 134) = 0.54$$

Calculation of $\dot{V}O_2$ max

$$\dot{V}O_2 \text{ max (ml kg}^{-1}\text{ min}^{-1})$$
$$= 61.8 + 0.54\,((220 - 38) - 172) = 67$$

Prediction of $\dot{V}O_2$ max (cycle ergometry protocol)

Cycle ergometry data of the example are shown in Table 9.2.

Table 9.2 Cycle ergometry data

	Stage 1	Stage 2
Work rate (kg m min^{-1})	900 (147 W)	1200 (196 W)
Heart rate	124	138

Calculation of submaximal $\dot{V}O_2$
Stage 1:

$$\dot{V}O_2 \text{ (ml)} = (900 \text{ kg m min}^{-1} \times 2 \text{ ml kg min}^{-1}) + (86 \text{ kg} \times 3.5 \text{ ml kg}^{-1}\text{ min}^{-1}) = 2101$$

$$\dot{V}O_2 \text{ (ml kg}^{-1}\text{ min}^{-1}) = 2101 \text{ ml} / 86 \text{ kg} = 24.4$$

Stage 2:

$$\dot{V}O_2 \text{ (ml min}^{-1}) = (1200 \text{ kg m min}^{-1} \times 2 \text{ ml kg}^{-1}\text{ min}^{-1}) + (86 \text{ kg} \times 3.5 \text{ ml kg}^{-1}\text{ min}^{-1}) = 2701$$

$$\dot{V}O_2 \text{ (ml kg}^{-1}\text{ min}^{-1}) = 2701 \text{ ml} / 86 \text{ kg} = 31.4$$

Calculation of slope (b)

$$b = (31.4 - 24.4) / (138 - 124) = 0.50$$

Calculation of $\dot{V}O_2$ max for cycle ergometry

$$\dot{V}O_2 \text{ (ml kg}^{-1}\text{ min}^{-1})$$
$$= 31.4 + 0.50\,((220 - 38) - 138) = 53$$

(b) Determining the exercise prescription

Once a maximal aerobic capacity has been determined, it is possible to prescribe a running speed/work-rate that corresponds to a given exercise intensity. In the following example, the exercise intensity corresponding to 70% $\dot{V}O_2$ max is determined, for running and for cycling for RGE.

For running

In the above example the $\dot{V}O_2$ max was determined to be 67 ml kg^{-1} min^{-1}; 70% of this is 46.9 ml kg^{-1} min^{-1}.

By substitution into the formula:

$$\dot{V}O_2 = (\text{m min}^{-1} \times 0.2 \text{ ml m}^{-1} \text{ min}^{-1}) + 3.5$$

The running speed (m min^{-1})
$$= (\dot{V}O_2 - 3.5) / 0.2 = (46.9 - 3.5) / 0.2$$
$$= 217 \text{ m min}^{-1} (3.61 \text{ m s}^{-1})$$

This equates to a running speed of 13 km h^{-1} (8.1 mph) or a running pace of 4 min 36 s per km or 7 min 24 s per mile on a level gradient.

For cycling

In the above example the $\dot{V}O_2$ max was determined to be 53 ml kg^{-1} min^{-1}; 70% of this is 37.4 ml kg^{-1} min^{-1}. This value is multiplied by mass (86 kg) to give an absolute $\dot{V}O_2$ = 3216 ml.

By substitution into the formula

$$\dot{V}O_2 \text{ (ml min}^{-1}) = (\text{kg m min}^{-1} \times 2 \text{ ml kg}^{-1}) + (3.5 \text{ ml kg}^{-1} \text{ min}^{-1} \times \text{mass})$$

The work rate (kg m min^{-1})

$$= (\dot{V}O_2 - (3.5 \times \text{mass})) / 2$$
$$= (3216.4 - (3.5 \times 86)) / 2$$
$$= 1457.7 \text{ kg m min}^{-1} (238 \text{ W})$$

The next thing to decide is the preferred cycling frequency. Clearly, the higher the pedal frequency, the lower the load. If we assume that one pedal revolution is equal to a forward motion of 6 m (as per a Monark cycle ergometer; Monark Exercise AB, Varberg,

Sweden), the loading can be calculated by the formula:

$$\text{Load (kg)} = (\text{kg m min}^{-1}) / (6 \text{ m} \times \text{rev min}^{-1})$$

Thus, for a pedal frequency of 50 rev min^{-1} the loading will be 4.86 kg, and for a pedal frequency of 70 rev min^{-1} it would be 3.47 kg. At both pedalling speeds, the power output = 1457 kg m min^{-1} or 238 W.

(c) Estimation of energy expenditure

The concept of energy expenditure and metabolic rate is reviewed by Cooke in Chapter 6. The total energy expenditure can be calculated on the basis that 1 MET (3.5 ml kg^{-1} min^{-1}) is equivalent to an energy expenditure of approximately 4.2 kJ kg h^{-1} (1 kcal kg^{-1} h^{-1}). Thus, an 86 kg person would expend approximately 361 kJ min^{-1} (86 kcal min^{-1}) at rest. In the above example, to run at a pace equal to 70% $\dot{V}O_2$ max, the metabolic equivalent is about 13.4 METs. Thus, the energy expenditure per hour is 86 kg $\times$ 13.4 kcal kg^{-1} h^{-1} = 1152 kcal h^{-1} (4817 kJ h^{-1}). If the person runs for 30 minutes, the theoretical energy expenditure at this level can be calculated by the appropriate time proportion, i.e. 30 / 60 = 576 kcal (2409 kJ). This method is sometimes used to estimate a predicted weight loss. For example, on the basis that 1 g of substrate of mixed carbohydrate and fat (assuming an RER of 0.85) yields an energy content of 7.2 kcal (30 kJ), the weight loss in the above example would be about 2409 kJ / 30 kJ g^{-1} (576 kcal / 7.2 kcal g^{-1}) which equals 80 g. This may not seem much for all that effort, but an energy deficit of this magnitude for 7 days a week over one month would lead to a weight loss of (7 d $\times$ 80 g $\times$ 4.2 wk) about 2352 g (5.2 lb).

9.4.2 USING HEART RATE TO PRESCRIBE EXERCISE INTENSITY

The advent of non-encumbering telemetry methods has made the accurate measurement of heart rate a relatively straightforward process. Since heart rate and oxygen uptake share a positive, linear relationship regardless of age and sex, target heart rate ranges may be selected to correspond with $\dot{V}O_2$ max values (Karvonen and Vuorimaa, 1988). This method is used in a variety of field tests and exercise protocols to approximate and monitor exercise intensity.

As a general rule, maximal aerobic power improves if exercise is sufficiently intense to increase heart rate to about 70% of maximum; equivalent to about 50–55% of $\dot{V}O_2$ max. This is a level of intensity thought to be the minimal stimulus required to produce a training effect (Gaesser and Rich, 1984), which will vary according to initial fitness status. Estimation of $\dot{V}O_2$ max from percentage HR is subject to error in all populations because of the need for a true maximal heart rate value. This can be attained from 2–4 minutes of 'all-out' exercise in the activity of interest. Such a procedure demands sound health coupled with a high level of commitment from an individual and is only really appropriate for competitive athletes. For this reason, maximum heart rate is usually arrived at by subtracting an individual's age from a theoretical maximum of 220 beats min^{-1} regardless of gender and age.

Although all people of the same age (or gender) do not possess the same maximal heart rate, the loss in accuracy for individual variation of approximately ±10 beats min^{-1} as one standard deviation at any age-predicted heart rate is usually considered to be of small significance in establishing an effective exercise programme for healthy individuals. Nevertheless, caution is required with this predictive procedure because, within normal variation, only 68% of 20-year-olds will have a heart rate maximum between 190 and 210 beats min^{-1} (i.e. 220 − 20 ±10 beats min^{-1}). This formula is also inappropriate for certain types of activity such as swimming, because flotation in the supine position and the cooling effect of water reduce heart rate values to an average of about 10–13 beats min^{-1} lower than in running. The assessment of intensity for swimming should therefore be at least 10 beats min^{-1} lower than the age-predicted maximum heart rate (McArdle *et al.*, 1991).

A preferred method to prescribe exercise intensity is the percentage maximal heart rate reserve method (%HRR$_{max}$) as described by Karvonen and Vuorimaa (1988). This method uses the percentage difference between resting and maximal heart rate added to the resting heart rate. When compared to the %HR$_{max}$ method, %HRR$_{max}$ yields at least a 10 beat min^{-1} higher training heart rate when calculated for exercise intensities between 60% and 85% $\dot{V}O_2$ max. This method equates more closely with given submaximal $\dot{V}O_2$ max values in both healthy adults and cardiac patients (Pollock *et al.*, 1982).

The procedure for calculating %HRR$_{max}$ values to determine exercise heart rates and the method of calculating %HRR$_{max}$ from exercise heart rates is shown below.

To calculate %HRR$_{max}$ from an exercising heart rate the following formula is used:

$$\%HRR_{max} = \frac{Exercise\,HR - RHR}{HR_{max} - RHR}$$

$$e.g.\ \frac{154-60}{195-60} = 70\%HRR_{max}$$

where:
RHR = resting heart rate
HRR = heart rate reserve
%HRR$_{max}$ = percentage maximal heart rate reserve
HR$_{max}$ = 220 − age (e.g. at age 25 the predicted HR$_{max}$ = 195 beats min^{-1})
HRR = HR$_{max}$ − RHR (e.g. if RHR = 60 then HRR = 195 − 60 = 135 beats min^{-1})
%HRR$_{max}$ = (training intensity (% of maximum) × HRR) + RHR

The training intensity at 70% of HRR$_{max}$ is therefore ((0.7 × 135) + 60) = 154 beats min^{-1}.

Table 9.3 provides data in support of the %HRR$_{max}$ method. Oxygen uptake and HR data were collected on RGE during a graded exercise test to maximum for treadmill running. The %HRR$_{max}$ values (column 1) correspond very closely to the %$\dot{V}O_2$ max values (column 7), and may be used to prescribe exercise intensity at a given %$\dot{V}O_2$ max. The %HRmax values tend to

Table 9.3   A comparison of %$\dot{V}O_2$ max at equivalent %HRRmax and %HRmax levels

%HR level	HR at %HRmax	$\dot{V}O_2$ (ml kg^{-1} min^{-1})	%$\dot{V}O_2$ max	HR at %HRRmax	$\dot{V}O_2$ (ml kg^{-1} min^{-1})	%$\dot{V}O_2$ max
40	73	8	13	105	26	41
50	91	21	33	118	33	52
60	109	28	44	131	38	60
70	127	37	59	144	46	73
80	140	43	68	157	52	82
90	164	56	89	169	58	92
100	182	63	100	182	63	100

Figure 9.1 A comparison of %$\dot{V}O_2$ max values at equivalent %HRRmax and %HRmax levels for RGE.

underestimate the %$\dot{V}O_2$ max values (column 4), as exemplified in Figure 9.1.

9.4.3 RATING OF PERCEIVED EXERTION (RPE)

(a) The concept of effort perception

The realization that physical performance emanates from a complex interaction of both perceptual, cognitive, and metabolic processes occurred a long time ago (see discussion by Borg, 1998, pp. 2–6). Perceived exertion is known to play an important role in the regulation of exercise intensity. Use of the Rating of Perceived Exertion Scale was first adopted as a principle in the exercise testing guidelines of the ACSM in 1986. Since then more detail has been added on the use of this important tool by both the ACSM (1995; 1998), BASES (1997) and of course by Borg (1998) himself.

The reasoning behind the use of what appears to be 'cardboard technology' is that humans possess a well-developed system for sensing the strain involved in physical effort.

This system is in constant use. A person can sense whether he/she is able to continue during vigorous exercise. Furthermore, during a bout of exercise, one is able to report both current, overall feelings of exertion and the locus of particular strain (say, in the chest or arms). With some experience of various levels of exercise, people have little difficulty in numerically scaling or at least ordering samples of exercise to which they have been subjected.

(b) Rating of perceived exertion scales

Attempts have been made to establish a basis for interpreting bodily sensations during exercise. By applying established principles of psychophysics (Stevens, 1957; Ekman, 1961) to gross motor action, Borg determined relative stimulus–response (S–R) functions and then developed two rating scales, the 6–20 Category Scale (RPE, Borg, 1970) and the Category-Ratio 10 Scale (CR10, Borg, 1982). Both scales have been revised since their inception. The latest revisions documented by Borg (1998) are used here. By far, the most commonly used device is the RPE Scale (RPE, Table 9.4). With this scale, the RPE increases linearly as exercise intensity increases. It is most closely correlated with the physiological responses that increase linearly, for example, heart rate and oxygen consumption. The CR10 Scale (Table 9.5) was constructed by Borg to take advantage of the properties of Stevens's ratio scaling (Stevens, 1957, 1971) and category scaling, so that verbal expressions and numbers could be used in a way that is congruent with the non-linear characteristics of sensory perception and physical stimulation. Basically, the psychophysical characteristics of the relationship between perceived exertion (Response, R) and exercise intensity (Stimulus, S) can be described as $R = c \times S^n$, where n is the exponent which reflects the growth function. The CR10 Scale may therefore be considered more appropriate to reflect the psychophysical characteristics of those variables which increase as a curvilinear

Table 9.4 The Borg 6 to 20 RPE Scale (Borg, 1998)

6	No exertion at all
7	
8	Extremely light
9	Very light
10	
11	Light
12	
13	Somewhat hard
14	
15	Hard (heavy)
16	
17	Very hard
18	
19	Extremely hard
20	Maximal exertion

function of power output, such as blood lactate and ventilation.

In both scales, numbers are anchored to verbal expressions. However, in the Category-Ratio Scale, unlike the 6–20 Category Scale, the numbers are not fixed. Half numbers or decimals can be used, e.g. 0.7 or 2.3. The numerical values also have a fixed relation to one another. For example, an intensity (I) judgement of 5 would be gauged to be half that of 10. It is important to note that in the CR10 Scale, a rating of 10 is not truly maximal. Borg (1998) indicated that this level is 'as hard as most people have ever experienced before in their lives'. If during the exercise test the subjective intensity exceeds this level, the person is free to choose any number in proportion to 10 that describes the proportionate growth in the sensation of effort. For example if the exercise intensity feels 20% harder than 10, the RPE would be 12. Instructions and rationale for using the two RPE Scales are provided in more detail by Borg (1998).

Table 9.5 The Borg CR10 Scale (Borg, 1998)

0	Nothing at all	'No I'
0.3		
0.5	Extremely weak	Just noticeable
0.7		
1	Very weak	
1.5		
2	Weak	Light
2.5		
3	Moderate	
4		
5	Strong	Heavy
6		
7	Very strong	
8		
9		
10	Extremely strong	'Max I'
11		
⌐		
●	Absolute maximum	Highest possible

(c) Exercise intensity and effort perception

Investigators who have examined the relationship between perceived exertion ratings and the indices of relative intensity discussed above (%$\dot{V}O_2$ max, %HR_{max} and so on) for graded exercise testing have generally reported high and positive correlation values ($r = 0.85$ and above). Also, perceived exertion, HR, and blood lactate La, for cycling, running, walking and arm ergometry are related in a consistent manner in that the incremental curve for perceived exertion can be predicted from a simple combination of HR and La (Borg *et al.*, 1987). Furthermore, criterion group differences (such as trained versus untrained, lean versus obese) observed at equivalent absolute work-rates diminish at the same %$\dot{V}O_2$ max. These results apply to both intermittent and continuous protocols.

Pollock *et al.* (1982) compared the validity of the RPE scale for prescribing exercise intensity with the two HR methods in young adult, old adult and cardiac patients. They observed that the %HRR_{max} method coupled with RPE was a much better indicator of exercise intensity and that the differences in RPE were greatly diminished at equivalent %HRR_{max} levels.

The empirical evidence supporting the notion that the regulation of exercise intensity is a psychophysiological process has led to the assertion that perceived exertion alone may be a sufficient basis for gauging exercise intensity (Borg, 1971). Ratings of 12 to 13 on the Borg 6 to 20 scale correspond to about 60–80% of $\dot{V}O_2$ max during treadmill running in most individuals (Eston *et al.*, 1987; Lamb *et al.*, 1999) and ratings of 16 to 17 are approximately 90% $\dot{V}O_2$ max (Eston *et al.*, 1987). For cycle ergometry the exercise intensities elicited at RPEs 13 and 17 tend to be somewhat lower, ranging from about 45% to 80% $\dot{V}O_2$ max, respectively (Eston and Williams, 1988; Parfitt *et al.*, 1996; Eston and Thompson, 1997).

(d) Applications for preferred exercise intensity

Although the association between RPE and preferred exercise intensity was included in Borg's published PhD thesis (Borg, 1962, pp. 31–32), it is only fairly recently that the use of RPE in this way has been applied in studies on preferred exercise intensity (Dishman *et al.*, 1994; Eston *et al.*, 1998; Parfitt *et al.*, 2000). Parfitt *et al.* (1996) investigated the differences in psychological affect and interest–enjoyment between prescribed treadmill intensity (based on 65% $\dot{V}O_2$ max) and preferred intensity exercise sessions, each of 20 minutes. Participants exercised at a higher intensity in the preferred versus a prescribed exercise condition, although there were no differences in RPE. It seems that the participants perceived that they were exercising at the same level in both conditions. This may indicate a positive perception for the preferred exercise intensity session as the participants worked harder but reported similar RPEs. In addition, work-rate and RPE increased over the duration of the exercise session. The apparent warm-up strategy during the preferred exercise intensity session confirmed findings from a previous study by Eston *et al.* (1998). In the latter study, preferred exercise intensity during a 30 minute cycle ride with both active and inactive healthy men, equated with a mean RPE of 13.

(e) Prediction of maximal heart rate

Often, it is not possible to measure maximal heart rate (HR_{max}) for practical or medical reasons. In such circumstances, prediction from the formula 220 beats min^{-1} minus age is used, although it has been indicated that this is only a rough estimate. As the relationship between RPE, $\dot{V}O_2$ and HR is linear over most of its range, it is theoretically possible to estimate maximal heart rate on the basis of submaximal RPE:HR responses, because RPE has a maximal value of 20. In fact, in our experience, a rating of 20 is rarely given by the subject. It is more common to record RPEs of 18 or 19, 'which for most people is the most strenuous exercise they have ever experienced' (Borg, 1998). The prescription of appropriate exercise intensities on the basis of this relationship, i.e. prediction of maximal heart rate from the linear extrapolation of submaximal RPEs, taken from a graded exercise test, has been applied in a number of studies (e.g. Wilmore *et al.*, 1986; Eston and Williams, 1986). Although less frequently used, perhaps indicating a short-sighted approach by researchers in the field, the prediction of HR_{max} can be derived from an effort-production rather an effort-estimation procedure. With this method an effort level of perceived magnitude to points on the RPE scale is produced. Eston and Thompson (1997) used this method to predict maximal heart rate in patients receiving beta blockade treatment to help quantify appropriate exercise intensity levels. Prediction of HR_{max} from RPE estimation and production protocols is demonstrated using data from RGE in the laboratory practical later in this chapter.

(f) Reliability of RPE production and estimation procedures

A worthwhile practical application is to use the rating scale as a frame of reference for regulating various intensities of exercise. Such an approach is clearly applicable to endurance training in various sports, but also applies to the attainment of general fitness and rehabilitation. As a rule it seems sensible to encourage people to 'tune' to their effort sense and develop sufficient awareness for determining an appropriate exercise intensity without recourse to external devices.

Several studies have confirmed the validity of self-regulation guided by effort rating procedures. In other words, the rating of perceived exertion can be used to regulate exercise intensities by enabling a subject to repeat a given physiological measure or exercise level from trial to trial. This has been demonstrated for treadmill running in adults (Smutok *et al.*, 1980; Eston *et al.*, 1987; Dunbar *et al.*, 1992; Glass *et al.*, 1992), cycling (Eston and Williams, 1988; Dunbar *et al.*, 1992; Buckley *et al.*, 2000), wheelchair exercise in children (Ward *et al.*, 1995) and cycling in children (Eston and Williams, 1986; Williams *et al.*, 1991; Eston *et al.*, 2000). This approach has also been used to predict $\dot{V}O_2$ max or maximal work-rate (e.g. Eston and Thompson, 1997).

An important consideration of the plausibility of determining exercise intensity through perceived exertion is that much of the research in this area has been undertaken in controlled laboratory conditions. As indicated above, a number of studies employing the RPE production mode have evaluated the reliability of RPE during treadmill exercise, track walking and running and/or cycle ergometry. With the exception of the study by Eston and Williams (1988), the target production mode RPE levels were determined from a passive estimation protocol measured during an initial graded exercise test (GXT). Byrne and Eston (1997) recommended caution when inferring a target production RPE from GXT estimation mode responses. They reported a mismatch of exercise intensities at a given RPE between estimation and production modes. Eston and Williams (1988) evaluated multiple-trial production mode reliability using pre-selected, randomly assigned RPEs of 9, 13 and 17 during cycle ergometry, and concluded that reliability improves after a period of initial practice. Such an application would seem relevant for field-work, where the practical problems and safety issues of administering an initial GXT are alleviated. Although this study has been widely cited when RPE reliability is discussed, it has only recently been replicated (Buckley *et al.*, 2000). The study by Eston and Williams (1988) and more recent studies by Lamb *et al.* (1999), Buckley *et al.* (2000) and Eston *et al.* (2000), which have used more rigorous measures for assessing reliability, provide evidence that the accuracy of effort perception is dependent on familiarization and practice for both production and estimation procedures.

If exercise prescription is to be based on RPE, then the exercise mode must be specified because the source of the effort percept varies and influences the magnitude of the rating (Pandolf, 1983). When different modes of exercise are performed, the RPE is greater for work involving small muscle groups (Berry *et al.*, 1989). The classic study by Ekblom and Goldbarg (1971) which differentiated between local and central effort percepts showed that the RPE for a given submaximal oxygen uptake or heart rate was higher for cycling compared to running. Also, Eston and Williams (1988) showed that RPE was higher for a given $\%\dot{V}O_2$ max value for cycling compared to running, when RPE was used to self-regulate exercise intensity. In addition, local and central factors are influenced by pedalling rate on a cycle ergometer (Robertson *et al.*, 1979). Higher RPE values were reported for pedalling rates of 40 rev min^{-1} compared to 80 rev min^{-1}. Furthermore, the timing of the measurement of RPE has been found to be an important consideration. For example, Parfitt and Eston (1995) observed that RPEs measured during cycle ergometry were significantly higher in the final 20 s of a 4-minute exercise bout, compared to the same point 2 minutes into the exercise bout for both men and women.

Dunbar *et al.* (1992) observed that there was greater test–retest reliability when RPE was estimated during cycle ergometry compared to treadmill running. This was attributed to the greater localization of muscle fatigue during cycle ergometry, allowing for a more accurate assessment of the intensity of the peripheral signal. They reported that a comparatively greater attentional focus on these intense regionalized perceptual signals might sharpen input to the perceptual cognitive framework. It follows from this finding that the production of a target RPE on the cycle should be facilitated. Another possible explanation advanced by Dunbar *et al.* (1992) was that the more stable position of the subject during cycle ergometry results in greater consistency in the RPE estimation. They postulated that the task of maintaining balance on a moving belt, as on a treadmill while running, may distract the individual from the quantity and intensity of the perceptual signals.

Although the process is not the same, the role of dissociation, as a method of alleviating the discomfort associated with exercise-induced fatigue, has been the subject of interest for some time (Benson *et al.*, 1978). It has been claimed to be a useful coping mechanism (Morgan *et al.*, 1983), although Rejeski (1985) has reported that theoretical explanations of why and how it works are lacking. He suggested that dissociative strategies provide a relief from fatigue by occupying limited channel capacity critical to bringing a percept into focal awareness. In addition, the subject is faced with the task of regulating speed and gradient of the treadmill and it is likely that the perception of speed is fundamentally different from the perception of exertion for whole-body exercise.

Those involved in assessing and giving advice on exercise prescription should be aware of the numerous factors that might influence this process. Apart from gender and age, contrasting styles of sensory processing may predispose individuals to modulate intensity (Robertson *et al.*, 1977). Furthermore, perceptual reactance mediated by sensory processing probably interacts with personality traits (characteristic ways of behaving). Whereas such variables may well be randomized out in general in research on perceived exertion, these are important considerations for individual exercise prescription. Reference should be made to Morgan (1981), Williams and Eston (1985, 1986, 1989), Cioffi (1991) and Watt and Grove (1993) for discussions of these variables.

9.5 EFFORT PERCEPTION IN CHILDREN

Consideration of the validity and reliability of an RPE scale for children should not ignore age, reading ability, experience, and conceptual understanding. The latter is a developmental issue, influenced by the extent of children's experiences of exercise, which was recognized some time ago by two of the leading proponents of RPE (Bar-Or, 1977; Borg, 1977). In recognition of the difficulties associated with the application of Borg's 6 to 20 Rating of Perceived Exertion (RPE) scale with children (Williams *et al.*, 1991), Williams *et al.* (1993, 1994) proposed and validated a 1–10 scale (Children's Effort Rating Table, CERT, Table 9.6) which contained fewer possible responses, a range of numbers more familiar to children, and more simple verbal expressions identified by children through a series of exercise sessions. Although CERT appears to have acceptable validity (Eston *et al.*, 1994; Lamb, 1995, 1996), it nevertheless requires the child to interpret words and numbers alone.

For a child to perceive effort accurately, and subsequently to produce exercise intensity level from a predetermined RPE, it is logical to assume that learning must occur. A production protocol was incorporated into the early research procedures during the development of CERT (Williams *et al.*, 1993) and it was found that children in the 6- to 8-year age range were

Table 9.6 Children's Effort Rating Table (CERT) (Williams *et al.*, 1994)

1	Very, very easy
2	Very easy
3	Easy
4	Just feeling a strain
5	Starting to get hard
6	Getting quite hard
7	Hard
8	Very hard
9	Very, very hard
10	So hard I am going to stop

unable to gauge even roughly intermediate levels of exercise intensity. Learning is a more or less permanent change in behaviour which is reflected by a change in performance brought about by practice as well as maturation (Buskist and Gerbing, 1990). Thus, the child must have developed the relevant cognitive capacity to comprehend the task as well as the direct experience and practice of the activity. According to Piaget's (1972) stage model of development, children around the age of 7–10 years can understand categorization, but find it easier to understand and interpret pictures and symbols rather than words and numbers. Contemporary paediatric exercise research has addressed this problem.

Recently, investigators have incorporated a variety of symbols and pictures to represent categories of effort in paediatric versions of effort perception scales. These developments recognize the need for verbal descriptors and terminology that are more pertinent to a child's cognitive development, age, and reading ability. The first published attempt was by Nystad *et al.* (1989) who depicted various stages of fatigue with stick figures to improve understanding of the Borg 6 to 20 scale in a group of 10–12-year-old asthmatic children. However, they still observed that children had difficulty interpreting the scale. Robertson *et al.* (2000) have produced the 0–10 Omni Scale, which depicts a child on a bicycle, at various stages of physical exertion, on a uniform gradient set at about 45°. This study validated the scale on separate ethnic groups of children.

As a consequence of reviewing the existing scales and concern with their limitations, Eston *et al.* (2000) proposed a symbolic Cart and Load Effort Rating scale (CALER, Figure 9.2). The CALER scale presents a child on a bicycle, at various stages of exertion, pulling a cart that is loaded progressively with bricks along a non-incremental path. The number of bricks in the cart corresponds with the numbers on the scale. The wording on the scale has been selected from the CERT. Other variants, including a four effort level scale anchored with versions of the well-known 'smiley' face and scaled directly from CERT and RPE, have been developed. Early research with 7-year-olds in the USA indicates that children readily identify and discriminate effort level with the various facial expressions (Williams and O'Brien, 2000).

As previously indicated, data on adults suggest that the accuracy of repeated effort production procedures is improved with practice. Eston *et al.* (2000) assessed the reliability of effort production at CALER 2, 5 and 8 across four occasions separated by one to two weeks in 20 boys and girls aged 7–10 years. A 'levels of agreement' and correlation analysis (for a discussion of these procedures, refer to Volume 1, Chapter 10 by Nevill and Atkinson) provided strong evidence that practice improves the reliability of effort perception and preliminary evidence for the validity of the CALER Scale. A more detailed discussion of effort perception in children, with examples of symbolic scales, is provided by Eston and Lamb (2000).

The next stage for the reader is to gain practical experience of determining exercise intensity which involves the measurement of perceived exertion and heart rate. Three practical exercises, an effort estimation, a heart rate production, and effort production protocol, are described. The data shown in Tables 9.7, 9.8 and 9.9 were taken on RGE over three consecutive days in 1994.

Figure 9.2 The Cart and Load Effort Rating Scale (Eston *et al.*, 2000).

9.6 PRACTICAL 1: USE OF RATINGS OF PERCEIVED EXERTION TO DETERMINE AND CONTROL THE INTENSITY OF CYCLING EXERCISE

9.6.1 ESTIMATION PROTOCOL

(a) Purpose

To determine the relationships between heart rate (HR), rating of perceived exertion (RPE), and power output for cycle ergometry

(b) Procedure

The subject is prepared for exercise with a heart rate monitoring device and informed that consecutive bouts of exercise will be performed on a cycle ergometer for 4 minutes. In the last 15 s of each 2-minute period the HR is recorded and the subject is requested to provide a rating of how hard the exercise feels. After the 4-minute period the resistance is increased by 25 W and the procedure repeated. The subject continues exercising in this way until 85% of the predicted maximal heart rate (220 minus age) is reached. At this point the resistance is removed and the subject is allowed a 5-minute warm-down period. All data are recorded as in Table 9.7.

Table 9.7   RPE estimation protocol

Name	Roger Eston		Age	38		HT 1.78 m
Body mass	83 kg		Date	21st Sept '94		Rest HR 45 beats min^{-1}

Power (W)	Time (min)	HR	RPE	%HR$_{max}$	%HRR$_{max}$
50	2	67	6	37	16
	4	73	7	40	20
75	2	81	7	44	26
	4	82	7	45	27
100	2	86	9	47	30
	4	92	10	50	34
125	2	96	10	53	37
	4	97	10	53	38
150	2	117	11	64	53
	4	122	12	67	56
175	2	135	12	74	66
	4	140	13	77	69
200	2	148	14	81	75
	4	153	15	84	79
225	2	157	15	86	82
	4	160	16	88	84
250	2	163	16	90	86
	4	165	17	91	88

Immediately prior to exercising, each subject is introduced to Borg's 6 to 20 Rating of Perceived Exertion Scale. It is essential that the subjects clearly understand that an accurate interpretation of the overall feeling of exertion brought about by the exercise is required when requested by the investigator. To do this, the participant uses the verbal expressions on the scale to provide a numerical rating of effort during exercise. It is recommended that standardized instructions are used to introduce the scale, as described in Borg (1998) and that complete comprehension of the process is checked during a brief warm-up period. Customized instructions may be needed for special applications of RPE. We have found that the perceptual 'anchoring' of the scale can be facilitated by manipulating the work-rates so that the participant experiences how hard the exercise feels at RPEs of 8–9 and RPEs of 16–17.

9.6.2 PRODUCTION PROTOCOL

(a) Purpose

To use heart rate and a given perceived exertion rating to produce exercise intensity levels on a cycle ergometer

(b) Procedure

The subjects, apparatus, exercise mode and general organization remain the same as in the Estimation Protocol (Section 9.6.1). However, in this task the approach is quite different. Two protocols are followed. Both are representative of procedures used in the determination of exercise intensity. The investigator should register the results into a record as shown in Tables 9.8 and 9.9, which also serves as a guide to each step in the process.

(c) HR Production Test: use of heart rate to produce selected levels of exercise intensity (Table 9.8)

The subject is allowed a brief period to habituate and warm-up for exercise. Following this the investigator increases power output randomly to elicit steady-state heart rate levels of 110, 130, 150 and 170 beats min^{-1} for between 3 and 4 minutes. The RPE (Category Scale) is applied in the final 15 s of the exercise period.

Table 9.8 Using heart rate to control exercise intensity

HR	Power output (W)	RPE	%HRR$_{max}$
110	159	11	47
130	188	12	62
150	223	14	77
170	260	18	91

(d) RPE Production Test: use of RPE to produce selected levels of exercise intensity (Table 9.9)

The subject uses Borg's 6 to 20 category scale as a frame of reference to determine selected levels of exercise intensity using only his or her bodily sensations arising

Table 9.9 Using RPE to control exercise intensity

RPE	Power output (W)	HR	%HRR$_{max}$
11	105	107	45
13	182	135	66
15	217	150	77
17	253	165	88

from the exercise. All visual (except pedalling frequency, which is constant) and auditory information feedback is removed. The subject exercises and self-adjusts power output until steady-state levels of RPE 11, 13, 15 and 17 are established and maintained for between 3 and 4 minutes. The investigator records power output at steady state and heart rate in the final 15 s of exercise, when the subject is confident that he or she is exercising at a constant RPE.

(e) Tasks/questions

1. Using linear regression analysis on data from the estimation protocol at minute 4, comment on the relationship between power output, heart rate and the rating of perceived exertion.
2. Using related *t* tests, compare the HR and RPE data from minute 2 and 4. How could this difference affect the prediction of maximal values for power output and HR?
3. Draw a simple graph to compare the relationship between HR and RPE for each of the three protocols. Put HR on the *x* axis so that the relationships can be directly compared.
4. Compare / correlate the power output and RPE values predicted from the estimation test at HR 110, 130, 150, 170 to the actual RPE and power output values produced in the HR production test.
5. Using RPEs of 19 and 20, predict the HRmax from both the estimation and production protocol. How does this compare to 220 – age?

9.7 BRIEF ANALYSIS OF THE EFFORT ESTIMATION AND PRODUCTION TEST DATA SHOWN IN TABLES 9.7, 9.8 AND 9.9

9.7.1 RPE ESTIMATION TEST

Table 9.7 contains an example of data collected during an 'estimation test' on one of the authors (RGE). It is possible to determine relationships between power output, heart rate and the rating of perceived exertion. It is evident from these data that there is a strong correlation between HR, RPE and power output, with correlations around 0.98. The importance of allowing sufficient time to adapt to the work-rate is also evident. A related *t* test indicates a significantly lower HR and RPE at minute 2 compared to minute 4 ($p < 0.01$).

The data from the estimation test can be compared with data derived from the production test. As already indicated above, the high correlations between HR, power output and RPE allow predictions of HR and power output to be made from RPE in both the estimation protocol (Table 9.8) and the effort production test (Table 9.9). The following section provides an example of such calculations. Note that only steady-state values have been used. The RPE data for each protocol could also be plotted against HR to compare the relationship.

In the estimation test, the regression equation for HR and power output is: power output = 1.9 (HR) – 79 ($r = 0.99$, SEE = 12 W). Thus, with prescribed heart rates of 110, 130, 150 and 170 beat min^{-1} the predicted power output values are 130, 168, 206 and 244 W respectively. A similar analysis on HR:RPE reveals that the predicted RPEs at these heart rates are 10.8, 12.9, 14.9 and 17 (RPE = 0.102 (HR) – 0.4; $r = 0.98$, SEE = 0.7). These values compare fairly well to the obtained values in the production test.

9.7.2 RPE PRODUCTION TEST

To compare how well the manipulation of RPE in the effort production protocol was at producing target heart rates, it is necessary to re-compute the linear regression equation for RPE:HR, with RPE as the predictor variable. The regression equation for RPE and HR is: HR = 9.47 (RPE) + 7.8 ($r = 0.98$, SEE = 11 beats min^{-1}). Thus, for an RPE of 11, 13, 15 and 17, the predicted HR values are 112, 131, 150 and 169, which compare extremely well with the target heart rates used to prescribe exercise intensity in Table 9.8. A similar analysis reveals that the predicted power output values at these RPEs are 134 W, 171 W, 208 W and 244 W, respectively. The regression equation for this prediction is: power output = 18.4 (RPE) − 68.4 ($r = 0.99$, SEE = 22 W). The reliability of the predicted versus actual HR and power output values at the prescribed RPEs is 0.99 and 0.98, respectively. Related t tests revealed no significant difference between the means.

As subjects rarely report a maximal RPE of 20, it is recommended that an RPE of 19 and 20 is inserted into the regression equation to predict a HR$_{max}$ range. The predicted HRmax is 188 to 197 for RPE 19 and 20, respectively. A HR$_{max}$ of 192 (RPE 19) was recorded on RGE one year later during a graded exercise test on the treadmill. This value compares to an age-predicted HR$_{max}$ of $(220 - 39) = 181$. For this individual therefore, the RPE estimation of maximal heart rate is closer.

For RGE the exercise test provided useful data which enabled him to regulate subsequent exercise intensities using both RPE and HR information obtained in the estimation test. One should remember, however, that the subject was an experienced user of the RPE scale and that practice improves the reliability of RPE for prescribing exercise intensities (Eston and Williams, 1988; Buckley *et al.*, 2000; Eston *et al.*, 2000).

9.8 PRACTICAL 2: RELATIONSHIP BETWEEN POWER OUTPUT, PERCEIVED EXERTION (CR10), HEART RATE AND BLOOD LACTATE

9.8.1 PURPOSE

To determine the relationship between perceived exertion (R), using Borg's CR10 Scale, with equal and gradual increments in exercise intensity (Stimulus, S) of 30–40 W. The psychophysical characteristics of the relationship can primarily be described as $R = c \times S^n$, where n is the exponent which reflects the growth function.

9.8.2 PROTOCOL

After explanation of the procedures, exercise intensity commences at 30–40 W and increases by similar increments until the participant responds at about 8 on the CR10 Scale. The participant should be reminded that he/she does not have to stick to the numbers on the scale. The scale is continuous and decimals (e.g. 0.8 or 2.3) can be used. If the participant is able, he/she should continue to maximal volitional exhaustion. The predicted maximal work-rate from extrapolation of the 'curve of best fit' can then be compared to the actual maximal work-rate.

9.8.3 TO DO

1. Plot the raw values of power output against the CR10 Scale on the vertical axis. You should observe that the relationship is curvilinear in nature.
2. *Calculation of the exponent by log-log regression analysis.* The curve of best fit can be calculated by performing a simple linear regression analysis on the natural log values (ln) from the CR10 Scale and the power output (PO) values. Table 9.10 gives an example using the sample class data: The ln:ln regression equation for the above data is $R = -5.496 + S (1.42)$. In this case, the exponent is 1.42.
3. *Prediction of maximal work rate using CR10 as the independent variable.* Using a similar procedure, in Table 9.10 it should be possible to predict the maximal work rate from the above submaximal data by entering a CR10 value of 10. The ln:ln regression equation for the above, using R as the x value is:

   $S = 3.872 + 0.703(R)$. The antilog of 3.872 is 48.04. The exponent is 0.703.

   Then from the equation $y = bx^a$:

   Maximal power output at $CR10 = b$
   $CR10^{0.703} = 48.04 \times (CR10)^{0.703} = 242$ W

Table 9.10   Example data for Practical 2

Stimulus (S in watts)	Response (R, CR10)
40	0.8
80	2.0
120	3.5
160	5.5
200	8.0

Table 9.11   Relationship between power output, perceived exertion (CR10), heart rate and blood lactate (female aged 24, 182 cm, 78 kg)

Power output (W)	CR10 value	HR	La
40	0.5	94	2.5
80	1.0	102	2.4
120	2.5	135	1.9
160	3.5	154	3.9
200	4.5	166	4.1
240	7.5	184	6.1
280	9.5	191	10.1
320	11.0	193	12.9
3 min post			12.1

As a check, enter ln 250 into the equation in paragraph 2, which uses PO as the independent factor, i.e., $R = -5.496 + 1.42 (5.52) = \ln 2.344$. Antilog of 2.344 = 10!

4. It would be interesting to compare the predicted maximal power output to the actual maximum obtained. The data in Table 9.11 were derived from a female participant (Elaine) during a workshop with Gunnar Borg at the University of Wales, Bangor in April 2000. You could compare the power output versus lactate relationship using similar procedures.

The ln : ln regression equation (of values up to CR 7.5) to calculate exponent:

$$R = -4.871 + S (1.18) \qquad \text{Exponent} = 1.18$$

The ln: ln regression equation using CR10 as the independent variable:

Max S at $CR10 = 4.271 + R (0.64)$ Exponent = 0.64   Antilog of intercept = 71.6

The equation of the curve to predict maximal power output (POmax) at CR10 ($y = bx^a$):

$$71.6 \times CR10^{0.64}$$

Predicted POmax at CR10 = 313 W   Actual POmax at CR11 = 320 W

What does this indicate about the efficacy of the CR10 Scale to predict maximal functional capacity?

9.9 PRACTICAL 3: THE BORG CYCLING STRENGTH TEST WITH CONSTANT LOAD

9.9.1 PURPOSE

To determine the maximal power output that can be sustained for a period of 30 s, using the Borg RPE Scale. The rationale and development of this test, which could be considered as the forerunner to the well-established Wingate Test (described in Chapter 11 by Winter and Maclaren) is presented in greater detail by Borg (1998, pp. 57–58).

9.9.2 PROTOCOL

In this laboratory experiment, the participant cycles for a series of 30 s bouts at constant work rates of 50, 100, 150, 200, 250, 300 … W, to an RPE of about 16–17. Pedalling speed should be kept constant at 60 or 70 rpm. The work intervals are separated by 2 minutes rest/active recovery. RPE and HR are recorded in the final 5 s. The predicted maximal work-rate range is calculated by extrapolating to RPE 19–20. This can be done by linear regression or pen and paper. After five minutes the subject cycles at the predicted work rate (W1) that he/she can sustain for 30s. The time is recorded. This is T1. The load is then adjusted using time to exhaustion (T1) at W1 using the formula in the next section. See data in Table 9.12.

9.9.3 TO DO

1. Plot the raw values of PO versus RPE and HR for each increment.
2. Extrapolate the PO:RPE and the PO:HR relationships to RPE = 20 and HR = maximal heart rate, respectively.
3. Compare the predicted work rates from the perpendicular at RPE (20) and the predicted HR_{max}.
4. The equation describing the curvilinear relationship for this kind of exercise is:
   Time on task = $c \times W^{-4}$

   (see Borg, 1998, pp. 57–58)
5. In Borg's example (1998, p. 58), the predicted maximal work rate that can be sustained for 30 s is 275 W. This is W1. The subject now pedals at this level for as long as possible, which in Borg's example is 44 s (T1). The power output is then corrected according to the formula:

$$W2 = W1 \times (T1/30s)^{0.25}$$

i.e. $W2 = 275 \times (44/30)^{0.25} = 302$ W.

Table 9.12 Data example from the Borg Cycling Strength Test with constant load

Power output (W)	RPE value	HR
50	7	94
100	7	109
150	11	131
200	11	134
250	13	146
300	14	151
350	14	152
400	15	170
450	16	178

After a rest of 5 minutes the subject pedals as close to the desired 30 s PO (W2) and the time is recorded. Table 9.12 contains data from a female participant (Elaine, age 24, ht 182 cm, 78 kg) collected during the RPE Symposium at Bangor in April 2000 to exemplify the procedure.

Regression analysis for RPE (x) and W (y) produced the following equation:

$$W = -231 + 40 \, (RPE) \quad (r = 0.96) \quad \text{Predicted} \quad PO_{max} \text{ at RPE } 19-20 = 529 - 569W$$

Regression analysis for HR (x) and W (y) produced the following equation:

$$W = -446 + 4.95 \, (HR) \quad (r = 0.98) \quad \text{Predicted} \quad PO_{max} \text{ at } HR_{max} \, (196) = 524 \, W$$

Trial 1. Time (s) at predicted PO_{max} using RPE = 46 s
Trial 2. Time (s) at 'corrected PO_{max}' based on formula: $W2 = W1 \times (T1/T2)^{0.25}$

$$W2 = 569 \times (46/30)^{0.25} = 633 \, W$$

After a 5-minute recovery Elaine managed to sustain the above power output for 29 s. For Elaine, therefore, the procedure seems to have worked well.

9.10 SUMMARY

1. Beneficial effects of exercise accrue when individuals engage in activity with appropriate frequency, duration, and intensity. The interplay of all three dimensions is important, but the determination of appropriate intensity requires careful consideration because of the impact of numerous variables.

2. One approach to determining intensity is to base judgements on physiological information. The usual method is to recommend intensity levels relative to actual or predicted maximal capacity based on measures of heart rate response, oxygen utilization, ventilation and blood lactate.

3. A comprehensive approach to setting exercise intensity is desirable. This requires the coupling of indices of bodily response during exercise with information on how hard the individual perceives the exercise to be. The most commonly used perceived exertion device used in this process has been the Borg 6 to 20 Category Scale. The Category Ratio 10 Scale deserves greater attention than it has previously received, particularly as it tends to reflect a classical stimulus–response pattern for perceived exertion and exercise intensity. For young children, the Children's Effort Rating Table (CERT) has been recommended. More recently, pictorial scales such as the CALER and OMNI Scales have been suggested.

4. Perceived exertion ratings have been mainly used in two ways, namely the response or estimation method and the production method. In the former, the subject provides a rating for a power output selected by the investigator. In the latter, the subject is requested to produce a power output which is judged to correspond with a given RPE.

5. The predictions of exercise intensity and maximal functional capacity using the RPE must consider the process by which it is used, owing to the essential differences in the process of estimation and production.

6. Whilst the correlation between physiological information and perceived exertion ratings measured in an exercise physiology laboratory for both response and production methods is usually high, 25% of the variance in the relationship between the two methods remains unaccounted for. The remnant is probably due to individual differences which predispose people to modulate their interpretation of intensity. Thus, the fine-tuning of exercise intensity within an exercise programme comes down to

individual decision-making emanating from effort sense. The exercise scientist's role is to arrive at balanced judgements from a psychophysiological perspective by taking into account the variables discussed.

The purpose of this chapter has been to introduce the reader to the concept of exercise intensity determination as a multifaceted process which requires consideration of both physiological and psychological information about the individual relative to specific activities. Through reading the introductory material, following up some of the primary reference material and undertaking the practical tasks which were suggested, a sound knowledge base for decision-making in this area should have been acquired.

REFERENCES

American College of Sports Medicine (1995). *Guidelines for Exercise Testing and Prescription*, 5th edn. (Williams and Wilkins, Baltimore, MD).

American College of Sports Medicine Position Stand (1998). The recommended quantity and quality of exercise for developing and maintaining cardiorespiratory and muscular strength and flexibility in healthy adults. *Medicine and Science in Sports and Exercise*, **30**, 975–91.

Bar-Or, O. (1977). Age-related changes in exercise perception. In *Physical Work and Effort*. ed. G. Borg (Pergamon Press, Oxford), pp. 255–66.

Benson, H., Dryer, T. and Hartley, H. (1978). Decreased consumption during exercise with elicitation of the relaxation response. *Journal of Human Stress*, **4**, 38–42.

Berry, M.J., Weyrich, A.S., Robergs, R.A., *et al.* (1989). Ratings of perceived exertion in individuals with varying fitness levels during walking and running. *European Journal of Applied Physiology*, **58**, 494–9.

Borg, G.A.V. (1962). *Physical performance and perceived exertion*. Studia Psychologica et Paedagogica. Series altera, Investigationes XI. (Gleerup, Lund, Sweden).

Borg, G.A.V. (1970). Perceived exertion as an indicator of somatic stress. *Scandinavian Journal of Rehabilitation Medicine*, **2**, 92–8.

Borg, G.A.V. (1971). La sensation de fatigue consécutive au travail physique. *Psychologie Médicale*, **3**, 761–73.

Borg, G.A.V. (1977). *Physical Work and Effort*. (Pergamon Press, Oxford), pp. 289–93.

Borg, G.A.V. (1982). Psychophysical basis of perceived exertion. *Medicine and Science in Sports and Exercise*, **14**, 377–81.

Borg, G.A.V. (1998). *Borg's Perceived Exertion and Pain Scales*. (Human Kinetics, Champaign, IL).

Borg, G.A.V., Van de Burg, M., Hassmen, P., *et al.* (1987). Relationships between perceived exertion, HR, and La in cycling, running, and walking. *Scandinavian Journal of Sports Science*, **9**, 69–77.

British Association of Sports & Exercise Sciences. (1997). *Physiological Testing Guidelines*. 3rd edn. eds. S. Bird and R. Davison (BASES, Leeds, UK).

Buckley, J.P., Eston, R.G. and Sim, J. (2000). Ratings of perceived exertion in Braille: validity and reliability in 'production' mode. *British Journal of Sports Medicine*, **34**, 297–302.

Buskist, W. and Gerbing, D.W. (1990). *Psychology: Boundaries and Frontiers*. (Harper Collins, New York), pp. 376–414.

Byrne, C. and Eston, R.G. (1997). Use of ratings of perceived exertion to regulate exercise intensity: a study using effort estimation and effort production (abstract). *Journal of Sports Sciences*, **16**, 15P.

Cioffi, D. (1991). Beyond attentional strategies: a cognitive-perceptual model of somatic interpretation. *Psychological Bulletin*, **109**, 25–41.

Dishman, R.D., Farquhar, K.P. and Cureton, K.J. (1994). Responses to preferred intensities of exercise in men differing in activity levels. *Medicine and Science in Sports and Exercise*, **26**, 780–3.

Dunbar, C., Robertson, R., Baun, R., *et al.* (1992). The validity of regulating exercise intensity by ratings of perceived exertion. *Medicine and Science in Sports and Exercise*, **24**, 94–9.

Ekblom, B. and Goldbarg, A.N. (1971). The influence of physical training and other factors in the subjective rating of perceived exertion. *Acta Physiologica Scandinavica*, **83**, 399–406.

Ekman, G. (1961). A simple method for fitting psychophysical power functions. *Journal of Psychology*, **51**, 343–50.

Eston, R. and Williams, J.G. (1988). Reliability of ratings of perceived effort for the regulation of exercise intensity. *British Journal of Sports Medicine*, **22**, 153–4.

Eston, R., Davies, B. and Williams, J.G. (1987). Use of perceived effort ratings to control exercise intensity in young, healthy adults. *European Journal of Applied Physiology*, **56**, 222–4.

Eston, R., Lamb, K.L., Bain, A., *et al.* (1994). Validity of CERT: a perceived exertion scale for children: a pilot study. *Perceptual and Motor Skills*, **78**, 691–7.

Eston, R.G. and Williams, J.G. (1986). Exercise intensity and perceived exertion in adolescent boys. *British Journal of Sports Medicine*, **20**, 27–30.

Eston, R.G. and Thompson, M. (1997). Use of ratings of perceived exertion for prediction of maximal exercise levels and exercise prescription in patients receiving atenolol. *British Journal of Sports Medicine*, **31**, 114–9.

Eston, R.G. and Lamb, K.L. (2000). Effort Perception. In *Paediatric Exercise Science and Medicine*. eds. N. Armstrong and W. Van Mechelen (Oxford University Press, Oxford), pp. 85–91.

Eston, R.G., Parfitt, G. and Tucker, R. (1998). Ratings of perceived exertion and psychological affect during preferred exercise intensity in high- and low-active men. *Journal of Sports Sciences*, **16**, 82–3.

Eston, R.G., Parfitt, C.G., Campbell, L. and Lamb, K.L. (2000). Reliability of effort perception for regulating exercise intensity in children using the Cart and Load Effort Rating (CALER) Scale. *Pediatric Exercise Science*, **12**, 388–97.

Gaesser, G.A. and Rich, E.G. (1984). Effects of high performance and low intensity training on aerobic capacity and blood lipids. *Medicine and Science in Sports and Exercise*, **16**, 269–74.

Glass, S., Knowlton, R. and Becque, M.D. (1992). Accuracy of RPE from graded exercise to establish exercise training intensity. *Medicine and Science in Sports and Exercise*, **24**, 1303–7.

Karvonen, J. and Vuorimaa, T. (1988). Heart rate and exercise intensity during sports activities. *Sports Medicine* **5**, 303–12.

Lamb, K.L. (1995). Children's ratings of effort during cycle ergometry: an examination of the validity of two effort rating scales. *Pediatric Exercise Science*, **7**, 407–21.

Lamb, K.L. (1996). Exercise regulation during cycle ergometry using the CERT and RPE scales. *Pediatric Exercise Science*, **8**, 337–50.

Lamb, K.L., Eston, R.G. and Corns, D. (1999). The reliability of ratings of perceived exertion during progressive treadmill exercise. *British Journal of Sports Medicine*, **33**, 336–9.

McArdle, W.D., Katch, F. and Katch, V.L. (1991).

Exercise Physiology: Energy, Nutrition and Human Performance. (Lea & Febiger, Philadelphia, PA).

Morgan, W. (1981). Psychophysiology of self-awareness during vigorous physical activity. *Research Quarterly for Exercise and Sport*, **52**, 385–427.

Morgan, W.P., Horstman, D.J., Cymerman, A. and Stokes, J. (1983). Facilitation of physical performance by means of a cognitive strategy. *Cognitive Therapy and Research*, **7**, 251–64.

Nystad, W., Oseid, S. and Mellbye, E.B. (1989). Physical education for asthmatic children: the relationship between changes in heart rate, perceived exertion, and motivation for participation. In *Children and Exercise XIII*. eds. S. Oseid and K. Carlsen (Human Kinetics, Champaign, IL), pp. 369–77.

Pandolf, K.D. (1983). Advances in the study and application of perceived exertion. In *Exercise and Sport Sciences Reviews*. ed. R. L. Terjung (Franklin Institute Press, Philadelphia, PA), pp. 118–58.

Parfitt, G. and Eston, R.G. (1995). Changes in ratings of perceived exertion and psychological affect in the early stages of exercise. *Perceptual and Motor Skills*, **80**, 259–66.

Parfitt, G., Eston, R.G. and Connolly, D.A. (1996). Psychological affect at different ratings of perceived exertion in high- and low-active women: a study using a production protocol. *Perceptual and Motor Skills*, **82**, 1035–42.

Parfitt, G., Rose, E. and Markland, D. (2000). The effect of prescribed and preferred intensity exercise on psychological affect and the influence of baseline measures of affect. *Journal of Health Psychology*, **5**, 231–40.

Piaget, J. (1972). Intellectual evolution from adolescence to adulthood. *Human Development*, **15**, 1–12.

Pollock, M.L., Foster, C., Rod, J.L. and Wible, G. (1982). Comparison of methods of determining exercise training intensity for cardiac patients and healthy adults. In *Comprehensive Cardiac Rehabilitation*. ed. J. J. Kellermann (S Karger, Basel, Switzerland), pp. 129–33.

Rejeski, W.J. (1985). Perceived exertion: an active or a passive process. *Journal of Sport Psychology*, **7**, 371–8.

Robertson, R.J., Gillespie, R.L., Hiatt, E. and Rose, K.D. (1977). Perceived exertion and stimulus intensity modulation. *Perceptual and Motor Skills*, **45**, 211–18.

Robertson, R.J., Gillespie, R.L., McArthy, J. and Rose, K.D. (1979). Differentiated perceptions of exertion: Part 1: mode of integration and regional signals. *Perceptual and Motor Skills*, **49**, 683–9.

Robertson, R.J., Goss, F.L., Boer, N.F., *et al.* (2000). Children's OMNI Scale of perceived exertion: mixed gender and race validation. *Medicine and Science in Sports and Exercise*, **32**, 452–8.

Smutok, M.A., Skrinar, G.S. and Pandolf, K.B. (1980). Exercise intensity: subjective regulation by perceived exertion. *Archives of Physical Medicine and Rehabilitation*, **61**, 569–74.

Stevens, S.S. (1957). On the psychophysical law. *The Psychological Review*, **64**, 153–81.

Stevens, S.S. (1971). Issues in psychophysiological measurement. *The Psychological Review*, **78**, 426–50.

Ward, D. S., Bar-Or, O., Longmuir, P. and Smith, K. (1995). Use of RPE to control exercise intensity in wheelchair-bound children and adults. *Pediatric Exercise Science*, **7**, 94–102.

Watt, B. and Grove, R. (1993). Perceived exertion: antecedents and applications. *Sports Medicine*, **15**, 225–42.

Williams, J.G. and Eston, R.G. (1985). Personality and effort perception in adolescent males. *Journal of Sports Sciences*, **3**, 228–9.

Williams, J.G. and Eston, R.G. (1986). Does personality influence the perception of effort? *Physical Education Review*, **9, 2,** 94–9.

Williams, J.G. and Eston, R.G. (1989). Determination of the intensity dimension in vigorous exercise programmes with particular reference to the use of the Rating of Perceived Exertion. *Sports Medicine*, **8**, 177–89.

Williams, J.G. and O'Brien, M. (2000). A Children's Perceived Exertion Picture Scale. Unpublished data. University of West Chester, PA, USA.

Williams, J.G., Eston, R. and Stretch, C. (1991). Use of the Rating of Perceived Exertion to control exercise intensity in children. *Pediatric Exercise Science*, **3**, 21–7.

Williams, J.G., Eston, R. and Furlong, B.A.F. (1994). CERT: a perceived exertion scale for young children. *Perceptual and Motor Skills*, **79**, 1451–8.

Williams, J.G., Furlong, B., Mackintosh, C. and Hockley, T.J. (1993). Rating and regulation of exercise intensity in young children. *Medicine and Science in Sports and Exercise*, **5 (Suppl. 25)**, S8.

Wilmore, J.H., Roby, F.B., Stanforth, M.J., *et al.* (1986). Ratings of perceived exertion, heart rate and power output in predicting maximal oxygen uptake during submaximal bicycle riding. *The Physician and Sports Medicine*, **14**, 133–43.

LIMITATIONS TO SUBMAXIMAL EXERCISE PERFORMANCE

Andrew M. Jones and Jonathan H. Doust

10.1 AIMS

The aims of this chapter are to:
- describe the three domains of submaximal exercise in terms of changes in acid-base status and respiratory gas exchange,
- review the methods that have been used to delineate the transition from moderate to heavy submaximal exercise, in particular the lactate and ventilatory thresholds,
- review the methods that have been used to delineate the transition from heavy to severe submaximal exercise, in particular the direct measurement or estimation of the maximal lactate steady-state,
- highlight the importance of a knowledge of the exercise domains in predicting the physiological response to exercise, and in prescribing and regulating exercise intensity within endurance training programmes,
- provide a series of practical exercises which explore the methods that have been used to identify the boundaries between the various domains of submaximal exercise.

10.2 INTRODUCTION

Maximal exercise is defined here as exercise of an intensity that requires 100% of the maximal oxygen uptake ($\dot{V}O_2$ max). Exercise that has an oxygen requirement above an individual's $\dot{V}O_2$ max (and that therefore is associated with an obligatory anaerobiosis to meet the energy demand) can thus be described as supramaximal, while exercise that requires an oxygen uptake below $\dot{V}O_2$ max can be termed submaximal. Maximal exercise can be sustained for only about 4–8 minutes before exhaustion occurs (Billat *et al.*, 1994b). Therefore, most forms of recreational exercise, and indeed many sports, can be considered to be submaximal. Continuous submaximal exercise can also be termed endurance exercise. The causes of fatigue during submaximal exercise are manifold and complex but may depend upon whether the exercise is of a sufficiently low intensity that adenosine triphosphate (ATP) resynthesis is almost completely aerobic or whether supplementary anaerobiosis is required, resulting in a progressive accumulation of blood lactate. For low-intensity submaximal exercise, fatigue may result from substrate depletion, dehydration, hyperthermia, or loss of motivation associated with central fatigue (Newsholme *et al.*, 1992). For high-intensity submaximal exercise, fatigue may result from the effects of acidosis on muscle contractile function or on inhibition of key glycolytic enzymes (Edwards, 1981). Understanding the physiological limitations to submaximal exercise is important in developing training programmes to enhance endurance performance.

10.3 EXERCISE DOMAINS

Three domains of intensity have been identified during submaximal exercise based on the characteristic responses of blood acid-base status and pulmonary gas exchange (Whipp

Kinanthropometry and Exercise Physiology Laboratory Manual: Tests, Procedures and Data. 2nd Edition, Volume 2: Exercise Physiology
Edited by RG Eston and T Reilly. Published by Routledge, London, June 2001

and Mahler, 1980; Whipp and Ward, 1990). These are moderate exercise, heavy exercise, and severe exercise (Figure 10.1). The metabolic, physiological and perceptual responses to exercise differ considerably according to the exercise domain that is studied. The boundaries between these different domains can be demarcated by the physiological 'landmarks' of the 'lactate threshold', and the maximal lactate steady state or critical power, while the $\dot{V}O_2$ max marks the boundary between severe submaximal exercise and supramaximal exercise. The lactate threshold (T_{lac}), which marks the transition between moderate and heavy intensity exercise, can be defined as the $\dot{V}O_2$ above which blood [lactate] exceeds the resting concentration during incremental exercise (Wasserman *et al.*, 1973). The maximal lactate steady state (MLSS) or critical power (P_{crit}), which mark the transition between heavy and severe intensity exercise, can be defined as the highest exercise intensity that allows blood [lactate] to be stabilized during long-term exercise (Poole *et al.*, 1988; Beneke and Von Duvillard, 1996).

If constant-load *moderate* exercise (below the T_{lac}) is commenced from a resting baseline, pulmonary $\dot{V}O_2$ rises in a mono-exponential fashion to attain a steady-state value within 2–3 minutes. The deficit between the energy demand and the oxygen uptake during this initial period of exercise is covered by intramuscular oxygen stores, depletion of phosphocreatine, and a small and transient increase in the rate of anaerobic glycolysis resulting in 'early lactate'. This lactate is rapidly cleared as exercise proceeds so that blood [lactate] will remain at or close to resting values during continuous moderate-intensity exercise.

If constant-load *heavy* exercise (i.e. above the T_{lac} but below the MLSS) is commenced from a resting baseline, $\dot{V}O_2$ rises to attain its predicted steady-state value within 2–3 minutes. As exercise is sustained, $\dot{V}O_2$ continues to rise until it reaches a steady-state value that is higher than the expected value. This continued increase in $\dot{V}O_2$, until a delayed and elevated steady state is attained, is due to the emergence of the $\dot{V}O_2$ 'slow component' (Whipp and Ward, 1990). If serial blood samples are taken and analysed for lactate concentration during continuous heavy exercise, it is seen that, following a transient overshoot in the first 5 minutes, blood [lactate] will eventually stabilize at an elevated level of around 2–5 mM.

In the transition from rest to severe exercise (i.e. above the MLSS but below $\dot{V}O_2$ max), the development of the $\dot{V}O_2$ slow component after 2–3 minutes also causes $\dot{V}O_2$ to rise above the expected steady-state value. In contrast to

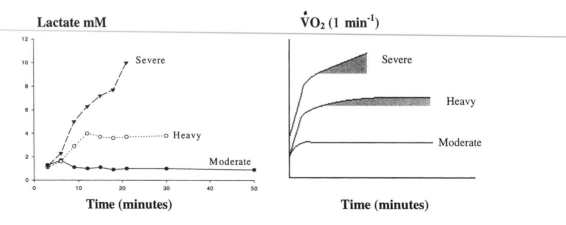

Figure 10.1 Blood lactate and oxygen uptake responses during moderate, heavy, and severe intensity submaximal exercise. The shaded areas in the oxygen uptake panel represent the increase in $\dot{V}O_2$ above the expected steady-state level.

heavy exercise, however, during *severe* exercise, $\dot{V}O_2$ will not attain a steady state but will continue to rise until the exercise is terminated and/or $\dot{V}O_2$ max is attained (Poole *et al.*, 1988). The $\dot{V}O_2$ slow component can account for as much as $0.5–1.0\,l\,min^{-1}$ of $\dot{V}O_2$ and result in the attainment of $\dot{V}O_2$ max during high-intensity *submaximal* exercise. The physiological mechanisms responsible for this reduction in efficiency (i.e. an increased oxygen cost for the same external power output) during sustained exercise above T_{lac} are not known with certainty. However, it has been demonstrated that ~86% of the $\dot{V}O_2$ slow component can be attributed to increased oxygen utilization in the exercising limbs (Poole *et al.*, 1991). This suggests that motor unit recruitment patterns and the increased energetic cost of contraction of type II muscle fibres might be important in the mediation of the $\dot{V}O_2$ slow component (Whipp, 1994; Barstow *et al.*, 1996). If severe exercise is continued and blood [lactate] is determined at regular intervals, it can be observed that blood [lactate] never attains a steady state but continues to increase with time. Typically, the exercise is terminated by the subject when the blood [lactate] reaches 8–12 mM.

During *supramaximal* exercise (exercise that requires a $\dot{V}O_2$ above the $\dot{V}O_2$ max), the exercise duration (1–5 minutes) is often too short to discern a $\dot{V}O_2$ slow component, and $\dot{V}O_2$ appears to project mono-exponentially to $\dot{V}O_2$ max. Likewise, the increased contribution of anaerobic glycolysis to ATP resynthesis in this domain causes lactate to accumulate very rapidly in the blood as lactate production outstrips its removal.

The profound differences in the physiological responses to moderate, heavy, and severe exercise make it essential that the boundaries that demarcate these intensities can be accurately measured. This is important not only in terms of exercise and training prescription but also for the prediction of functional or performance capability. It should be recognized that setting exercise intensity in relation to $\dot{V}O_2$ max

alone may result in vastly different responses to exercise even in individuals with identical $\dot{V}O_2$ max values (Katch *et al.*, 1978). This is because exercise at, for example, 65% $\dot{V}O_2$ max may be above the T_{lac} in some subjects but below this threshold in others. Likewise, exercise at 85% $\dot{V}O_2$ max will be above T_{lac} in most subjects but it could be above the MLSS in some subjects and below MLSS in others. Therefore, setting exercise intensity relative to $\dot{V}O_2$ max alone is unlikely to 'normalize' exercise stress across a group of subjects. If an equivalent exercise intensity is required in a group of subjects, then this should, ideally, be calculated using measurements of T_{lac}, MLSS and $\dot{V}O_2$ max. Exercise physiologists have acknowledged this and their attempts to gain greater precision in the prescription and control of exercise intensity have led to the evolution of numerous methods to determine the boundaries between moderate, heavy and severe exercise in different population groups and in different settings (for example, field vs. laboratory).

10.4 FROM MODERATE TO HEAVY EXERCISE: THE LACTATE / VENTILATORY THRESHOLD

10.4.1 THE LACTATE THRESHOLD

The lactate threshold (T_{lac}) was originally defined as the first increase in blood [lactate] above resting values during incremental exercise (Figure 10.2; Wasserman *et al.*, 1973). The exercise intensity at the T_{lac} is associated with a non-linear increase in $\dot{V}_E$ (the ventilatory threshold, T_{vent}) due to bicarbonate buffering of the lactic acidosis (see below). As outlined previously, constant-intensity exercise below T_{lac} can be sustained without an appreciable increase in blood [lactate]. Heart rate and ventilation reach an early steady state and subjects perceive the exercise to be relatively easy. Exercise below T_{lac} can be sustained for several hours but will eventually be terminated by substrate depletion, dehydration, musculoskeletal injury or by psychological factors. If exercise at a constant intensity just above the T_{lac} is performed, blood [lactate] increases above resting levels, eventually stabilizing at 2–5 mM. Exercise above T_{lac} is associated with a non-linear increase in metabolic, respiratory and perceptual stress (Katch *et al.*, 1978; Whipp and Ward, 1990). Furthermore, exercise above T_{lac} is associated with more rapid fatigue, either through the effects of metabolic acidosis on contractile function or through an accelerated depletion of muscle glycogen (Jones *et al.*, 1977; Roberts and Smith, 1989).

The exercise intensity at the T_{lac} / T_{vent} is a powerful predictor of endurance exercise performance (Farrell *et al.*, 1979; Fay *et al.*, 1989). Numerous studies also testify to the sensitivity of the T_{lac} and T_{vent} to endurance training. A rightward shift of the T_{lac} / T_{vent} to a higher power output or running speed is characteristic of successful endurance training programmes (Henritze *et al.*, 1985; Weltman *et al.*, 1992; Carter *et al.*, 1999b). This adaptation allows a higher absolute (running speed or power output) and relative (%$\dot{V}O_2$ max) exercise intensity to be sustained without the accumulation of blood lactate as a result of training. In athletes who have trained for competition for several years, the T_{lac} (and performance) may continue to improve despite a relatively stable $\dot{V}O_2$ max (Pierce *et al.*, 1990). Furthermore, endurance training is associated with a reduction in the degree of lactacidaemia for any given absolute or relative exercise intensity. This means the power output or running speed corresponding to arbitrary 'blood lactate reference values' such as 2 mM or 4 mM blood lactate is increased following a period of endurance training (Farrell *et al.*, 1979; Hurley *et al.*, 1984). An improvement in the T_{lac} / T_{vent} with training is therefore a clear marker of an enhanced endurance capacity. The T_{lac} / T_{vent} is typically found at 60–80% $\dot{V}O_2$ max even in highly trained subjects, and it therefore occurs at a lower exercise intensity than is maintained by endurance athletes during most forms of endurance competition. The maximal lactate steady state (MLSS), which is the highest exercise intensity at which blood lactate does not

Figure 10.2 Determination of exercise intensity at lactate threshold (T_{lac}, first increase in blood lactate above resting values) and at 4 mM blood lactate ('OBLA') from an incremental treadmill test before (squares) and after (circles) a period of endurance training.

accumulate over time, may be of more importance to success in these events.

Several authors have hypothesized that T_{lac} represents the optimal intensity for improvement of endurance fitness (Weltman *et al.*, 1990; Mader, 1991). Training at T_{lac} should provide a high-quality aerobic training stimulus without the accumulation of lactate that would compromise training duration (Weltman, 1989). The effect of training intensity on improvements in the T_{lac} / T_{vent} has recently been reviewed (Londeree, 1997). In general, it appears that training at intensities close to or slightly above the existing T_{lac} / T_{vent} is important in eliciting significant improvements in this parameter (Henritze *et al.*, 1985; Acavedo and Goldfarb, 1989; Weltman *et al.*, 1992). For example, increasing training intensity through the use of fartlek training on three days per week (Acavedo and Goldfarb, 1989) or adding a 20-minute run at speed corresponding to T_{lac} to the weekly training programme (Sjodin *et al.*, 1982) caused an improvement in T_{lac} with no change in $\dot{V}O_2$ max in runners. Athletes with access to heart rate telemetry can regulate their training intensity in relation to their T_{lac} by recording the heart rate at T_{lac} measured during an incremental exercise test in a physiology laboratory (Jones, 1996).

The physiological mechanisms responsible for the increase in blood [lactate] at the T_{lac} have been much debated (Walsh and Banister, 1988). It was originally considered that muscle hypoxia was the main cause of this increase (Wasserman *et al.*, 1973). Despite the possibility that there may be regional inequalities in muscle perfusion, it is hard to accept that O_2 availability may be limited at the submaximal exercise intensities associated with the T_{lac}. Indeed, some studies have demonstrated an increase in lactate production without any evidence for the existence of hypoxic loci in the contracting muscle tissue (Jobsis and Stainsby, 1968; Connett *et al.*, 1984). It has been proposed that lactate produced in muscle during submaximal exercise may be important as a cytosolic reserve for carbohydrate and reducing equivalents, thereby maintaining optimal coupling of cytosolic supply to mitochondrial utilization (Connett *et al.*, 1985; Honig *et al.*, 1992). The effect of catecholaminergic stimulation of glycolysis should also be considered. Some studies have shown similar patterns of increase and simultaneous 'thresholds' in plasma lactate and plasma catecholamines (Mazzeo and Marshall, 1989). Greater oxidative enzyme activity following training may reduce lactate production by limiting the ability of the enzyme lactate dehydrogenase (LDH) to compete with the mitochondria for pyruvate and reducing equivalents. An augmented rate of entry of pyruvate into the mitochondria would diminish the possibility of a mass action effect, although study of the lactate / pyruvate ratio has indicated no role for mass action in lactate production at T_{lac} (Wasserman *et al.*, 1985). It is possible that T_{lac} represents a transient imbalance between mechanisms of lactate production and lactate removal from the blood (Brooks, 1991). Certainly, the rate of blood lactate accumulation should be considered to be the difference between the rate of lactate production and the rate of lactate clearance in tissues such as red skeletal muscle

fibres, and the heart, liver and kidneys (Donovan and Pagliassotti, 1990; MacRae *et al.*, 1992). It has been suggested that lactate produced in type II muscle fibres might be used as a fuel by adjacent type I muscle fibres before lactate ever reaches the bloodstream, and that net lactate release by less active muscle during exercise may provide a convenient method to distribute carbohydrate stores from glycogen-replete to glycogen-depleted areas (Talmadge *et al.*, 1989; Brooks, 1991). Finally, the close correlation between the percentage of type I fibres in the active muscles and the T_{lac} (Ivy *et al.*, 1980) suggests that T_{lac} may coincide with a greater recruitment of type II fibres as exercise intensity increases (Nagata *et al.*, 1981).

The notion of a 'threshold' in lactate accumulation is not universally accepted. Some groups believe that blood [lactate] increases as a continuous function of exercise intensity (Hughson *et al.*, 1987). Although lactate may increase exponentially above T_{lac}, an exponential curve does not provide a good fit to exercise data in the region of interest (1–4 mM) (Wasserman *et al.*, 1990). The exercise protocol is also of importance if a clear identification of T_{lac} is required. Firstly, it is critical that the exercise test is started at a sufficiently low exercise intensity so that the baseline blood [lactate] can be established. If precision is required in the identification of T_{lac} then numerous stages (7–9) with small increments between incremental stages are recommended (Jones and Doust, 1997a). The $\dot{V}O_2$ at T_{lac} is independent of the rate at which the exercise intensity is increased during incremental or ramp exercise tests. Yoshida (1984) demonstrated that the $\dot{V}O_2$ at T_{lac} was the same when exercise was increased by 25 W every 1 minute or by 25 W every 4 minutes. However, the exercise intensity (power output or running speed) at the T_{lac} depends upon the incremental rate used (Ferry *et al.*, 1988), so if the identification of power output or running speed at T_{lac} is required for training prescription, then a protocol using 'steady state' stages of at least 3–4 minutes duration is recommended. The 'real' exercise intensity at T_{lac} can be estimated from ramp or incremental tests if the data are corrected for the lag time in $\dot{V}O_2$ at the onset of exercise. This is generally equivalent to subtracting 75% of the ramp rate from the measured value. For example, if the power output at T_{lac} is 200 W when using a ramp exercise test with a ramp rate of 20 W min^{-1}, then the 'corrected' power output at $T_{lac} = 200 - (0.75 \times 20) = 185$ W.

The T_{lac} is routinely used in laboratory-based physiological assessments of endurance capacity. Subjects commonly perform a single incremental protocol involving a number of short (3–5 minute) stages of increasing intensity. Blood samples for the determination of blood [lactate] are obtained at the end of each stage before the exercise intensity is increased. Assessment of T_{lac} is usually by scrutiny of data plots by one or more reviewers. While this practice has been shown to be highly reliable both within and between reviewers (Davis, 1985), some authors have criticized this approach for its subjectivity (Yeh *et al.*, 1983). Until relatively recently, the measurement of blood lactate was confined to the exercise laboratory. However, the advent of portable and robust blood lactate analysers has enabled blood [lactate] and the T_{lac} to be assessed in field conditions (Figures 10.3a and 10.3b).

10.4.2 REFERENCE BLOOD LACTATE CONCENTRATIONS

To circumvent problems associated with the subjective assessment of T_{lac}, some authors have chosen to define T_{lac} as the $\dot{V}O_2$, power output or running speed at which an absolute blood lactate concentration is reached. Examples of this are interpolation to blood [lactate] of 2 mM (Lafontaine *et al.*, 1981), 2.5 mM (Hurley *et al.*, 1984) and 1 mM above resting lactate levels (Coyle *et al.*, 1983). It should be borne in mind that absolute blood lactate concentrations are affected by factors such as the incremental rate used in the exercise protocol (Foxdal *et al.*, 1994), muscle glycogen levels (Hughes *et al.*, 1982), the blood sampling site (artery, vein, or fingertip) and the choice of assay (whole blood, lysed blood, or plasma) (Robergs *et al.*, 1990; Williams *et al.*, 1992). Despite these limitations, the reduction in blood [lactate] for a given absolute exercise intensity following endurance training means that this method can be useful in demonstrating

a

b

Figure 10.3a and b Lactate measurement in the laboratory and in the field on two members of the British Figure Skating team.

an improved endurance capacity provided that the same methods are used longitudinally. Another method that has been used to increase objectivity of T_{lac} assessment is the D_{max} method (Cheng *et al.*, 1992). This procedure involves fitting a curve to the blood lactate response to exercise and then drawing a line between the first and the last data points. The 'T_{lac}' is defined as the running speed that is furthest away from this line. A problem with the D_{max} method is that determination of the 'T_{lac}' may be skewed by error in either the first or last blood [lactate] measurement.

10.4.3 THE VENTILATORY THRESHOLD

The T_{lac} can be assessed non-invasively by consideration of the gas exchange responses to exercise. Due to its low pK, lactic acid will be almost completely dissociated on formation. The liberated protons will be buffered predominantly by intracellular and plasma bicarbonates, resulting in the liberation of large amounts of 'non-metabolic' CO_2. This is detected by the peripheral chemoreceptors and causes a disproportionate increase in $\dot{V}_E$ and $\dot{V}CO_2$ at what is known as the ventilatory threshold (T_{vent}) (Figure 10.4). The most sensitive approaches to the measurement of the T_{vent} is the disproportionate increase in $\dot{V}CO_2$ known as the V-slope method (Beaver *et al.*, 1986), and the increase in the ventilatory equivalent for O_2 ($\dot{V}_E / \dot{V}O_2$) without a concomitant increase in the ventilatory equivalent for CO_2 ($\dot{V}_E / \dot{V}CO_2$) (Caiozzo *et al.*, 1982). While it is possible to dissociate the T_{lac} from the T_{vent} by using a variety of manipulations of protocol and dietary status owing to the complexity of both lactate accumulation and ventilatory control, in most situations the T_{lac} and T_{vent} are coincident.

The T_{vent} can be measured during multistage exercise protocols with stage durations of 3–4 minutes, but ventilatory breakpoints are sharper when fast incremental or ramp protocols are used to bring subjects to exhaustion in

Figure 10.4 Determination of exercise intensity at ventilatory threshold (T_{vent}) from an incremental treadmill test.

around 10 minutes. It is possible to measure T_{vent} by collecting expired air into Douglas bags during each stage of an incremental test but breath-by-breath gas analysis allows a greater density of respiratory gas exchange measures and a more reliable assessment of the T_{vent}. During fast incremental or ramp exercise tests, a second ventilatory breakpoint known as the respiratory compensation threshold can be identified. For a short period of time during incremental exercise above the T_{vent}, there is an 'isocapnic buffering' region in which $\dot{V}_E$ increases in direct proportion to $\dot{V}CO_2$. Above this point, $\dot{V}_E$ increases at a faster rate than $\dot{V}CO_2$ to achieve respiratory compensation for the metabolic acidosis. The respiratory compensation threshold can be observed as a second breakpoint in $\dot{V}_E$ when plotted against $\dot{V}O_2$, or, more easily, as a single breakpoint when $\dot{V}_E$ is plotted against $\dot{V}CO_2$. While measurement of the T_{vent} can be convenient, the requirement for sensitive and sophisticated gas analysis equipment means that it is limited to laboratory use.

10.4.4 BREATHING FREQUENCY THRESHOLD

The increase in $\dot{V}_E$ during incremental exercise is caused by changes in tidal volume (breathing depth) and ventilatory frequency (breathing rate). Tidal volume typically attains a plateau at ~50% $\dot{V}O_2$ max, so that further increases in $\dot{V}_E$ are mediated mainly by changes in ventilatory frequency. It has been suggested that a non-linear increase in ventilatory frequency might be used to determine T_{vent} without the requirement for the analysis of expired air (James *et al.*, 1989). This would allow for the T_{lac} / T_{vent} to be determined non-invasively outside the laboratory and for exercise intensity to be prescribed and/or monitored using ventilatory frequency. However, factors such as the entrainment of ventilatory frequency to exercise rhythm (cadence) and disruption of the ventilatory pattern by coughing, swallowing, and speech limit the utility of monitoring breathing frequency to give information on the proximity to T_{vent} in the field situation (Jones and Doust, 1998a).

10.5 FROM HEAVY TO SEVERE EXERCISE: THE MAXIMAL LACTATE STEADY STATE

10.5.1 THE MAXIMAL LACTATE STEADY STATE

The maximal lactate steady state (MLSS), the exercise intensity above which blood [lactate] (and $\dot{V}O_2$) will rise continuously during continuous exercise, demarcates the boundary between heavy and severe exercise and it is considered by some to be the criterion measure of endurance fitness. Measurement of the MLSS requires that subjects perform a series of prolonged constant-intensity exercise bouts with blood [lactate] determined serially over a range of exercise intensities. As an example, a subject may be required to complete five treadmill runs each of 30 minutes duration at different running speeds on separate days (see Figure 10.5). The MLSS is defined as the highest running speed or power output at which blood [lactate] will stabilize during prolonged exercise (Beneke and von Duvillard, 1996;

Jones and Doust, 1998b). Measurement of MLSS, however, is not suitable for routine diagnostic use. Measurement of MLSS is time-consuming, requiring several days to complete the series of exercise bouts. Additionally, a large number of blood samples must be taken in order to define MLSS accurately (e.g. 30 samples for 5 × 30 minute exercise bouts with blood samples taken at rest and then every 5 minutes during exercise). This is unpleasant for the subject and is expensive in costs of consumables. Another problem is the precise definition of MLSS. While several methods have been used to define MLSS, Londeree (1986) recommended an increase of no more than 1 mM in blood [lactate] measured between 10 and 30 minutes of a sustained exercise bout and this criterion has been applied by other authors (Snyder *et al.*, 1994; Beneke and Von Duvillard, 1996; Jones and Doust, 1998b). This criterion would appear to be reasonable given the small error inherent in capillary blood sampling and assay and the changes in muscle substrate and plasma volume that might be expected with exercise of this duration and intensity.

For exercise above the MLSS, the time to exhaustion will be a function of the rate at which $\dot{V}O_2$ increases towards $\dot{V}O_2$ max and the rate at which muscle and blood [lactate] rises to fatiguing levels. Therefore, it is not surprising that the MLSS has been shown to be an important predictor of endurance exercise performance. Jones and Doust (1998b) demonstrated that the MLSS was better correlated with 8 km running performance ($r = 0.92$) than a number of other physiological measures including T_{lac}, T_{vent}, blood [lactate] reference values, and $\dot{V}O_2$ max. Theoretically, the exercise intensity at the MLSS can be sustained for one hour during competition, but under laboratory conditions an exercise duration of 40–50 minutes is more common. Therefore, it appears that the MLSS dictates the running speed that can be sustained during competition in running races at distances of 10 km to 10 miles.

Figure 10.5 Determination of the running speed at the maximal lactate steady state (MLSS) from 5 treadmill runs of 30 minutes duration at different speeds. In this example, the MLSS occurs at 16.5 km h⁻¹.

Despite the great theoretical and practical interest in the direct determination of the MLSS, the requirement for several laboratory sessions and numerous blood samples has led exercise physiologists to devise simpler tests for the estimation of the MLSS.

10.5.2 CRITICAL POWER

Monod and Scherrer (1965) noted a hyperbolic relationship between power output and time to exhaustion in isolated muscle groups and transformed this into a linear relationship between total work done and time to exhaustion. The critical power (P_{crit}) was later defined as the slope of the regression of work done on time to exhaustion, and was considered to represent the highest exercise intensity that could be sustained for long periods without fatigue (Moritani *et al.*, 1981). The critical power can also be defined as the intercept of the regression equation describing the relationship between power output and the inverse of time to exhaustion (1 / *t*), (Figure 10.6). The P_{crit} concept has also been applied to other sports including running (Hughson *et al.*, 1984; Pepper *et al.*, 1992) and swimming (Wakayoshi *et al.*, 1992), but in these sports the term critical velocity is used. The measurement of P_{crit} requires that subjects exercise to exhaustion at several (ideally 4–6) constant power outputs on separate days. In theory, the P_{crit} should represent the same

exercise intensity as the MLSS and provide a direct measure of the boundary between heavy and severe exercise. Poole *et al.* (1988) demonstrated that blood lactate and $\dot{V}O_2$ attained steady-state values below the P_{crit} but rose over time during exercise above the P_{crit}. It has also been demonstrated that P_{crit} is sensitive to endurance training (Poole *et al.*, 1990; Jenkins and Quigley, 1992) and that the $\dot{V}O_2$ slow component which is most evident for exercise

Figure 10.6 Determination of the critical power (P_{crit}). In this example, the subject performed three exercise bouts to exhaustion at three power outputs on a cycle ergometer. The intercept of the regression equation relating power output to the inverse of time to exhaustion is the P_{crit}, while the anaerobic work capacity (AWC) is given by the gradient of the regression line.

above the P_{crit} is attenuated with endurance training (Casaburi *et al.*, 1987; Womack *et al.*, 1995). However, time to exhaustion at the P_{crit} has varied considerably between studies and it has been reported that exercise at P_{crit} cannot be sustained beyond about 45 minutes (Poole *et al.*, 1988; Housh *et al.*, 1989; Jenkins and Quigley, 1990; Overend *et al.*, 1992). The differences in time to exhaustion at the P_{crit} noted in different studies may relate to the range of exercise intensities that are used to calculate the P_{crit}. Exhaustive trials of less than 3 minutes duration may not sufficiently tax the aerobic system, while trials requiring greater than 15 minutes may be prematurely curtailed as subjects lose motivation (Hill, 1993).

The critical power has obvious relevance as a theoretical construct. However, the necessity for subjects to perform a number (3–6) of exhaustive efforts on separate days precludes its routine use as means of identifying the boundary between heavy and severe exercise.

10.5.3 NEUROMUSCULAR FATIGUE THRESHOLD

The neuromuscular fatigue threshold (NFT) was first described by De Vries *et al.* (1982). Determination of the NFT requires subjects to exercise at a number of severe and supra-maximal power outputs while electromyographic activity (EMG) in the working muscles is measured continuously. The slope of the increase in the integrated EMG (iEMG) over time in each of these exercise bouts is recorded. Subsequently, the slope of the iEMG is plotted against the respective power output and the intercept of this relationship is defined as the NFT (i.e. the NFT therefore represents the highest power output at which iEMG will remain stable over time). The NFT has been shown to occur at a similar power output to the P_{crit} (Housh *et al.*, 1991a; Housh *et al.*, 1991b). This coincidence may indicate that the transition from heavy to severe exercise is associated with an increased firing frequency of already recruited muscle fibres or with a progressive recruitment of low-efficiency type II muscle fibres as fatigue ensues. The latter scenario

may also explain the increase in blood [lactate] over time and the emergence of the $\dot{V}O_2$ slow component for exercise above the P_{crit} / MLSS (Poole *et al.*, 1988; Barstow *et al.*, 1996).

Measurement of the NFT has not proved popular as a method for defining the boundary between the heavy and severe exercise intensity domains due to the requirement for subjects to complete several exercise bouts and for equipment to measure and analyse electromyographic activity.

10.5.4 LACTATE TURNPOINT

During multistage and incremental exercise tests, some authors have identified two lactate thresholds from plots of blood [lactate] against $\dot{V}O_2$ or exercise intensity (Ribeiro *et al.*, 1986; Aunola and Rusko, 1992; Hofmann *et al.*, 1994). These correspond to the traditional *first* lactate threshold where blood [lactate] first increases above baseline, and a *second* 'sudden and sustained' lactate threshold or lactate turnpoint at around 2.5–4.0 mM. Skinner and McLellan (1980) first argued for the existence of two transition points in both the blood lactate and ventilatory responses to incremental exercise, and these authors also speculated on the possible physiological mechanisms that may underpin these phenomena. It has been noted that the lactate turnpoint may be more meaningful in terms of the endurance race performance characteristics of highly trained subjects than is the T_{lac} (Ribeiro *et al.*, 1986; Aunola and Rusko, 1992; Hoffman *et al.*, 1994). It is not known whether any similarity between the exercise intensity at the lactate turnpoint and the P_{crit} / MLSS is coincidental or whether both are related to the same underlying mechanism. If incremental exercise tests utilize stage durations that are sufficiently long and intensity increments that are sufficiently small to allow the measured blood [lactate] to reflect entry of lactate and its removal from the blood, it is possible that the lactate turnpoint can provide a reasonable estimate of the MLSS. Identification of the lactate turnpoint is subjective and it is often impossible to identify a *second* lactate threshold.

10.5.5 FIXED BLOOD LACTATE CONCENTRATIONS (OBLA)

Mader *et al.* (1976) defined the 'aerobic–anaerobic transition' as the point at which blood [lactate] reached 4 mM in an incremental exercise test (Figure 10.2). This rationale may have been based on the suggestion that muscle lactate transporters become saturated at approximately 4 mM muscle [lactate] (Jorfeldt *et al.*, 1978). Support for the 4 mM concept was provided by Kindermann *et al.* (1979) and Heck *et al.* (1985) who demonstrated that the *mean* blood [lactate] at MLSS was approximately 4.0 ± 0.7 mM (range: 3.1–5.5 mM). Jones and Doust (1998b) also recently reported that the mean blood [lactate] at MLSS in a group of runners was close to 4 mM, but noted that individual values could be as low as 2.5 mM or as high as 6.0 mM. The 4 mM blood [lactate] reference value evaluated during incremental exercise was termed the 'onset of blood lactate accumulation' (OBLA) by Sjodin and Jacobs (1981). This is something of a misnomer given that 4 mM blood [lactate] is reached at a significantly higher exercise intensity than the T_{lac} (Jones and Doust, 1994).

The use of OBLA, and other fixed values such as 3 mM (Borch *et al.*, 1993), certainly improves the objectivity with which exercise lactate data can be evaluated and may be useful in demonstrating a reduced reliance on anaerobic metabolism during submaximal exercise following training. This procedure takes no account of inter-individual differences in the rate of blood lactate accumulation, and the dependency of blood [lactate] on substrate availability (Ivy *et al.*, 1981), exercise protocol (Ferry *et al.*, 1988), and on the site of blood sampling and the assay medium (Williams *et al.*, 1992) brings the validity of this practice into question. Coincidentally, the exercise intensity at 4mM blood [lactate] may be similar in some subjects to the exercise intensity at the lactate turnpoint, which, in turn, may provide a good estimate of the MLSS. It should be remembered, however, that blood lactate responses during incremental exercise tests rarely allow the blood lactate response during prolonged exercise at a constant intensity to be predicted (Orok *et al.*, 1989; Aunola and Rusko, 1992). If subjects are asked to exercise continuously at the exercise intensity corresponding to 4 mM blood [lactate] derived from an incremental test, blood [lactate] rises throughout the exercise bout and exhaustion occurs relatively quickly (Mognoni *et al.*, 1990; Oyono-Enguille *et al.*, 1990). This suggests that, in most subjects, the exercise intensity at which 4 mM blood [lactate] is reached in an incremental test overestimates the exercise intensity at the MLSS. This may be especially true in elite subjects who may not increase their blood [lactate] to greater than 4 mM until they reach $\geq 95\% \dot{V}O_2$ max (Jones and Doust, 1994).

10.5.6 INDIVIDUAL ANAEROBIC THRESHOLD

Investigations by Stegmann *et al.* (1981) and Stegmann and Kindermann (1982) into individual blood lactate kinetics during exercise and recovery led to the concept of the individual anaerobic threshold (IAT). The calculation of IAT involves the measurement of blood [lactate] during a standard incremental exercise test and during the subsequent recovery period. The IAT concept makes several important assumptions including that the lactate clearance kinetics during recovery reflect those that are operating during exercise. An exponential curve is fitted to the blood [lactate] response to exercise and a third-order polynomial is fitted to the data for blood [lactate] during the recovery period. Then, a horizontal line is drawn to connect the peak exercise blood [lactate] to the equivalent blood [lactate] in recovery. A second line is then drawn from this point on the 'recovery blood [lactate] curve' tangential to the 'exercise blood [lactate] curve'. The point at which this line cuts the 'exercise blood [lactate] curve' is defined as the IAT and is assumed to represent the exercise intensity at which the elimination of blood lactate is both maximal and equal to the rate of diffusion of lactate from working muscle to blood (Stegmann *et al.*, 1981). The physiological rationale for this approach has never been transparent, and misgivings exist as to the validity of a number of the assumptions made in the IAT concept, including that the rate of blood lactate clearance reaches a plateau during submaximal exercise. Although the IAT is sensitive to endurance training (Keith *et al.*, 1992), the time to exhaustion at IAT varied considerably in different studies. Stegmann *et al.* (1981) reported that exercise at IAT could be sustained for 50 minutes in all subjects tested , whereas Orok *et al.* (1989) found that exercise at IAT could only be sustained for 3–36 minutes. Jones and Doust (1998c) reported that in well-trained runners, the IAT overestimated the running speed at both T_{lac} and at 4 mM blood [lactate]. The differences between studies may be related to variations in the protocols used to derive IAT including the incremental rate and stage duration employed in the incremental test, whether the exercise test is continued to exhaustion, and the use of a passive or active recovery period (McLellan and Jacobs, 1993). The requirement for complex data analysis in the determination of IAT precludes routine use of IAT by athlete and coach, and the method has not proved popular.

10.5.7 LACTATE MINIMUM SPEED

Tegtbur *et al.* (1993) suggested that the point at which blood [lactate] reaches a minimum before beginning to rise during an incremental exercise test initiated during lactacidosis provides a valid estimate of MLSS. The lactate minimum speed test requires subjects to perform: (1) two supramaximal exercise bouts for 60 s and 45 s (separated by a 60 s recovery period) at an intensity of ~120% $\dot{V}O_2$ max; (2) an 8 minute walk to allow blood [lactate] to reach a peak in the blood; and (3) an incremental exercise test using ~3-minute stages with blood [lactate] measured at the end of each stage. The blood [lactate] response during the incremental portion of the test, which should be described using a cubic spline function, is characteristically U-shaped and the nadir on this curve can be termed the lactate minimum speed (LMS),

(Figure 10.7). Tegtbur *et al.* (1993) suggested that the decreasing blood [lactate] during the early stages of the incremental test indicated that the rate of blood lactate clearance was greater than the rate of lactate production, while the increasing blood [lactate] during the latter part of the test indicated that lactate production outstripped its removal. On this basis, the point at which blood [lactate] reaches a minimum should reflect the point at which lactate production and lactate clearance rates are equal, i.e. the MLSS. Tegtbur *et al.* (1993) showed that when 25 endurance runners ran for 8 km at the LMS they exhibited elevated but stable blood [lactate] values. When the subjects ran at a speed only 0.68 km h^{-1} above the LMS, there was a significant accumulation of blood lactate which caused 11 subjects to terminate the exercise bout before 8 km had been completed. The LMS test is attractive in that the LMS may be determined objectively, is robust to variations in stage duration during the incremental test provided that stages are of at least 800 m in length (or 2.5–3 minutes in duration), and is claimed not to be affected by glycogen depletion (Tegtbur *et al.*, 1993).

Several recent studies indicate that the LMS may not be valid for the estimation of MLSS. Jones and Doust (1998b) reported that the LMS was not significantly different from the running speed at T_{lac} but that it was significantly lower than the running speed at the MLSS in 10 trained runners. The LMS had poor discriminatory power between subjects, was poorly correlated with MLSS, and provided the worst estimate of the MLSS out of a range of other physiological measures including T_{lac}, T_{vent}, and OBLA. Carter *et al.* (1999a) have shown that the LMS is profoundly influenced by the exercise intensity at which the incremental portion of the lactate minimum test is started. These authors reported a positive linear relationship between the starting speed used in the incremental test and the speed at which the lactate minimum was found. Although it would be possible to choose a starting speed that would provide a reasonable value for LMS, this requirement for manipulating the test protocol does not inspire confidence in the validity of the LMS concept. In another study, Carter *et al.* (1999b) measured T_{lac} and the blood lactate response to a standard incremental treadmill test, the LMS, and $\dot{V}O_2$ max in 16 subjects before and after they completed a 6-week endurance training programme and in a further 8 subjects who acted as controls. In the control group, there were no changes in the running speeds at T_{lac} or 3 mM blood [lactate], LMS or $\dot{V}O_2$ max. In the experimental groups, there were significant improvements in the running speeds at T_{lac} and 3 mM blood [lactate], and a significant increase in $\dot{V}O_2$ max. However, despite this clear evidence of improvement in endurance fitness in the training group, the LMS was not significantly different before or after training. Although further work is needed, this lack of sensitivity to training, along with the protocol-dependency of the lactate minimum test, suggests that the LMS does not provide a valid estimate of MLSS.

10.5.8 HEART RATE DEFLECTION POINT

Conconi *et al.* (1982) reported that the speed at which the linearity in the heart rate (HR)–running speed relationship was lost in an incremental field test in runners, i.e. the heart rate deflection point, was highly correlated with ($r = 0.99$) and not significantly different from the running speed at T_{lac}. Droghetti *et al.* (1985) confirmed this relationship in a number of other sports and activities. Conconi *et al.* (1982) hypothesized that the $\dot{V}O_2$ spared by the increased anaerobic contribution to the total energy cost of exercise beyond T_{lac} would be reflected by a reduced rate of increase in HR above T_{lac}. Conconi's original method required subjects to run around an athletic track initially at a slow speed. Thereafter, there was a progressive increase in running speed every 200 m with HR recorded using an HR monitor at the end of each stage until athletes reached exhaustion. When HR is plotted against running speed, a deviation of heart rate at high speeds can sometimes be seen (Figure 10.8). Conconi *et al.*

Figure 10.7 Determination of the lactate minimum speed (LMS). In this example, an incremental treadmill test involving five exercise stages has been completed following prior sprint exercise. The blood lactate data are fitted with a cubic spline and the minimum point on the curve is termed the LMS.

Figure 10.8 Determination of the heart rate deflection point. The heart rate deflection point is the running speed at which heart rate begins to deviate from linearity.

(1982) claimed that the deflection point in HR could be observed in all subjects and that it occurred at the same running speed as the T_{lac}. However, the protocol used to assess T_{lac} was unusual and it was later suggested that the deflection in HR corresponded to the lactate turnpoint (Ribeiro *et al.*, 1985) or the MLSS (Hofmann *et al.*, 1994). Recently, Conconi's research group has modified the original Conconi test protocol (Grazzi *et al.*, 1999) in the face of criticism from the scientific community.

The interest in the possibility of a non-invasive field test for MLSS led to a large number of investigations into the validity of Conconi's method. Most of these studies have cast great doubt upon the validity, reliability, and underpinning theory of the Conconi test (Kuipers *et al.*, 1988; Tokmakidis and Leger, 1992; Jones and Doust, 1995; Jones and Doust, 1997b), although other groups have maintained that the test is valid and useful (Hofmann *et al.*, 1994; Bunc *et al.*, 1995). The physiological rationale for the existence of a deflection in heart rate and for its mechanistic link to increased blood lactate accumulation has never been clear. Conconi's original hypothesis that increased anaerobic metabolism spares $\dot{V}O_2$ is, however, untenable. The increased rate of ATP resynthesis through anaerobic glycolysis above the T_{lac} appears to supplement rather than spare the rate of ATP production through oxidative metabolism. During incremental tests which bring subjects to exhaustion in 8–12 minutes, a reduced rate of increase in $\dot{V}O_2$ during submaximal exercise has never been demonstrated, although there is generally a plateau in $\dot{V}O_2$ at maximal exercise ($\dot{V}O_2$ max). Rather, with longer stage durations, $\dot{V}O_2$ may demonstrate an upward curvilinearity as the $\dot{V}O_2$ slow component develops (Jones *et al.*, 1999). It has been suggested that the deflection in heart rate is an artefact of the specifics of the Conconi test protocol (Jones and Doust, 1997b). The increase in running speed every 200 m means

that the time between increases in exercise intensity becomes progressively shorter as the test proceeds. This may have two important effects. Firstly, measurements of HR become more frequent as HR approaches its maximum. When plotted against running speed, this will elongate the region at HR max and lead to the artificial appearance of a deflection point. Secondly, the decreasing exercise stage durations in the face of similar or slowed HR response kinetics may not allow sufficient time for HR to rise to its 'steady state' level.

Pokan *et al.* (1993) demonstrated that the existence of a deflection in HR depends on increases in the left ventricular ejection fraction. The same group have acknowledged that a deflection in HR is not always found because the HR response to incremental exercise may be perfectly linear up to HR_{max} or may even exhibit an upward deflection point (Pokan *et al.*, 1995). Difficulty in observing a deflection in HR in all subjects has been recognized as a limitation to the Conconi test (Kuipers *et al.*, 1988; Jones and Doust, 1995; Jones and Doust, 1997b) and these difficulties persist even when mathematical approaches to the identification of a deflection in HR are utilized (Tokmakidis and Leger, 1992). Jones and Doust (1995) assessed the test–retest reliability of the Conconi test in 15 subjects and reported that a deflection in HR was found in both tests in only 6 individuals. The deflection in HR has also been shown to occur at rather high submaximal exercise intensities, i.e. 90–95% HR_{max}, that are above both the T_{lac} and OBLA (Tokmakidis and Leger, 1992; Jones and Doust, 1997b). Two studies of running (Jones and Doust, 1997b) and cycling (Heck and Hollmann, 1992) have shown that the exercise intensity at the deflection in HR cannot be sustained without appreciable accumulation of blood lactate and premature fatigue. These studies suggest that a deflection in HR, when it can be determined, overestimates the exercise intensity at MLSS in most subjects.

10.5.9 OTHER ESTIMATES

Recently, other approaches have been used to estimate the boundary between heavy and severe exercise. Snyder *et al.* (1994) proposed that the exercise intensity at 85% HR_{max} provides a close estimate of the exercise intensity at MLSS. While this may be generally true, dangers in non-individual evaluation of the physiological response to exercise have been highlighted previously (Katch *et al.*, 1978). For example, in elite distance runners, exercise at the MLSS requires approximately 90% HR_{max} (Jones, 1998). Billat *et al.* (1994a) estimated the power output at MLSS during cycling by analysing the change in blood [lactate] between 20 and 30 minutes at two levels corresponding to ~65% and ~80% $\dot{V}O_2$ max. Effectively, these authors interpolated between a power output which incurred a decreased or constant blood [lactate] with time, and a power output which incurred an increased blood [lactate] with time, to predict a power output at which blood [lactate] would be maximal but stable. Clearly, there will be inherent error in using interpolation as opposed to direct measurement of MLSS and some precision will be lost. Nevertheless, this type of approach would seem to have some potential, since it might permit a working estimate of MLSS from two short exercise bouts performed on the same day. Further research is required to determine a simple and practical procedure for determination of MLSS or critical power that does not unduly sacrifice accuracy.

10.6 FROM SEVERE TO SUPRAMAXIMAL EXERCISE: THE $V - VO_2$ max

The boundary between severe submaximal exercise and supramaximal exercise (exercise having an energy cost greater than the $\dot{V}O_2$ max) is, by definition, the $\dot{V}O_2$ max. The $\dot{V}O_2$ max represents the maximal rate at which ATP can be generated aerobically. Numerous studies have shown that $\dot{V}O_2$ max is an excellent predictor of endurance performance in heterogeneous groups (e.g. Costill *et al.*, 1973).

Although a high $\dot{V}O_2$ max (>70 ml kg^{-1} min^{-1} for males, >60 ml kg^{-1} min^{-1} for females) is necessary for elite-level performance, other factors such as T_{lac}, MLSS, and exercise economy can discriminate performance differences in athletes with similar $\dot{V}O_2$ max values. In terms of the control of physical training, and the definition of exercise intensity domains, however, it is not the absolute or relative value of $\dot{V}O_2$ max (in units of l min^{-1} or ml kg^{-1} min^{-1}) that is important but rather the 'functional expression' of $\dot{V}O_2$ max in units of velocity or power output. In order to estimate the running velocity at $\dot{V}O_2$ max ($V - \dot{V}O_2$ max) it is necessary to make measurements of both $\dot{V}O_2$ max and the running economy characteristics of the subject. The latter is best done by measuring the steady-state $\dot{V}O_2$ at several sub-T_{lac} running speeds. A regression equation describing the relationship between $\dot{V}O_2$ and submaximal running speed can then be solved for $\dot{V}O_2$ max to give the estimated $V - \dot{V}O_2$ max (Morgan *et al.*, 1989). Two individuals with the same $\dot{V}O_2$ max values may have different $V - \dot{V}O_2$ max values if one subject is more economical than the other (Figure 10.9). In this example, the subject with the better economy

Figure 10.9 Determination of the running velocity at maximal oxygen uptake ($V - \dot{V}O_2$ max). This involves regressing $\dot{V}O_2$ on exercise intensity for submaximal exercise and extrapolating this relationship to $\dot{V}O_2$ max. The $V - \dot{V}O_2$ max can differ in two individuals with the same $\dot{V}O_2$ max (in ml kg^{-1} min^{-1}) if exercise economy differs in the two individuals.

would be able to run at a higher speed for the same exercise intensity such as 100% $\dot{V}O_2$ max. The $V - \dot{V}O_2$ max is highly correlated with endurance performance (Jones, 1998; Jones and Doust, 1998b). This is due, in part, to the fact that athletes sustain similar percentages of their $\dot{V}O_2$ max for given durations of exercise (Londeree, 1986). The $V - \dot{V}O_2$ max has also been shown to be sensitive to endurance training (Jones, 1998; Billat *et al.*, 1999). It has been suggested that the $V - \dot{V}O_2$ max represents an important exercise intensity if the goal is to improve $\dot{V}O_2$ max and endurance fitness (Billat and Koralsztein, 1996; Hill and Rowell, 1997).

10.7 CONCLUSION

This chapter has demonstrated the existence of several 'domains' of submaximal exercise (Figure 10.1). These are referred to as moderate exercise, heavy exercise and severe exercise. Moderate exercise is that performed below the lactate threshold. During moderate exercise, $\dot{V}O_2$ attains an early steady state and blood [lactate] remains close to resting levels. Heavy exercise is that performed above the lactate threshold but below the maximal lactate steady state or critical power. In this domain, both $\dot{V}O_2$ and blood lactate will attain a delayed but elevated steady state. Severe exercise is that performed above the maximal lactate steady state but below the exercise intensity corresponding to $\dot{V}O_2$ max. In the severe domain, both $\dot{V}O_2$ and blood [lactate] will rise continuously over time until $\dot{V}O_2$ max is reached and/or fatigue resulting from the metabolic acidosis terminates exercise. In the severe submaximal exercise domain, the time to exhaustion is predictable based upon the critical power and the anaerobic work capacity.

In order to define exercise intensity accurately, it is important to delineate the boundaries between the various exercise domains. In this chapter, the variety of methods that have been employed to measure or estimate the physiological parameters that define the transition from one domain to another have been reviewed. These methods differ in the degree to which the scientific literature supports their validity, reliability, and sensitivity to change following physical training. The possible advantages of practicality and simplicity of a method must be secondary to the principles of good scientific measurement. None of the measures reviewed above has received universal acceptance, but the weight of evidence suggests that the lactate threshold and MLSS are the criterial standards in terms of defining the boundaries between the submaximal exercise intensity domains. The $V - \dot{V}O_2$ max is widely accepted as a useful parameter that separates submaximal from maximal / supramaximal exercise. Table 10.1 summarizes the validity, reliability, sensitivity, objectivity, practicality, and acceptability of the methods that are most commonly used for evaluating endurance fitness.

Direct measurements (or estimates) of T_{lac}, MLSS, and $V - \dot{V}O_2$ max in an individual athlete allow for endurance performance capability and/or times to exhaustion at particular running speeds or power outputs to be estimated. This information can also be used to help in the prescription of a structured, balanced and appropriate training programme. For example, an individual who is new to regular exercise may initially be prescribed only moderate-intensity exercise because higher intensities ($>T_{lac}$) may be perceived to be unpleasant and stressful and this experience may adversely affect adherence to the exercise programme. In contrast, elite endurance athletes will generally perform exercise sessions at moderate, heavy, severe, and supramaximal intensities during a normal training week. The relative proportions of these sessions will depend on current fitness status, age, aspirations, training preferences, the time in the training macrocycle, and the specialist event. Excessive severe intensity exercise may impair recovery and eventually contribute to overtraining, while if moderate-intensity exercise is performed almost exclusively in a training

Table 10.1 The validity, reliability, sensitivity, objectivity, practicality and acceptability of the methods that are most commonly used for evaluating endurance fitness

Test	Strong evidence for validity?	Strong evidence for reliability?	Strong evidence for sensitivity?	Objective?	OK for field testing?	Athlete friendly?
Tlac	√	√	√	x	√	√
Tvent	√	√	√	x	x	√
MLSS	√	√	√	√	x	x
Pcrit	?	√	√	√	x	x
TlacP	?	?	?	x	x	√
OBLA	x	x	√	√	√	√
IAT	x	?	√	√	x	√
LMS	x	√	x	√	√	√
HRD	x	x	x	x	√	√
$\dot{V}-\dot{V}O_2$ max	√	√	√	√	x	√

programme then 'underperformance' may result. The training intensity can be regulated if an athlete has a portable heart rate monitor and knows his or her heart rate at the lactate threshold and at maximal lactate steady state as well as the maximal heart rate (Figure 10.10). The balance of training intensities (and hence durations) in a training programme can be specified and controlled with this systematic approach. Over time, this should maximize the effectiveness of training and result in improved performance.

Figure 10.10 Use of heart rate to regulate training intensity. The vertical lines represent the heart rate at lactate threshold, the heart rate at the lactate turnpoint (which may provide a reasonable estimate of the maximal lactate steady state) and the maximal heart rate. These heart rates and the corresponding running speeds can be used to prescribe and regulate training intensity within the moderate, heavy, severe, and supramaximal domains.

10.8 PRACTICAL EXERCISES

10.8.1 GENERAL GUIDELINES

Subject preparation: Subjects should be well rested, hydrated, and with full glycogen stores to ensure that the responses to exercise are not influenced by acute changes in physiological status. The following procedure is recommended.

- 48 hours before testing: Refrain from heavy exercise. Light exercise can be undertaken. A high-carbohydrate diet should be consumed.
- 24 hours before testing: No exercise should be undertaken. A high-carbohydrate diet should be consumed.
- The day of testing: No exercise should be undertaken. A light-carbohydrate meal 2 to 4 hours before testing should be consumed but nothing thereafter. Adequate fluids should be taken but no caffeine or high (>12%) carbohydrate drinks should be consumed in the four hours prior to testing.

Subjects should wear appropriate athletic clothing and training shoes. The laboratory should be well ventilated and at a comfortable temperature for exercise (17–20°C). Appropriate informed consent and pre-exercise health questionnaires should be completed (see Jones and Doust, 1997a).

10.8.2 ESTIMATING CAPABILITY

In a number of the experiments, an estimate of the subject's likely performance is required to guide the intensity of exercise in an incremental test. Prior testing for maximal oxygen uptake provides the best guidance, although estimations can be made based on knowledge of the subject's sporting performance. Table 10.2 offers guidance.

10.8.3 GENERAL METHODS

Heart rate is best obtained from a portable heart rate telemeter (Polar Sport Tester, Polar Electro Oy, Finland) or similar device set to 5 s recording intervals for immediate playback after exercise. Interpretation of data can be enhanced if the subject is instructed to press the electronic marker button at the commencement of each level of a staged protocol.

Oxygen uptake can be obtained from an on-line system or from Douglas bags. The former allows observation in real-time. If using Douglas bags, expired air should be collected for a whole number of breaths over a timed period of about 45 s during the final minute of each level of a staged protocol. Rating of perceived exertion can be obtained during the period of expired air collection.

Blood sampling can take place immediately after collection of air is completed. During

Table 10.2 Estimation of speed and work rate increments for graded exercise testing according to fitness status.

Standard	Running (male) (km h^{-1})	Running (female) (km h^{-1})	Cycling (male) (W)	Cycling (female) (W)
Fair	9, 10.5, 12, 13.5, 15	7, 8.5, 10, 11.5, 13	50, 80, 110, 140, 170	50, 75, 100, 125, 150
Average	11, 12.5, 14, 15.5, 17	9, 10.5, 12, 13.5, 15	110, 140, 170, 200, 230	80, 110, 140, 170, 200
Good	13, 14.5, 16, 17.5, 19	11, 12.5, 14, 15.5, 17	180, 210, 240, 270, 300	110, 140, 170, 200, 230
Excellent	15, 16.5, 18, 19.5, 21	13, 14.5, 16, 17.5, 19	250, 280, 310, 340, 370	140, 170, 200, 230, 260

Fair would be a typical student who keeps fit but does not take part in competitive sport
Average would be a typical student who plays team sports
Good would be a typical student endurance athlete
Excellent would be a competitive endurance athlete

treadmill running, blood sampling is most easily achieved by the subject jumping astride the moving belt at the end of each stage. This allows a finger to be held stable for sampling. During the sampling period the treadmill speed can be increased to the next level and once sampling is complete the subject can recommence running. The advantages of achieving a quick and neat sample from a stationary hand outweigh the disadvantages of the short (~30 s) interruption to exercise which, given the slow kinetics of lactate change, is unlikely to significantly influence the data (Gullstrand *et al.*, 1994). In cycling exercise, a finger can easily be stabilized and no interruption to exercise is required. Laboratory health and safety guidelines must be adhered to when handling blood (see Chapter 4 by Maughan *et al.*).

Fingertip capillary sampling is the most convenient method for blood collection although the ear lobe is preferred by some. Lactate concentration is affected by the site of sampling and the post-sampling treatment (see Williams *et al.*, 1992). The general pattern of change will be similar whatever the method used but absolute values will differ.

Treadmill grade should be set to 1% to reflect the energetic cost of outdoor running (Jones and Doust, 1996). An electronically braked cycle ergometer, where power is kept constant even if pedalling rate changes, will allow superior results to those obtained with a friction-braked cycle ergometer.

Where a laboratory practical is being undertaken with inexperienced students to show the basic phenomena, the use of larger increments (1.5 km h^{-1} or 30 W) will provide clear data and allow easy understanding but poor precision. More precise identification of the T_{lac} requires smaller step changes and the guidance given in the Guidelines of the British Association of Sport and Exercise Sciences (Jones and Doust, 1997a) should be followed.

10.8.4 GENERAL FURTHER ANALYSIS OPPORTUNITIES

If more than one of the following practicals can be completed over the course of a teaching unit, the running speed or power output obtained by the different methods can be ranked and cross-correlated. This would allow discussion of how the data fit into the theoretical framework (see main text) and the extent of similarity between the parameters.

Confirmation (or otherwise) of the validity of any of the parameters can be shown by a 'verification' test. Following identification of the running speed or power output at T_{lac}, subjects may undertake constant load exercise at this intensity on a separate day. Heart rate, oxygen uptake and blood [lactate] can be determined at 5-minute intervals. This test can be undertaken on a running track with heart rate monitored continuously and a blood sample taken every 800 m (running) or 2400 m (cycling) for analysis of blood [lactate].

10.9 PRACTICAL 1: T_{LAC} (LACTATE THRESHOLD) AND OBLA (ONSET OF BLOOD LACTATE ACCUMULATION)

10.9.1 GENERAL PROTOCOL (CYCLING OR RUNNING)

Following a 5-minute jogging or cycling warm-up, the subject completes an incremental test of five 4-minute stages. Oxygen uptake is measured over the final minute of each stage. A blood sample is taken at the end of each stage for the determination of lactate concentration. The intensities can be estimated from Table 10.2.

10.9.2 ADDITIONAL HINTS

- This practical can be performed equally well on a treadmill or a cycle ergometer.
- Only a short warm-up is required due to the early, sub-threshold stages of the protocol.
- A resting blood [lactate] value may give some insight into carbohydrate status.

10.9.3 DATA ANALYSIS

Blood lactate concentration should be plotted against exercise intensity (speed or power output). The data points may be joined by straight lines. If available, a cubic spline program provides the best form of curve fitting. It is not recommended that any form of best-fit poly-nomial curve is used since there is no physiological justification for such an approach.

The OBLA is determined as the exercise intensity at a blood lactate concentration of 4 mM. The lactate threshold is judged by visual inspection as the exercise intensity at which the blood [lactate] data show a sudden and sustained increase above baseline levels.

10.9.4 FURTHER ANALYSIS OPPORTUNITIES

- Determine inter-reviewer reliability by coding plots. Each person in a class can then be asked to identify T_{lac}.
- Does [lactate] at T_{lac} equal [lactate] at OBLA?

10.10 PRACTICAL 2: VENTILATORY THRESHOLD

10.10.1 GENERAL PROTOCOL (CYCLING OR RUNNING)

Following a 5-minute jogging or cycling warm-up, the subject completes an incremental test of seven 2-minute stages. Oxygen uptake is measured over the final minute of each stage. The exercise intensities can be estimated from Table 10.2.

10.10.2 ADDITIONAL HINTS

- This practical can be performed equally well on a treadmill or a cycle ergometer.
- Only a short warm-up is required due to the early, sub-threshold stages of the protocol.
- A ramp protocol can be used (20 W min^{-1} or 1 km h^{-1} min^{-1}) with oxygen uptake being measured continuously with an on-line system or with 45 s sequential Douglas bag collections.

10.10.3 DATA ANALYSIS

Ventilation (l min^{-1} STPD) should be plotted against exercise intensity (running speed or cycling power output). The data points may be joined by straight lines. If available, a cubic spline program provides the best form of curve fitting. It is not recommended that any form of best-fit polynomial curve is used since there is no physiological justification for such an approach.

Ventilatory threshold is judged as the intensity at which the linear relationship between $\dot{V}_E$ and exercise intensity is lost.

10.10.4 FURTHER ANALYSIS OPPORTUNITIES

- Plotting the ventilatory equivalent for oxygen (that is, $\dot{V}_E / \dot{V}O_2$) against exercise intensity may make the threshold clearer.
- Ventilatory parameters may be plotted against $\dot{V}O_2$ rather than speed or power output.
- Plotting three lines ($\dot{V}_E$, RER and $\dot{V}CO_2$) against exercise intensity offers the opportunity to discuss potential underlying physiological mechanisms associated with the respiratory compensation for metabolic acidosis.
- Determine inter-reviewer reliability by coding plots. Each person in a class can then be asked to identify T_{vent}.

10.11 PRACTICAL 3: CRITICAL POWER

10.11.1 GENERAL PROTOCOL (CYCLE)

Three tests to exhaustion are completed on three separate days. Each test is undertaken at a constant intensity and cadence. The intensity is set so that time to exhaustion is between 1 and 10 minutes. After a 5-minute submaximal warm-up, the intensity is increased to the desired value and the subject continues until unable to maintain the required cadence (>5 rev min^{-1} decrease for >5 s). Since the tests are maximal, strong verbal encouragement is appropriate.

The intensities can be judged from Table 10.2 by taking the fifth-stage intensity and cycling at this intensity (likely duration about 10 minutes), + 15% (likely duration about 6 minutes), and + 30% (likely duration about 1 minute).

10.11.2 ADDITIONAL HINTS

- Attempting to complete three tests on one day will not yield reliable results. Tests can be completed on consecutive days but should be given in a random order.
- Note the saddle height so this may be kept constant between tests.
- The exact intensities chosen for the three bouts are not critical since, in principle, exhaustion times anywhere between 1 and 30 minutes will be linearly related. However, the variability in time to exhaustion is greater with durations above 10 minutes.
- Ideally the intensities should be given in random order. If little is known about the subject, give the middle intensity first and the intensities for the subsequent two bouts can be adjusted to ensure the data span an adequate range of exercise intensity.
- The equivalent to critical power, the critical velocity, can be determined on the treadmill using three bouts of exhaustive running at different speeds. However, running to exhaustion on a fast-moving treadmill is a potentially dangerous procedure and not advisable as a student practical.

10.11.3 DATA ANALYSIS

The inverse of time to exhaustion (i.e. $1 / t$) is plotted against power output and a linear regression line is fitted. The intercept of the line gives critical power (P_{crit}) and the slope of the line gives anaerobic work capacity.

10.11.4 FURTHER ANALYSIS OPPORTUNITIES

Adjusting one of the times to exhaustion by ~10% and recalculating P_{crit} and anaerobic work capacity will allow discussion of the sensitivity of these parameters to methodological variation due to subject's motivation to exercise to exhaustion.

10.12 PRACTICAL 4: LACTATE MINIMUM SPEED

10.12.1 GENERAL PROTOCOL (RUNNING)

The subject should warm up with 5 minutes of jogging, some stretching and three acceleration sprints where the treadmill speed is raised over 30 s from slow jogging to sprinting speed and back down again.

The test begins with two pre-test sprints at a speed that is 120% of the running speed at $\dot{V}O_2$ max. The subject should stand with legs astride the treadmill belt. The treadmill speed is increased to the required level and the subject lets go carefully and begins running. The first sprint is for 60 s and the second is for 45 s with a 60 s rest given between sprints. The treadmill speed is lowered to 4 km h^{-1} and the subject walks for 8 minutes, with a capillary blood sample taken after 7 minutes for the determination of lactate concentration. Five 3-minute incremental stages are then completed. The intensities can be judged from Table 10.2.

A capillary sample is obtained at the end of each stage for the determination of lactate concentration.

10.12.2 DATA ANALYSIS

Capillary lactate concentration is plotted against running speed for the five incremental stages. A cubic spline is fitted and the lactate minimum speed determined as the speed at which the lowest point occurs (i.e. a zero-gradient tangent) by visual inspection or mathematically. If a spline-fitting algorithm is not available the data may be connected by straight lines.

10.12.3 ADDITIONAL HINTS

- The lactate concentration after walking for 7 minutes allows confirmation that the pre-test sprints have induced a significant lactacidosis. If the value is < 5 mM the sprints were insufficiently intense and the test should be stopped and repeated on another day.
- The exact sprinting speed and the exact lactate concentration after the sprints is not important in illustrating the principle of the lactate minimum speed test.
- If running speed at $\dot{V}O_2$ max is not known, the speeds for the initial sprints can be estimated by adding 4 km h^{-1} to the fifth-stage speed shown in Table 10.2.

- It is not recommended that any form of best-fit polynomial curve is used since there is no physiological justification for such an approach.
- The test can be undertaken on a cycle ergometer. The sprint power can be estimated as 125% of the fifth-stage power output in Table 10.2. The same table gives estimates for the power output during the subsequent five stages.
- The test can be undertaken in the field using a running track. A pre-recorded tape and loudspeaker system is needed to control the running pace (see Tetgbur *et al.*, 1993).

10.13 PRACTICAL 5: HEART RATE DEFLECTION POINT (CONCONI TEST)

10.13.1 GENERAL PROTOCOL (RUNNING)

Following a 3-minute warm-up jog and some stretching, the subject completes an incremental protocol to maximal effort. The starting intensity is the lowest intensity shown in Table 10.2. Treadmill velocity is increased by 0.5 km h^{-1} every 200 m. Heart rate is recorded throughout using a short-range radio telemeter (Polar Sport Tester, Polar Electro Oy, Finland) or similar device set to 5 s recording intervals for immediate playback after exercise. The subject should press the electronic marker button on the telemeter at the end of each stage.

10.13.2 DATA ANALYSIS

Heart rate at the end of each 200 m stage is plotted against running speed. Heart rate deflection point is identified as the running speed at which linearity is lost in the HR–speed relationship.

10.13.3 ADDITIONAL HINTS

The test can be undertaken in the field using a running track. A pre-recorded tape and loudspeaker system are needed to control the running pace. The intensity should be increased according to distance covered (i.e. every 200 m) not according to time to remain true to Conconi's original work.

10.13.4 FURTHER ANALYSIS OPPORTUNITIES

- Determine inter-reviewer reliability by coding plots. Each person in a class can then be asked to identify the heart rate deflection point.
- Compare the heart rate deflection point determined by visual inspection with the same point determined using the software provided with the Polar Sport Tester radio telemetry unit.

ACKNOWLEDGEMENT

The authors would like to record their thanks to Dr Helen Carter for her help in the preparation of this chapter.

REFERENCES

Acavedo, E.O. and Goldfarb, A.H. (1989). Increased training intensity effects on plasma lactate, ventilatory threshold, and endurance. *Medicine and Science in Sports and Exercise, 21*, 563–8.

Aunola, S. and Rusko, H. (1992). Does anaerobic threshold correlate with maximal lactate steady state? *Journal of Sports Sciences, 10*, 309–23.

Barstow, T.J., Jones, A.M., Nguyen, P. and Casaburi, R. (1996). Influence of muscle fiber type and pedal frequency on oxygen uptake kinetics of heavy exercise. *Journal of Applied Physiology, 81*, 1642–50.

Beaver, W.L., Wasserman, K. and Whipp, B.J. (1986). A new method for detecting anaerobic threshold by gas exchange. *Journal of Applied Physiology, 60*, 2020–7.

Beneke, R. and Von Duvillard, S.P. (1996). Determination of maximal lactate steady state response in selected sports events. *Medicine and Science in Sports and Exercise, 28*, 241–6.

Billat, V., Blondel, N. and Berthoin, S. (1999). Determination of the longest time to exhaustion at maximal oxygen uptake. *European Journal of Applied Physiology, 80*, 159–61.

Billat, V.L. and Koralsztein, J.P. (1996). Significance of the velocity at $\dot{V}O_2$ max and time to exhaustion at this velocity. *Sports Medicine, 22*, 90–108.

Billat, V.L., Dalmay, F., Antonini, M.T. and Chassain, A.P. (1994a). A method for determining the maximal steady state of blood lactate concentration from two levels of submaximal exercise. *European Journal of Applied Physiology, 69*, 196–202.

Billat, V.L., Renoux, J.C., Pinoteau, J., *et al.* (1994b). Times to exhaustion at 100% of velocity at $\dot{V}O_2$max and modelling of the time-limit / velocity relationship in elite long-distance runners. *European Journal of Applied Physiology, 69*, 271–3.

Borch, K.W., Ingjer, F., Larsen, S. and Tomten, S.E. (1993). Rate of accumulation of blood lactate during graded exercise as a predictor of "anaerobic threshold". *Journal of Sports Sciences, 11*, 49–55.

Brooks, G.A. (1991). Current concepts in lactate exchange. *Medicine and Science in Sports and Exercise, 23*, 895–906.

Bunc, V., Hofmann, P., Leitner, H. and Gaisl, G. (1995). Verification of the heart rate threshold. *European Journal of Applied Physiology, 70*, 263–9.

Caiozzo, V.L., Davis, J.A., Ellis, J.F., *et al.* (1982). A comparison of gas exchange indices used to detect the anaerobic threshold. *Journal of Applied Physiology, 53*, 1184–9.

Carter, H., Jones, A.M. and Doust, J.H. (1999a). Effect of incremental test protocol on the lactate minimum speed. *Medicine and Science in Sports and Exercise, 31*, 837–45.

Carter, H., Jones, A.M. and Doust, J.H. (1999b). Effect of six weeks of endurance training on the lactate minimum speed. *Journal of Sports Sciences, 17*, 957–67.

Casaburi, R., Storer, T.W., Ben-Dov, I. and Wasserman, K. (1987). Effect of endurance training on possible determinants of $\dot{V}O_2$ during heavy exercise. *Journal of Applied Physiology, 62*, 199–207.

Cheng, B., Kuipers, H., Snyder, A.C., *et al.* (1992). A new approach for the determination of ventilatory and lactate thresholds. *International Journal of Sports Medicine, 13*, 518–22.

Conconi, F., Ferrari, M., Ziglio, P.G., *et al.* (1982). Determination of the anaerobic threshold by a non-invasive field test in runners. *Journal of Applied Physiology, 52*, 869–73.

Connett, R.J., Gayeski, T.E.J. and Honig, C.R. (1984). Lactate accumulation in fully aerobic, working, dog gracilis muscle. *American Journal of Physiology, 246*, 120–8.

Connett, R.J., Gayeski, T.E.J. and Honig, C.R. (1985). Energy sources in fully aerobic work-rest transitions: a new role for glycolysis. *American Journal of Physiology, 248*, 922–9.

Costill, D.L., Thomason, H. and Roberts, E. (1973). Fractional utilisation of the aerobic capacity during distance running. *Medicine and Science in Sports. 5*, 248–52.

Coyle, E.F., Martin, W.H., Ehsani, A.A., *et al.* (1983). Blood lactate threshold in some well-trained ischemic heart disease patients. *Journal of Applied Physiology, 54*, 18–23.

Davis, J.A. (1985). Anaerobic threshold: review of the concept and direction for future research. *Medicine and Science in Sports and Exercise, 17*, 6–18.

De Vries, H.A., Moritani, T., Nagata, A. and Magnussen, K. (1982). The relation between critical power and neuromuscular fatigue as estimated from electromyographic data. *Ergonomics, 25*, 783–91.

Donovan, C.M. and Pagliassotti, M.J. (1990). Enhanced efficiency of lactate removal after endurance training. *Journal of Applied Physiology*, **68**, 1053–8.

Droghetti, P., Borsetto, C., Casoni, I., *et al.* (1985). Non-invasive determination of the anaerobic threshold in canoeing, cross-country skiing, cycling, roller and ice-skating, rowing and walking. *European Journal of Applied Physiology*, **53**, 299–303.

Edwards, R.H.T. (1981). Human muscle function and fatigue. In *Human Muscle Fatigue: Physiological Mechanisms*. eds. R. Porter and J. Whelan (CIBA Foundations Symposium No. 82, Pitman Medical, London), pp. 1–18.

Farrell, P.A., Wilmore, J.H., Coyle, E.F., *et al.* (1979). Plasma lactate accumulation and distance running performance. *Medicine and Science in Sports*, **11**, 338–44.

Fay, L., Londeree, B.R., Lafontaine, T.P. and Volek, M.R. (1989). Physiological parameters related to distance running performance in female athletes. *Medicine and Science in Sports and Exercise*, **21**, 319–24.

Ferry, A., Duvallet, A. and Rieu, M. (1988). The effect of experimental protocol on the relationship between blood lactate and workload. *Journal of Sports Medicine and Physical Fitness*, **28**, 341–7.

Foxdal, P., Sjodin, B., Sjodin, A. and Ostman, B. (1994). The validity and accuracy of blood lactate measurements for prediction of maximal endurance running capacity: dependency of analysed blood media in combination with different designs of the exercise test. *International Journal of Sports Medicine*, **15**, 89–95.

Grazzi, G., Alfieri, N., Borsetto, C., *et al.* (1999). The power output / heart rate relationship in cycling: test standardization and repeatability. *Medicine and Science in Sports and Exercise*, **31**, 1478–83.

Gullstrand, L., Sjodin, B. and Svedenhag, J. (1994). Blood sampling during continuous running and 30-second intervals on a treadmill: effects on the lactate threshold results? *Scandinavian Journal of Science and Medicine in Sports*, **4**, 239–42.

Heck, H. and Hollmann, W. (1992). Identification, objectivity, and validity of Conconi threshold by cycle stress tests. *Osler Journal Sportsmedizin*, **22**, 35–53.

Heck, H., Mader, A., Hess, G., *et al.* (1985). Justification of the 4 mmol/l lactate threshold. *International Journal of Sports Medicine*, **6**, 117–30.

Henritze, J., Weltman, A., Schurrer, R.L. and Barlow, K. (1985). Effects of training at and above the lactate threshold on the lactate threshold and maximal oxygen uptake. *European Journal of Applied Physiology*, **54**, 84–8.

Hill, D.W. (1993). The critical power concept: a review. *Sports Medicine*, **16**, 237–54.

Hill, D.W. and Rowell, A. L. (1997). Response to exercise at the velocity associated with $\dot{V}O_2$ max. *Medicine and Science in Sports and Exercise*, **29**, 113–6.

Hofmann, P., Bunc, V., Leinter, H., *et al.* (1994). Heart rate threshold related to lactate turnpoint and steady-state exercise on a cycle ergometer. *European Journal of Applied Physiology*, **69**, 132–9.

Honig, C.R., Connett, R.J. and Gayeski, T.E.J. (1992). O_2 transport and its interaction with metabolism: a systems view of aerobic capacity. *Medicine and Science in Sports and Exercise*, **24**, 47–53.

Housh, D.J., Housh, T.J. and Bauge, S.M. (1989). The accuracy of the critical power test for predicting time to exhaustion during cycle ergometry. *Ergonomics*, **32**, 997–1004.

Housh, T.J., De Vries, H.A., Housh, D.J., *et al.* (1991a). The relationship between critical power and the onset of blood lactate accumulation. *Journal of Sports Medicine and Physical Fitness*, **31**, 31–6.

Housh, T.J., Johnson, G.O., McDowell, S.L., *et al.* (1991b). Physiological responses at the fatigue threshold. *International Journal of Sports Medicine*, **12**, 305–8.

Hughes, E.F., Turner, S.C. and Brooks, G.A. (1982). Effects of glycogen depletion and pedalling speed on "anaerobic threshold". *Journal of Applied Physiology*, **52**, 1598–607.

Hughson, R.L., Cook, C.J. and Staudt, L.E. (1984). A high velocity treadmill running test to assess endurance running potential. *International Journal of Sports Medicine*, **5**, 23–5.

Hughson, R.L., Weisiger, K.H. and Swanson, G.D. (1987). Blood lactate concentration increases as a continuous function in progressive exercise. *Journal of Applied Physiology*, **62**, 1975–81.

Hurley, B.F., Hagberg, J.M., Allen, W.K., *et al.* (1984). Effect of training on blood lactate levels during submaximal exercise. *Journal of Applied Physiology*, **56**, 1260–4.

Ivy, J.L., Withers, R.T., Van Handel, P.J., *et al.* (1980). Muscle respiratory capacity and fiber type as determinants of the lactate threshold. *Journal of Applied Physiology*, **48**, 523–7.

Ivy, J.L., Costill, D.L., Van Handel, P.J., *et al.* (1981). Alteration in the lactate threshold with changes in substrate availability. *International Journal of Sports Medicine*, **48**, 523–7.

James, N.W., Adams, G.M. and Wilson, A.F. (1989). Determination of the anaerobic threshold by breathing frequency. *International Journal of Sports Medicine*, **10**, 192–6.

Jenkins, D.G. and Quigley, B.M. (1990). Blood lactate in trained cyclists during cycle ergometry at critical power. *European Journal of Applied Physiology*, **61**, 278–83.

Jenkins, D.G. and Quigley, B.M. (1992). Endurance training enhances critical power. *Medicine and Science in Sports and Exercise*, **24**, 1283–9.

Jobsis, F.F. and Stainsby, W.N. (1968). Oxidation of NADH during contractions of circulated mammalian skeletal muscle. *Respiration Physiology*, **4**, 292–300.

Jones, A.M. (1996). Heart rate, lactate threshold and endurance training. *Coaching Focus*, 12–13.

Jones, A.M. (1998). A five year physiological case study of an Olympic athlete. *British Journal of Sports Medicine*, **32**, 39–43.

Jones, A.M. and Doust, J.H. (1994). Disparity between exercise intensity at lactate threshold and at the 4 mM blood lactate reference value increases with maximal aerobic power in runners (abstract). *Journal of Sports Sciences*, **12**, 141.

Jones, A.M. and Doust, J.H. (1995). Lack of reliability in Conconi's heart rate deflection point. *International Journal of Sports Medicine*, **16**, 541–4.

Jones, A.M. and Doust, J.H. (1996). A 1% treadmill grade most accurately reflects the energetic cost of outdoor running. *Journal of Sports Sciences*, **14**, 321–7.

Jones, A.M. and Doust, J.H. (1997a). Specific considerations for the assessment of middle distance and long distance runners. In *British Association of Sport and Exercise Sciences Physiological Testing Guidelines*, 3rd edn. eds. S. Bird and R. Davison (BASES, Leeds, UK), pp. 108–11.

Jones, A.M. and Doust, J.H. (1997b). The Conconi test is not valid for estimation of the lactate turnpoint in runners. *Journal of Sports Sciences*, **15**, 385–94.

Jones, A.M. and Doust, J.H. (1998a). Assessment of the lactate and ventilatory thresholds by breathing frequency in runners. *Journal of Sports Sciences*, **16**, 667–75.

Jones, A.M. and Doust, J.H. (1998b). The validity of the lactate minimum test for determination of the maximal lactate steady state. *Medicine and Science in Sports and Exercise*, **30**, 1304–13.

Jones, A.M. and Doust, J.H. (1998c). The relationship between the individual anaerobic threshold, the lactate threshold, and the 4 mM blood lactate reference value during incremental treadmill exercise (abstract). *Journal of Sports Sciences*, **16**, 53.

Jones, A.M., Carter, H. and Doust, J.H. (1999). A disproportionate increase in $\dot{V}O_2$ coincident with lactate threshold during treadmill exercise. *Medicine and Science in Sports and Exercise*, **31**, 1299–306.

Jones, N.L., Sutton, J.R., Taylor, R. and Toews, C.J. (1977). Effect of pH on cardiorespiratory and metabolic responses to exercise. *Journal of Applied Physiology*, **43**, 959–64.

Jorfeldt, L., Juhlin-Dabbfelt, A. and Karlsson, J. (1978). Lactate release in relation to tissue lactate in human skeletal muscle during exercise. *Journal of Applied Physiology*, **44**, 350–2.

Katch, V., Weltman, A., Sady, S. and Freedson, P. (1978). Validity of the relative percent concept for equating training intensity. *European Journal of Applied Physiology*, **39**, 219–27.

Keith, S.P., Jacobs, I. and McLellan, T.M. (1992). Adaptations to training at the individual anaerobic threshold. *European Journal of Applied Physiology*, **65**, 316–23.

Kindermann, W., Simon, G. and Keul, J. (1979). The significance of the aerobic-anaerobic transition for the determination of work load intensities during endurance training. *European Journal of Applied Physiology*, **42**, 25–34.

Kuipers, H., Keizer, H.A., De Vries, T., *et al.* (1988). Comparison of heart rate as a non-invasive determinant of anaerobic threshold with the lactate threshold when cycling. *European Journal of Applied Physiology*, **58**, 303–6.

Lafontaine, T.P., Londeree, B.R. and Spath, W.K. (1981). The maximal steady state versus selected running events. *Medicine and Science in Sports and Exercise*, **13**, 190–3.

Londeree, B.R. (1986). The use of laboratory test results with long distance runners. *Sports Medicine*, **3**, 201–13.

Londeree, B.R. (1997). Effect of training on lactate / ventilatory thresholds: a meta-analysis. *Medicine and Science in Sports and Exercise*, **29**, 837–43.

McLellan, T.M. and Jacobs, I. (1993). Reliability, reproducibility and validity of the individual anaerobic threshold. *European Journal of Applied Physiology*, **67**, 125–31.

MacRae, H., Dennis, S.C., Bosch, A.N. and Noakes, T.D. (1992). Endurance training vs. lactate production and removal. *Journal of Applied Physiology*, **73**, 2206–7.

Mader, A. (1991). Evaluation of the endurance performance of marathon runners and theoretical analysis of test results. *Journal of Sports Medicine and Physical Fitness*, **31**, 1–19.

Mader, A., Liesen, H., Heck, H., *et al.* (1976). Zur Beurteilung der sportartspezifischen Ausdauerleistungsfähigkeit im Labor. *Sport und Medizin*, **27**, 80–112.

Mazzeo, R.S. and Marshall, P. (1989). Influence of plasma catecholamines on the lactate threshold during graded cycling. *Journal of Applied Physiology*, **67**, 1319–22.

Mognoni, P., Sirtori, M.D., Lorenzelli, F. and Cerretelli, P. (1990). Physiological responses during prolonged exercise at the power output corresponding to the blood lactate threshold. *European Journal of Applied Physiology*, **60**, 239–43.

Monod, H. and Scherrer, J. (1965). The work capacity of a synergic muscle group. *Ergonomics*, **8**, 329–38.

Morgan, D.W., Baldini, F.D., Martin, P.E. and Kohrt, W.M. (1989). Ten kilometer performance and predicted velocity at $\dot{V}O_2$ max among well-trained male runners. *Medicine and Science in Sports and Exercise*, **21**, 78–83.

Moritani, T.A., Nagata, A., De Vries, H.A. and Muro, M. (1981). Critical power as a measure of physical work capacity and anaerobic threshold. *Ergonomics*, **24**, 339–50.

Nagata, A., Muro, M., Moritani, T. and Yoshida, T. (1981). Anaerobic threshold determination by blood lactate and myoelectric signals. *Japanese Journal of Physiology*, **31**, 85–97.

Newsholme, E.A., Blomstrand, E. and Ekblom, B. (1992). Physical and mental fatigue: metabolic mechanisms and importance of plasma amino acids. *British Medical Bulletin*, **48**, 477–95.

Orok, C.J., Hughson, R.L., Green, H.J. and Thomson, J.A. (1989). Blood lactate responses in incremental exercise as predictors of constant load performance. *European Journal of Applied Physiology*, **59**, 262–7.

Overend, T.J., Cunningham, D.A., Paterson, D.H. and Smith, W.D.F. (1992). Physiological responses of young and elderly men to prolonged exercise at critical power. *European Journal of Applied Physiology*, **64**, 187–93.

Oyono-Enguille, S., Heitz, A., Marbach, J., *et al.* (1990). Blood lactate during constant-load exercise at aerobic and anaerobic thresholds. *European Journal of Applied Physiology*, **60**, 321–30.

Pepper, M.L., Housh, T.J. and Johnson, G.O. (1992). The accuracy of the critical velocity test for predicting time to exhaustion during treadmill running. *International Journal of Sports Medicine*, **13**, 121–4.

Pierce, E.F., Weltman, A., Seip, R.L. and Snead, D. (1990). Effects of training specificity on the lactate threshold and $\dot{V}O_2$ peak. *International Journal of Sports Medicine*, **11**, 267–72.

Pokan, R., Hofmann, P., Preidler, K., *et al.* (1993). Correlation between inflection of heart rate / work performance curve and myocardial function in exhausting cycle ergometer exercise. *European Journal of Applied Physiology*, **67**, 385–8.

Pokan, R., Hofmann, P., Lehmann, M., *et al.* (1995). Heart rate deflection related to lactate performance curve and plasma catecholamine response during incremental cycle ergometer exercise. *European Journal of Applied Physiology*, **70**, 175–9.

Poole, D.C., Ward, S.A. and Whipp, B.J. (1988) The effects of training on the metabolic and respiratory profile of high-intensity cycle ergometer exercise. *European Journal of Applied Physiology*, **59**, 421–9.

Poole, D.C., Ward, S.A., Gardner, G.W. and Whipp, B.J. (1990). Metabolic and respiratory profile of the upper limit for prolonged exercise in man. *Ergonomics*, **3**, 1265–79.

Poole, D.C., Schaffartzik, W., Knight, D.R., *et al.* (1991). Contribution of exercising legs to the slow component of oxygen uptake kinetics in humans. *Journal of Applied Physiology*, **71**, 1245–53.

Ribeiro, J.P., Fielding, R.A., Hughes, V., *et al.* (1985). Heart rate breakpoint may coincide with the anaerobic and not the aerobic threshold. *International Journal of Sports Medicine*, **6**, 224–34.

Ribeiro, J.P., Hughes, V., Fielding, R.A., *et al.* (1986). Metabolic and ventilatory responses to steady state exercise relative to lactate thresholds. *International Journal of Sports Medicine*, **6**, 220–4.

Robergs, R.A., Chwalbinska-Moneta, J., Mitchell, J.B., *et al.* (1990). Blood lactate threshold differences between arterialised and venous blood. *International Journal of Sports Medicine*, **11**, 446–51.

Roberts, D. and Smith, D.J. (1989). Biochemical aspects of peripheral muscle fatigue: a review. *Sports Medicine*, **7**, 125–38.

Sjodin, B. and Jacobs, I. (1981). Onset of blood lactate accumulation and marathon running performance. *International Journal of Sports Medicine*, **2**, 23–6.

Sjodin, B., Jacobs, I. and Svedenhag, J. (1982). Changes in onset of blood lactate accumulation

(OBLA) and muscle enzymes after training at OBLA. *European Journal of Applied Physiology*, **49**, 45–57.

Skinner, J.S. and McLellan, T.H. (1980). The transition from aerobic to anaerobic metabolism. *Research Quarterly for Exercise and Sports*, **51**, 234–48.

Snyder, A.C., Woulfe, T., Welsh, R. and Foster, C. (1994). A simplified approach to estimating the maximal lactate steady state. *International Journal of Sports Medicine*, **15**, 27–31.

Stegmann, H., Kindermann, W. and Schnabel, A. (1981). Lactate kinetics and individual anaerobic threshold. *International Journal of Sports Medicine*, **2**, 160–5

Stegmann, H. and Kindermann, W. (1982). Comparison of prolonged exercise tests at the individual anaerobic threshold and the fixed anaerobic threshold of 4 mmol/l lactate. *International Journal of Sports Medicine*, **3**, 105–10.

Talmadge, R.J., Scheide, J.I. and Silverman, H. (1989). Glycogen synthesis from lactate in a chronically active muscle. *Journal of Applied Physiology*, **66**, 2231–8.

Tegtbur, U., Busse, M.W. and Braumann, K.M. (1993). Estimation of an individual equilibrium between lactate production and catabolism during exercise. *Medicine and Science in Sports and Exercise*, **25**, 620–7.

Tokmakidis, S.P. and Leger, L. (1992). Comparison of mathematically determined blood lactate and heart rate 'threshold' points and relationship with performance. *European Journal of Applied Physiology*, **641**, 309–17.

Wakayoshi, K., Yoshida, T., Udo, M., *et al.* (1992). The determination and validity of critical speed as an index of swimming performance in the competitive swimmer. *European Journal of Applied Physiology*, **64**, 153–7.

Walsh, M.L. and Banister, E.W. (1988). Possible mechanisms of the anaerobic threshold – a review. *Sports Medicine*, **5**, 269–302.

Wasserman, K., Beaver, W.L. and Whipp, B.J. (1990). Gas exchange theory and the lactic acidosis (anaerobic) threshold. *Circulation*, **81** (**Suppl II**), 14–30.

Wasserman, K., Whipp, B.J., Koyal, S.N. and Beaver W.L. (1973). Anaerobic threshold and respiratory gas exchange during exercise. *Journal of Applied Physiology*, **35**, 236–43.

Wasserman, K., Beaver, W.L., Davis, J.A., *et al.* (1985). Lactate, pyruvate, and the lactate-to-pyruvate ratio during exercise and recovery. *Journal of Applied Physiology*, **59**, 935–40.

Weltman, A. (1989). The lactate threshold and endurance performance. *Advances in Sports Medicine and Fitness*, **2**, 91–116.

Weltman, A., Snead, D. and Seip, R. (1990). Percentages of maximal heart rate, heart rate reserve and VO$_2$ max for determining endurance training intensity in male runners. *International Journal of Sports Medicine*, **11**, 218–22.

Weltman, A., Seip, R.L., Snead, D., *et al.* (1992). Exercise training at and above the lactate threshold in previously untrained women. *International Journal of Sports Medicine*, **13**, 257–63.

Whipp, B.J. (1994). The slow component of O$_2$ uptake kinetics during heavy exercise. *Medicine and Science in Sports and Exercise*, **26**, 1319–26.

Whipp, B.J. and Mahler, M. (1980). Dynamics of pulmonary gas exchange during exercise. In *Pulmonary Gas Exchange (Vol. II)*. ed. J.B. West (Academic Press, New York), pp. 33–96.

Whipp, B.J. and Ward, S.A. (1990). Physiological determinants of pulmonary gas exchange kinetics during exercise. *Medicine and Science in Sports and Exercise*, **22**, 62–71.

Williams, J.R., Armstrong, N. and Kirby, B.J. (1992). The influence of the site of sampling and assay medium upon the measurement and interpretation of blood lactate responses to exercise. *Journal of Sports Sciences*, **10**, 95–107.

Womack, C.J., Davis, S.E., Blumer, J.L., *et al.* (1995). Slow component of O$_2$ uptake during heavy exercise: adaptation to endurance training. *Journal of Applied Physiology*, **79**, 838–45.

Yeh, M.P., Gardner, R.M., Adams, T.W., *et al.* (1983). 'Anaerobic threshold': problems of determination and validation. *Journal of Applied Physiology*, **55**, 1178–86.

Yoshida, T. (1984). Effect of exercise duration during incremental exercise on the determination of anaerobic threshold and the onset of blood lactate accumulation. *European Journal of Applied Physiology*, **53**, 196–9.

Edward M. Winter and Don P. MacLaren

11.1 AIMS

The aims in this chapter are to:
- provide students with an understanding of techniques for assessing maximal-intensity exercise,
- describe the development of cycle ergometer-based assessments of peak power output,
- describe the concept of anaerobic capacity,
- describe techniques for direct (invasive) and indirect (non-invasive) estimation of anaerobic metabolism.

11.2 INTRODUCTION

Maximal-intensity exercise refers to exercise that is performed 'all-out'. It should not be confused with intensities of exercise which elicit a maximal physiological response. For instance, maximal oxygen uptake ($\dot{V}O_2$ max) can be elicited by intensities of exercise that are only a third or quarter of maximal-intensity exercise (Williams, 1987).

Movement does not always occur during maximal-intensity exercise. The scrum in rugby and maintenance of the crucifix and balance in gymnastics are examples where maximal force production occurs during isometric muscle activity. Durations of exercise are short and range from approximately 1 to 2 seconds in discrete activities like the shot-put and golf swing to 20 to 45 seconds of sprinting during running and cycling. Even in these latter activities, there is probably an element of pacing rather than genuinely all-out effort. Also,

associated mechanisms of energy release are predominantly anaerobic but they are not exclusively so. During 30 s of 'flat out' cycling, for example, 13–29% of energy provision could come from aerobic sources (Inbar *et al.*, 1976; Bar-Or, 1987).

The purpose of this section is to outline current developments in assessments of maximal-intensity exercise. Special attention is given to those that use cycle ergometry, and investigations into accompanying metabolism.

11.3 TERMINOLOGY

Maximal-intensity exercise can be assessed in different ways, and care should be taken to ensure that descriptions of performance adhere to principles of mechanics. These descriptions can be categorized into one of three broad groups. First, and the most basic, are scalar quantities such as time (s), distance (m) and speed ($m s^{-1}$). In the field, time is probably the most widely used measure and is employed to assess performance in activities such as running, swimming and cycling; distance is used to assess performance in activities which involve throwing and jumping, either for height or distance; and speed can be used to assess performance when both time taken and distance moved are known.

Next are vector quantities such as force (F), impulse (N s) and momentum ($kg m s^{-1}$), which are assessments that tend to be laboratory, rather than field, based. Thirdly, there are measures of energy which also tend to be laboratory-based and concern either energy expended (J) or mechanical power output (W). Clearly, power output is only one measure of maximal-intensity exercise, yet there is a tendency to assume it is the only measure of this type of performance. Indeed, Adamson and Whitney (1971) and Smith (1972) addressed this point in detail and suggested that, in explosive activities such as jumping, the use of power is meaningless and unjustified. Horizontal velocity in sprinting and vertical velocity in jumping are determined by impulse. Consequently, it is the impulse-generating capability of muscle, not its power-producing capability, that is the determinant of effective performance.

Unless the units of performance are watts, performance cannot be described as power. Even when these units are used and the description appears to be sound, underlying theoretical bases might not be sustainable.

These considerations are important because they influence the purpose of assessments. Performance per se could be the focus in studies that investigate the effects of training. An assessment could also be used to investigate changes in metabolism brought about by training or growth. The integrity of the procedure has to be sound, otherwise the insight into underlying mechanisms could be obscured. An understanding of principles of mechanics is a prerequisite of effective test selection and subsequent description of measures.

11.4 HISTORICAL BACKGROUND

Concerted interest in maximal-intensity exercise has a long history which can be traced back to 1885, when Marey and Demeney introduced a force platform to investigate mechanisms that underpinned jumping (Cavagna, 1975). Investigations into how muscle functions were based on studies of isolated mammalian and amphibian tissue (Hill, 1913). Attention turned to humans and investigations into $\dot{V}O_2$ at running speeds that were in excess

of those that could be maintained at steady state (Hill and Lupton, 1922; Sargent, 1926; Furusawa *et al.*, 1927) and attempts to determine mechanical efficiency and equations to describe motion during maximal-intensity exercise (Lupton, 1923; Best and Partridge, 1928, 1929).

In 1921 D.A. Sargent introduced a jump test which is still used today. Shortly afterwards, L.W. Sargent (1924) suggested that the test could be used as a measure of power, and the Lewis nomogram (Fox *et al.*, 1988) has been suggested as a means to estimate power output from vertical jump data in spite of the forcible objections stated earlier by Adamson and Whitney (1971) and Smith (1972).

Investigations into the mechanics of bicycle pedalling during high-intensity exercise also have a long history (Dickinson, 1928; Fenn, 1932; Hill, 1934). So too have attempts to increase the sensitivity of assessment in this type of exercise. Kelso and Hellebrandt (1932) introduced an ergometer that used a direct current generator to apply resistive force, and Tuttle and Wendler (1945) modified the design so that alternating current could be used. It was not until Fleisch (1950) and Von Döbeln (1954) introduced their forerunners that inexpensive friction-braked devices became available commercially. It was a further twenty or so years before these types of ergometer had a marked impact on studies into maximal intensity exercise (Cumming, 1974). Moreover, developments in microprocessor-based data logging systems (McClenaghan and Literowitch, 1987) improved the sensitivity and practicality of assessments.

In 1938 Hill published one of the most influential reports on muscle function ever written, in which he described the relationship between the force a muscle can exert and the accompanying speed with which it can shorten. This has become known as the muscle force–velocity relationship. Hill was remarkably modest about this work and claimed later that he 'stumbled upon it' (Hill, 1970, p. 3) and that Fenn and Marsh (1935) had actually outlined a similar relationship already. A major point to be emphasized here is that peak power output is produced by an optimum load; if the load is either too great or too low, a muscle or group of muscles will not exert peak power output. This presents major implications for meaningful assessments of peak power output during maximal-intensity exercise.

11.5 SCREENING

Tests of maximal-intensity exercise are strenuous and might produce feelings of nausea or giddiness. It is important that potential subjects are recruited by means of suitable pre-test medical questionnaires.

11.6 PROCEDURES FOR ASSESSING MAXIMAL-INTENSITY EXERCISE

There is a variety of procedures for assessing maximal-intensity exercise. Cycle ergometer tests are the most common and these can be categorized into one of four groups; (a) 'Wingate' type procedures, (b) optimization procedures, (c) correction procedures, (d) isokinetic procedures. The first three of these procedures use friction-braked devices, whereas the isokinetic group uses more elaborate control systems which restrain pedalling to constant velocity. Other procedures include other forms of isokinetic testing, treadmill and field assessments. Details of laboratory procedures for the above tests are outlined at the end of this chapter.

11.6.1 WINGATE TYPE PROCEDURES

The Wingate Anaerobic Test, so named because it was developed at the Wingate Institute in Israel, was introduced as a prototype by Ayalon *et al.* (1974). Since then it has been refined and a comprehensive description was published later (Bar-Or, 1981) and subsequently reviewed (Bar-Or, 1987). Its use has become widespread. Subjects have to pedal flat out for 30 s on a cycle ergometer against an external resistive load which usually is equivalent to 7½% of body weight for Monark-type ergometers and 4% on Fleisch systems (see Practical 1).

In the original Wingate Anaerobic Test, three measures of performance were recorded: peak power output, mean power output and power decay. For the purposes of recording, the test was subdivided into six 5-s blocks and peak power output invariably occurred in the first 5 seconds. Although mean power output was demonstrated to be a robust measure and could withstand variations above and below the proposed optimum (Dotan and Bar-Or, 1983), reservations were expressed about the integrity of peak power output. Sargeant *et al.* (1981) suggested that the fixed load of 7½% of body weight was unlikely to satisfy Hill's force–velocity relationships, so casting doubt on this particular measure. Later, Bar-Or (1987) acknowledged that this might be the case, and confirmation was provided by Winter *et al.* (1987, 1989). Consequently, it is advisable to omit this measure from data summaries.

Time to peak power can be of interest, although the importance placed upon this particular measure depends to a large extent on the timing system that is used. With rolling starts, the precise beginning of the test is difficult to identify. While a stationary start would resolve this issue, it is difficult to set the system in motion from standstill.

After the highest value of power output is produced, and although maximal effort is continued, performance begins to deteriorate as fatigue sets in. At first sight it is tempting to suggest that mechanisms of adenosine triphosphate (ATP) synthesis are being demonstrated and that performance can be partitioned into alactic and lactacid phases. However, studies that have used muscle biopsy techniques have demonstrated clearly that lactic acid is produced from the moment all-out exercise begins, not when phosphocreatine stores are depleted (Boobis, 1987). Consequently, use of the terms alactacid and lactacid should be avoided.

Blood lactate provides some insights into underlying metabolism, although there are some points of caution that have to be considered. Peak blood lactate concentration [HLa] occurs some minutes after exercise has ended and, coincidentally, tends to correspond with feelings of nausea. Efflux of lactic acid from muscle cells into interstitial fluid and then into blood takes time, and not all of the lactic acid that is produced enters the circulation. Some of it is used by muscle cells as substrate (Brooks, 1986) and some is removed from the circulation before subsequent sampling occurs. This is a timely reminder that, although blood lactate can be a useful indicator of metabolism, when non-steady-state exercise is under examination, it might well provide a less than clear window through which mechanisms can be viewed.

Differences in performance are partly attributable to differences in body size between subjects, so ways to partition out size have to be introduced. This scaling, as it is called, is currently an area of renewed interest (Nevill *et al.*, 1992; Winter, 1992) although early considerations date back more than forty years ago (Tanner, 1949). It is now appreciated that the construction of straightforward ratio standards, in which a performance variable is simply divided by an anthropometric characteristic such as body mass, probably misleads by distorting the data under investigation. Comparisons between subjects, especially when there are marked differences in size – say, between men and women, or adults and children – should be based on *power function ratios* (Nevill *et al.*, 1992; Welsman *et al.*, 1993; Winter *et al.*, 1993; Eston *et al.*, 1997) that are obtained from the allometric relationship between performance and anthropometric variables (Schmidt-Nielsen, 1984). This issue is discussed in more detail in Volume 1, Chapter 11 by Winter and Nevill.

Another feature that appears to be clear, but upon further investigation is seen to be more complicated, is the expression of fatigue profiles. It would be tempting to suggest that after training, the difference between peak power output and the succeeding lowest value would

decrease, but this is not necessarily the case (Bird and Davison, 1997). Training can produce a higher peak so that fatigue appears actually to increase, and there is no clear explanation for this observation. Possibilities could be a change in force–velocity characteristics of muscle that are not accommodated by the fixed resistive load, technicalities over the way in which performance is expressed, or other as-yet-unidentified factors associated with the skill required to perform the test. This is a rich area for further research.

In summary, the Wingate Anaerobic Test is a useful laboratory procedure to demonstrate how fatigue occurs. The fixed external resistive force might not satisfy muscle force–velocity relationships, so values of peak power output are probably affected adversely. Blood lactate does not necessarily provide a full insight into the underlying metabolism. Fatigue profiles are ambiguous. Differences in the size of subjects should be scaled out using allometry (see Volume 1, Chapter 11 by Winter and Nevill).

11.6.2 OPTIMIZATION PROCEDURES

Anxieties about the potential inability of fixed external loads to satisfy muscle force–velocity relationships led to the development of alternative procedures which provide theoretically sound indications of peak power output. The concern is not simply with a single isolated muscle, but groups of muscles *in vivo* whose leverage characteristics undergo constant change throughout a complete mechanical cycle.

The availability of 'drop-loading' basket ergometers has played a key role in developments whose origins date back over seventy years to when Dickinson (1929) identified an inverse linear relationship between peak pedalling rate and applied load. Vandewalle *et al.* (1985) and Nakamura *et al.* (1985) used the principle to calculate optimized peak power output on the basis of flywheel-derived data. Acknowledging the reservations about the use of instantaneous values of power output expressed by Adamson and Whitney (1971) and Smith (1972), Winter *et al.* (1991) modified the protocol and recorded movements of the pedals.

The relationship between peak pedalling rate in rev min^{-1} (R) and applied load (L) is in the form:

$$R = a + bL$$

where:

a = intercept of the line of best fit
b = slope of the line of best fit.

On Monark ergometers, one revolution of the pedal crank moves a point on the flywheel a distance of 6 m. Consequently, an expression for power output (W) can be produced as:

$$1\,W = 1\,J\,s^{-1} = 1\,N\,m\,s^{-1}$$

$$\text{then Power} = \frac{R}{60} \times 6\,m \times L\,(\text{newtons})$$

$$\therefore \text{Power} = \frac{(a+bL)}{60} \times 6\,m \times L\,(\text{newtons})$$

$$\therefore \text{Power} = \frac{aL}{10} + \frac{bL^2}{10}$$

We can use differential calculus to help us interpret the relationship. By differentiating the power / load expression, which is a quadratic relationship, the gradient at any point on the curve can be identified:

$$\frac{dW}{dL} = a + 2bL$$

At the top of the curve, the gradient is zero:

$$\therefore 0 = a + 2bL$$

$$\therefore L = \frac{-a}{2b}$$

Substituting this value of L in the original equation yields the optimized peak power output:

$$\text{Optimized peak power} = \frac{a\left(\dfrac{-a}{2b}\right)}{10} + \frac{b\left(\dfrac{-a}{2b}\right)^2}{10}$$

$$= \frac{-0.025a^2}{b}$$

Thus, three key measures of performance can be identified: the optimized peak power output; the load corresponding to the optimized peak power output, and the pedalling rate corresponding to optimized peak power output. Assessment of these measures is exemplified in Practical 2.

Seemingly, optimization procedures are useful and they increase the sensitivity with which maximal intensity exercise can be assessed. However, the protocols are considerably longer than the Wingate Anaerobic Test, even if, as Nakamura *et al.* (1985) suggested, only three loads are used to establish the regression equation that provides the basis for calculating the optimized peak power output. Furthermore, while peak values are identified, the protocols do not assess fatigue profiles, and this is a distinct limitation. Nevertheless, the protocols have one distinct advantage; because body weight is supported, they isolate activity to the legs and remove potentially contaminating effects from the trunk, head and arms. Similarly, they could be applied to investigations of performance characteristics of the arms. Coupled with this is an especially useful anthropometric technique that can assess the total and lean volume of the leg (Jones and Pearson, 1969) and meaningful comparisons of performance capabilities between groups can be made.

Winter *et al.* (1991) and Eston *et al.* (1997) compared maximal-intensity exercise of men and women and found that there were distinct differences in performance that were independent of differences in the size of the leg. These studies also demonstrated the importance of applying correct scaling procedures. Similarly, the techniques have been used to compare children and adults (Winter *et al.*, 1993) where it is suggested that traditional ratio standard measures overestimate children's maximal intensity exercise.

In summary, optimization procedures appear to satisfy muscle force–velocity relationships and produce theoretically sound assessments of peak power output. Useful studies can be performed when optimization is coupled with anthropometric procedures that assess limb volumes. Optimization procedures do not produce valid fatigue profiles.

11.6.3 CORRECTION PROCEDURES

Optimization procedures are not the only tests that have been proposed for friction-braked cycle ergometers. The completeness of calculations that are used to determine the optimized peak power output have been questioned by Lakomy (1986) who pointed out that the external resistive load does not necessarily account for all the forces applied to the pedals and transmitted to an ergometer's flywheel. Clearly, as the flywheel is accelerated, a force greater than the resistive load is applied to the system and this extra force is ignored in traditional calculations of mechanical work done and hence power output.

Lakomy (1986) determined an 'acceleration balancing load' (*EL*) which was identified by plotting deceleration of the flywheel from 150 rev min^{-1} against the conventional resistive force. As a result, the effective load, i.e. the actual force applied could be calculated as:

Effective load (*F*) = resistive load (*RL*) + excess load (*EL*)

The value of *F* could then be multiplied by the velocity of the flywheel to provide an instantaneous value of power output. By introducing this correction, Lakomy (1985) demonstrated that the lightest loads produced peak power output. A commercially available kit (Concept II, Nottingham, UK) which contains a flywheel-mounted generator and related computer software can be used with Monark friction-braked ergometers. A similar system was developed by Bassett (1989). By using the kit, simultaneously data can be logged from the flywheel to calculate corrected peak power output, and from the pedals to calculate the optimized peak power output.

As can be seen from the data generated in Practical 3, although the relationship between data generated by optimization and correction procedures is high, the two methods can produce different results. The explanation for this could be technical in that it is associated with the precision of measurement, but the sensitivity of measurement procedures suggests

that this is unlikely. The reason could still be technical because of the procedures for calculating power output which are, of course, distinctly different. The value for the optimized peak power output is calculated at peak velocity for a complete mechanical cycle of activity, whereas the corrected peak power output is based on products of force and instantaneous velocity. This latter procedure has been questioned by Adamson and Whitney (1971) and Smith (1972). While these products yield the units of power, the meaningfulness of using W is still not clear. Correction procedures are based on systems in which acceleration occurs, and in Section 11.3 it was pointed out that acceleration and hence change in momentum is attributable not to power but to preceding impulse. Hence, it is the impulse-generating capability of muscle that is manifest, but it is described in terms of power. Nevertheless, although there is a difference between the optimized peak power output and the corrected peak power output, the difference is systematic and the association between the variables is particularly strong.

Clearly, this unresolved debate impacts directly on our understanding of how muscle functions and, in particular, how it functions in concert with skeletal, neurophysiological and metabolic systems *in vivo*. Winter *et al.* (1996) have compared the optimized peak power output and the corrected peak power output, but no studies have been undertaken to compare the way in which these values reflect changes in performance brought about by training. From a practical point of view, correction procedures are easier to administer than optimization tests because only one bout of exercise has to be performed. On the other hand, optimization procedures satisfy muscle force–velocity relationships and appear to be sound theoretically. This area is still a rich field for further investigation.

11.6.4 ISOKINETIC SYSTEMS

Before the advent of optimization and correction procedures, isokinetic systems were introduced to assess peak power output in a way that satisfied muscle force–velocity relationships.

Sargeant *et al.* (1981) designed an ergometer in which the pedals were driven at constant angular velocity by an external electric motor and forces applied to the pedals were detected by strain gauges attached to the pedal cranks. By altering pedalling rate externally, force–velocity relationships were explored. McCartney *et al.* (1983) developed a similar system but, in this case, the pedals of the ergometer are driven by the subject until an electric motor restricts any further acceleration of the system.

The acquisition of data from these systems is demanding. Data have to be transmitted from a rotating device via a slip ring, and this can introduce noise into the signals which can be difficult to suppress. Also, previously questioned instantaneous values of power output are calculated from the products of force and velocity. Conversely, calibration is easier than in friction-braked systems. In the latter, frictional losses from the chain and bearing assemblies are not usually considered, whereas in the former, especially with the motor-driven version, these losses are irrelevant. The assessment of peak power output using a conventional isokinetic dynamometry system has also been compared to the traditional Wingate test (Baltzopoulos *et al.*, 1988).

11.6.5 NON-MOTORIZED TREADMILLS

While cycle ergometry has a number of key advantages, there is one major limitation: it is task-specific and does not necessarily reflect performance in running. Within the last decade attempts have been made to redress this problem by means of non-motorized treadmills in which the subject drives the belt of the treadmill. These systems can be used to assess power output whilst running horizontally (Lakomy, 1984). Subjects are tethered to the apparatus by a suitable harness that contains a force transducer that registers the horizontal forces exerted. These forces and the treadmill speed provide the basis for calculation.

It has been reported that substantial periods of habituation are required before valid data can be obtained (Gamble *et al.*, 1988). Nevertheless, this type of assessment has been used successfully to examine mechanical characteristics of running (Cheetham and Williams, 1985; Cheetham *et al.*, 1986).

Recent developments in the design of treadmills have renewed interest in the use of this form of ergometry to assess exercise capabilities of humans (Jaskólski *et al.*, 1996; Jaskólska *et al.*, 1999). Jaskólski *et al.* (1996) attempted to identify optimal resistances that maximized external peak power output, and Jaskólska *et al.* (1999) compared muscle force–velocity relationships during treadmill running and cycling. The improved sensitivity of these systems and their continued development suggest that they will be used in further studies of exercise performance and underlying metabolism.

11.6.6 MULTIPLE-SPRINT TYPE PROTOCOLS

Maximal-intensity exercise might have to be performed in repeated bouts interspersed with periods of rest. This intermittent form of exercise is typified in what have been termed multiple-sprint sports (Williams, 1987) such as soccer, hockey and racket games, and is probably the most common type of activity in sport. Common though it is, this type of activity is difficult to model, but the challenge has been met by proposals of field-based and laboratory-based procedures.

Léger and Lambert (1982) devised a shuttle running type protocol in which subjects ran 20 m lengths in time to a metronome. Running speed increased progressively until volitional exhaustion occurred. Since then this system has been commercialized (Brewer *et al.*, 1988).

Wootton and Williams (1983) used cycle ergometry, and subjects performed 5 bouts of exercise, each of which lasted 6 s with a 30 s rest between bouts. Bird and Davison (1997) suggested 10 × 6 s sprints and outlined other field- and laboratory-based procedures. Non-motorized treadmills have been used (Hamilton *et al.*, 1991; Nevill *et al.*, 1993) in which up to 30 repeated sprints are required. By various means, there have been concerted attempts to develop protocols that model multiple-sprint activities in controlled ways.

Studies have investigated the effects of: hot environments on shuttle running performance (Morris *et al.*, 1998); creatine supplementation in repeated sprint swimming (Peyrebrune *et al.*, 1998); and branched-chain amino acids and carbohydrate on fatigue during intermittent, high-intensity running (Davis *et al.*, 1999). Muscle soreness induced by shuttle running has also been examined (Thompson *et al.*, 1999), as has the effect of intermittent high-intensity exercise on neuromuscular performance (Mercer *et al.*, 1998). It is likely that these types of assessment will be used increasingly as investigations into metabolism and mechanisms of fatigue continue.

11.7 ASSESSMENT OF METABOLISM

There have been developments in procedures for assessing maximal-intensity exercise, and both the sensitivity and integrity of measures have been improved in recent years. While performance can be quantified and underlying metabolic processes demonstrated, quantification of this underlying metabolism is still a considerable challenge. By way of comparison, the criterial standard for aerobic exercise is maximum oxygen uptake ($\dot{V}O_2$ max), but as Williams (1990) queried: why should this be so? The problem is to measure the contribution from anaerobic energy releasing mechanisms up to and including the maximum contribution, i.e. a person's anaerobic capacity. Immediately a dilemma is presented: anaerobic capacity could be expressed as an amount, but the concern is more likely to be with the rate at which energy can be released and the length of time for which this release can be sustained. Furthermore, it was reported in Section 11.2 that, even in a short-duration test like the Wingate Anaerobic Test, aerobic mechanisms account for ~20% of total energy provision. We have also already seen that previous suggestions that maximal-intensity exercise could be

partitioned into alactacid and lactacid phases are now known to be simplifications; energy release from high-energy phosphagens and glycolysis occurs simultaneously, not sequentially.

In spite of these difficulties, techniques that attempt to assess anaerobic capacity have been devised and can be categorized into 'direct' and 'indirect' determinations (Bangsbo, 1997). The direct measures include the use of muscle biopsies before and immediately after any form of muscle contractions, or the use of ^{31}P magnetic resonance spectroscopy if the muscle is electrically stimulated or made to perform isometrically. Indirect measures, on the other hand, are based on the concept of the oxygen deficit.

11.7.1 DIRECT ESTIMATION OF ANAEROBIC METABOLISM

During maximal- and high-intensity exercise, decreases in muscle ATP and in phosphocreatine (PCr) are observed along with an increase in lactate. It is possible therefore to quantify the anaerobic energy production if determinations of the changes in these metabolites are made immediately following the exercise. This quantification has only been made possible after the introduction of the muscle biopsy technique (Bergström, 1962). In essence, the process requires the muscle under investigation to be identified before a small area on the surface is sterilized and then a local anaesthetic injected beneath the surface of the skin. A small incision of the skin and subcutaneous tissue is made initially before cutting through the muscle fascia. A hollow biopsy needle can then be inserted through the incision to the depth required before aspiration is applied. Aspiration causes a small portion of the muscle to 'bulge' into a small window at the side of the biopsy needle where it is cut by a sharp blade inside the hollow of the needle. The needle is then withdrawn and the sample is immediately frozen in liquid nitrogen. When this process is used for the determination of phosphagen stores (i.e. ATP + PCr) following high-intensity exercise, speed of sampling and freezing the muscle tissue is necessary since some resynthesis is possible.

Table 11.1 provides data from selected studies in which the muscle biopsy technique has been used for the estimation of anaerobic energy production from phosphagens and glycolysis before and immediately after maximal-intensity exercise of varying time periods. The findings are based on calculations of the decrease in muscle ATP and PCr, and the increase in muscle lactate from muscle samples taken both at rest and immediately after exercise. The highest rates of anaerobic energy production for PCr and for glycolysis during dynamic exercise lasting up to 10 s are 5·1 and 9·3 mmol $kg^{-1} s^{-1}$ respectively. When the dynamic exercise is increased to 30 s, the highest rates of ATP produced anaerobically from PCr and glycolysis are 1.9 and 5·9 mmol $kg^{-1} s^{-1}$ respectively. These values are mean rates over the 10 or 30 s exercise bouts, and the actual peak rates would be expected to occur within the first second or so. Indeed the change in power output during a 30 s Wingate test reflects the maximal rates of ATP being engendered within the muscle from these anaerobic sources as well as the aerobic contribution.

There are problems with the estimations calculated from the muscle biopsy data. First, there is the time delay in getting the muscle sample frozen following exercise. This procedure involves stopping the activity, immobilizing the leg, taking the biopsy, and then transferring the sample to the liquid nitrogen; a series of events that can take between 10 and 20 s. Nevertheless, Soderlund and Hultman (1986) have shown that ATP and PCr concentrations in muscle biopsy samples are not significantly affected by a delay in freezing. A second problem is the difficulty in determining the muscle mass involved in whole-body exercise, and therefore the metabolic response of the biopsied muscle may not be representative of all those muscles engaged in the exercise. Finally, the amount of energy related to the release of lactate into the blood from the

muscle is not taken into account in the calculations presented in Table 11.1, so the anaerobic energy production from glycolysis is underestimated. It is difficult to determine the volume in which lactate is diluted. Bangsbo (1997) suggested that the likely underestimation for a 75 kg individual is between 5.2% and 25.6% for maximal-intensity exercise of 30 s duration. The lower value is based on a dilution volume of 6 litres (i.e. blood volume), whereas the higher value is based on a dilution volume of 30 litres (i.e. total body fluids). Even these calculations do not take account of the lactate metabolized by inactive muscles and by the heart.

In spite of these limitations outlined above, there is a consistency in the data on rates of anaerobic ATP production during maximal-intensity exercise from the various studies. Indeed, the data from a recent study involving twenty electrically evoked maximal isometric actions of the anterior tibialis muscle using both magnetic resonance spectroscopy and muscle biopsy demonstrated that there was little difference in the muscle concentration of PCr, although differences were found in the estimates of ATP and changes in lactate (Constantin-Teodosiu *et al.*, 1997). The significantly higher muscle lactate concentrations estimated using magnetic resonance spectroscopy accounted for ~30% greater estimation of ATP turnover.

All the studies reported so far have documented the metabolic response of mixed muscle to maximal intensity exercise without recourse to possible variations in fibre type. Some recent investigations have separated single fibres and measured ATP, PCr, and glycogen of one fibre type at rest, during muscle action and in recovery (Soderlund *et al.*, 1992; Greenhaff *et al.*, 1994; Casey *et al.*, 1996). The conclusions from these studies are that during maximal-intensity exercise, type II fibres compared with type I fibres produce a greater rate of PCr degradation, a greater rate of glycolysis and a slower rate of resynthesis of PCr.

As many sports can be classified as multiple-sprint sports, there have been developments in

Table 11.1 Estimated total anaerobic ATP production, rate of anaerobic ATP production and % contribution from PCr and glycolysis during dynamic exercise

Reference	Type of exercise	Duration (s)	Total ATP produced (mmol kg⁻¹)	Rate of ATP produced (mmol kg⁻¹ s⁻¹)		% contribution	
				PCr	Glycolysis	PCr	Glycolysis
Boobis *et al.* (1982)	Cycle	0–6	63	4.9	4.8	47	53
		0–30	189	1.9	4.0	30	64
Jones *et al.* (1985)	Isokinetic cycle 60 rpm	0–10	166	5.1	8.0	42	58
		0–30	291	1.4	5.8	21	79
	140 rpm	0–10	173	4.4	9.3	35	65
		0–30	240	0.7	6.5	11	89
McCartney *et al.* (1986)	Isokinetic cycle 100 rpm	0–30	228	1.4	5.9	23	77
Cheetham *et al.* (1986)	Run	0–30	183	1.9	3.8	38	62
Nevill *et al.* (1989)	Run	0–30	186	1.9	4.1	33	67

assessing the metabolic requirements of repeated high-intensity exercise. Casey *et al.* (1996) reported metabolic responses of different fibre types during repeated bouts of maximal isokinetic cycling. Exercise consisted of two bouts of 30 s cycling with a 4-minute passive recovery between bouts. The authors reported that a 4-minute recovery period was insufficient to allow total resynthesis of ATP and PCr in type II muscle fibres although recovery was complete in type I fibres. Furthermore, utilization of ATP and PCr was less in type II fibres during the second bout of exercise without a corresponding change in type I fibres. Performance was also significantly reduced.

A major reason for performing tests of anaerobic capacity, speed, power output and the like is to examine the effect of training on these parameters. Sprint training normally results in an increase in the ability to perform maximal intensity exercise. Are these performance changes reflected in an enhanced capacity for generation of anaerobic ATP production? Boobis *et al.* (1983) trained subjects for 8 weeks by means of sprinting on a cycle ergometer and analysed muscle samples at rest and after 30 s of maximal cycling before and after the training programme. Training increased the mean power output by 8%, a change mirrored by an increase in anaerobic energy production from glycolysis. The energy produced anaerobically from PCr and ATP was not significantly affected. Similar results were obtained in a study in which recreational runners were sprint-trained for 8 weeks (Nevill *et al.*, 1989). A 6% increase in mean power output was matched by a 20% increase in anaerobic energy production from glycolysis but not from the phosphagen stores.

11.7.2 INDIRECT ESTIMATIONS OF ANAEROBIC METABOLISM

Direct measures of metabolites in muscle are needed to determine anaerobic capacity accurately, but owing to the invasive nature of this approach an alternative technique is often desirable. The most commonly used indirect estimation of anaerobic capacity is maximal accumulated oxygen deficit (MAOD) during short, intense exercise. This measure arose from the original idea of the oxygen deficit and was first proposed by Hermansen (1969). The method requires establishing a linear relationship between oxygen uptake and exercise intensity over a number of visits (since oxygen uptake is measured over a 4 to 10 minute period for each intensity), then extrapolating the line beyond maximal oxygen uptake to a value corresponding to 120% $\dot{V}O_2$ max. The subject then exercises at this intensity to exhaustion. The MAOD is calculated as the difference in oxygen estimated as needed to exercise at that intensity (from the extrapolated data) and the actual oxygen consumed during the exercise corresponding to 120% $\dot{V}O_2$ max (see Medbø *et al.*, 1988). Although there appears to be similarity in the estimation of anaerobic energy provision between the MAOD and data from muscle biopsies in isolated muscle groups (Bangsbo *et al.*, 1990), there are conflicting views about the implications for whole-body exercise. For details of the debate taking place in the literature readers are advised to consult Bangsbo (1996a, 1996b) and Medbø (1996a, 1996b). Practical 4 provides a modified version of the MAOD assessment procedure.

11.7.3 AEROBIC CONTRIBUTION

The data presented above are exclusively concerned with rates of anaerobic energy production, with no recourse to aerobic contribution. Indirect estimates of the anaerobic and aerobic contribution to intense isolated knee extension exercise of 30 s are 80% and 20% respectively (Bangsbo *et al.*, 1990). These values change to 45%:55% and 30%:70% anaerobic:aerobic as the exercise duration increases from 60 to 90 s and 120 to 192 s. During the first 10 s of a 30 s Wingate test, the estimated contribution from aerobic metabolism is 3% (Serresse *et al.*, 1988), whereas the mean values of the aerobic contribution for the 30 s Wingate test have been reported as being between 16% and 28% (Serresse *et al.*, 1988; Smith and Hill, 1991).

Even if a subject does not breathe, myoglobin and haemoglobin stores can provide oxygen for aerobic energy provision and assessment of anaerobic capacity needs to take account of the likely aerobic energy contribution.

11.7.4 POSSIBLE RELATIONSHIP BETWEEN METABOLISM AND FATIGUE

The power output profile of an individual undergoing a 30 s Wingate test shows a peak in the first few seconds followed by a decline. This profile has a parallel in the decrease in rate of ATP production from both PCr and glycolysis (Table 11.1). It should also be recognized that aerobic contribution increases with time. The greatest rate of decrease in energy production is attributable to the depletion of PCr stores. This is noticeable in the type II muscle fibres, where after 10 s of activity 70% of these stores are used and after 20 s they are nearly depleted. The maximal rate of ATP production from glycolysis probably occurs at around 20 s and is maintained thereafter until the build-up of lactate and inorganic phosphate inhibit glycolytic enzyme activity. The switch from generation of ATP from PCr predominantly to glycolysis and then to aerobic metabolism necessitates a decrease in the maximal rate of ATP production. If ATP can only be generated at given (reducing) rates, then power output must decrease in a like manner. So the power output profile over 30 s is a function of maximal rate of ATP production from a changing energy source and is unlikely to be due solely to increases in lactate production and concomitant increases in hydrogen ions.

11.8 SUMMARY AND CONCLUSION

There has been considerable progress in assessments of maximal intensity exercise that involve brief single and repeated bouts of exercise. Similarly, successful field- and laboratory-based attempts have been made to model multiple-sprint type sports. Unequivocal quantification of accompanying metabolism is a challenge that has yet to be met.

11.9 PRACTICAL 1: WINGATE TEST

11.9.1 AIM

The aim of this practical is twofold: first, to describe external power output characteristics during the Wingate anaerobic test and, second, to examine changes in blood lactate concentration.

11.9.2 EQUIPMENT

A Monark 824E (Monark Exercise AB, Varberg, Sweden) basket-loading cycle ergometer with microprocessor-linked data logging facilities is used to record movements of either the flywheel or pedals; a separate ergometer can be used during the warm-up. Figure 11.1 shows the general arrangement for the test, and Figures 11.2 and 11.3 illustrate detection systems for logging data from movements of the flywheel and pedals respectively.

11.9.3 METHODS

1. Subjects should wear shorts and a T-shirt.
2. Take a finger-prick blood sample at rest. Collect the blood in duplicate, i.e. in two microcapillary tubes. One tube is labelled *a*, the other *b*, (see Chapter 4 by Maughan *et al.* for details on blood sampling).

Figure 11.1 General layout of the equipment used in the Wingate Anaerobic Test. The cycle ergometer is bolted to the floor and has a modified load hanger. Note also the use of toe clips and a restraining belt.

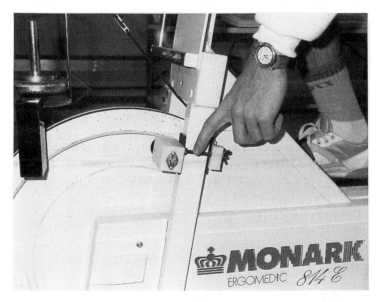

Figure 11.2 Data logging from the flywheel by means of a precision DC motor (Lakomy, 1986).

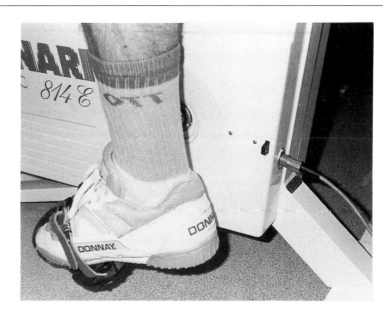

Figure 11.3 Data logging from the passage of the left pedal by means of a optoelectronic sensor housed in the chain guard (Winter *et al.*, 1991; Winter *et al.*, 1996).

3. Subjects have a 5-minute warm-up at 100 W with a flat-out sprint for 5 s at 3 minutes, followed by a 5-minute rest.
4. During this time subjects transfer to the test machine. Seat height is adjusted for comfort (Hamley and Thomas, 1967; Nordeen-Snyder, 1977), toe clips are secured (La Voie *et al.*, 1984), the resistive load (usually 7.5% ± 0.5 N of body weight) is positioned and a restraining harness should be fixed to ensure that the subject cannot rise from the saddle.
5. Subjects pedal at 50–60 rev min^{-1} with the external load supported. Upon the command, '3, 2, 1, go!' the load is applied abruptly, subjects begin to pedal flat out and data logging is started.
6. Subjects pedal for 30 s.
7. At the end of the test subjects undertake a suitable warm-down, e.g. two minutes of cycling at 100 W.
8. Take blood samples as in step 2 immediately at the end of exercise, and 7½ minutes and 12½ minutes later, and determine blood lactate concentration (HLa). This can be done by means of fast-response analysers but this practical uses Maughan's (1982) fluorimetric technique, which has greater control over the precision of measurement.
9. Complete the results sections (Tables 11.2–11.5).

11.9.4 SAMPLE RESULTS

Plot the calibration curve including the regression analysis.

The regression equation for the data in Table 11.3, which minimizes the sum of squares of residuals about the regression line in a *horizontal* direction, is equal to:

$$x = 0.015 + 0.139 \, y$$

Table 11.2 Raw data for WAnT on a small sample of 20-year-old male college students

Subject	Time to peak power (s)	Mean power (W)	Decay (W)
1	4.50	635	456
2	2.87	806	538
3	3.45	745	426
4	5.34	813	562
5	3.83	830	446
Mean	4.00	766	486
SD	0.96	80	60

Mean power output ranges from 400 to 900 W, although differences in participant size account for some of the variation. Other factors such as muscle fibre type and training status are also influential. Time to peak power output ranges approximately from 2 to 6 s, very early in the test, and decay, the difference between the highest value of peak power output and the subsequent lowest value is approximately 40–60 % of the mean value. Blood lactate concentrations tend to peak some 7 to 8 minutes after exercise has ended.

Table 11.3 Calibration data for blood lactate (Hla). This is a six-point calibration, i.e. a blank and five standards are used. Each is analysed in duplicate.

Standards	$(mmol\ l^{-1})$					
Tube	Blank	2.5	5.0	7.5	10.5	12.5
1	0	18	35	53	70	91
2	0	18	37	54	72	90
Mean	0	18.0	36.0	53.5	71.0	90.5

Table 11.4 Samples (fluorimeter reading). Note how each of the capillary tubes is analysed in duplicate.

Tube	Rest		0		7.5 min PE		12.5 min PE	
	a	b	a	b	a	b	a	b
1	5	6	64	66	75	75	68	61
2	5	6	62	64	76	75	70	62

Table 11.5 Blood lactate values in mmol l^{-1}. Use the regression data from Table 11.3 to convert the instrument readings in Table 11.4. Note how each blood sample is analysed in quadruplicate.

Tube	Rest a	Rest b	0 a	0 b	7.5 min a	7.5 min b	12.5 min a	12.5 min b
1	0.71	0.85	8.92	9.19	10.45	10.45	9.47	8.50
2	0.71	0.85	8.64	8.92	10.58	10.45	9.75	8.64
Mean	0.71	0.85	8.78	9.06	10.52	10.45	9.61	8.57
Mean	0.78		8.92		10.49		9.09	

Table 11.6 Sample results for WAnT

	Mean	SD	Range
Time to peak power (s)	3.6	1.2	2–6
Mean power (W)	650	80	400–900
Decay (W)	300	50	150–500

Table 11.7 Sample results for blood lactate following performance of the Wingate Anaerobic Test (values are mean, SD).

	Blood lactate (mmol l^{-1})
Rest	0.70, 0.15
Immediately post-exercise	9.6, 2.1
7.5 min post-exercise	12.5, 2.4
12.5 min post-exercise	11.0, 2.1

11.10 PRACTICAL 2: OPTIMIZATION PROCEDURES

11.10.1 AIMS

The purposes of this practical are
- to assess optimized peak power output, optimized load and the optimized pedalling rate
- to compare these measures with Wingate-derived data
- to establish the extent to which muscle force–velocity relationships are not satisfied by the Wingate Anaerobic Test.

11.10.2 EQUIPMENT

The same as for the Wingate Anaerobic Test.

11.10.3 METHODS

1. Dress, warm-up and screening procedures are the same as for the Wingate Anaerobic Test.
2. After a 5-minute warm-up, subjects perform four bouts of all-out exercise against randomly assigned loads. Each bout lasts 10 s and is followed by 1 minute of warm-down. A period of rest is allowed such that each exercise bout is separated in total by 5 minutes. Each bout is started in the same way as for the Wingate Anaerobic Test. Loads are assigned according to body mass, and guidelines are given in Table 11.8. These loads should produce peak pedalling rates within the range 100–200 rev min^{-1}.

Table 11.8 Suggested loads in newtons for the optimization procedure according to body mass (9.81 N = 1 kg force)

| Load | Body mass (kg) | | | | | |
	< 50	*50–59.95*	*60–69.95*	*70–79.95*	*80–89.95*	*> 90*
1	20.0	25.0	25.0	25.0	30.0	30.0
2	30.0	35.0	37.5	40.0	45.0	47.5
3	Wingate	Wingate	Wingate	Wingate	Wingate	Wingate
4	50.0	55.0	62.5	70.0	75.0	82.5

3. The order for applying the loads is: Wingate (i.e. 7½% of body weight), load 2, load 4 and finally load 1.
4. Record peak pedalling rate for each load and calculate the optimized peak power output, optimized load and optimized pedalling rate.
5. Compare the Wingate-derived values of peak power output and peak pedalling rate with the optimized values.

11.10.4 SAMPLE RESULTS

Table 11.9 gives peak pedalling rate and applied load data for a female sports studies student. Pearson's product-moment correlation coefficient and regression data are as follows:

$r = -0.998$

$R = 212.5 - 1.969\,L$

i.e. $a = 212.5$

$b = -1.97$

Substituting these values of a and b:

$$\text{Optimized peak power output} = \frac{-0.025a^2}{b} = 573\,\text{W}$$

$$\text{Optimised load} = \frac{-a}{2b} = 53.9\,\text{N}\,(5.49\,\text{kg force})$$

Optimized pedalling rate = $a + bL = 106.2$ rev min^{-1}

The relationship between peak pedalling rate, applied load and power output is illustrated in Figure 11.4. Tables 11.10 and 11.11 illustrate some typical results. The calculation of the optimized peak power output, optimized load and optimized pedalling rate depends on the linearity of the relationship between peak pedalling rate and applied load. In this example, r was -0.996 ± 0.005 for the men and -0.996 ± 0.006 for the women, so the required linearity is clearly illustrated. Values of peak power output derived from the Wingate Anaerobic Test were only ~88% of the optimized peak power output in men and ~90 % in women. In addition, the reductions were not consistent. Although values of r were significant ($p < 0.001$), ~20% of the variance of the optimized peak power output in men and ~16 % in women is not accounted for by the relationship with Wingate-derived peak power output values.

Table 11.9 Sample results for peak pedalling rate and applied load

Load (N)	Peak pedalling rate (rev min^{-1})	Peak power output (W)
44.1	128	564
34.3	144	493
53.9	105	566
24.5	164	402

Figure 11.4 An example of the way in which peak pedalling rate and power output are related to the applied braking force.

The results demonstrate clearly that the optimized peak power output is greater than Wingate-derived peak power output (WPP) and that the pedalling rate that accompanied WPP is greater than the pedalling rate that accompanied the optimized peak power output. Consequently, these data confirm the suggestion (Sargeant *et al.*, 1981) that the Wingate load of 7½% of body weight does not necessarily satisfy muscle force–velocity relationships. Optimized pedalling rate is ~115 rev min^{-1} in men (Sargeant *et al.*, 1984; Nakamura *et al.*, 1985; Winter *et al.*, 1991) and ~105 rev min^{-1} in women (Sargeant *et al.*, 1984; Winter *et al.*, 1991). Pedalling rate at WPP is some 15–20 % higher in each case. The higher pedalling rate is at the expense of effective force production and hence power output. This reduction in effectiveness is also illustrated by OL (optimized load), which is ~11% of body weight in both men and women, and considerably higher than the Wingate value.

Table 11.10 Sample results for optimized and WAnT-derived data in men, n = 19. Values are mean, SEM (Winter *et al.*, 1987)

	Optimum	*Wingate*	*r*	*t*	*V%*
Peak power (W)	1 012, 30	883, 21	0.898[a]	−9.029[a]	5.8
Pedal rate	118.4, 1.8	155.9, 2.5	0.589[b]	−19.078[a]	5.4

[a] $p < 0.001$.
[b] $p < 0.01$.

Table 11.11 Sample results for optimized and WAnT-derived data in women, n = 28. Values are mean, SEM (Winter *et al.*, 1987)

	Optimum	*Wingate*	*r*	*t*	*V%*
Peak power (W)	640, 20	579, 17	0.918[a]	9.22[a]	6.8
Pedal rate	103.8, 1.6	134.5, 1.7	0.582[b]	−22.571[a]	6.7

[a] $p < 0.001$.
[b] $p < 0.01$.

11.11 PRACTICAL 3: CORRECTION PROCEDURES

11.11.1 AIMS

The purpose of this practical is to compare optimized peak power output values to corrected values for peak power output, as suggested by Lakomy (1985).

11.11.2 METHODS

1. Warm-up procedures as for Practical 1.
2. Subjects perform the optimization procedure outlined in Practical 2.

3. During the 'Wingate Load' bout, i.e. bout one, data are also recorded using the Concept II system and the corrected peak power output is calculated.
4. Record the corrected peak power output, the optimized peak power output and the pedalling rates for both.

11.11.3 SAMPLE RESULTS

Table 11.12 Sample data for optimized and corrected peak power output in men, $n = 19$, women $n = 18$. Values are mean, SEM (Winter *et al.*, 1996)

	Optimized	Corrected	r	t	V%
Men					
Peak power (W)	915, 35	1 005, 32	0.92[a]	−6.79[a]	5.6
Pedal rate (rev min⁻¹)	111, 2	128, 2	0.64[b]	−11.77[a]	5.1
Women					
Peak Power (W)	673, 33	777, 39	0.96[a]	−9.38[a]	5.8
Pedal rate (rev min⁻¹)	101, 1	111, 2	0.51[b]	−4.71[a]	7.9

[a] $p < 0.001$.
[b] $p < 0.01$.

The important points to note are that the corrected peak power output is greater than the optimized peak power output and similarly, pedalling rate is higher for the corrected peak power values.

The value for the corrected peak power output is ~10% greater than the optimized peak power output, although the relationship between the measures is strong, with 85% of the variance in the corrected peak power output accounted for by its relationship with the optimized peak power output. Similarly, the pedalling rate for the corrected peak power output is ~15% greater, but in this case only 41% of the variance in this value is accounted for by its relationship with the optimized equivalent. However, the coefficient of variation is smaller than for the optimized peak power output and this is a good example of the caution that has to be taken when r is interpreted. The magnitude of r is influenced by the range in the data and it does not necessarily give a clear indication of the relationship between variables. This is a reminder of the care that has to be taken when using r (Sale, 1991).

11.12 PRACTICAL 4: ASSESSMENT OF MAXIMAL ACCUMULATED OXYGEN DEFICIT (MAOD)

The original method for the determination of MAOD as described by Medbø *et al.* (1988) required subjects to perform ~20 runs on a treadmill at varying speeds up to a speed corresponding to maximal oxygen uptake. Each run lasted for 10 minutes, with the treadmill gradient set at 10.5%. Oxygen uptake was determined in the last two minutes of each run, and because only one run was performed on a particular day, the whole process took three weeks. Clearly this would be impractical for testing athletes or for student laboratory classes. However, to illustrate the principles a scaled-down version can be used over two testing sessions as follows:

11.12.1 METHODS

1. The subject runs at 4 submaximal speeds on a treadmill with a gradient set at 10.5% for 4 minutes each during which oxygen uptake is measured in the last two minutes. From these data, it is possible to establish a linear relationship between oxygen uptake and running speed.
2. After the final 4-minute run, the treadmill speed is progressively increased every minute until volitional exhaustion occurs, so that maximal oxygen uptake can be determined.
3. Produce graph of $\dot{V}O_2$ vs. running speed and determine the oxygen demand and running speed equivalent to 120% of $\dot{V}O_2$ max. This is achieved by extrapolating the straight line relationship beyond $\dot{V}O_2$ max. Alternatively, it may be predicted from the regression equation derived from the relationship between oxygen uptake (x) and running speed (y).
4. On a separate day, the subject runs to exhaustion on the treadmill (set at 10.5% gradient) at the speed corresponding to 120% $\dot{V}O_2$ max. Oxygen uptake is monitored throughout this test, which normally results in fatigue between 2 and 6 minutes.
5. The MAOD is calculated from the difference between the oxygen demand for that running speed (i.e. time to fatigue × $\dot{V}O_2$ extrapolated to 120% $\dot{V}O_2$ max) and the actual total oxygen consumption during the run.

Using this brief method, it is possible to distinguish between sprint-trained and endurance-trained populations, but it is probably not sensitive enough to distinguish subtle changes due to training. The use of four 4-minute bouts of running in one session as well as continuing to $\dot{V}O_2$ max might account for this lack of sensitivity.

11.12.2 SAMPLE RESULTS

The following data provide an example of oxygen uptake values collected on a male college sprinter using the above protocol.
(i) Day One (Table 11.13)
    120% of $\dot{V}O_2$ max (1.2 × 69) = 83 ml kg^{-1} min^{-1}
    Regression equation for $\dot{V}O_2$ (x) versus speed (y):
    Speed (m min^{-1}) = 23.2 + 2.758 ($\dot{V}O_2$) r = 0.99
    Therefore, the speed corresponding to 120% $\dot{V}O_2$ max = 251.5 m min^{-1}

Table 11.13 Running speeds and equivalent oxygen uptake values

Run	Speed (m min^{-1})	$\dot{V}O_2$ (ml kg^{-1}min^{-1})
1	161	49
2	174	56
3	188	60
4	201	64
5	214	69

Table 11.14 Oxygen uptake at specific times while running at 251.5 m min^{-1} at a gradient of 10.5%

Time (s)	$\dot{V}O_2$ (ml kg^{-1}min^{-1})
30	27
60	49
90	55
120	60
150	62

(ii) Day Two (Treadmill speed = 251.5 m min^{-1} at a gradient of 10.5%) (Table 11.14)

$$\text{Calculation of MAOD} = (2.5 \text{ min} \times 83 \text{ ml kg}^{-1}) - ((27 + 49 + 55 + 60 + 62)/2)$$
$$= 207.5 - 126.5 = 81 \text{ ml kg}^{-1}$$

$$\text{Aerobic contribution} = (126.5 / 207.5) \times 100 = 61\%$$

The following are typical values for MAOD (ml kg^{-1}):

Before training (males)	66.4
After training (males)	79.8
Before training (females)	69.6
After training (females)	80.9

(Ramsbottom *et al.*, 1991)

Values of 55 ml kg^{-1} and 72 ml kg^{-1} have been observed for endurance-trained and sprint-trained men in the exercise physiology laboratory in Don MacLaren's laboratory.

REFERENCES

Adamson, G.T. and Whitney, R.J. (1971). Critical appraisal of jumping as a measure of human power. In *Medicine and Sport 6, Biomechanics II.* eds. J. Vredenbregt and J. Wartenweiler (S. Karger, Basel, Switzerland), pp. 208–11.

Ayalon, A., Inbar, O. and Bar-Or, O. (1974). Relationships among measurements of explosive strength and anaerobic power. In *International Series on Sport Sciences (Vol. I, Biomechanics IV).* eds. R.C. Nelson and C.A. Morehouse (University Press, Baltimore, MD), pp. 572–7.

Baltzopoulos, V., Eston, R.G. and Maclaren, D.A. (1988). A comparison of power measures between the Wingate test and tests of using an isokinetic device. *Ergonomics*, **3**, 1693–9.

Bangsbo, J. (1996a). Oxygen deficit: a measure of the anaerobic energy production during intense exercise? *Canadian Journal of Applied Physiology*, **21**, 350–63.

Bangsbo, J. (1996b). Bangsbo responds to Medbø's paper. *Canadian Journal of Applied Physiology*, **21**, 384–8.

Bangsbo, J. (1997). Quantification of anaerobic energy production during intense exercise. *Medicine and Science in Sports and Exercise*, **30**, 47–52.

Bangsbo, J., Gollnick, P.D., Graham, T.E., *et al.* (1990). Anaerobic energy production and the O deficit-debt relationship during exhaustive exercise in humans. *Journal of Physiology*, **422**, 539–59.

Bar-Or, O. (1981). Le test anaérobie de Wingate: caractéristiques et applications. *Symbioses*, **13**, 157–72.

Bar-Or, O. (1987). The Wingate Anaerobic Test: an update on methodology, reliability and validity. *Sports Medicine*, **4**, 381–94.

Bassett, D.R. (1989). Correcting the Wingate Test for changes in kinetic energy of the ergometer flywheel. *International Journal of Sports Medicine*, **10**, 446–9.

Bergström, J. (1962). Muscle electrolytes in man. *Scandinavian Journal of Clinical Laboratory Investigation*, **14**, (**Suppl 68**), p. 110.

Best, C.H. and Partridge, R.C. (1928). The equation of motion of a runner exerting maximal effort. *Proceedings of the Royal Society Series B*, **103**, 218–25.

Best, C.H. and Partridge, R.C. (1929). Observations on Olympic athletes. *Proceedings of the Royal Society Series B*, **105**, 323–32.

Bird, S. and Davison, R. (1997). *Physiological Testing Guidelines*, 3rd edn. (British Association of Sport and Exercise Sciences, Leeds).

Boobis, L.H. (1987). Metabolic aspects of fatigue during sprinting. In *Exercise: Benefits, Limitations and Adaptations.* eds. D. Macleod, R. Maughan, M. Nimmo, *et al.* (E. and F.N. Spon, London), pp. 116–43.

Boobis, L.H., Williams, C. and Wootton, S.A. (1982). Human muscle metabolism during brief maximal exercise. *Journal of Physiology*, **338**, 21P–22P.

Boobis, L.H., Williams, C. and Wootton, S.A. (1983). Influence of sprint training on muscle metabolism during brief maximal exercise in man. *Journal of Physiology*, **342**, 36P–37P.

Brewer, J., Ramsbottom, R. and Williams, C. (1988). *Multistage Fitness Test – a progressive shuttle-run test for the prediction of maximum oxygen uptake.* National Coaching Foundation, Leeds, UK.

Brooks, G.A. (1986). The lactate shuttle during exercise and recovery. *Medicine and Science in Sports and Exercise*, **18**, 355–64.

Casey, A., Constantin-Teodosiu, D., Howell, S., *et al.* (1996). Metabolic response of type I and II muscle fibres during repeated bouts of maximal exercise in humans. *American Journal of Physiology*, **271**, E38–E43.

Cavagna, G.A. (1975). Force platforms as ergometers. *Journal of Applied Physiology*, **39**, 174–9.

Cheetham, M.E. and Williams, C. (1985). Blood pH and blood lactate concentrations following maximal treadmill sprinting in man. *Journal of Physiology*, **361**, 79P.

Cheetham, M.E., Boobis, L.H., Brooks, S. and Williams, C. (1986). Human muscle metabolism during sprint running in man. *Journal of Applied Physiology*, **61**, 54–60.

Constantin-Teodosiu, D., Greenhaff, P.L., McIntyre, D.B., *et al.* (1997). Anaerobic energy production in human skeletal muscle in intense contraction: a comparison of ^{31}P magnetic resonance spectroscopy and biochemical techniques. *Experimental Physiology*, **82**, 593–601.

Cumming, G. (1974). Correlation of athletic performance and anaerobic power in 12–17-year-old children with bone age, calf muscle and total body potassium, heart volume and two indices of anaerobic power. In *Paediatric Work Physiology.* ed. O. Bar-Or (Wingate Institute, Isreal), pp. 109–34.

Davis, J.M., Welsh, R.S., DeVolve, K.L. and Alderson, N.A. (1999). Effects of branched-chain amino acids and carbohydrate on fatigue during intermittent, high-intensity running. *International Journal of Sports Medicine*, **20**, 309–14.

Dickinson, S. (1928). The dynamics of bicycle pedalling. *Proceedings of the Royal Society Series B*, **103**, 225–33.

Dickinson, S. (1929). The efficiency of bicycle pedalling as affected by speed and load. *Journal of Physiology*, **67**, 242–55.

Dotan, R. and Bar-Or, O. (1983). Load optimization for the Wingate Anaerobic Test. *European Journal of Applied Physiology*, **51**, 409–17.

Eston, R.G., Winter, E. and Baltzopoulos, V. (1997). Ratio standards and allometric modelling to scale peak power output for differences in lean upper leg volume in men and women. *Journal of Sports Sciences*, **15**, 29.

Fenn, W.O. (1932). Zur Mechanik des Radfahrens im Vergleich zu der des Laufens. *Pflügers Archiv für gesante Physiologie*, **229**, 354–66.

Fenn, W.O. and Marsh, B.S. (1935). Muscular force at different speeds of shortening. *Journal of Physiology*, **85**, 277–97.

Fleisch, A. (1950). Ergostat à puissances constantes et multiples. *Helvetica Medica Acta Series A*, **17**, 47–58.

Fox, M.L., Bowers, R.W. and Foss, M.L. (1988). *The Physiological Basis of Physical Education and Athletics*, 4th edn. (Saunders, Philadelphia, PA).

Furusawa, K., Hill, A.V. and Parkinson, J.L. (1927). The energy used in "sprint" running. *Proceedings of the Royal Society Series B*, **102**, 43–50.

Gamble, D.J., Jakeman, P.M. and Bartlett, R.M. (1988). Force velocity characteristics during non-motorised treadmill sprinting. *Journal of Sports Sciences*, **6**, 156.

Greenhaff, P.L., Nevill, M.E., Soderlund, K., et al. (1994). The metabolic responses of human type I and II muscle fibers during maximal treadmill sprinting. *Journal of Physiology*, **478**, 149–55.

Hamilton, A.L., Nevill, M.E., Brooks, S. and Williams, C. (1991). Physiological responses to maximal intermittent exercise: differences between endurance-trained runners and games players. *Journal of Sports Sciences*, **9**, 371–82.

Hamley, E.J. and Thomas, V. (1967). Physiological and postural factors in the calibration of the bicycle ergometer. *Journal of Physiology*, **193**, 55P–57P.

Hermansen, L. (1969). Anaerobic energy release. *Medicine and Science in Sports*, **1**, 32–8.

Hill, A.V. (1913). The absolute mechanical efficiency of the contraction of an isolated muscle. *Journal of Physiology*, **46**, 435–69.

Hill, A.V. (1934). The efficiency of bicycle pedalling. *Journal of Physiology*, **82**, 207–10.

Hill, A.V. (1938). The heat of shortening and the dynamic constants of muscle. *Proceedings of the Royal Society Series B*, **126**, 136–95.

Hill, A.V. (1970). *First and Last Experiments in Muscle Mechanics*. (Cambridge University Press, London).

Hill, A.V. and Lupton, H. (1922). The oxygen consumption during running. *Journal of Physiology*, **56**, xxxii–xxxiii.

Inbar, O., Dotan, R. and Bar-Or, O. (1976). Aerobic and anaerobic components of a thirty-second supramaximal cycling task. *Medicine and Science in Sports*, **8**, 51.

Jaskólska, A., Goossens, P., Veenstra, B., et al. (1999). Comparison of treadmill and cycle ergometer measurements of force-velocity relationships and power output. *International Journal of Sports Medicine*, **20**, 192–7.

Jaskólski, A., Veenstra, B., Goossens, P., et al. (1996). Optimised resistance for maximal power during treadmill running. *Sports Medicine and Training Rehabilitation*, **7**, 17–30.

Jones, N.L., McCartney, N., Graham, T., et al. (1985). Muscle performance and metabolism in maximal isokinetic cycling at slow and fast speeds. *Journal of Applied Physiology*, **59**, 132–6.

Jones, P.R.M. and Pearson, J. (1969). Anthropometric determination of leg fat and muscle plus bone volumes in young male and female adults. *Journal of Physiology*, **204**, 63P–66P.

Kelso, L.E.A. and Hellebrandt, F.A. (1932). The recording electrodynamic brake bicycle ergometer. *Journal of Clinical and Laboratory Medicine*, **19**, 1105–13.

Lakomy, H.K.A. (1984). An ergometer for measuring the power generated during sprinting. *Journal of Physiology*, **354**, 33P.

Lakomy, H.K.A. (1985). Effect of load on corrected peak power output generated on friction loaded cycle ergometers. *Journal of Sports Sciences*, **3**, 240.

Lakomy, H.K.A. (1986). Measurement of work and power output using friction loaded cycle ergometers. *Ergonomics*, **29**, 509–17.

La Voie, N., Dallaire, J., Brayne, S. and Barrett, D. (1984). Anaerobic testing using the Wingate and Evans-Quinney protocols with and without toe stirrups. *Canadian Journal of Applied Sport Sciences*, **9**, 1–5.

Léger, L.A. and Lambert, J. (1982). A maximal multistage 20m shuttle run test to predict O_2 max. *European Journal of Applied Physiology*, **49**, 1–5.

Lupton, H. (1923). An analysis of the effects of speed on the mechanical efficiency of human muscular movement. *Journal of Physiology*, **57**, 337–53.

McCartney, N., Heigenhauser, G.J.F. Sargeant, A.J. and Jones, N.L. (1983). A constant-velocity cycle ergometer for the study of dynamic muscle function. *Journal of Applied Physiology: Respiratory, Environmental and Exercise Physiology*, **55**, 212–17.

McCartney, N., Spriet, L.L., Heigenhauser, G.J.F., *et al.* (1986). Muscle power and metabolism in maximal intermittent exercise. *Journal of Applied Physiology*, **60**, 1164–9.

McClenaghan, B.A. and Literowitch, W. (1987). Fundamentals of computerised data acquisition in the human performance laboratory. *Sports Medicine*, **4**, 425–45.

Maughan, R.J. (1982). A simple rapid method for the determination of glucose, lactate, pyruvate, alanine, b hydroxybutyrate and acetoacetate on a single 20 ml blood sample. *Clinica Chimica Acta*, **122**, 231–40.

Medbø, J.I. (1996a). Medbø responds to Bangsbo's paper. *Canadian Journal of Applied Physiology*, **21**, 364–9.

Medbø, J.I. (1996b). Is the maximal accumulated oxygen deficit an adequate measure of the anaerobic capacity? *Canadian Journal of Applied Physiology*, **21**, 370–83.

Medbø, J.I., Mohn, A., Tabata, I., *et al.* (1988). Anaerobic capacity determined by the maximal accumulated oxygen deficit. *Journal of Applied Physiology*, **64**, 50–60.

Mercer, T.H., Gleeson, N.P., Claridge, S. and Clement, S. (1998). Prolonged intermittent high intensity exercise impairs neuromuscular performance of the knee flexors. *European Journal of Applied Physiology*, **77**, 560–2.

Morris, J.G., Nevill, M.E., Lakomy, H.K.A., *et al.* (1998). Effect of a hot environment on performance of prolonged, intermittent, high-intensity shuttle running. *Journal of Sports Sciences*, **16**, 677–86.

Nakamura, Y., Mutoh, Y. and Miyashita, M. (1985). Determination of the peak power output during maximal brief pedalling bouts. *Journal of Sports Sciences*, **3**, 181–7.

Nevill, A.M., Ramsbottom, R. and Williams, C. (1992). Scaling measurements in physiology and medicine for individuals of different size. *European Journal of Applied Physiology*, **65**, 110–7.

Nevill, M.E., Boobis, L.H., Brooks, S. and Williams, C. (1989). Effect of training on muscle metabolism during treadmill sprinting. *Journal of Applied Physiology*, **67**, 2376–82.

Nevill, M.E., Williams, C., Roper, D., *et al.* (1993). Effect of diet on performance during recovery from intermittent sprint exercise. *Journal of Sports Sciences*, **11**, 119–26.

Nordeen-Snyder, K. (1977). The effect of bicycle seat height variation upon oxygen consumption and lower limb kinematics. *Medicine and Science in Sports and Exercise*, **9**, 113–17.

Peyrebrune, M.C., Nevill, M.E., Donaldson, F.J. and Cosford, D.J. (1998). The effect of oral creatine supplementation on performance in single and repeated sprint swimming. *Journal of Sports Sciences*, **16**, 271–9.

Ramsbottom, R., Nevill, A.M., Nevill, M.E. and Williams, C. (1991). Effect of training on maximal accumulated oxygen deficit and shuttle run performance. *Journal of Sports Sciences*, **9**, 429–30.

Sale, D.G. (1991). Testing strength and power. In *Physiological Testing of the High-Performance Athlete*, 2nd edn. eds. J.D. MacDougall, H.A. Wenger and H.A. Green (Human Kinetics, Champaign, IL), pp. 21–106.

Sargeant, A.J., Hoinville, E. and Young, A. (1981). Maximum leg force and power output during short term dynamic exercise. *Journal of Applied Physiology: Respiratory, Environmental and Exercise Physiology*, **53**, 1175–82.

Sargeant, A.J., Dolan, P. and Young, A. (1984). Optimal velocity for maximal short-term (anaerobic) power output in cycling. *International Journal of Sports Medicine*, **5**, 124–5.

Sargent, D.A. (1921). The physical test of a man. *American Physical Education Review*, **26**, 188–94.

Sargent, L.W. (1924). Some observations on the Sargent Test of Neuromuscular Efficiency. *American Physical Education Review*, **29**, 47–56.

Sargent, R.M. (1926). The relation between oxygen requirement and speed in running. *Proceedings of the Royal Society Series B*, **100**, 10–22.

Schmidt-Nielsen, K. (1984). *Scaling: why is animal size so important?* (Cambridge University Press, Cambridge).

Serresse, O., Lortie, G., Bouchard, C. and Boulay, M.R. (1988). Estimation of the contribution of the various energy systems during maximal work of short duration. *International Journal of Sports Medicine*, **9**, 456–60.

Smith, A.J. (1972). *A study of the forces on the body in athletic activities, with particular reference to jumping*. Unpublished Doctoral Thesis, University of Leeds, UK.

Smith, J.C. and Hill, D.W. (1991). Contribution of energy systems during a Wingate power test. *British Journal of Sports Medicine*, **25**, 196–9.

Soderlund, K. and Hultman, E. (1986). Effects of delayed freezing on content of phosphagens in human skeletal muscle biopsy samples. *Journal of Applied Physiology*, **61**, 832–5.

Soderlund, K., Greenhaff, P.L. and Hultman, E. (1992). Energy metabolism in type I and II human muscle fibres during short term electrical stimulation at different frequencies. *Acta Physiologica Scandinavica*, **144**, 15–22.

Tanner, J.M. (1949). Fallacy of per-weight and per-surface area standards and their relation to spurious correlation. *Journal of Applied Physiology*, **2**, 1–15.

Thompson, D., Nicholas, C.W. and Williams, C. (1999). Muscular soreness following prolonged intermittent high-intensity shuttle running. *Journal of Sports Sciences*, **17**, 387–95.

Tuttle, W.W. and Wendler, A.J. (1945). The construction, calibration and use of an alternating current electrodynamic brake bicycle ergometer. *Journal of Laboratory and Clinical Medicine*, **30**, 173–183.

Vandewalle, H., Pérès, G., Heller, J. and Monod, H. (1985). All out anaerobic capacity tests on cycle ergometers: a comparative study on men and women. *European Journal of Applied Physiology*, **54**, 222–9.

Von Döbeln, W. (1954). A simple bicycle ergometer. *Journal of Applied Physiology*, **7**, 222–4.

Welsman, J., Armstrong, N., Winter, E. and Kirby, B.J. (1993). The influence of various scaling techniques on the interpretation of developmental changes in peak O_2. *Pediatric Exercise Science*, **5**, 485.

Williams, C. (1987). Short term activity. In *Exercise: Benefits, Limits and Adaptations*. eds. D. Macleod, R. Maughan, M. Nimmo, *et al*. (E and F.N. Spon, London), pp. 59–62.

Williams, C. (1990). Metabolic aspects of exercise. In *Physiology of Sports*, eds. T. Reilly, N. Secher, P. Snell and C. Williams (E. and F.N. Spon, London), pp. 3–40.

Winter, E.M. (1992). Scaling: partitioning out differences in body size. *Pediatric Exercise Science*, **4**, 296–301.

Winter, E.M., Brookes, F.B.C. and Hamley, E.J. (1987). A comparison of optimized and non-optimized peak power output in young, active men and women. *Journal of Sports Sciences*, **5**, 71.

Winter, E.M., Brookes, F.B.C. and Hamley, E.J. (1989). Optimized loads for external power output during brief, maximal cycling. *Journal of Sports Sciences*, **7**, 69–70.

Winter, E.M., Brookes, F.B.C. and Hamley, E.J. (1991). Maximal exercise performance and lean leg volume in men and women. *Journal of Sports Sciences*, **9**, 3–13.

Winter, E.M., Brookes, F.B.C. and Roberts, K.W. (1993). The effects of scaling on comparisons between maximal exercise performance in boys and men. *Pediatric Exercise Science*, **5**, 488.

Winter, E.M., Brown, D., Roberts, N.K.A., *et al*. (1996). Optimized and corrected peak power output during friction-braked cycle ergometry. *Journal of Sports Sciences*, **14**, 513–21.

Wootton, S. and Williams, C. (1983). The influence of recovery duration on repeated maximal sprints. In *Biochemistry of Exercise*. eds. H.G. Knuttgen, J.A. Vogel and J. Poortmans (Human Kinetics, Champaign, IL), pp. 269–73.

APPENDIX: RELATIONSHIPS BETWEEN UNITS OF ENERGY, WORK, POWER AND SPEED

Table A.1 Energy and work units (The joule is the SI unit for work and represents the application of a force of 1 newton (N) through a distance of 1 metre. A newton is the force producing an acceleration of 1 metre per second every second (1 m s^{-2}) when it acts on 1 kg.)

1 joule (J)	=	1 newton metre (N m)
1 kilojoule (kJ)	=	1000 J
	=	0.23892 kcal
1 megajoule (MJ)	=	1000 kJ
1 kilocalorie (kcal)	=	4.1855 kJ = 426.8 kg m

Table A.2 Relationships between various power units (The watt is the SI unit for power and is equivalent to 1 J s^{-1}.)

	W	kcal min^{-1}	kJ min^{-1}	kg m min^{-1}
1 watt (W)	1.0	0.014	0.060	6.118
1 kcal min^{-1}	69.77	1.0	4.186	426.78
1 kJ min^{-1}	16.667	0.2389	1.0	101.97
1 kg m min^{-1}	0.1634	0.00234	0.00981	1.0

Table A.3 Conversion table for units of speed (m s^{-1} is the SI unit for speed.)

km h^{-1}	m s^{-1}	mph
1	0.28	0.62
2	0.56	1.24
3	0.83	1.87
4	1.11	2.49
5	1.39	3.11
6	1.67	3.73
7	1.94	4.35
8	2.22	4.98
9	2.50	5.60
10	2.78	6.22

INDEX